D1083429

NARRATIVES OF THE
CORONADO EXPEDITION

AMS PRESS
NEW YORK

COMPOSTELA, CAPITAL OF NEW GALICIA IN 1540, AS IT LOOKS TODAY

Narratives of the Coronado Expedition 1540-1542

GEORGE P. HAMMOND
The University of New Mexico

and

AGAPITO REY
Indiana University

The University of New Mexico Press
Albuquerque
1940

Library of Congress Cataloging in Publication Data

Hammond, George Peter, 1896- ed. and tr.
    Narratives of the Coronado expedition, 1540-1542.

    Reprint of the 1940 ed. published by the University
of New Mexico Press, Albuquerque, which was issued as
v. 2 of Coronado cuarto centennial publications,
1540-1940.
    Includes index.
    1. Vázquez de Coronado, Francisco, 1510-1549.
    2. Southwest, New—Discovery and exploration.
    3. Explorers—Southwest, New—Biography. I. Rey,
Agapito, 1892- II. Title. III. Series: Coronado
cuarto centennial publications, 1540-1940; v. 2.
E125.V3H4   1977   979.1'01'0924 [B]   75-41126
ISBN 0-404-14669-4

Reprinted from the edition of 1940, Albuquerque
First AMS edition published in 1977
Manufactured in the United States of America

AMS PRESS INC.
NEW YORK, N.Y.

PREFACE

The history of New Mexico, rich in tradition, dates back not only to the great exploration of the Southwest by Francisco Vázquez de Coronado four hundred years ago, but a thousand or more years to the civilization of the Pueblo Indians, who still inhabit a large portion of the beautiful valleys of this region.

When, in 1935, the New Mexico legislature created the Coronado Cuarto Centennial Commission to promote a state-wide celebration in honor of the ancient pioneers of the Southwest, the leaders who sponsored the movement were determined that the Centennial should be established on a sound historical basis. It was their conviction that no greater tribute could be paid the history, anthropology, the folklore and literature of the region than by presenting them in their true perspective. The Commission's aim was to inspire in the people an appreciation of the state's great heritage, for a people cannot survive with honor without recognizing its obligations to the past, and to the efforts of its forefathers to make the land a better place in which to pursue peacefully the arts and tasks of civilization.

The Coronado Historical series, of which this volume is the second, was authorized by the Coronado Cuarto Centennial Commission in order to encourage the preservation of our historical literature, and every member of the Commission enthusiastically supported this endeavor to preserve, on the printed page, a record of man's achievements in the Southwest. Their enthusiasm was absorbed by the political leaders of the state, and, be it said to their honor, they gave immense encouragement to this broad historical celebration.

By emphasizing the long sweep of history in the Southwest, New Mexico, which is today a place where one may escape from the conflict of man and seek the peaceful solitude of its mesas, sierras, and valleys, presents to the world an invitation to preserve the glory of bygone days, and to pass on to posterity the torch of civilization.

ix

It is for us a great pleasure to pay tribute to those who have borne the heavy burden of planning and directing the Coronado Cuarto Centennial celebration. To Dr. J. F. Zimmerman, president of the New Mexico Coronado Cuarto Centennial Commission and president of the University of New Mexico, is due much of the credit for the realization of the whole program. His vision, energy, and leadership, his capacity for enlisting men and women who would sacrifice their own interests for the welfare of the state have made the Coronado Centennial a reality. To Erna Fergusson, vice-president of the Commission, and to Gilberto Espinosa, its secretary—both members of distinguished New Mexico families—we are grateful for their adherence to ideas of permanent spiritual and cultural value. No less may be said for the other members of the Commission: Charles M. Martin, one of the first to suggest this four-hundredth year commemoration; Ruth Laughlin Alexander, author; Riley M. Edwards, merchant; B. C. Hernández, former congressman; Orval Ricketts, editor and publisher; and Concha Ortiz y Pino, social and political leader.

This acknowledgment would not be complete without voicing our gratitude to Clinton P. Anderson, managing director of the New Mexico Coronado Cuarto Centennial Commission and the United States Coronado Exposition Commission, and G. C. Dickens, executive officer of the federal commission. They have given unstinted support to the Coronado Historical series and the wider, cultural aspects of the Centennial program.

GEORGE P. HAMMOND
AGAPITO REY

Albuquerque, May 29, 1940

CONTENTS

CONTENTS *(Continued)*

INTRODUCTION

In 1510, in the flourishing university city of Salamanca, Spain, a son was born to blue-blooded Juan Vázquez de Coronado and Doña Isabel de Luján, who christened him Francisco Vázquez. Grandparents of the infant were old Juan Vázquez de Coronado and Berenguela Vázquez. When Grandfather Juan died—after taking a second wife, María Fernández—to son Juan went his entire estate, amid the protests of the offspring by his second marriage, who sued for a share of the property.[1]

Son Juan, bolstered by his legacy, prospered, and was appointed corregidor of Burgos in 1512. Wary of inheritance tangles, in 1520 he created a *mayorazgo*, leaving to eldest son, Gonzalo Vázquez de Coronado, his estate, to be passed down through first sons. Francisco Vázquez, younger brother of Gonzalo Vázquez, and their other brothers received outright settlements, and endowments were made to convents housing their two sisters who had become nuns.[2] Gonzalo and Francisco had two brothers, both named Juan Vázquez de Coronado; one became an adelantado in Costa Rica and the other comendador of the order of St. John of the encomienda of Cubillas.[3]

There is no record of Francisco Vázquez de Coronado's early life. Historians' best guess is that he was given the education his social status demanded, and that he afterwards indulged in the idleness and fripperies common to 16th century gentlemen of high birth.

When Antonio de Mendoza, newly appointed viceroy of Mexico, sailed from Spain in 1535 to assume his charge, he took along his court friend, 25-year old Francisco Vázquez de Coronado, as a member of his train. His inheritance having possibly dwindled, and barred from further participation in the paternal estate, it is likely that Coronado welcomed the

1. A. S. Aiton and A. Rey, "Coronado's Testimony in the Viceroy Mendoza Residencia," in *New Mexico Historical Review*, XII (1937), p. 289.
2. *Loc. cit.*
3. Archivo General de Indias, *Indiferente*, legajo 1240.

opportunity to seek his fortune in the New World. He first set foot on New Spain's soil in October, 1535, and accompanied the viceroy's triumphal procession into Mexico city the following month.[4]

Backed by Mendoza's friendship and patronage, Coronado quickly gained prominence in the capital. When, in 1537, revolting negro miners at Amatepeque elected a "king" and threatened considerable trouble, the viceroy dispatched him to quell the uprising with the help of Indians. After some fighting, the revolt was suppressed, and a score of the rebels hanged and quartered.[5] The following year, Coronado having acquired citizenship in Mexico city, Mendoza brushed aside the customary formality of royal sanction and made his protege a member of the city council. The young fortune seeker was admitted to that body on June 14, 1538, and retained the post for the remainder of his life.[6]

Nor was Francisco Vázquez's prominence solely political; he was active socially as well, being an organizer and charter member of the *Brotherhood of the Blessed Sacrament for Charity*, a laymen's charitable society founded in Mexico city in 1538 to aid the needy and educate orphan girls.[7]

Further enhanced were Coronado's prestige and fortunes when he married a wealthy heiress, Beatriz de Estrada, daughter of New Spain's late royal treasurer, Alonso de Estrada, labeled by gossip a son of his Catholic Majesty, Don Ferdinand. From his mother-in-law, Doña Marina, came a wedding gift of a large country estate—"half of Tlapa," wrote Viceroy Mendoza. In some manner Coronado also acquired the lands of one Juan de Burgos, who wanted to return to Spain.[8]

4. A. S. Aiton, *Antonio de Mendoza*, Durham, 1927, pp. 41-42.

5. Letter of Mendoza to the king, December 10, 1537, in Pacheco y Cárdenas, *Colección de documentos inéditos relativos al descubrimiento, conquista, y organización de las antiguas posesiones españolas en América y Oceanía*, Madrid, 1864-1884, II, pp. 198-199.

6. A. S. Aiton, "The Later Career of Coronado," in *American Historical Review*, xxx (1925), pp. 298-299.

7. Lota Spell, "The First Philanthropic Organization in America," in *American Historical Review*, xxxii (1927), pp. 546-549.

8. The grant of Tlapa was investigated by the audiencia, and Coronado apparently did not get it. Pacheco y Cárdenas, *op. cit.*, II, pp. 194-195; H. H. Bancroft, *History of Mexico*, II, p. 465.

Five children came from the conquistador's marriage, one son, Juan Vázquez, and four daughters, Doña Isabel de Luján, Doña Marina Vázquez, Doña Luisa de Estrada, and Doña Gerónima Vázquez. Son and heir Juan and Doña Gerónima died young. Doña Isabel married Bernardino Pacheco de Bocanegra, but had no children. Doña Luisa married twice, Luis Ponce de León and the factor, Martín de Iriguyen, but likewise had no children. Doña Marina Vázquez, who married Nuño de Chavez Bocanegra y Córdoba, was the only one of the five children to have heirs.[9]

Coronado's climb to affluence continued apace. In New Galicia, Mexico's wild, sparsely-settled northwestern province, Spanish affairs were in bad shape at this time. Its governor, infamous Nuño de Guzmán, later jailed for his crimes, had precipitated a native revolt in 1538 by enslaving and mistreating the Indians. Diego Pérez de la Torre, established as an investigating judge in the province, had supplanted Guzmán's rule, and suppressed the rebellion temporarily, but was badly injured in the fighting and soon died.[10]

Meanwhile, Cabeza de Vaca and his three companions, survivors of the disastrous Narváez expedition to Florida, arrived in Mexico city in 1536 with wondrous tales of large Indian cities in the mysterious country to the north. Shipwrecked on the Texas coast, the quartet had made its way across the continent to Mexico's west coast and thence to the capital.

Inspired by their stories, Viceroy Mendoza launched preparations for a small exploring party under Fray Marcos de Niza to verify Vaca's accounts. At the same time, considering New Galicia as an ideal base and starting point for a larger expedition, he set the stage for such an enterprise in August, 1538, by appointing his friend, Francisco Vázquez de Coronado, to investigate the injured Torre's administration and to become acting governor as well.[11]

9. Baltasar Dorantes de Carranza, *Sumaria Relación de las Cosas de la Nueva España*, Mexico, 1902, p. 279; A. G. I., *Audiencia de Mexico*, legajo 124.

10. See Letter of Coronado to the king, December 15, 1538, *infra*, pp. 35-41.

11. *Ibid.*, p. 35, which dispels Winship's speculations as to Coronado's appointment; see also Fray Antonio Tello, *Libro Segundo de la Crónica Miscelánea de la Santa Provincia de Xalisco*, Guadalajara, 1891, p. 303.

Off to New Galicia went Coronado, and the winter and spring of 1538-1539 were busy times for the future conquistador. In a letter to the king on December 15, 1538, Coronado wrote that, upon his arrival in the province, he found Torre dead and most of the Indians at war, "some because they have not been conquered, and others who, after being subjugated . . . have revolted." The Spanish settlers there, he complained, did not bother to convert the natives to the Christian faith, but "bend their efforts to exploiting them more than they should." Indians, declared Coronado, were made to carry excessive loads from Mexico city, and "free" and "unbranded" natives were bought and sold by the Spaniards. He had taken steps to correct these abuses, he assured the monarch, and would try to pacify the revolting Indians "by good deeds and by according them good treatment."

Rich gold and silver deposits had lured the Spaniards to New Galicia, whose four principal villages were Guadalajara, Compostela, Purificación, and Culiacán. As in all frontier settlements, the province's architecture was flimsy and makeshift. After appointing regidores for Guadalajara and approving Compostela's elected magistrates,[12] Coronado promulgated a royal decree that all houses built thereafter must be of stone, brick, or adobe, and designed after the style of Spain's dwellings, "so that they might be permanent and an adornment to the cities." Upon petition of its citizens that fall, Coronado had the village of Compostela moved to a location nearer the mines.[13]

During the winter, an official of the village of San Miguel de Culiacán, northernmost Spanish outpost, arrived in New Galicia with the news that San Miguel's residents, harassed by privations and an Indian revolt, were about to abandon the town and return south. He entreated Coronado to go to Culiacán and attempt to remedy the situation, but the latter was not able to leave Compostela until spring owing to disturbed conditions there.

With early spring, also, came Fray Marcos de Niza and

12. *Loc. cit.*
13. Letter of Coronado to the king, December 15, 1538, *infra*, pp. 39-40.

party, en route north on their exploring mission to verify the gilded stories of Cabeza de Vaca. Coronado accompanied them to Culiacán, and, after providing the friar with Indians and provisions, turned his attention to the revolt in that province and succeeded in quelling it. Ayapín, leader of the uprising, he captured and had quartered, Coronado informed King Charles in a letter.[14]

While in Culiacán, Francisco Vázquez heard of a rich region to the north called Topira. It was thickly populated, he wrote Viceroy Mendoza, and "the natives wear gold and emeralds and other precious stones." In April Coronado set out from Culiacán with 350 men to explore this fabulous region. He returned, says Pedro de Castañeda, member and chronicler of the Cíbola expedition, without finding "any signs of good lands."[15]

Back in New Galicia, Coronado plunged into the work of improving and extending Guadalajara with such success that the following summer the king dignified it with the title of "city" and granted it a coat of arms.[16]

On April 18, 1539, Francisco Vázquez was officially appointed governor of the province. His annual salary was set by King Charles at 1,500 ducats, but the monarch stipulated that the royal treasury would not be responsible for payment in case the revenue from the province did not yield this sum.[17]

Early in the autumn of 1539 Marcos de Niza returned from Cíbola with glowing accounts. When he passed through New Galicia, Coronado met him and together they hurried to tell the viceroy what the friar had seen and heard. Plans for the great entrada into the north were begun at once. Governor Coronado remained in the capital until fall, when he returned to New Galicia to send forth another reconnoitering party on November 17, under Melchior Díaz and Juan de Zaldívar,

14. Letter of Coronado to the king, July 15, 1539, *infra*, pp. 45-49.
15. Letter of Coronado to Mendoza, March 8, 1539, *infra*, pp. 42-44; letter of Mendoza to the king, 1539, *infra*, p. 53; Castañeda, *infra*, pp. 199-200.
16. George Parker Winship, "The Coronado Expedition, 1540-1542," in *Fourteenth Annual Report*, Bureau of Ethnology, Washington, 1896, p. 381, after Tello's Fragmento in Joaquín Garcia Icazbalceta, *Colección de documentos para la Historia de Mexico*, Mexico, 1858-1866, II, p. 371.
17. "Appointment of Francisco Vázquez de Coronado as Governor of New Galicia," *infra*, pp. 54-57.

and then hurried back to Mexico city to continue preparations for his expedition. Viceroy Mendoza officially commissioned Coronado as leader of the enterprise on January 6, 1540.[18]

This appointment was made by virtue of a cédula of 1535 by which the viceroy was authorized to disregard the pretensions of Hernán Cortés and to select some other leader for further explorations.[19] Slighted continually in America, Cortés repaired to the court of Charles V in 1540 to seek redress against what he claimed to be the usurpation of his rights and privileges in America, but the crown failed to heed his remonstrances.

While the principal reasons for the exploring enterprise were undoubtedly the lure of riches and glory, and to add new possessions to Spain's empire, other theories have been advanced. Adolph F. Bandelier, noted scientist, says of the expedition: "One of the chief objects seems to have been to free Mexico from an idle and unruly element. Hence exaggerated accounts of the northern regions, of the culture of their inhabitants, and of their mineral resources were purposely spread abroad."[20] And Spanish officials, according to evidence presented to Viceroy Mendoza on February 26, 1540, declared at the time that there were only two or three men in the entire army who had been permanent residents of New Spain, that

18. *Infra*, p. 83; letter of Mendoza to the king, April 17, 1540, *infra*, p. 157.

19. *Infra*. The contest between Cortés and his rivals was long and acrimonious and dated from the time of his conquest of Mexico, Tenochtitlán, in 1521. Shortly afterward he made the disastrous expedition to Honduras to safeguard his interests there, owing to the defection of his lieutenant, Olid. His long absence from the capital—he was even reported dead—gave his enemies in Mexico a period in which to consolidate their grasp on the government and to undermine Cortés, who carried the issue to Charles V, in 1528, by personally appearing at court to thwart his enemies. But Charles V was wary of too powerful subjects, and when Cortés returned to New Spain in 1530, it was with the appearance of power, not the substance. The establishment of the viceroyalty in Mexico five years later and Mendoza's appointment as viceroy pushed Cortés further into the background, for the king was determined that his own officials headed by the viceroy rather than a fortunate conqueror should be in charge of any new conquests such as now appeared likely in the northern interior.

20. A. F. Bandelier, in *Catholic Encyclopedia*. It must be borne in mind that there was a contest between Mendoza and Cortés for supremacy in New Spain and that Mendoza was possibly seeking to protect himself from criticism by the adherents of Cortés.

these few had been unable to make a living as settlers, and that the country was well rid of the entire force.[21] Whatever the actual motives, by February preparations for the expedition were complete and men and supplies converged on Compostela, the starting point. Pedro de Castañeda termed the assemblage "the most brilliant company ever assembled in the Indies to go in search of new lands," a sentiment re-echoed by Tello.[22]

On Sunday, February 22, 1540, Viceroy Mendoza and other dignitaries who had journeyed the 500 miles from Mexico to bid the army Godspeed held a review and muster roll of the great force.[23] In keeping with Spanish legalistic practice, the muster roll was drawn up before a judge and a notary, each member of the expedition giving his name, the number of horses he was bringing, and his military equipment. The whole force comprised, according to the notary's record, 230 men with horses and 62 without, but this did not include the friars nor their escort. Nor did it include any late arrivals, except Captain Melgosa, who was specifically included in the muster roll though he had not yet arrived from Mexico, nor any who joined at Culiacán or elsewhere along the way, nor did it make mention of Alarcón's armada, then being organized. Naturally there was no mention of the Indian allies in the official record, as only Spanish soldiers were listed.

We get a more complete picture of the nature of Coronado's force by piecing together the scattered records that have survived. We learn from Castañeda, for example, that there were 1,000 horses and 600 pack animals. Mota Padilla gave the figure as 1,000 horses, not including mules and pack animals. Coronado himself testified in 1547, in the Mendoza residencia, that there were 1,500 animals, horses, mules, and stock, by actual count.[24] As this is the most direct and authoritative statement on the subject, we may conclude that it is pretty accurate.

21. "Hearing on Charges of Depopulating New Spain," *infra*, p. 109.
22. Castañeda's Narrative, *infra*, p. 202.
23. See below, "The Muster Roll," pp. 87-108.
24. Castañeda's Narrative, *infra*, pp. 206 and 278; Mota Padilla, p. 112; Aiton and Rey, *New Mexico Historical Review*, xii, p. 314.

The Indian allies swelled Coronado's force greatly, but again there is no certainty as to the total number. Castañeda's figure of 1,000 is the one usually given, which is the same as Mota Padilla's. Viceroy Mendoza testified in his visita that no more than 300 Indians were taken from New Spain. This would, presumably, not include any from New Galicia, for in his residencia Mendoza claimed that 1,300 Indians voluntarily accompanied Coronado from Culiacán, which was corroborated by Coronado in his testimony.[25] Thus it is evident that a very large Indian force from Mexico took part in the great Coronado entrada to Cíbola and the new lands in the north.

The military equipment of the Spanish soldiers was no less heterogeneous than the human element that made up the expedition. Castañeda wrote that they had six or seven bronze pieces, *pedreros,* which were stone mortars. They were not of much use in the fighting with the pueblo Indians, as the same author makes disparaging remarks in this regard. Four of these guns were left with the pueblo of Zia for safe keeping and because they were useless.[26]

According to the muster roll, the only official inventory of the army, 27 soldiers had harquebuses, 19 had crossbows, and others swords, daggers, lances, and various odd pieces. Coronado himself was glitteringly arrayed in a suit of gilded armor, with a fine helmet ornamented with plumes.[27] Ten others wore full armor, while about forty had coats of mail. A good many soldiers had various pieces of head armor, and many also were protected by a buckskin coat, the most common armor in the whole force.

Castañeda relates that there was a surgeon to watch over the health of the army and tend its wounds, but he adds that he had no medicines and was in fact an incompetent newsmonger.[28] The muster roll makes no reference to any medical man.

25. Consult the same sources as in note 24.
26. Castañeda, *infra,* p. 233.
27. The description of Coronado's armor is given in his letter to Mendoza, August 3, 1540, p. 169; Traslado de las Nuevas, p. 180.
28. Castañeda's Narrative, *infra,* pp. 229 and 266.

To coöperate with Coronado's force, a sea expedition was organized, for it was thought that the new lands in the north bordered on the ocean and that additional food supplies and munitions for the army could best be provided in this manner.

The commander of the fleet was Hernando de Alarcón,[29] who was instructed to take command of the vessels, one ship and a sloop, in the port of Navidad, load them with artillery, provisions, and munitions, and proceed up the Gulf of California. As usual in such cases he was to keep a notarial record of his men and all the equipment and supplies. Alarcón was to sail for Culiacán to get in touch with Coronado, but if he missed him there he was instructed to proceed to Los Puertos. Beyond this point he was to land in every place possible to establish contact with Coronado or to learn of his whereabouts. In case of failure, Alarcón was to continue to the Buena Guía river, leaving landmarks and letters wherever he put in to shore, and proceed up this stream in the sloop as far as possible to inquire about Coronado and Cíbola.

The friars who accompanied Coronado's forces are not listed in the muster roll, which merely says that they had gone on in advance with an escort, nor is there any other source which states categorically who they were or how many. This has led to considerable confusion, especially as later chroniclers have cast shadows on this subject rather than light. We now have some new information on this phase of early southwestern history, chiefly from the trial records of Coronado, Cárdenas, and other members of the expedition.

The identity of four friars who went on the journey has been pretty definitely established. Fray Antonio de Victoria was one of these. We learn of him through an accident, for he broke a leg after leaving Culiacán and was sent back to recover.[30] Castañeda leaves the impression that he accompanied the main army under Don Tristán de Arellano, but there is nothing to substantiate this.

Fray Marcos de Niza, though little is said about him, was

29. Alarcón's instructions for his second voyage are translated below, pp. 117-123; those for the first voyage are not known to exist.
30. Castañeda's Narrative, *infra*, p. 207.

the chief guide, and he accompanied Coronado's advance force and was present at the capture of Cíbola, after which he returned to Mexico.[31]

Fray Juan de Padilla was with the expedition throughout its sojourn in the north, taking part in numerous scouting parties and remaining in the land to convert the natives. He accompanied Tovar to Tusayán, Alvarado to Cicuye, and Coronado to Quivira. It is believed that he was martyred at Quivira, whither he had returned to carry on his missionary labors.[32] This information is from the accounts of the Portuguese do Campo and others who escaped.

Fray Juan de Padilla was from Andalusia. He came to New Galicia with Nuño de Guzmán on his arrival there in 1529, becoming the first to minister the sacraments at Tepic. For some time he worked among the Indians at Pontzitlán, Tuchpán, and Tzapotlán, later served as guardian at Tulantzingo, in the province of the Holy Evangel, and accompanied Guzmán in his activities.[33] Fray Juan's frontier activities mark him as a zealous and fearless missionary.

According to Mendieta, Fray Juan de Padilla was accompanied by two oblates when he went to Quivira on Coronado's departure for Mexico. These were Sebastián and Lucas, but nothing more is known of them.[34]

Fray Luis de Escalona is the last of the friars of whom we are certain, though his name is sometimes given as Fray Luis de Ubeda, from which some confusion has resulted. Tello, Mota Padilla, Vetancurt, and Figueroa have called him Ubeda, but there appears to be no question but that Escalona and Ubeda were one and the same person. This friar also remained among the pueblos, at Cicuye, Coronado giving him some goats,

31. *Ibid.*, p. 210; Cárdenas' trial, *infra*, p. 345.

32. Castañeda, *infra*, pp. 263 and 270; Mendieta, *op. cit.*, pp. 742-745. López de Gómara, published in 1552, has only the following comment on the friars: "Fray Juan de Padilla se quedó en Tiguex con otro fraile francisco," and "Los de Quivira mataron a los frailes."

33. Tello, *Crónica*, pp. 67, 78, 88, 100, 137, 201, 484-494.

34. These oblates, Sebastián and Lucas, were first mentioned by Fray Gerónimo de Mendieta, whose history was written in 1596. *Historia Eclesiástica Indiana*, Mexico, 1870, pp. 744-745. Later Tello, Mota Padilla, and others repeated Mendieta's account.

sheep, and articles for gifts or trade.[35] No more was heard of him; it is supposed that he was martyred at Pecos amid his missionary labors.

The identity of Fray Juan de la Cruz has caused considerable controversy, some insisting that there was a friar by this name on Coronado's expedition and others contending that this was merely the monastic name for Fray Luis de Escalona.[36]

As to the latter point, it appears that there was a Fray Juan de la Cruz, a Frenchman from Aquitaine, who served as guardian of the convent of Tuchpán during the Coronado expedition, according to Tello, though elsewhere he contradicts himself and says that Fray Juan de la Cruz remained in Tiguex with the other friars. Actually Tello followed Mendieta, who finished his great history in 1596.[37] This confusion has been repeated by later chroniclers; there appears to be no contemporary document, however, to show that Fray Juan de la Cruz was with the expedition. Pending further proof it may be assumed that he remained in Mexico.

A Fray Daniel appears in some documents as a member of Coronado's band. Tello records that he was an Italian and remained at Tuchpán with Fray Juan de la Cruz during the period of the Coronado expedition.[38] When Coronado wrote to Mendoza on August 3, 1540, describing the clash with the Indians before reaching Cíbola, he mentioned two friars, Daniel and Luis, as present at that time.[39] This was the testimony also of Pedro de Ledesma, one of the soldiers, who said that Fray Daniel and the notary were together at Cíbola when the arrows began to fly.[40] Castañeda, on the contrary, mentions him as going with Fray Marcos in 1539.[41] Later writers add nothing to clarify the picture.

35. See Castañeda and Jaramillo, *infra.*, pp. 270 and 306.
36. See Bandelier's discussion of this point in *New Mexico Historical Review*, v (1930), pp. 174-184.
37. Tello, *Crónica*, pp. 406 and 489. Fray Gerónimo de Mendieta, *Historia Eclesiástica Indiana*, Mexico, 1870, pp. 742-745.
38. *Ibid.*, p. 106.
39. Coronado to Mendoza, August 3, 1540, *infra*, p. 167.
40. A. G. I., *Justicia*, legajo, 1021.
41. Castañeda, *infra*, p. 197.

Still another friar is mentioned by Coronado, on two different occasions. This was Fray Antonio de Castilblanco. Coronado's first reference to him was during his testimony in his own residencia on September 1, 1544, when he mentioned him in connection with some Indian slaves in New Galicia. Two days later, in his testimony on the conduct of the expedition, Coronado said that he "called to his quarters Fray Juan de Padilla and Fray Antonio de Castilblanco" to ask their advice about attacking one of the recalcitrant Tiguex pueblos.[42] There is no further mention of this Fray Antonio.

Two friars, Remundo and Antonio, were to accompany Alarcón's second expedition up the coast, but it is not known that it actually sailed, so we hear nothing more of them.

Pending further evidence in regard to the friars and lay brothers who accompanied the Coronado expedition, there is not much profit in speculating on the number that went.

At least three women accompanied the expedition, Francisca de Hozes, wife of Alonzo Sánchez, María Maldonado, wife of Juan de Paradinas, and the wife of Lope Caballero. Francisca de Hozes went with her husband and a son and accompanied the expedition from beginning to end. She later testified against Coronado, charging that he prevented her and other Spaniards from remaining in the new land to establish a colony.[43] María Maldonado, wife of Juan de Paradinas (or Paladinas), was described by witnesses as nursing the sick soldiers on the expedition, mending their clothes, and doing other good works. Her husband was a tailor by trade. He was a good soldier and Coronado named him camp marshal and appointed him to other posts.[44] The wife of Lope Caballero is described simply at a native woman, without the mention of her name.[45]

From the muster roll of the expedition and the court records accumulated during the trials of Coronado, Cárdenas,

42. See *infra,* p. 333.
43. Testimony in A. G. I., *Justicia,* legajo 1021, pieza 4.
44. See C. W. Hackett, *Historical Documents relating to New Mexico, Nueva Vizcaya, and Approaches Thereto, to 1773,* Washington, 1923, I, pp. 45-47.
45. Icaza, *Diccionario,* no. 987.

and other members of the army, as well as from applications for compensation or employment made later by ex-soldiers and colonizers, come the names of a number of foreigners. Most of these were Portuguese, five altogether. These were Andrés do Campo, a man of some wealth as indicated by the fact that he had three horses on the expedition. He remained with Fray Juan de Padilla and brought back from Quivira the news of the friar's death. Do Campo's countrymen were Gaspar Alvarez, Andrés Martín, one Aorta, each of whom brought one horse, and Fernández Páez, who invested two horses in the enterprise.[46]

Two Italians joined the northern adventure. The first was Simón García,[47] from Genoa, whose mother was Spanish. Not only did he go to Cíbola with Coronado, taking two horses, but he had taken part in the conquest of Peru.

The second Italian was Francisco Roxo Loro, a native of Sicily, who said he came to America with an expedition for conquest in Central America.[48] On his return from Cíbola, he settled at Compostela and Coronado gave him in encomienda some Indians in the sierras of Jalisco. He took three horses on the expedition.

Apparently there was one Frenchman, Cristóbal Bertao (Christophe Berteau), from Bernuel in the province of Rouen, in Coronado's army, evidently a foot soldier.[49]

There was one Scot in the expedition, celebrated as the first Scotchman to enter what is now the United States. He was Tomás Blaque (Thomas Blake), married to Francisca de Rivera, the widow of one of the first settlers in New Spain.[50]

The foreigner who played the most conspicuous role in the army seems to have been Juan Fioz, a native of Worms, Germany. As the bugler of the expedition, he was present at all the major actions, including the expedition to Quivira. He was, accordingly, an important witness at the investigation of

46. These names are in the Muster Roll.
47. Icaza, *Diccionario*, no. 791.
48. *Ibid.*, no. 1207.
49. *Ibid.*, no. 305.
50. *Ibid.*, no. 738; G. R. G. Conway, "A Scotsman in America in 1535," *Notes and Queries*, vol. 148, pp. 293-294.

Coronado's management of the expedition and appeared as a defense witness for both Coronado and Cárdenas.[51]

Other non-Spanish names are found among Coronado's men. There is Bartolomé Napolitano (the Neapolitan) ; Juan Bautista de San Vitorees, perhaps of French descent; a certain Galiveer, perhaps a Gulliver from the British Isles; Jaco de Brujas (Jack of Bruges), a Fleming; Lorenzo Genovés (the Genoese) ; and Juan Francés (the Frenchman) ;[52] while these names are foreign, it is not established that they were of foreign birth.

The exodus of so many people from Mexico caused criticism, for it was said that the country was being left unprotected and at the mercy of the hostile Indians, so recently outraged by Nuño de Guzmán. To forestall such charges, the viceroy instituted proceedings to refute contentions of critics. The legal inquiry took place on February 26, at Compostela, at Coronado's instigation, and the witnesses, who were the best qualified officials, testified that only three residents of Mexico were going. In fact they claimed that only transients, unemployed, and new arrivals planned to go and that Mexico would be better off without them.[53]

Legal formalities over, the great adventure began in earnest. The march from Compostela to Culiacán, last Spanish outpost to the north, required more than a month. It was uneventful save for the death of Lope de Samaniego, the army master,[54] at the hands of hostile Indians and for the slow and laborious progress of a large expedition through country covered with a jungle-like monte and inhabited by Indians whose normal existence had been shattered by the Spanish conquest. Discouraging news the expedition gleaned, also, from the scouting party under command of Melchior Díaz and Juan de Zaldívar which had been sent north the previous November and which now returned. Though the officials strove to keep their report confidential, the news spread and Fray Marcos

51. A. G. I., *Justicia*, legajo 1021, pieza 5.
52. These names are in the Muster Roll.
53. See *infra*, pp. 109-116; see also p. 6, note 20.
54. Castañeda, *infra*, p. 204.

was obliged to exert himself to reassure the men.[55] He himself had been there and they should wait and see for themselves, he claimed.

The small frontier town of Culiacán opened its doors wide in welcome to the seekers of new lands and wealth. Nor were the citizens ill repaid for their hospitality, for the soldiers here discarded their excess baggage and fancy raiment for more substantial needs, especially food supplies, of which Culiacán had an abundance, following a good harvest.[56] By this time the soldiers realized the seriousness of getting food along the way for such a large number of men and animals and the fact that they might have difficulty in keeping in touch with Alarcón's ships. At least, the fleet failed to meet them at Culiacán, as anticipated.

By this time Coronado had reached the decision that the expedition's progress must be speeded up and that he would go on in advance with a small party, unimpeded by unnecessary baggage, to spy out the new lands. So, after two weeks in Culiacán, Coronado set out on April 22, 1540, with approximately 75 horsemen and 25 foot soldiers, some Indian allies, and with cattle for food. The main army was placed in charge of Don Tristán de Arellano, who was to lead it in the wake of the faster moving advance party a fortnight later.[57]

Crossing from river valley to river valley, Coronado's party followed the old Indian trails, for his force was provided with native guides and accompanied also by Fray Marcos de Niza, who had already been through the land the previous year. From Culiacán the route led by way of Pericos, over the rolling hills and sharp dales, covered with a dense growth of the thick shrubs and trees that characterize the region. In the vicinity of Pericos, an ancient settlement, the country opens out into broad flat plains, much of it extremely fertile and supporting a tremendous growth of native vegetation; for this is a part of the coastal

55. *Loc. cit.,* and letter of Mendoza to the king, April 17, 1540, which incorporates the report of Díaz.
56. Castañeda, *infra,* p. 206.
57. *Ibid.,* p. 206; letter of Coronado to Mendoza, August 3, 1540, p. 162; Traslado de las Nuevas, p. 179; Narrative of Jaramillo, p. 295.

plain, the deep blue mountains rising ridge on ridge farther to the east and forming a barrier difficult to traverse.

For several hundred miles north of Pericos, the old trail to the north country varied but little, passing through Mocorito and Sinaloa and Fuerte, all situated in rich valleys that have always supported a considerable population. North of Fuerte, the lay of the land changed, becoming more rolling and less densely covered with vegetation, but from the Mayo to the Yaqui the route lay again through beautiful valleys, especially that of the Rio de los Cedros and then along the east bank of the Yaqui to Soyopa. Here, instead of entering the narrow canyon through which the Yaqui flows before it debouches into the coastal plain, the trail lay to the west, along Rebeico canyon to Mátape, and thence across to Ures in the Sonora valley, and up the latter. The Sonora river comes out of a canyon a few miles above modern Ures, a point that is unmistakably described by Fray Marcos de Niza and which all expeditions along this line of travel sought, for it provided an easy and practicable route to the interior, including water and food for man and beast, all so vital on these long marches.

From the Sonora valley, with its numerous Indian settlements, Coronado followed the regular trail northward by way of Arizpe and Bacoachi into the San Pedro valley, proceeding along its course for several days before striking Chichilti-calli near the Gila river. At Chichilti-calli the weary Spaniards halted for two days to prepare for the march through the forbidding country ahead. They were nearly exhausted, being on the verge of starvation, and they had already lost many of their animals.[58] Neither men nor animals were in any shape for a fight; in fact, many dropped by the wayside as they went on. Their only hope, however, lay in finding the rich province of Cíbola, for although they had heard from the natives that several ships, possibly Alarcón's, had been sighted along the coast, by now they were too far inland to make practical use of any reinforcements from that source.

Striking into the White Mountain Apache region of Arizona, Coronado and his men veered northeastward until they

58. Letter of Coronado to Mendoza, August 3, 1540, *infra*, pp. 164-166.

approached the place called Cíbola by Fray Marcos but which Coronado called Granada in honor of the viceroy's birthplace in Spain. The pueblo was the modern Hawikuh, now a pile of ruins a few miles southwest of Zuñi pueblo.[59]

Before coming to Cíbola, Coronado met Indians, but they fled, heedless of his protestations of friendship. Then, a scant three or four leagues from the pueblo, scouts reported a bad and rocky pass which might prove troublesome if hostile Indians should occupy it. Coronado sent López de Cárdenas to remain at the spot during the night until the whole party should arrive. This he did, camping there one night after trying to convince the Indians he encountered of his friendly intentions. But they would not be convinced, and that very night the natives attacked, causing some damage and upsetting the soldiers a good deal, for it was the first clash that Coronado and his men had had since leaving Culiacán.[60]

This disturbance took place on the night of July 6, and on the following day, when the Indians resisted all friendly overtures, Coronado and his men stormed and occupied the pueblo of Hawikuh.[61] During the invasion of the town, disaster all but overtook Coronado, for while leading his men into the narrow streets of the village and seeking to scale a ladder at one of the houses—there were no doorways on the ground floor—the enemy rained stones on his head and he was seriously stricken. Had it not been for López de Cárdenas and Maldonado, who loyally came to his aid and extricated his unconscious form from the thick of the battle, Coronado might not have lived to lead his men on, on to disillusionment and failure, failure to find the rich kingdoms he sought.

Cíbola was a tremendous disappointment to the little Spanish force, for they beheld no turquoise-studded doors, no silversmiths' shops in the streets, no gold—though they did find a goodly supply of maize, of which they were in greater need at

59. F. W. Hodge has summarized the evidence regarding the identification of Cíbola with Hawikuh. *History of Hawikuh, New Mexico*, Los Angeles, 1937.

60. Testimony of Coronado and Cárdenas, *infra*, pp. 322 and 344; letter of Coronado to Mendoza, August 3, 1540, *infra*, p. 167.

61. Traslado de las Nuevas, *infra*, pp. 179-181; testimony of Coronado and Cárdenas, pp. 322-323 and 344-345.

the time than of other golden treasure. Poor Fray Marcos. This was not what he had told about, and before long he returned to Mexico with some messengers, for he had become the butt of the soldiers' rage.

Recovered from the recent hardships, the Spaniards set out to explore, keeping Hawikuh as their base of operations. Even though they had not yet found the kingdoms they had been led to expect so confidently, these might be near at hand. Perhaps the kingdom of Tusayán, of which they heard from the Indians, was the place, so Coronado sent Don Pedro de Tovar with a force of twenty men and Fray Juan de Padilla to reconnoiter. Without incident, he reached the Hopi pueblos, as they are now called, and approached the pueblo one night, unobserved, and camped at the foot of a mesa below one of the villages. Early next morning the intruders were discovered, and the Indians rushed out to meet them "with bows, shields, and wooden maces." Defying the strange men before them, they drew lines on the ground and forbade them to cross. Through the interpreter, Tovar voiced his friendly intentions, but the Hopis would not let the invaders enter. During the conference an Indian, bolder than his fellows, struck one of the horses over the bridle, whereupon Fray Juan gave the signal to advance. In the resulting melee, the Indians soon abandoned their resistance to the strange men and their horses, "who ate people," so they had been told.[62] But Tusayán did not yield the treasures sought and Tovar and his men returned to Cíbola to report what they had learned.

On Tovar's return, Coronado sent out a party under López de Cárdenas to explore a great river to the west, of which the Hopis had informed Tovar. Taking twelve men, Cárdenas set out late in August, going first to Hopi-land where he was given guides and provisions for the rest of the journey. Reinforced in this manner, Cárdenas and his party traveled westward and discovered the Grand Canyon of the Colorado river. They were the first Europeans to gaze upon this tremendous gorge, appalling in its solitude and awful majesty. Frustrated in their efforts to reach the river at the bottom of the canyon, Cárdenas and his

62. Castañeda, pp. 213-215; Coronado to Mendoza, August 3, 1540, p. 175.

men returned to headquarters at Cíbola to tell of their experiences.[63]

Here Coronado had entertained visitors—Indians from a pueblo to the east called Cicuye, now known as Pecos. Among them was one named Bigotes because of his beard. Bigotes brought messages of friendship from his people and invited the Spaniards to visit their country. He brought gifts, also, gifts of buffalo skins, and in turn was regaled with gewgaws of various kinds which the Indians prized highly.

Captivated by the descriptions of these strange animals, the buffaloes, and eager to learn more of the country, Coronado sent Captain Hernando de Alvarado and Fray Juan de Padilla and twenty men, accompanied by Indian guides, to explore. Passing numerous ruins on the way, Alvarado's party, five days after leaving Hawikuh, arrived at the great rock of Acoma and marveled at the secure position of the pueblo atop its rocky mesa. The Acomans were peaceful and offered gifts of food and skins. Then Alvarado and his followers climbed the 357-foot rock, the first time that white men had visited this sky pueblo, still an object of wonder to visitors as it was four hundred years ago.

From Acoma the Spaniards headed eastward to the fertile Rio Grande valley and the province of Tiguex, stretching to the north and south of modern Albuquerque. The Tiguex Indians greeted their visitors peacefully.

So impressed was Captain Alvarado with the prosperity of the Rio Grande valley and its pueblos that he immediately dispatched messengers to Coronado, advising him to bring the army there for the winter. Meantime Alvarado's party spent several days in the province of Tiguex, and then struck out northeast to Cicuye. Here the natives welcomed home Bigotes and marveled at their strange guests. Cicuye, as promised by Bigotes, accorded the Spaniards an ovation, bringing them "into the pueblo with drums and flageolets, similar to fifes."[64]

At Cicuye the Spaniards met an Indian from a country farther to the east, a man who was to influence greatly Coronado and his expedition's fortunes. He was promptly dubbed "the

63. Castañeda, *infra,* pp. 215-217; Relación del Suceso, *infra,* pp. 287-288.
64. Castañeda, *infra,* p. 219.

Turk," because, said the Spaniards, "he looked like one." Guided by the Turk, Alvarado and his men explored to the east, crossed the mountains and followed the Canadian river into the plains of the Texas Panhandle. There they got their first glimpse of the buffaloes, of which the Indians had already told them.

The finding of the Turk relieved the Spaniards of whatever monotony and dullness had come over them since their discovery that Cíbola and neighboring provinces had turned out so poorly. Forgotten, now, were their sufferings and earlier disappointments, for the Turk told of a new land, something greater and more wonderful than even the sermons of Fray Marcos de Niza had led them to expect. This new land was called Quivira. Its riches defied description, for in it gold and silver were so plentiful that even ordinary kitchen utensils were made of these metals. The chase for the pot of phantom gold was about to begin again.

Meanwhile Don Tristán de Arellano and the main army, having left Culiacán with the pack animals, were plodding over the plains and mountains of northern Mexico, following the trails that Coronado and his party had blazed. At Corazones in the Sonora valley, about where the river emerges from the canyon known locally as La Tescalama, the army settled down to await orders from Coronado. There in the distant new land the Spaniards built houses and established a town, naming it San Gerónimo de los Corazones (St. Jerome of the Hearts). Anxious to contact Alarcón's fleet, Arellano dispatched a small force to the coast, but found no ships, only a tribe of giant Indians, one of whom was brought back to Corazones.[65]

In early September, Fray Marcos and the two soldiers whom Coronado had sent from Cíbola arrived at Corazones with orders for the army to proceed, leaving a force of eighty men at Corazones to maintain it as a supply station between the army in Cíbola and the ships or the homeland, depending on their success in finding the Alarcón expedition. Fray Marcos and Juan Gallego, meantime, returned to inform the viceroy of the discoveries up till that time.[66]

65. *Ibid.,* p. 209.
66. *Ibid.,* p. 210.

In command at Corazones Coronado had appointed Melchior Díaz and had given orders that he look for Alarcón's ships. With twenty-five men, Díaz pushed on to the Gulf of California and then northward to the junction of the Gila and Colorado rivers near modern Yuma. Because the Indians there carried firebrands to warm themselves, the Spaniards named the stream the Tizón or Firebrand river. Here the natives told of strange men and boats, and Díaz discovered on a tree these words: "There are letters at the foot of this tree." Digging down, he found the message that Alarcón had been there but that, after waiting in vain for news of Coronado, he had been obliged to leave because his ships were rotting.

Melchior Díaz and his men now crossed the river on rafts, after some difficulty with the Yuma Indians, and started down the west side of the Colorado river into Lower California. Finding their way blocked by beds of volcanic lava, they retraced their steps and set out for Corazones. But one night, Captain Díaz saw a dog harrying the expedition's sheep and started in pursuit on horseback. Galloping at full speed, he hurled his lance at the offending dog, but his aim missed, the weapon lodged in the ground, and, unable to swerve his horse, the lance pierced the rider's abdomen. The men carried their injured captain for some days, but he died before they reached Corazones on January 18, 1541.[67]

Diego de Alcaraz now succeeded to command at the midway station in the Sonora valley; he proved unequal to the task.

At Cíbola Coronado joyfully received Alvarado's report of the favorable outlook for food and supplies in the province of Tiguex, and immediately sent López de Cárdenas, just back from his journey to the Grand Canyon, to prepare winter quarters for the army in this fruitful valley. At this time the main army under Don Tristán de Arellano reached Cíbola from Corazones, after a comparatively uneventful journey. Once during the march some men became ill from eating prickly pear preserves; on another occasion they saw Rocky Mountain sheep, which created some diversion.

---

67. *Ibid.*, pp. 210-212 and 231-232. The date of Díaz's death is given in Tello, *Crónica*, p. 411.

A few days after the army's arrival, Francisco Vásquez, ordering Arellano's force to proceed to Tiguex after men and horses
had rested, set out with about thirty men to explore a province
called Tutahaco, situated evidently in the neighborhood of
Isleta or possibly beyond the Manzano mountains. This reconnaissance over, he soon joined López de Cárdenas at the pueblo
of Alcanfor, whither Alvarado and his men, accompanied by the
Turk, had also repaired.[68] The Spanish forces were to live
among these pueblos, extending from Isleta to Bernalillo, for
the next two years, but the exact site of Alcanfor has not been
finally determined.

The Spaniards listened avidly to the Turk's very glib and
graphic descriptions of the wonders in store for them. The new
land was far to the east, at a place called Quivira, he said, where
there was a river two leagues wide, and there were fish in it as
large as horses. Not only this, but there were hundreds of
canoes with more than twenty rowers on a side; these canoes
carried sails, and the chiefs lolled under awnings in the stern,
and on the prows there were great golden eagles. The high lord

68. Castañeda's Narrative, *infra*, pp. 220-221. Coronado and Cárdenas gave
the name of the pueblo of Alcanfor. *Infra*, pp. 326 and 347.
    After Coronado entered Cíbola and appropriated whatever provisions he
found there, he sent Alvarado, Cárdenas, and other captains ahead with small
forces to explore. Alvarado marched north as far as Cicuye (Pecos), and Braba
(Taos), which he named Valladolid. Cárdenas prepared lodging for the army at
the pueblo of Alcanfor, or Coofor, in the province of Tiguex. Both names are
given in the testimony of Coronado and Cárdenas.
    There were about fifteen pueblos in Tiguex province, almost equally dis-
tributed on both sides of the river. Two leagues from Alcanfor was Arenal, a
large pueblo attacked and entered by Cárdenas. Between Alcanfor and Arenal
was Alameda, according to the testimony of Coronado. Another large pueblo,
besieged for fifty days by Coronado and his men, was Moho or Mohi. It was
at the siege of this pueblo that Francisco de Ovando and other prominent
Spaniards were killed.
    The number of pueblos attacked and destroyed by the Spaniards in the
province of Tiguex was about thirteen, according to testimony. Domingo Martín
said that ten were destroyed; Juan de Contreras and Melchior Pérez gave the
number as thirteen. Cristóbal de Escobar said, "Que se tomaron tres pueblos
por fuerça, quel uno se llamaba el pueblo de la Cruz, y el otro el de la Alameda,
y el otro el del Circo. E despues de tomados quemaron la madera dellos."
    Melchior Pérez said that Braba (Taos) had 30,000 persons. While this figure
is grossly exaggerated, it shows that Taos made a strong impression on the
Spaniards.
    The testimony drawn upon in this note comes from A. G. I., *Justicia*, legajo
1021, pieza 4.

of the land took his afternoon siesta under a great tree on which hung little golden bells which lulled him to sleep as they tinkled in the breeze. Even the everyday dishes of the poorest natives there were made of wrought plate, and the jugs and bowls were of gold.[69]

The Promised Land? Indeed! Cabeza de Vaca and Fray Marcos were right after all!

Furthermore, said the Turk, he had brought some gold bracelets from Quivira, but the Cicuye Indians had taken them from him. Anxious to see the actual proof of these riches, Coronado sent Alvarado to Cicuye once more to demand the jewelry. But when he arrived there, Cicuye's residents denied all knowledge of the bracelets and jewels. The Turk, they claimed, was lying.

During that first winter in New Mexico, 1540-1541, peaceful relations prevailed between Spaniards and Indians for some time, even after the latter had moved in to live with their friends and relatives in order to turn over Alcanfor to the strangers.

But friction soon arose, chiefly over the gathering of food supplies and clothing from the pueblos, it seems, but doubtless over other misunderstandings as well. As the winter progressed, Spaniards and Mexican Indian allies, accustomed to warmer climes, suffered severely, and dire necessity drove Coronado and his officers to overrule tact and courtesy in procuring much-needed clothing from the Pueblo Indians. "There was nothing the natives could do," said Castañeda, "except take off their own cloaks and hand them over until the number that the Spaniards asked for was reached." In fact, reminisced the aging Castañeda, "if they saw an Indian with a better one, they exchanged it with him without any consideration or respect."[70]

To the Indians this was the last straw, and a few days later the storm broke. An Indian ally, in charge of the expedition's horses in a nearby pasture, staggered into Alcanfor, wounded and bleeding. Pueblo Indians, he revealed, had attacked and

---

69. Castañeda, p. 221.
70. *Ibid.*, p. 224. This episode played a considerable part in the Coronado and Cárdenas trials. *Infra*, pp. 329-330 and 351.

killed one of the horse guards, and had stampeded the horses and driven them off.

Coronado dispatched Captain López de Cárdenas with a few men to investigate. The party followed the tracks of the stampeded herd to the pueblo of Arenal, but found it enclosed by a stockade.[71] Inside pandemonium reigned. The terrified horses were milling madly about the grounds—"as in a bull ring," said Castañeda—with shouting Indians in hot pursuit, discharging arrows at them. Cárdenas and his men rounded up what horses they could find outside the pueblo and started back to give Coronado the disturbing news. From what they saw at other pueblos along the way they deduced—correctly—that the whole province was up in arms.

Threatened by a general revolt, Coronado and his advisers, including the friars, held an important council of war, at which it was decided that the Indian uprising must be suppressed. López de Cárdenas, as maestre de campo, was immediately sent to demand the surrender of Arenal, the offending pueblo. But the inhabitants, haughty and defiant, refused all peace overtures, and Cárdenas gave the signal for attack.

Combining strategy with superior weapons, the Spaniards not only attacked openly and gained possession of some of the terraces, but also used smudge fires to drive the Indians to submission, and some of them surrendered to Captains Melgosa and Diego López, who signified acceptance. Captain Cárdenas, unaware that the Indians had capitulated on a promise of safe keeping, as was claimed later, ordered his men "to make an example of the pueblo." They did so in exemplary fashion by preparing to burn the captives at the stake. Perhaps twenty-five or thirty suffered this punishment, but fifty or more of their companions in Cárdenas' tent, awaiting a similar fate, made a dash for freedom and some were killed in the ensuing melee.[72]

Guilt for the horrible massacre was never conclusively proved against any one. Captain Cárdenas, tried in Spain several years later for the atrocity, claimed that unruly soldiers had

---

71. Coronado gives the name of the pueblo; *infra*, p. 333.

72. These are the figures given in the Coronado and Cárdenas trials. *Infra*, pp. 334-335, 355. Castañeda states that the number was much larger. *Infra*, p. 226.

done it in the heat of battle without his orders. But he was convicted. It is hardly conceivable that Coronado, who had demonstrated beyond doubt his earnest desire for peaceful relations with the Indians, ordered such butchery. The most logical explanation is that it was a blundering misinterpretation of orders.

At this time Arellano's force arrived at Alcanfor from Cíbola, after floundering through heavy snowstorms which blotted out the trail. Each night it was necessary to clear the ground in order to make camp, and the falling snow covered the baggage, horses, and the men in their beds.

The fate of Arenal did not cow the Indians to submission, for at Mohi, called Tiguex by Castañeda, they again challenged the strange men on horseback. The trouble began when Captain Cárdenas and thirty men arrived at this fortified pueblo on a peace mission. At the solicitation of the Indians, Cárdenas advanced to meet them, unarmed, whereupon the Indians attacked him with clubs they had concealed behind their backs. He was saved by the quick action of two mounted Spaniards,[73] but Coronado and his staff, angered at this rejection of their peace offers, decided that the recalcitrant pueblo must be punished.

With a large force Coronado began the attack, which lengthened to a siege of fifty days, for the people of Mohi would not surrender to a conqueror they did not trust. In the end, the shortage of water within the pueblo forced the issue, even after a considerable number of women and children had been surrendered to the Spaniards. Two weeks later the defenders crept stealthily out of the pueblo one night and started across the plain. Guards sounded the alarm and the Spaniards took up the pursuit, overtaking the foe near the river. In a sharp engagement many of the Indians were killed. Survivors escaped across the ice.

These encounters at Arenal and Mohi were the most serious that winter, though some other clashes occurred. But, by the end of March the resistance of the pueblos was over and the

---

73. Testimony of Coronado and Cárdenas, *infra*, pp. 333 and 359, and Castañeda, *infra*, pp. 227-228.

valley settled down to a comparative calm. The Indians of the province of Tiguex were passive if not pacified.

Winter over and the country quieted, General Coronado's thoughts turned to Quivira and its riches, and preparations began for the journey to that fabulous land of dreams. With the Turk as a guide, the entire expedition evacuated Alcanfor on April 23, 1541, and moved slowly out of the Rio Grande Valley.[74] Silently the Indians watched their departure, but in a different spirit than they had shown on their arrival a few months earlier. At the pueblo of Pecos, the army halted to return Bigotes and to make sure of the friendship of these people. Their governor, Coronado's prisoner for a time, had already been restored to his people.

Leaving Cicuye, apparently with the good will and friendship of its inhabitants, the army was soon out upon the buffalo plains among nomadic tribes of Querecho Indians. These people, living entirely on the products of the buffalo, were different from their pueblo brothers, but they greeted the strange white people in friendly manner. They gave only vague, very vague, information about settlements to the east, so the Spaniards wandered forward—aimlessly on the limitless plains.

Spaniards and guides alike were confused. Patience and food supplies were nearly exhausted, and the army faced a crisis. Only the buffaloes were to be seen everywhere. On one occasion three horses, lost in a buffalo stampede, were buried in a ravine amid a bellowing mass of the awkward animals. Another time the army suffered severely in a terrific hailstorm which destroyed all the crockery and caused other damage.

Alarmed by the shortage of provisions and the slim prospects of obtaining any on the plains, Coronado and his staff decided that the general, with thirty horsemen and a few foot soldiers, should proceed in search of Quivira; the remainder of the army was to return to the Rio Grande valley and wait there for news from their leader.

Doubts about the Turk's veracity had beset Coronado since leaving Tiguex—a suspicion shared by most of the army. His

74. Letter of Coronado to the king, October 20, 1541, *infra,* p. 186; Castañeda, *infra,* p. 234.

directions for finding Quivira had been contradicted by the Querechos and the Teyas, tribes of plains Indians. Ysopete, another of the guides with the army and himself a plains Indian, had declared all along that the Turk was lying and that he was leading the army astray. Placing Ysopete in the van as guide and putting the Turk in chains, Coronado and his select band struck out boldly northward for the fabled Quivira.

Six weeks later another rainbow had evaporated into meaningless mist as Coronado and his troop discovered that Quivira, in central Kansas, was a populous province of the Wichita Indians, and all of them as poor in gold as his own men. The Turk, faced with the grim reality of being unmasked, now confessed that golden Quivira was a plot hatched to lead the expedition astray on the plains, and when they were out of food and water, the entire force would fall easy victims to the Indians of the Pueblo country if they had not already perished. The Turk was promptly garrotted.[75]

After exploring for a month in Quivira, Coronado and his men turned their weary footsteps toward the Rio Grande. It was a crestfallen band that rejoined their comrades at Alcanfor that autumn of 1541 to settle down to another gloomy winter in Pueblo land.

On the whole, that second winter was not as severe as the first, for even though the men suffered from want of clothing and adequate food, there were no major battles between Spaniards and Indians. Discontent grew steadily, however, for many were satisfied that it would be better to return to Mexico since all the accounts of treasure in the north had proved to be fables. Thoughts of home and its pleasures induced others to dissatisfaction with further exploration, and thus passed the winter, with much tugging and pulling as to whether to return to Mexico or to remain and continue the search for the "other Mexico" somewhere in that vast inland empire. Only occasionally were there scouting parties, but these overran pretty thoroughly all of the pueblos for food and provisions.

During the autumn Captain López de Cárdenas, who had suffered a broken arm on the way to Quivira, set out for Mexico

75. *Ibid.*, pp. 235-244; testimony of Coronado and Cárdenas, pp. 336, 361-362.

with a small group of disabled soldiers. Corazones, the midway station in Sonora, they found in ashes and the Indians up in arms. Retracing his steps, López de Cárdenas hastened to advise Coronado of the disaster. Most of the Corazones people, in fact, had been killed by the Indians, only a few escaping to Culiacán. Diego de Alcaraz, commander at Corazones, was among the dead, and well was it so, for his misconduct was said to have been responsible for the savage uprising.

Back at Alcanfor also disaster had struck sharply, for one day while racing with Captain Rodrigo Maldonado, Coronado's saddle girth broke and, falling under the hammering hoofs of Maldonado's horse, he received a dangerous wound on the head. Throughout the winter Coronado lay in a critical condition, a situation that was simulated rather than real, according to his critics, in order to force the return of the whole expedition to Mexico.

Though one group of sixty people wanted to remain in the new land, the other faction, supported by Coronado, won the day and all were required to join the return march.[76] So, early in the spring of 1542, the dejected colonists and soldiers turned their faces westward and set out on the homeward trek—past Acoma, Inscription Rock, Zuñi, the ruins of Corazones, back to Mexico and their friends, cool friends now, back to the travail of ordinary existence, back to everlasting fame.

Coronado's star sank rapidly after his return from Cíbola. Like all men holding high office in the Spanish realm, he soon had to undergo an official inspection, both of his stewardship of the Cíbola venture and of his administration as governor of New Galicia. On September 7, 1543, Judge Lorenzo Tejada of the audiencia of Mexico was appointed to investigate and verify reports of abuses, violences, and crimes committed by Coronado and his captains during the expedition to Cíbola.[77]

In the inquiry into the conduct of the expedition, Judge Tejada called in fourteen witnesses, to whom he submitted a number of questions. The first witness to appear was Francisca de Hozes, wife of Alonso Sánchez, who testified in Mexico on

76. Castañeda, pp. 264-268, 270-274; Relación del Suceso, infra, p. 293.
77. Tejada's commissions are given in this volume, pp. 313 and 315.

May 9, 1544. Among other witnesses were Juan de Zaldívar, Cristóbal de Escobar, and Rodrigo de Frías. Coronado testified at Guadalajara on September 3 of the same year. Upon the completion of the hearing Judge Tejada gave the report to Cristóbal de Benavente, fiscal or prosecuting attorney of the audiencia of Mexico, to study it and press charges if the evidence warranted. On March 21, 1545, the fiscal indicted Coronado on six counts and asked the audiencia to impose the most severe punishment possible in accordance with the law. Coronado, who had been under technical arrest in his home, was asked to appear before the audiencia. On February 19, 1546, at a public meeting, this body declared Coronado innocent of all charges resulting from his management of the expedition to Cíbola. This exculpating sentence was signed by Viceroy Mendoza, as president of the audiencia, and Judges Tejada, Tello de Sandoval, Ceynos, and Santillán.[78]

Judge Tejada was also required to conduct the residencia of Coronado as governor of New Galicia, of Cristóbal de Oñate, acting governor, and other officials, and began the inquiry on August 8, 1544. As was customary in such cases, all of the officials to be investigated were suspended from office by the appointment of a juez de residencia. The judge prepared a list of twenty-five elaborate questions which he submitted to twenty-eight witnesses, among whom were the men under investigation. From the mass of evidence gathered, he indicted Coronado on thirty-four counts ranging from accepting gifts, which was forbidden by law, to favoritism in the administration of justice.

In spite of Coronado's rebuttal evidence and the introduction of numerous character witnesses, Judge Tejada imposed sentence on some of the charges, leaving others to the discretion of the Council of the Indies.[79] The sentence imposed consisted wholly of fines and amounted to 607 pesos, one tomin, and three grains in gold bullion. Coronado appealed, but before this could be granted he had to deposit the amount of his sentence. Besides these fines, Coronado was deprived of the pueblos and Indians he had acquired. Eight years later, in 1553, Coronado

78. See *infra*, pp. 393-398.
79. See *infra*, pp. 369-392.

was still petitioning the audiencia at Guadalajara for the return of the pueblos and Indians taken from him.[80]

García López de Cárdenas, Coronado's chief officer on the expedition to Cíbola, suffered more severely than his chief. In his case the testimony of Judge Tejada's inquiry was sent to the Council of the Indies in Spain and Cárdenas was found guilty. During the long delays that intervened before the case was finally disposed of, Cárdenas spent five years in jail. In the end, he had to serve the king for one year on the frontier, pay a fine of two hundred ducats, and be banished from the Indies for ten years.[81]

Having finished his inquiry Judge Tejada returned to his post at the audiencia in Mexico. On March 11, 1545, he wrote to the king, on the discharge of the commissions entrusted to him,[82] a duty he had performed in thorough manner. Not only did he correct abuses and punish offenders, but he instituted much-needed reforms in the administration of New Galicia.

In his letter to the king, Judge Tejada tried to mollify his accusations against Coronado, stating that the latter's mind was not clear, a condition that was due to Coronado's head injury at Tiguex, according to report. Mota Padilla also writes that Coronado was not himself again after his fall.[83] Coronado's daughter's son, Don Francisco Pacheco de Córdoba y Bocanegra, said that as a result of injuries and illnesses contracted in the expedition, Coronado died prematurely, after spending 50,000 ducats in the venture.[84]

Upon the end of his governorship of New Galicia, Coronado returned to Mexico city and settled down to the routine of his position as a councilman of the city, a position he held until his death. When not ill, he discharged his duties with clock-like regularity.[85]

80. A. G. I., *Justicia*, legajo 336.

81. See the amended sentence of López de Cárdenas, *infra*, p. 367.

82. Letter of Tejada to the king, Mexico, March 11, 1545, in Francisco del Paso y Troncoso, *Epistolario de Nueva España*, IV, pp. 183-190.

83. Mota Padilla, p. 166, "Se fué de la silla, y dando la boca en el suelo, quedó sin sentido, y aunque después lo recobró, el juicio le quedo diminuto."

84. A. G. I., *Mexico*, legajo 124.

85. A. S. Aiton, "The Later Career of Coronado," *American Historical Review*, XXXII, p. 302.

Like many other conquistadors, Coronado often wrote to the Council of the Indies, setting forth his services to the crown and recounting his poverty after spending his fortune in the expedition to Cíbola. He sought an appointment as corregidor (judge). By a royal cédula of November 9, 1549, the king instructed the viceroy and audiencia of Mexico to provide Coronado with a corregimiento when one became vacant, provided he was properly qualified.[86] It seems that the two conditions never materialized.

Relations between Coronado and his protector, Viceroy Mendoza, seem to have remained friendly throughout the years, for failure of the viceroy to appoint Coronado to other important posts must be attributed to Coronado's limitations rather than to ill will of his friend. Be that as it may, the viceroy never failed to defend Coronado and his conduct of the expedition against the attacks of Cortés and his followers. In more than two years of extensive explorations in strange lands, said Mendoza, during which Coronado and his men experienced unusual and inclement weather, lack of provisions, and trouble with the natives, they did not lose more than twenty men, counting Spaniards and Indian allies. In so far as this figure can be checked against the documents relating to the expedition this does not seem to be an exaggeration.

In 1551 Mendoza was promoted to the viceroyalty of Peru. He was in poor health, but he considered it his duty to accept; he died in Lima on July 21, 1552. Coronado's health was likewise on the decline. He often had to take vacations from his duties because of ill health and finally died in November, 1554, his death being recorded in the register of the city council on November 12.[87] It is believed that Coronado was buried in the convent of Santo Domingo that had been founded by his late father-in-law, Alonso de Estrada, and supported by Coronado's wife, Doña Beatriz.[88]

These translations of documents relating to the Coronado expedition have been based on photostatic copies of the origin-

86. A. G. I., *Mexico,* legajo 1089.
87. Aiton, *op. cit.,* p. 303.
88. Paul A. Jones, *Coronado and Quivira,* Lyons, Kansas, 1937, pp. 170-173.

als whenever possible. With the exception of material relating to the Coronado and Cárdenas trials, the remainder have for the most part been printed previously, but even in these cases we have compared the documents diligently with the manuscript copies. In most cases, variations were of a minor nature, though sometimes the changes were more serious. The reader will at once note the differences between our translation and others on comparison. While we have sought to make our rendering of the Spanish into English as smooth as possible, we have adhered strictly to the meaning according to our interpretation. Castañeda's narrative is without doubt the most difficult document in the collection. This is not due to any serious errors in Winship's Spanish edition of the manuscript, which contains but few paleographic errors, but rather to Castañeda, himself, whose style would hardly be called literary.

Except for the accounts of the Coronado and Cárdenas trials, the other documents have been translated on previous occasions. Henri Ternaux-Compans presented a French translation of Castañeda's narrative and related documents in 1838. Though this is a work that is often cited, we have found it of no value in our study. Much more accurate and meritorious is the English translation of George Parker Winship, published originally in the *Fourteenth Annual Report* of the Bureau of Ethnology, which has stood as the standard work on the subject since its publication in 1896. While the present translation has been made independently of any previous work, we are under great obligation to those students who have delved into the story of Coronado in years past. Not only are we under a deep debt of gratitude to Winship but also to Frederick Webb Hodge, whose annotation of the Castañeda narrative in 1907 in *The Spanish Explorers in the United States, 1542-1706,* and his annotation of this and related documents in 1933, published by the Grabhorn Press under the title, *The Journey of Francisco Vázquez de Coronado, 1540-1542,* will always be of importance. Without the guidance provided by the pioneer labors of Winship and Hodge, our task would have been more difficult and the results of our study less perfect.

In the various documents presented here for the first time

in English translation, we have exercised great care to make sure of their accuracy. We regret particularly that the limitations of this series have not permitted us to publish the original Spanish texts.

Practical limitations have likewise made impossible extensive textual annotation and discussion of controversial points suggested by the documents. Our purpose has been to present the documents; their study and interpretation and the place of the Coronado expedition in American history will be met by Professor Herbert E. Bolton's more general story to be published as Volume One in this Coronado Historical series during the summer of 1940.

LETTER OF CORONADO TO THE KING

LETTER FROM FRANCISCO VÁZQUEZ DE CORONADO TO THE EMPEROR AND KING OF SPAIN. FROM COMPOSTELA, NEW GALICIA, DECEMBER 15, 1538.[1]

Holy Cæsarean Catholic Majesty:

The viceroy of New Spain gave me a royal order from your Majesty by which you command me to come to this province of New Galicia to take charge of it and to hold the residencia of Licentiate de la Torre,[2] the former judge of residencia[3] here. In compliance with what your Majesty ordered me, I set out from Mexico City immediately upon receiving your order. Upon reaching this province, I found that Licentiate de la Torre, whose residencia your Majesty had instructed me to hold, had died.

In the town of Guadalajara of this province, where the licentiate lived and died, I proclaimed the residencia against the estate left to his heirs. In this way I investigated some matters that were of importance to the service of your Majesty.

As I was about to leave for this city of Compostela, the solic-

1. Translated from a photostatic copy of the original in the Archives of the Indies, *Audiencia de Guadalajara*, legajo 5. There are two identical copies, with the exception that one has marginal endorsements and the other does not. The Spanish text of one of these copies was published by A. S. Aiton in the *Hispanic American Historical Review*, XIX (August, 1939), pp. 306-313.

2. In March, 1536, the king appointed Diego Pérez de la Torre of Extremadura as judge of residencia to investigate Nuño de Guzmán and to serve as governor of New Galicia in his place. He proceeded to New Galicia, put Guzmán in prison, and was himself mortally wounded in a battle with the Indians near Tonalá in 1538. Cristóbal de Oñate then served as governor until the appointment of Francisco Vázquez de Coronado in the latter part of the year 1538. Fray Antonio Tello, *Libro Segundo de la Crónica Miscelánea de la Santa Provincia de Xalisco*, Guadalajara, 1891, pp. 257-314; Martías de la Mota Padilla, *Historia de la Conquista de la Nueva Galicia*, Mexico, 1870, pp. 104-110; H. H. Bancroft, *History of Mexico*, San Francisco, 1883, II, p. 457 *et seq.*

3. The residencia was an official investigation conducted at the close of a man's term of office. All officials, from the highest to the lowest, had to undergo this inquiry; it was the king's most effective means for keeping a check on his administrative representatives throughout the Spanish empire. See L. E. Fisher, *Viceregal Administration in the Spanish-American Colonies*, Berkeley, 1926, pp 44-50.

itor of the town of San Miguel in the province of Culiacán
came to tell me that the residents of that town were about to
abandon it and return, and that the whole province was on
the verge of being lost. He entreated me, in the name of your
Majesty, to proceed there at once in order to remedy the situation. He affirmed that if I failed to go within forty days the
residents would leave, because of the many privations they were
enduring and the great harm done to them by Ayapín, an
Indian who was up in arms. I asked the solicitor for a report
and he gave me one that was more complete than I should have
wanted, because it showed that the residents of the town of
San Miguel and the Indians living there peacefully are suffering great hardships.

With this letter I am sending your Majesty the petition
addressed to me, and the report, in order that you may be
pleased to have them examined and learn the condition in
which that province finds itself.

I was already planning to come to its assistance as soon as I
was free from other duties, for I had been ordered to do so by
the viceroy of New Spain in the name of your Majesty. The
viceroy furnished me with some relief to take to the residents
of that town of San Miguel, knowing their plight and fearing
what might happen, which would be the desertion and abandonment of the town. I shall leave here within a week and
would have started out sooner except that I wanted to complete
my work here in your service. I shall do everything possible to
help that town and province and shall see whether it is to the
service of your Majesty to maintain it. I shall furnish a report
of it all to you.

Your Majesty must have been informed by now concerning
this province of New Galicia and those who have governed it
for you. For this reason, and because I have been here only a
short time, I shall not inform you for the present, not until I
have examined everything carefully. I shall simply give you
an account here of the condition in which I found it.

Your Majesty may know that most of the Indians there are
at war, some because they have not been conquered, and others
who, after being subjugated and brought under your authority,

have revolted. Of those who are at peace, Nuño de Guzmán and three or four retainers and friends of his have the best and the most of them. For this reason and because there are so few friendly Indians, many Spaniards who have served your Majesty in the conquest here, and others who have come here to settle, are in straitened circumstances; therefore they do not take any interest in instructing the Indians in matters of the faith, but bend their efforts to exploiting them more than they should. For, as the Indians of this province have not been assigned the amount of tribute they are to pay, the Spaniards use them for personal services, because very few Indians of this province pay tribute, except the ones Nuño de Guzmán holds in encomienda, and these do not pay him much, even though they are numerous.

The manner in which the residents of this province who have Indians in encomienda support themselves is that in the gold mines most of the towns give their encomenderos Indians to get out the gold for them. Some of those who deal in Indians buy and sell unbranded and free Indians as slaves. These living conditions have prevailed since the mines were discovered about three years ago. This happens because of the scarcity of slaves in this province, for, although they were taken there in large numbers, they have all been taken away to be sold. And because of this scarcity of slaves the mines are being worked by Indian slaves and free Indians.

I went to the mines called Nuestra Señora de la Concepción in order to establish some order in this matter and to find out how the workers in them are being treated. I held public and secret inquiries among the Indians themselves, and I found that they are well treated, both in that their work is moderate and that they receive adequate food and clothing in keeping with their way of living, and they are being taught the matters of the faith. On the other hand, I have not seen an Indian in the whole province with the slightest trace of being a Christian, except the ones I saw at the mines. For this reason it seemed best to me to leave everything in the present state without disturbing anything, as was done by those who governed before, until I give an account of it to your Majesty so that you may command what you deem most appropriate.

He did right, and his service is appreciated

There was another way in which the residents of this province, before my going there, exploited the Indians whom they held in encomienda. This was that they hired them out to Mexico city and from there they were brought back loaded with merchandise. This was done so brazenly that when I came from Mexico I met them in groups of forty and fifty, loaded, traveling back and forth, dead from hunger, because they were not given enough food to bear the work. In the name of your Majesty I have ordered that no one may take a free Indian out of this province, under severe penalties, because it was to the great detriment of the natives of the province that some traveled a distance of eighty leagues from their homes with such loads. The residents of this province resented my action so much that they say they are going to complain to your Majesty.

To the viceroy: have it issued in blank so he may assign the tribute with the governor

In your royal decree you order that I heed the letters and instructions sent by your Majesty to Licentiate de la Torre as if they had been issued to me. Among them there is one in which you order Licentiate de la Torre and the protector of the Indians,[4] Cristóbal de Pedraza, to assess the tributes which the Indians of this province are to pay the persons who hold them in encomienda for your Majesty. But since the protector is not in the province, I shall not carry out the order until I receive instructions from you. It is urgent that the Indians be assessed, because, although they pay but little tribute, as long as they are not assessed they are being employed in personal service at will. Therefore, your Majesty will relieve your royal conscience by ordering this appraisal.

When this decree of your Majesty to have the Indians assessed was made public there were some who began requiring the Indians whom they have in encomienda to give much larger tributes than they usually pay or could pay. This was done in the belief that when the assessors find the tribute high, their assessments will be set at that level. And although I believe

4. The viceroy as the crown's representative, was the protector of the Indians and was required to appoint protectors for the Indians. Lawsuits involving Indians went to the audiencia, but, when it became too busy with other matters, a special court for Indian cases, known as the Juzgado de Indios, was created. Fisher, *op. cit.*, pp. 163-164, 173. *Recopilación de Leyes de Los Reynos de Las Indias*, 2nd ed., Madrid, 1756, Book VI, Title VI, Laws I-XIV.

that they are mistaken, still I thought I should notify you of it.

As soon as I return from Culiacán, which will be as soon as I put things in order there, I shall try to pacify the Indians of this province who are in revolt. I shall do it by good deeds and by according them good treatment and with the aid of the friars that the viceroy of New Spain said he would send for this purpose. If we should be unable to bring them to the knowledge of the faith and the service of your Majesty, I shall still strive, by all means within my power, to bring them under your authority.

Good

Licentiate de la Torre allotted, in this province, many Indians who had neither been conquered nor seen. He gave them to whoever asked him for them, granting fifteen or twenty leagues of land with all the Indians thereon. Although there were some repartimientos of more than fifty leagues in extent, and the owners are holding their cédulas, waiting until the country is pacified, may your Majesty order what seems proper in this respect. Those who have served and labored for you in the conquest and pacification of this land would be offended if others who had not done so should reap all the benefits.

What was not done in the life of the Licentiate need not be carried out

In the district of this city of Compostela there are thirty repartimientos entrusted to its residents, and only ten houses in the whole city. The owners would not establish a home there, some claiming that the Indians they have in repartimiento are at war, and others saying that they brought them no profit. The absence of the owners is, in part, the cause for this locality not being pacified and the main reason for the Indians not being taught the matters of the faith. In this regard there has been too much neglect, for, as I have told your Majesty, I have not seen an Indian in this entire province who gave any indication of being a Christian, except those living at the mines, and five or six boys left here by the protector.

Good

Now the residents of this city of Compostela have asked to move to some place where they would be closer to the Indians who work for them. Seeing that the town's location is not good, and that the Indians would benefit by not going so far from their homes to work, I have selected a place where the townspeople may move to. I have issued a proclamation to the effect that all those who have Indians in this city must come to live there within a certain time, with the warning that, in the name of your Majesty, their Indians would otherwise be given in encomienda to other persons who live there and who would instruct the Indians in the matters of the faith. May your Majesty be pleased to order what should be done in this connection, because, in order that this province may be pacified and the Indians taught, it is important that those who have them in encomienda should reside on their encomiendas.

In the residencia of Licentiate de la Torre, no one brought charges against him, except Nuño de Guzmán, who made four demands for certain Indians which the latter held in encomienda and whom the licentiate used. As the secret investigation failed to reveal anything for which charges could be brought against his heirs, although many could have been lodged against him personally, and since he has now rendered an account of them before God, I am not forwarding it to your Majesty for inspection. The licentiate did not have any lieutenants in this jurisdiction of whom we might hold a residencia. There were not even alcaldes in the city of Guadalajara when I arrived there, as I myself appointed them and the regidores in the name of your Majesty.

Licentiate de la Torre audited the accounts of the officials who had charge of the royal treasury of your Majesty in this province. When I came here I found that your treasurer had in his possession all the accounts, the balance, and the sentence[5] issued there. For, upon the death of the licentiate, the treasurer remained here by official order and by instructions and decrees of your Majesty, and he audited his accounts. Now he claims that the licentiate charged him with certain items. The treasurer asks that he be given a certified copy of the accounts, the balance, the sentence, and proceedings. It has been given to him, and, although I do not know that there was anything improper in the accounts, it seemed to me that I should report the matter to you.

The order whereby your Majesty commands me to come and take charge of this province does not indicate the salary.

He did properly (margin note)

Let him re-examine them (margin note)

5. Of Licentiate de la Torre. See note 2 above.

I beg you to grant what you will, so that I may be able to support myself in this costly land, where expenses are great, Provided because it is too far removed from the port and from Mexico city.

May the Lord keep and prosper your Sacred Cæsarean Catholic Majesty with the addition of other great kingdoms and dominions, as your Majesty desires.

From this city of Compostela, New Galicia, December 15, 1538.

Your Majesty's vassal and servant who kisses your royal hands and feet,

FRANCISCO VÁZQUEZ DE CORONADO

Sacred Cæsarean Catholic Majesty

LETTER OF CORONADO TO VICEROY MENDOZA, MARCH 8, 1539

Copy of the Letter of Francisco Vázquez de
Coronado, Governor of New Galicia, to Don
Antonio de Mendoza, Viceroy of New Spain.
Dated at Culuacán.[1]

*Concerning the difficult navigation from San Miguel of Culua-
cán to Topira; description of this province, and of another
neighboring one rich in gold and precious stones; number
of people taken along by Vázquez to go thither; and the
respect shown Fray Marcos de Niza by the Indians of
Petatlán.*

God willing, on April 10 I shall leave this land of San
Miguel de Culuacán for Topira. It cannot be done sooner, for
at that time the powder and fuse which your Lordship is sending me will arrive. I believe it must have reached Compostela
by now. Furthermore, I must travel a good many leagues along
mountains so high that they rise to the sky, and by a river so
large and swollen at present that there is no place to cross it.
By starting on the above date it is said that we may be able to
cross it. I had been told that it is only fifty leagues from here
to Topira, and I have found that it is over eighty.

I do not recall if I have written your Lordship about the
information I have of Topira, or whether I have made any
report; therefore, since I have obtained some new information,
I shall report it to you in this present letter. You may know,
then, that I have been told that Topira is a thickly populated
province, located between two rivers; that there are more than
fifty inhabited places; that a little farther on there is another
larger province. The Indians could not tell me its name. It
contains abundant provisions of maize, beans, peppers, melons,

---

1. Translated from the Italian in Ramusio, *Delle Navigationi et Viaggi*,
Venetia, 1556, III, ff. 354-355. A French translation is found in H. Ternaux-
Compans, *Voyages, Relations et Mémoires*, Paris, 1838, IX, pp. 352-354.

calabashes, and large numbers of native chickens. The natives wear gold and emeralds and other precious stones. They make general use of gold and silver, with which they cover their houses. The leaders wear finely worked large gold chains around their necks. They dress in painted blankets. There are numerous cattle, but not domestic ones. I am advised not to go in search of them, since there are few people here, and the Indians are numerous and brave. I have heard the aforesaid from the accounts of two Indians, their neighbors.

I shall set out on the stated date, taking with me 150 mounted men, twelve replacement horses, and 200 foot soldiers as crossbowmen and harquebusiers. I am taking along pigs, sheep, and everything that I could buy.

Your Lordship may rest assured that I shall not return to Mexico until I can report to you with more certitude, and until we find something in that land from which benefit may be derived. I shall remain until you order what we are to do.

If, unfortunately, we do not find anything, I shall proceed one hundred leagues farther inland, where, God willing, something will be found with which your Lordship may be able to reward these gentlemen and those who may follow later. It seems to me that I shall not fail to be hindered by the water, the weather, and the nature of the land. What I experience on the way will determine what I shall do.

Fray Marcos, together with Esteban, proceeded farther inland on the seventh of last February.[2] When I took leave of them I left them in the care of more than one hundred Indians from Petatlán and from the section whence they had come. They carried the padre on the palms of their hands, pleasing him in everything they could. It would be impossible to relate or describe his trip better than has been done in every report included in my letters from Compostela; and at San Miguel I wrote to you with all the detail possible. Even if only one-tenth were true, it would be marvelous.

With this letter I am enclosing one for your Lordship that I have received from the said padre. The Indians tell me they

2. The date is given as March 7 in Fray Marcos' own report; see below, p. 63.

all adore him. And so I believe he must have traveled two thousand leagues inland.[3] He says that he will write to me when he finds good country, and I shall not fail to inform you. I trust in God that in one way or another we may be able to locate something worth while.

3. Since Fray Marcos left on March 7, 1539, the time given in his own report, it is obvious that the viceroy could not have received any news from him by March 8, 1539, which is the date given by Ramusio for this letter. Evidently this date is erroneous.

LETTER OF CORONADO TO THE KING

Letter from Francisco Vázquez de Coronado to the Emperor, July 15, 1539.[1]

Holy Cæsarean Catholic Majesty:

Immediately upon my arrival, by order of your Majesty, in this province of New Galicia, I reported, in my letters to you, on the condition in which I found the affairs of this province and of how I was asked by the town of San Miguel in the province of Culiacán to come and remedy the difficulties of the residents of the town. This was because the natives of that province, or most of them, were in revolt under the leadership of a cacique named Ayapín, who was the leader and chief of the uprising. As it seemed to me that the trip would redound to the service of your Majesty, I departed for that province as quickly as I could. When I arrived there I found that most of the residents were already on the point of abandoning the town, both because of the straits to which Ayapín's raids had reduced them, and because they were very poor, not being able to derive any benefit from the land as the Indians they had in repartimiento would not work for them.

Upon my arrival and the succor that the viceroy of New Spain sent them, in the name of your Majesty, the settlers became calm again. In addition, I distributed among them a few small villages which Nuño de Guzmán had in repartimiento there. I distributed them, with the advice and consent of Nuño de Guzmán, because, seeing that it was to the service of your Majesty and that the settlers could not sustain themselves without them, he agreed to it, pending other orders from you.

After doing this I set out through the province in order to bring an end to the bloodshed by all ways and means that I

---

1. Translated from a photostatic copy of the original in the Archives of the Indies, *Audiencia de Guadalajara,* legajo 5. An extract of this letter was published by C. Pérez Bustamante, *Don Antonio de Mendoza,* Santiago, 1928, p. 151. See also H. R. Wagner in the *New Mexico Historical Review,* IX, pp. 336-337.

could find. Little by little I succeeded in pacifying the natives and in bringing them to the service of your Majesty. I explained to them that they are your vassals, that it is your royal will that they become Christians, and that they be well treated. Seeing that their uprising had been due more to ignorance and bad treatment than to malice, I promised them in your name to pardon them for their past misdeeds, providing that they would submit to the service of your Majesty of their own free will and would not do anything for which they might deserve punishment. Having explained this to them through interpreters, whom they understood well, most of those who were in rebellion submitted peacefully, without there being any executions or other punishment.

When Ayapín saw that all, or most, of the people were deserting him and coming to me peacefully, he fled to the fastness of some very rough mountains, where, pursuing him relentlessly, I apprehended him. After capturing him, I brought him to trial, where he was found guilty and sentenced to death, and I ordered him quartered. This execution completed the task of stabilizing and pacifying all that land.

Since the Indians had all been wandering in the sierras until then because of the uprising, they had neither houses nor planted fields. They have now commenced to build houses and to plant their fields. They returned to the places where they formerly had their settlements, although of those who used to live in this province many people are missing on account of the famines, wars, and butcheries that have afflicted it. However, as it is a very fertile country and abundant in all things for the sustenance of life, I trust in God that it will be rebuilt and that the Spanish settlers of that town will remain there, as the land is very good and many indications of gold and silver have been found which could be exploited more than they have been up to the present.

I took with me to this province of Culiacán a friar of the order of St. Francis, named Fray Marcos de Niza. The viceroy of New Spain had recommended that I send him inland, because he was going at his command, in the name of your Majesty, to explore, by land, the coast of this New Spain in order to learn its secrets and to gain knowledge of the lands and peoples that are now unknown. In order that he might travel with greater safety, I sent some Indians, of those who had been made slaves in this province of Galicia and whom the viceroy had freed, to the towns of Petatlán and Cuchillo,[2] nearly sixty leagues beyond Culiacán. I asked them to enlist some native Indians of those pueblos and to tell them not to be afraid, since your Majesty has ordered that no hostilities be waged against them or bad treatment accorded them, or that they be made slaves. In view of this and the fact that the messengers who came to appeal to them were free, which astounded them not a little, over eighty men came to me.

After having taken particular pains to make clear to them your royal will, namely, that at present you do not want anything else from them except that they become Christians and recognize God and your Majesty as their lords, I charged them to take Fray Marcos and Esteban, a negro, to the interior of the land, with all assurance. The viceroy bought the negro for this purpose from one of those who escaped from Florida. His name is Esteban. They did so, treating them very well.

Traveling their normal days' journeys,[3] the Lord willed that they should come to a very fine country, as your Majesty will see by the report of Fray Marcos and by what the viceroy is writing to you, and inasmuch as he is doing so I shall not go into details here. I hope that God and your Majesty will be well served not only by the greatness of the country which Fray Marcos tells about but also by the planning and activity which the viceroy has displayed in discovering it and that he will employ in pacifying and bringing it under the authority of your Majesty.

I have already reported to you concerning the need for friars in this province of Galicia to teach its natives, for there is hardly a man in the entire province who shows any indication

2. Petatlán, or Petlatlán, from petates, reed mats, the modern Sinaloa; Cuchillo was fifty leagues from Culiacán, according to Fray Marcos.

3. Dr. Henry R. Wagner has suggested that the Spanish should perhaps read "seis jornadas" for "sus jornadas," but the word is clearly "sus." See his note of "Addition" to "Fr. Marcos de Niza," *New Mexico Historical Review,* IX (July, 1934), pp. 336-337.

of being a Christian, except those who live and associate with
the Spaniards at the mines. I have tried by all means to obtain
some friars. They have written to me that they would come
very soon. I trust in God that, by their teaching and good
example, they will reap much fruit in this province. In addition to the above, I have ordered that churches be built in all
the towns where the natives may assemble for religious instruc-
tion. Some of the people who were in rebellion have submitted
peacefully, although there still remain many other Indians who
are in revolt. I shall try to win them over with good deeds and
kindness, but if I should fail I shall try to do it by whatever
means should be more suitable to the service of God and your
Majesty.

I have received an order from you in which you command
that all Spaniards living in this province should build houses
of stone or adobe, and a letter from you decreeing that the order
be enforced. As soon as I received it I put into effect what you
commanded. It was proclaimed in this city of Compostela and
in other towns of this province. It will be done as you order,
without injury to the settlers, for with the gold they are obtaining they are beginning to be able to afford houses.

A decree from your Majesty orders that we check the
accounts of administrators of the estates of deceased persons,
and that the balance obtained be forwarded to the Casa de la
Contratación of the Indies or to your officials of it. So, as soon
as I arrived in the province I began an audit of the administrators' accounts. The property of deceased persons which they
hold consists mostly of deeds, which were given by persons who
have moved away or died without leaving anything with which
to pay. These contracts have been passing from administrator
to administrator for more than six or seven years, because the
estates of the deceased were sold at public auctions or on credit,
as at that time there was no gold in this province. The governor, Nuño de Guzmán, had ordered that the administrators
inform one another of what could not be collected in those contracts. May your Majesty be pleased to order what should be
done in this matter, because those who at present are holding
estates of deceased persons value these estates at less than two

hundred castellanos, while the total in the contracts amounts to more than thirteen hundred.

May the Lord protect and honor the Sacred Cæsarean Catholic person of your Majesty and bring you greater kingdoms and dominions, as we, your servants, desire.

From Galicia in New Spain. Compostela, July 15, 1539.

The humble servant of your Majesty who kisses your royal feet,

FRANCISCO VÁZQUEZ DE CORONADO

LETTER OF MENDOZA TO THE KING

LETTER WRITTEN BY HIS EXCELLENCY, DON ANTONIO DE MENDOZA, VICEROY OF NEW SPAIN, TO HIS MAJESTY, THE EMPEROR. 1539.[1]

Telling about the gentlemen who have endured great hardships in order to discover the limits of the mainland of New Spain beyond the sierra, the coming of Vázquez and Fray Marcos to San Miguel of Culiacán, the former with instructions, as governor, to reassure the Indians and not to take any more of them as slaves.

In the last fleet in which Miguel de Vsnago sailed, I sent a letter to your Majesty relating how I had sent two friars of the order of St. Francis to discover the limits of this mainland in the region across the mountains. And since their trip is an event of greater importance than was thought, I shall relate this matter from the beginning.

Your Majesty must recall that whenever I wrote to you I expressed my eagerness to learn where the limits of the province of this New Spain were, it being such an extensive land, and there being no information as to its limits. I have not been the only one who expressed this desire, for Nuño de Guzmán left this city with four hundred mounted men and fourteen thousand footmen, natives of these Indies, the best people and the best organized expedition that had ever been seen in these parts. He accomplished so little that most of them were consumed in the undertaking, and he was not able to go beyond the territory already explored. Later, while this said governor was at New Galicia, he sent out some captains with mounted men, but they did not obtain better results than he had.

Likewise the Marqués del Valle, Hernando Cortés, sent a captain with two ships to explore the coast. The ships and the captain himself were lost. Later, Cortés again sent two other

---

1. Translated from the Italian in Ramusio, *Viaggi*, III, fol. 355; translated into French in Ternaux-Compans, *Voyages*, IX, pp. 285-290.

ships, one of which became separated from the other. The pilot, with a few sailors, took control of the ship and murdered the captain. This done, they sailed into an island where, upon landing, the pilot and some sailors were killed by the native Indians, who took the landing boat. The ship, with the men who had remained on board, returned to the coast of New Galicia, where it foundered.[2] The Marqués obtained information of the land they had discovered from the men who came in this ship. Immediately, either because of some disaffection with the bishop of Santo Domingo and the judges of this royal audiencia, or, likely, because everything in New Spain had turned out so well for him, without waiting to obtain further verification of what was to be found on that island, he sailed in that direction with three ships and some footmen and horsemen, and none too well provided with the necessary things. The whole thing turned out so different from what he expected that most of the men he had with him starved to death. And, even though he had ships and the land was very suitable, with an abundance of provisions, he had no means of conquering it.[3] It seemed as if God drew it away from him supernaturally. And he returned home without accomplishing anything.

After this, having here with me Andrés Dorantes, one of those who went in the expedition of Pánfilo de Narváez, I consulted with him many times. It seemed to me that he could render great service to your Majesty if he were sent with forty or fifty horsemen to lay bare the mysteries of that region. On that account I spent considerable money in providing what was necessary for his journey, and I do not know how it was that the

2. On the return of Cortés from Spain in 1530, he organized a fleet and sent it to sea under command of his cousin, Diego Hurtado de Mendoza, on June 30, 1532, and was finally lost at sea. A few of the men reached Guzmán's territory and were promptly seized by him. Undaunted by these disasters, Cortés prepared another fleet and sent it up the coast to explore. It was commanded by Captain Diego Becerra and Hernando de Grijalva and sailed on October 30, 1533. Captain Becerra was murdered by his pilot, Fortún Ximénez, who sailed to Lower California and was in turn destroyed by the Indians. Some survivors who reached the mainland fell victims to Guzmán's ferocity. H. I. Priestley, *The Mexican Nation*, New York, 1923, pp. 46-47.

3. In April, 1535, Cortés himself sailed for Lower California with the purpose of establishing colonies. The inhospitable land and the treacherous Gulf of California frustrated his plans. *Ibid.*, p. 47.

plan fell through and the undertaking was abandoned. Of the arrangements made for this plan, I retained a negro who had come with Dorantes, some slaves whom I bought, and a few native Indians of that region whom I had gathered. I sent them with Fray Marcos de Niza and a companion of his, a friar of the order of St. Francis, men long trained in the hardships of this region, experienced in the affairs of the Indies, earnest persons of exemplary lives, whom I obtained from their provincial. Thus they accompanied Francisco Vásquez de Coronado, governor of New Galicia, to the town of San Miguel de Culiacán, the last outpost of the Spaniards in that region, two hundred leagues from this city.

When the governor arrived with the friars at this place, he asked some Indians of those I had given him to return to their land and tell the people there that your Majesty had ordered that no more slaves be taken from among them, that they should lose all fear and return to their homes and live peacefully in them, and that since they had been greatly abused in the past by the treatment they had been accorded, his Majesty would punish those who were responsible for this. After twenty days some four hundred came back with these Indians. Appearing before the governor, they told him that they came on behalf of all the natives to tell him that they wanted to see and know the person who had done them so much good by allowing them to return to their homes and plant maize so that they would have food. They had been wandering and hiding in the mountains like wild beasts for years, they said, for fear of being made slaves, and now they and all the others were ready to do what was ordered of them. The governor reassured them with kind words and ordered them fed, keeping them with him for three or four days.

During these days the friars taught them to make the sign of the cross and to say the name of Jesus Christ, our Lord, which they did in earnest. At the end of this time, the governor sent them back to their homes, telling them not to be afraid and to remain calm. He gave them clothes, pater nosters, knives, and other things of this nature which I had given him for such purposes. They went away very happy, saying that whenever he sent for them again they and many others would come to do what he commanded them.

The entry thus prepared, Fray Marcos and his companion, before setting out, spent ten or twelve days with the negro and the other slaves and Indians that I had given him.

And as I had also received information of a province called Topira, situated back of the mountains, and had arranged with the governor that he should find means of learning about it, considering this of primary importance, he decided to go in person to explore it. He arranged with Fray Marcos as to what part of the mountain he would turn at in order to meet him at a town named Corazones, one hundred and twenty leagues from Culiacán. He traveled through this province and found it to conform to what I have written in my letters. There is a great scarcity of provisions, and the mountain range was so rough that he could not find anywhere a way of proceeding ahead, and he was forced to return to San Miguel.

Consequently, because of the poor choice of the route and the inability to find a way, everyone thought that God our Lord wanted to close the door to all those who wished to carry out this undertaking by human force, and open it to a poor barefooted friar. In this manner Fray Marcos began to march inland. Since the way had been so well prepared, he was well received. As he has written about all that befell him on the whole trip, following the instructions I gave him for this journey, I shall not extend myself further, but simply transcribe for your majesty all that has been related by him.

CORONADO'S APPOINTMENT AS GOVERNOR, APRIL 18, 1539[1]

Don Carlos, emperor by divine grace, etc.

Whereas, in another order of appointment, we instructed you, Francisco Vázquez Coronado, as is told more at length in the said order of appointment, to go to the province of New Galicia in New Spain and hold the residencia of Licentiate de la Torre, our judge of residencia there, now dead, and of his officials, and since the term of the said residencia has already expired and there is no governor to exercise and administer our justice: therefore, accepting your qualifications and ability, and considering that it is fitting to our service and the good government of the said province and the administration and execution of justice, it is our will and command that now and henceforth, subject to our will and command, you be our governor and captain general of the said province of New Galicia, that you hear cases and administer civil and criminal justice in coöperation with the judicial offices there in the cities, towns, and villages that are or may be established in the said province. By this our letter we command the councils, judges, regidores, caballeros, escuderos, and good men in all the cities, towns, and villages that are or may be established in the said province, and our officials and other persons living there, and each one of them, that whenever they are summoned, without any tarrying or delay, without inquiring or consulting us or waiting for or expecting any other letter or order from us, without a second or third command, they must obey you and your lieutenants. The latter you may appoint, and with the proper oaths and formalities that the case may require, which you must observe, you may

1. At a meeting of the alcaldes and regidores at the cabildo of Guadalajara, Coronado presented this royal cédula of appointment as governor of New Galicia. See Fray Antonio Tello, *Libro Segundo de la Crónica Miscelánea de la santa provincia de Xalisco*, Guadalajara, 1891, pp. 311-314. Critics have assumed that Viceroy Mendoza had a commission in blank for appointment of a new governor of New Galicia and that he merely filled in Coronado's name on the above date. *Cf.* H. R. Wagner, *The Spanish Southwest*, I, pp. 217-219.

dismiss or remove them whenever you wish to do so and think it desirable. Thereupon they must accept, receive, and respect you as our governor, captain general, and magistrate of the said province during the time that it may be our will and command, as has been stated. They must allow and permit you and your lieutenants to discharge freely the said offices and to carry out and execute our justice there in the offices of governor, captain general, alguacil, and other offices relating or pertaining to the said governorship. You must be allowed to conduct investigations in law cases, inquiries, and all other matters concerning the said offices. You and your lieutenants will concern yourselves with what relates to our service and the administration of justice, the settling and government of the said lands and provinces, in the most suitable manner.

To discharge the said functions and carry out and execute our justice, every one, themselves and their retainers, must submit to you. They must dispense and grant you all the favor and aid you may demand and need. Every one must obey, respect, and comply with your orders and those of your lieutenants. They must not offer or allow any one to offer any obstacle in the matter. By these presents we accept you and consider you accepted in the said offices and in the performance and discharge of them.

In case you should not be accepted by them, or by any one of them, we command, by this present letter, any person or persons holding rods of authority in the said province to deliver their commissions at once to you, Francisco Vázquez Coronado, thus depriving them of authority and power, and that they make no use of them without our special order or command, under the penalties incurred by private individuals who hold public and royal offices. By these presents we suspend and consider such officials suspended.

Further, in matters which pertain to our exchequer and treasury in which you or your lieutenants and alcaldes may make condemnation for our said exchequer and treasury, you must execute and cause such acts to be executed, delivered, and handed over to our treasurer in the said province.

Further, it is our wish that if you, the said Francisco Váz-

quez Coronado, should endeavor to perform our service and
the administration of our justice, that any persons who are or
may be present in the province, or those who may be away and
not present then, must appear before you. You may so order
in our name. You may force them to leave the province in
accordance with a decree covering the case. You must explain
to the persons so banished the reasons why you are banishing
them. If you think it desirable that the matter should remain
secret, you must give the message to them privately and sealed,
sending us at the same time a copy so that we may be informed
of the matter. You must keep in mind that should you banish
any one, it must be for a very serious reason. For all of the
above and for the discharge of the said offices as our governor
and captain general of the said provinces and for performing
and executing our justice there, we grant you full authority in
every respect.

It is our will and command that you be assigned and paid
1,500 ducats per year, which amounts to 562,000 maravedís,
which are to be paid to you from our income and revenue in
the said province. Should there be no revenue in the province,
we are not under obligation to order any portion of your salary
to be paid. We order that you shall begin to receive this salary
from the date of this letter, and until this day you are to
receive the one thousand ducats salary that had been assigned to
you. The salary that we now assign to you, you are to enjoy
during the whole time that you hold the said office and post as
our governor and captain general of the said province; and we
order our treasurer there to give and pay you the said sum each
year, and to obtain your receipt of payment, upon presentation
of which and a signed copy of this letter we order the said
1,500 ducats to be paid. And no controversy shall be started in
regard to this matter by any one under penalty of our disfavor
and a fine of 10,000 maravedís to be paid into our treasury by
each and every one who shall act contrary to these presents.

Given at Toledo on April 18, 1539.

I, the king. I, Juan de Sámano, secretary of his Cæsarean
and royal Majesty, had it written by his order.

When the alcaldes and regidores of the said city saw the

order of appointment, they said that they obeyed it as a letter from their king and natural lord, and that they obeyed the said Francisco Vázquez as governor, as therein stated. They took the oath with the formality prescribed by law, and delivered to him their rods of office and signed their names.

FRANCISCO VÁZQUEZ CORONADO. DIEGO PROAÑO, TORIBIO DE BOLAÑOS, alcaldes. JUAN DEL CAMINO, MIGUEL DE IBARRA, HERNANDO LÓPEZ, PEDRO DE PLACENCIA, FRANCISCO DE LA MOTA.

INSTRUCTIONS TO FRAY MARCOS DE NIZA

INSTRUCTIONS OF THE VICEROY TO FRAY MARCOS DE NIZA, NOVEMBER, 1538.

This is what you, Fray Marcos de Niza, are to observe in the expedition which you are undertaking for the honor and glory of the Holy Trinity and for the exaltation of the holy Catholic faith.[1]

First: Upon arriving at the province of Culuacán, you are to exhort and urge the Spaniards residing in the town of San Miguel to treat the peaceful Indians well and not to employ them in excessive tasks, assuring them that, by so doing, they will be granted favors and rewarded by his Majesty for the hardships they have endured there, and that they will find in me a

1. These Fray Marcos de Niza documents, the Instructions and the Relation, are translated from a photostatic copy of the original in the Archives of the Indies, *Patronato,* legajo 20. There are two separate copies in this legajo; they are sewn together and are identical except as to title. The one reads: "Relation of the journey to and discovery of Seven Cities in the Indies by Fray Marcos de Niza, Friar Observant of the order of Saint Francis, by order of the viceroy of New Spain, Don Antonio de Mendoza, 1539. Done in Mexico on August 26, 1539." The other reads: "Relation of the journey from the province of Culuacán in New Spain made by Fray Marcos de Niza, a Franciscan friar, by order of the viceroy of New Spain, Don Antonio de Mendoza, who instructed him to note the good or bad measures taken by Francisco Vázquez Coronado, who was going as governor of that province of Culuacán. Mexico, September 2, 1539."
The Spanish text is given in Pacheco y Cárdenas, *Colección de Documentos Inéditos relativos al descubrimiento, conquista y colonización de las posesiones Españolas en América y occeania,* Madrid, 1864-1884, III, pp. 325-351. English translations from this printed text have been made by Dr. Percy M. Baldwin, published in the *New Mexico Historical Review,* I (1926), pp. 193-223, also reprinted together with the Spanish text; Bonaventure Oblasser, O. F. M., Topawa, Arizona, 1939,—does not contain the instructions; R. Hakluyt, *The Principall navigations, voiages and discoveries of the English Nation,* several editions; Mrs. Fannie Bandelier, in *The Journey of Alvar Nuñez Cabeza de Vaca,* New York, 1905. An Italian translation is found in Ramusio, *Viaggi,* III, ff. 355-359; a French version is contained in Ternaux-Compans, *Voyages,* IX, pp. 356-373. For a critical discussion of the Fray Marcos expedition, consult H. R. Wagner, "Fray Marcos de Niza," *New Mexico Historical Review,* IX (1934), pp. 184-227, 336-337; Carl Sauer, "The Discovery of New Mexico Reconsidered," *ibid.,* XII (1937), pp. 270-287; and Carl Sauer, "The Road to Cíbola," *Ibero-Americana: 3,* Berkeley, 1932.

good supporter for their claims. And if they do the opposite they will incur punishment and disfavor.

You shall make clear to the Indians that I am sending you, in the name of his Majesty, to tell them that the Spaniards shall treat them well, to let them know that he regrets the abuses and harm they have suffered, and that, from now on, they shall be well treated and those who may mistreat them shall be punished.

Likewise you are to assure them that no more slaves shall be taken from among them and that they are not to be taken away from their lands; on the contrary, they shall be left alone, as free people, without suffering any harm; tell them that they should not be afraid, but acknowledge God, our Lord, who is in heaven, and the emperor, as he has been placed on earth by His hand to rule and govern it.

Since Francisco Vázquez de Coronado, whom his Majesty has appointed governor of that province, will go with you as far as the town of San Miguel de Culuacán, you shall inform me of how he provides for the affairs of that town, in matters pertaining to the service of God, our Lord, and the conversion and good treatment of the natives of that province.

If, with the aid of God, our Lord, and the grace of the Holy Spirit, you should find a way to go on and penetrate the land in the interior, you shall take along Esteban de Dorantes as guide. I command him to obey you in whatever you may order him, as he would obey me in person. If he should not do so, he will be at fault and incur the penalties falling on those who disobey the persons empowered by his Majesty to command them.

Likewise the said governor, Francisco Vázquez, is taking along the Indians who came with Dorantes and others from those regions who could be brought together, so that if he and you deem it advisable that some of them should go along, you may employ them in the service of our Lord as you deem fitting.

You are always to endeavor to travel the safest way possible, informing yourself first as to whether the Indians are at peace or at war among themselves, so that they may not do any violence to your person that would give cause to taking up arms against them and punishing them, because, in this case, instead of helping and enlightening them, this would do just the opposite.

You shall be very careful to observe the number of people that there are, whether they are few or many, and whether they are scattered or living together. Note also the nature, fertility, and climate of the land; the trees, plants, and domestic and wild animals there may be; the character of the country, whether it is broken or flat; the rivers, whether they are large or small; the stones and metals which are there; and of all things that can be sent or brought, send or bring samples of them in order that his Majesty may be informed of everything.

Endeavor always to learn if there is any information about the seacoast, both of the North and South seas, for it may be that the land narrows and that a sea inlet reaches the interior of the land. If you should reach the coast of the South sea, leave letters buried at the headlands, at the foot of some tree outstanding for its size, telling of what you think should be known. Mark the tree with a cross where the letters are left, so that they may be found. Likewise, at the mouths of rivers and suitable harbors, on prominent trees near the water, make the same sign, a cross, and leave letters. Thus if I send ships, they will be advised to look for this sign.

Try always to send reports through Indians, telling how you are faring, how you are received, and particularly what you may find.

If God, our Lord, should will it that you find some large settlement which you think would be a good place for establishing a monastery and for sending friars who would devote themselves to conversions, you are to send a report by Indians, or return, yourself, to Culuacán. Send back reports with the utmost secrecy so that appropriate steps may be taken, without disturbing anything, because, in the pacification of what is discovered, the service of our Lord and the welfare of the natives shall be taken into consideration.

Although the whole land belongs to the emperor, our lord, you shall take possession of it for his Majesty in my name and draw up the documents and set up the markers that you feel are required for this purpose. You must explain to the natives of the land that there is only one God in heaven, and the emperor on earth to rule and govern it, whose subjects they must all become and whom they must serve.—Don Antonio de Mendoza.

Acceptance of Fray Marcos

I, Fray Marcos de Niza, of the Observant Friars of Saint Francis, state that I received a copy of these instructions signed by his Excellency, Don Antonio de Mendoza, viceroy and governor of New Spain. It was delivered to me by order of his Lordship and in his name by Francisco Vázquez de Coronado, governor of this New Galicia. The said copy was taken from these instructions, word for word, checked against the original, and corrected. These said instructions I promise to carry out faithfully, and not to exceed or violate anything contained therein, now or at any time. And since I will thus observe and follow them, I attached my name hereto, at Tonalá, which is in the province of New Galicia, November 20, 1538, where were given and delivered to me in the said name the said instructions. —Fray Marcos de Niza.

Certification of the Provincial

I, Fray Antonio de Ciudad Rodrigo, friar of the order of the Minorites, and at the present time father provincial for the province of the Holy Evangel in this New Spain, state that it is true that I sent Fray Marcos de Niza, priest, friar, presbyter, and religious, a man of much virtue and piety; that I and my brothers, the definers, commissioned for the purpose, took cognizance of the arduous and difficult tasks, and that he was chosen and considered ideal and competent to undertake this journey and exploration, both because of the aforesaid personal ability, as well as because he is learned, not only in theology, but even in cosmography and navigation. Thus having consulted and determined that he should go, he went, with another companion, a lay brother named Fray Onorato, by order of Don Antonio de Mendoza, viceroy of this said New Spain. His Excellency provided him with all the equipment and provisions needed for the said trip and expedition, and also with these instructions here recorded, which I saw and which his Lordship communicated to me, asking me what I thought of them. As they seemed to me appropriate, they were given to the said Fray Marcos by Francisco Vázquez de Coronado. He received them without fail and carried them out faithfully, as has been shown in fact. Since the aforesaid is true and contains no misstatement, I have added this verification and testimony, and signed it with my own name. Dated in Mexico, August 26, 1539.—FRAY ANTONIO DE CIUDAD RODRIGO, minister provincial.

REPORT OF FRAY MARCOS DE NIZA

With the aid and favor of the blessed Virgin Mary, our Lady, and our seraphic father, Saint Francis, I, Fray Marcos de Niza, a professed friar of the order of Saint Francis, in fulfillment of the above-contained instructions from the illustrious Don Antonio de Mendoza, his Majesty's viceroy and governor of New Spain, set out from the town of San Miguel in the province of Culuacán on Friday, March 7, 1539, taking along Father Fray Onorato as companion. I also took with me Esteban de Dorantes, a negro, and some Indians from among those whom the said viceroy had liberated and bought for this purpose. They were delivered to me by Francisco Vázquez de Coronado, governor of New Galicia. I also took a large number of Indians from Petatlán and from the town called Cuchillo, distant some fifty leagues from the said town. These Indians came to the valley of Culuacán, showing great joy because they had been reassured by the liberated Indians, whom the said governor had sent ahead to tell them of their freedom and to assure them that they would not be made slaves, nor war waged against them, nor harmed in any way, and to tell them that this is the will and command of his Majesty.

In this company, I continued on my way until reaching the town of Petatlán.[1] I was greeted along the way with many receptions and presents of food, roses, and other such things, and houses of branches and mats which they built for me at all places where there were no settlements.

At this pueblo of Petatlán I stopped for three days because my companion, Fray Onorato, was taken ill, and I found it advisable to leave him there.[2] Observing the aforesaid instructions, I continued on my way wherever the Holy Spirit, without my deserving it, guided me. I was accompanied by the said Esteban de Dorantes, a negro, some of the freed Indians, and

---

1. Modern Sinaloa.
2. Fray Onorato appeared as a character witness for Coronado on September 8, 1544. A. G. I., *Justicia*, legajo 339.

numerous people of the land. Everywhere they received me with receptions, gladness, and triumphal arches, giving me of whatever food they had, although it was but little, because they said it had not rained for three years, and because the Indians of that region put more effort into hiding than into sowing, for fear of the Christians from the town of San Miguel, who used to come that far to wage war on them and to take slaves. In this whole distance, which must have been twenty-five or thirty leagues beyond Petatlán, I did not see anything worth recording here, except that some Indians from the island visited by the Marqués del Valle came to see me. From them I assured myself that it is an island and not the mainland, as some claim. I saw that they passed from it to the mainland and back again on rafts. The distance between the island and the mainland may be half a nautical league, more or less.[3] I was likewise visited by some Indians from another larger island located farther on. From them I learned that there are thirty other small islands, which are inhabited and poor in food, except two, which they said had maize.

These Indians wore, hanging around their necks, many shells of the kind that often contain pearls. I showed them a pearl which I was carrying as a sample, and they told me that some like it were found in the islands, but I did not see any among these Indians.

I continued my march over a despoblado[4] for four days, being accompanied by Indians both from the islands mentioned as well as from the settlements which I had left behind. At the end of the despoblado, I met other Indians who marveled at seeing me, because they knew nothing at all of Christians, as these natives do not trade with those farther back owing to the despoblado. These people accorded me fine receptions and gave me much food. They tried to touch my garments, and called me *Sayota,* which in their language means "man from heaven." I explained to them, as best I could through inter-

3. Evidently this refers to the islands in the vicinity of Topolobampo.
4. Throughout we have left this word untranslated in order to leave the critic free to make his own interpretation. It may mean uninhabited or barren region.

preters, the significance of my instructions, namely, their acknowledgment of our Lord in heaven and his Majesty on earth. I always tried by all possible means to learn about a country with many settlements and with people more advanced and cultured than those I met. I obtained no other information except that they told me that four or five days inland, where the cordilleras of the sierras end, there is an open valley[5] of large extent in which they said there were many very large settlements and in which there were people clothed in cotton. When I showed them some metals which I had brought with me to learn about the metals of the country, they took the gold metal and said that there were vessels of it among the people of the valley,[6] and that they wore some round articles of that gold hanging from their noses and ears and that they have some small blades made of it, with which they scrape and remove their sweat.

As this valley[7] draws away from the coast—and my instructions were not to go away from it—I decided to leave the coast until my return, because then it could be more easily visited. So I traveled for three days through settlements of those same people, by whom I was received as by the others before. I came to a good-sized settlement named Vacapa,[8] where they gave me a fine reception and much food, which they had in abundance, as this was all irrigated land. It is forty leagues from this settlement to the sea. Finding myself so far away from the sea, and it being two days before Passion Sunday, I decided to remain there until Easter to inform myself in regard to the islands, of which, as I said above, I had reports. So I sent Indian messengers to the sea by three different routes. I charged them to bring me people from the coast and from some of the islands, in order to obtain information from them.

In a different direction I sent Esteban de Dorantes, a negro, whom I instructed to go fifty or sixty leagues toward the north to see whether, by that route, information could be obtained of

5. The word is *abra*.
6. *Abra.*
7. *Abra.*
8. Vacapa, between the Mayo and the Fuerte rivers.

something important of what we were seeking. I arranged with him that, should he learn of some inhabited and rich country, something really important, he should not go any farther but return in person or send me Indians bearing the following sign we had agreed upon: If it were something moderate, he should send me a white cross a span in size; if it were of greater importance, he should send one two spans in size; and if it were something greater and better than New Spain, he should send me a large cross. Thus the negro Esteban took leave of me on Passion Sunday, after dinner, and I remained at this settlement, which, as I have said, is called Vacapa.

Four days later messengers from Esteban arrived carrying a very large cross the height of a man, and they told me on Esteban's behalf that I should set out immediately and follow him, because he had met people who informed him of the greatest thing in the world; that he had Indians with him who had been there, of whom he sent me one. The latter told me so many marvels of the land that I postponed believing them until after seeing them or having further verification of the matter. He told me that there was thirty days' travel from the place where Esteban was to the first city of the land, which is called Cíbola.

As it seems to me worth recording here what this Indian, sent to me by Esteban, says about the country, I shall proceed to do so. He says and maintains that, in the first province, there are seven very large cities, all under one ruler, with large houses of stone and lime. The smaller ones are one story high with a terrace above; others are two and three stories high, and the ruler's house is four stories high; these houses are all joined in orderly manner. He says that the doorways to the best houses have many decorations of turquoises, of which there is a great abundance, and that the people in these cities are very well clothed. He told me many other details, both of these seven cities and of other provinces farther on, each one of which he claims to be much more important than these seven cities. In order to find out from him how he came to know this, we had a good many questions and answers, and I found him quite able to express himself. I rendered thanks to our Lord.

I postponed my departure in the footsteps of Esteban de

Dorantes, believing that he would wait for me, as I had arranged with him, and also because I promised the messengers whom I had sent to the sea that I would wait for them, for I had determined to be very truthful with the people with whom I had any dealings. The messengers arrived on Easter Sunday, and with them came people from the coast and from two islands. From them I learned that the islands previously mentioned are poor in food, as I had heard before, and that they are inhabited by people. They wore shells on their foreheads and said that they contain pearls. They assured me that there were thirty-four islands, all close together, whose names I am writing in another paper in which I am recording the names of the islands and settlements. The people from the coast say that they, as well as the inhabitants of the islands, have little food, and that they trade with one another by means of rafts. Here the coast turns almost directly north. These Indians from the coast brought me shields made of hides of the cattle, finely fashioned and large, which covered them from head to foot, with holes above the hilt in order to be able to see from behind them. They are so strong that I believe a crossbow will not pierce them.

On this day, three Indians of those called the Pintados came to see me, their faces, chests, and arms all decorated.[9] Their settlements form a circle toward the east, and some of their territory borders on that near the seven cities. They said that they came to see me because they had heard of me. Among other things, they gave me much information of the seven cities and provinces of which Esteban's Indian had told me, and their accounts were about the same as those that Esteban had sent me.

So I dismissed the coast people, but two Indians from the islands said that they wanted to travel with me for seven or eight days. Accompanied by them and the three Pintados I have mentioned, I set out from Vacapa on the second day after Easter Sunday, following the road and direction taken by Esteban. I had received other messengers from him, bringing another cross the size of the first one he had sent. He urged me to hurry, affirming that the land I was seeking was the best and

9. Tattooed, or painted? See p. 243, note 3.

greatest that had ever been heard of. The messengers told me individually what the previous one had said, without omitting the slightest detail; on the contrary, they told much more and gave me a clearer explanation.

So I traveled that day, the second after Easter, and two additional days, traversing the same distances that had been covered by Esteban. At the end of this time I met the people who had told him about the seven cities and the country beyond. They told me that from there they went to the city of Cíbola, which is the first of the seven, in thirty days. I was told this not by one but by many. They told me most particularly about the size of the houses and their construction, the same as had been told me by the first Indians. They advised me that, besides these seven cities, there are three other kingdoms called Marata, Acus, and Totonteac. I wanted to know, then, why they went so far away from their homes, and they said that they went after turquoises, hides of the cattle, and other things, all of which they have in that pueblo in abundance. I also wanted to know what they traded for those things, and they replied that they gave their sweat and personal service. They said that they went to the first city, called Cíbola, and worked there tilling the soil and doing other tasks, and for their services the inhabitants gave them hides of the cattle, of the kind they had there, and turquoises.

The people of this pueblo all wear beautiful and good turquoises hanging from their ears and noses. They say that the principal doorways at Cíbola are decorated with them. They told me that the type of dress of the people of Cíbola consisted of some cotton shirts, reaching to the ankle, with a button at the neck, from which hangs a long cord. The sleeves of these shirts are wide, both at the top and the bottom. As I understand it, it is like Bohemian dress. They say that they girdle themselves with turquoise sashes, and that over the shirts some wear very fine blankets and others very well-tanned hides of the cattle, which they consider the best clothes, and of which there are great numbers in that country. The women, too, dress in the same manner, covered to their feet.

These Indians received me very well and took much care

to learn the day of my departure from Vacapa in order to provide me with food and lodging along the way. They brought their sick to me that I might heal them, and they tried to touch my garments. I recited the gospel over them. They gave me some hides of the cattle so well tanned and worked that they all looked as if they had been made by men of higher culture. The natives all said that the hides came from Cíbola.

On the next day I continued on my way, taking along the Pintados, who would not leave me. I came to another settlement, where I was well received by its people. They, too, tried to touch my garments and gave me as detailed accounts of the country where I was going as had the people farther back. They said that people from there had accompanied Esteban Dorantes for four or five days' travel. Here I found a large cross that Esteban had left for me as proof that the information about the good country was always increasing. He left word for me to hurry, that he would wait for me at the edge of the first despoblado. I erected two crosses here and took possession in accordance with the instructions, because this seemed to me a better country than the one we had left behind, and it seemed proper to institute acts of possession from here on.

Thus I traveled for five days, always finding settlements, good lodging, excellent reception, and many turquoises, hides of the cattle, and the same information regarding the country. The inhabitants all spoke to me of Cíbola, and of that province, since they knew I was in search of it. They told me that Esteban was ahead, and here I received messengers from him—some residents of that pueblo who had gone with him. He always persisted in telling me about the greatness of the country, and that I should hasten. Here I learned that in a journey of two more days I would come to a despoblado of four days' travel, in which there was no food, but that they had already arranged to put up houses for me and bring me food. I hastened forward, thinking that I would meet Esteban at the end of it, because he had sent me word that he would wait for me there.

Before reaching the despoblado I came to a pueblo, in green irrigated land, where many people came to meet me, both men and women. They were clothed in cotton, some wearing skins of the cattle, which in general they consider better material than cotton. In this pueblo they were all bedecked with turquoises, which hung from their noses and ears and which they call *cacona*. Among them came the ruler of this pueblo and two of his brothers, very well dressed in cotton, adorned, and each wearing a turquoise necklace. They brought me much game, consisting of deer, rabbits, and quail, and maize and piñol,[10] all in great abundance. They offered me many turquoises and skins of the cattle, very fine vases, and other things, of which I did not take anything, for that has been my practice ever since I entered the land where they had not heard of us.

Here I was given the same report which I said I had received before concerning the seven cities, kingdoms, and provinces. I was wearing a habit of gray cloth, of the kind called Zaragoza, which was obtained for me by Francisco Vázquez de Coronado, governor of New Galicia. The chief of this pueblo and other Indians felt my habit with their hands and told me that there was much cloth like it at Totonteac, that it was worn by the natives there. I laughed at this and said that perhaps it was only cotton blankets they wore. They replied, "Do you think we do not know that what you wear and what we wear is different? Know that at Cíbola all the houses are filled with this cloth we are wearing, but at Totonteac there are some small animals from which they obtain that with which to make this cloth you are wearing." I was startled, because I had never heard of such a thing until I reached this place. I wanted to get very detailed information about this matter, and they told me that the animals are the size of the two Castile greyhounds Esteban was taking along. They said there were many at Totonteac. I could not figure out what sort of animals they could be.

The next day I entered the despoblado, and at the place where I was to eat I found huts and plenty of food near an arroyo. At night I found houses and also food, and this continued during the four days which I spent in the despoblado. At the end of this distance I came into a valley well settled with

10. Piñol seems to mean piñon nuts. Fernández de Oviedo uses it to mean roasted corn.

people. Here at the first pueblo many men and women came out to meet me with food. They all wore many turquoises, suspended from their noses and ears, and some wore necklaces of turquoise, of the variety I mentioned as being worn by the chief and his brothers at the pueblo before coming to the despoblado, except that the latter had only one string and these had three or four. They had very good blankets and skins of the cattle. The women wore similar turquoises in their noses and ears, and fine skirts and shirts.

They knew as much here about Cíbola as they know in New Spain about Mexico, or in Peru about Cuzco. They described in much detail the construction of the houses, and the town, its streets and plazas, as people who had been there many times and had brought from there the fine things they obtained in exchange for personal service, as had the people farther back. I told them it was not possible that the houses could be constructed the way they described, and to explain it to me they took dirt and ashes, mixed them with water, and showed me how they set the stone and reared the building, using mortar and stone until it was up. I asked the men of the country if they had wings to ascend to those terraces. They laughed and pictured a ladder for me as clearly as I might do it myself. They took a stick, placed it over their heads, and said that this would be the height from terrace to terrace.

At this place I was also told of the woolen cloth of Totonteac, where, they said, the houses are like those at Cíbola, but better, and that there are many more of them, and that it is a very extensive place, without limit.

Here I learned that the coast turns west very abruptly, for up to the time of entering this first despoblado which I crossed, the coast extended always to the north. Since the turning of the coast is very important, I wanted to verify it, and so I went in search of it, and I saw clearly that at a latitude of thirty-five degrees it turns to the west. This brought me no less joy than the good information of the country.

So I returned to proceed on my way and marched through that valley for five days. It is so thickly settled by attractive people and so bountiful in food that it could provision more than three hundred men and horses. All is irrigated; it is like a garden. There were villages every half or quarter of a league. In each one of these pueblos I obtained very extensive reports of Cíbola, and they spoke to me very minutely about it, for they go there every year to earn their living. Here I met a man, native of Cíbola, who said that he fled from the person whom the ruler has appointed in Cíbola, because the lord of these seven cities lives and has his seat in one of them, which is named Ahacus, and in the others he has placed persons who govern in his name.

This resident of Cíbola is a man of good presentation, rather old and much more intelligent than the natives of this valley or the ones farther back. He said that he wanted to go with me so that I might obtain his pardon. I questioned him closely, and he told me that Cíbola was a big city in which there are many people, streets, and plazas, that in some sections of the city there are some very large houses ten stories high, and that the leaders assemble in them on certain days of the year. They say that the houses are of stone and lime, of the type described by the people farther back, that the portals and fronts of the chief houses are of turquoise. He told me that the other seven cities are like this one, some even larger, and that the principal one is Ahacus. He says that to the southeast there is a kingdom named Marata, which used to have many and very large settlements, and that all of them had these stone houses and terraces.

These people, he said, have been and are at war with the lord of these seven cities, and because of this war the kingdom of Marata has declined a great deal, although it is still independent and at war with the others. He also said that toward the southeast there is the kingdom called Totonteac. He says that it is the biggest in the world, with the most people and riches, and that there they wear clothes of the material of which mine are made, and other finer materials, obtained from the animals that they had described to me before. These people are very orderly, he declared, and different from the people I have seen. He informed me that there is another very large kingdom and province which is called Acus—there are both Ahacus and Acus. A[ha]cus, with the aspiration, is one of the seven cities, the main one; Acus, without the aspiration, is a kingdom and province by itself.[11] He told me that the dress they wear at Cíbola is as described by the people farther back. He said that all the people in that city sleep in beds high above the ground, and that they have bedclothes, and canopies which cover the beds. He told me that he would go with me as far as Cíbola, and beyond, if I would take him. This same report was given to me at this pueblo by many other persons, although not in such detail.

I marched through this valley for three days, the natives entertaining me with all the fiestas and celebrations they could. Here in this valley I saw more than two thousand skins of the cattle, extremely well tanned. I saw a much larger quantity of turquoises and strings of them in this valley than in all the country I had traversed before. The natives all say that it comes from the city of Cíbola, of which place they have as much information as I have of the things I handle every day. They are similarly acquainted with the kingdoms of Marata, Acus, and Totonteac.

Here in this valley they brought me a hide half as large again as that of a big cow. They told me that it was from an animal which has only one horn in the front, and that this horn is curved toward its breast, then turns in a straight point, and which they say is so strong that it does not fail to tear anything it strikes, however strong it may be. They say that there are many of these animals in that country. In color the skin rather resembles that of a buck, and the hair is as long as a finger is thick.

Here I received messengers from Esteban, who told me on his behalf that he was already in the last despoblado, and very elated, because he was more certain of the riches of the country than before. He sent word to me that since he had taken leave of me he had never caught the Indians in a lie, that thus far he had found everything as it had been described to him, and that he expected to find the rest the same. I believe it to be true,

11. The writing of Acus and Ahacus is slightly confused in the original. Pacheco y Cárdenas corrected the sentence to conform to the meaning, and we give the latter rendering.

because the fact is that from the very first day when I heard of the city of Cíbola, until now, everything that the Indians told me I have verified. They always told me what pueblos I would find on the way, and their names. In the regions where there were no settlements, they informed me where I would find food and lodging, without ever making the slightest mistake, even though, from the first time when I heard about the land to this day, I have traveled one hundred and twelve leagues, which makes the veracity of these people quite worth recording.

Here in this valley, as in the other pueblos farther back, I erected crosses and performed the proper legal acts and proceedings in accordance with my instructions. The natives of this village begged me to rest here for three or four days, because the despoblado began four days'[12] travel from here, and from its beginning until coming to the city of Cíbola is fifteen long days' travel. They wanted to prepare food and provide me with what I needed for the journey. They told me that more than three hundred men from here had accompanied the negro Esteban, carrying food for him, and that many also wanted to go with me, to serve me, because they hoped to come back rich. I thanked them and told them to get things ready quickly, because each day seemed a year to me, such was my desire to see Cíbola.

So I delayed three days without going farther. In this time I constantly tried to obtain information about Cíbola and all the other places, doing nothing else but taking Indians aside to question each one of them separately. They all agreed in their accounts. They told me of the multitude of people, the arrangement of the streets, the bigness of the houses, and the type the doorways, all as others had described them before.

The three days being over, many people gathered to go with me. I selected about thirty prominent men, all very well dressed, wearing turquoise necklaces, some with five and six loops. In addition, I chose the necessary people to carry the provisions for them and for me, and set out on my way. Thus marching, I entered the despoblado on May 9.

12. The manuscript copy reads *jornadas;* Pacheco y Cárdenas have *leguas,* III, p. 342.

We traveled as follows: On the first day we marched over a wide and much-used road. We arrived for dinner at a spring which the Indians had indicated to me, and then at another one, where we slept. Here I found a shelter, which they had just built for me, and another one, in which Esteban had slept when he passed here. There were also old shacks and many signs of dead fires of the people who had traveled this road on their way to Cíbola. In this manner I traveled twelve days, always well supplied with provisions of deer, hares, and partridges of the same color and taste as those of Spain, although slightly smaller.

Here I was met by an Indian, a son of one of the chiefs who accompanied me and who had gone ahead with the negro Esteban. He arrived very grieved, exhibiting great sadness in his countenance, his face and body covered with sweat. He told me that one day's travel before reaching Cíbola, Esteban sent messengers ahead with his gourd, just as he was in the habit of doing, so that they might know he was coming. The gourd had some strings of jingle bells, and two feathers, one white and the other red. When the messengers arrived at Cíbola, they appeared before the man appointed there by the ruler and gave him the gourd. When he took it in his hands and saw the jingle bells, he at once hurled the gourd to the ground with much anger and wrath. He told the messengers to leave immediately, for he knew what sort of people they represented, and that they should tell them not to enter the city or he would kill them all. The messengers went back and told Esteban what had happened. He told them that it was of no importance, that those who showed anger received him better.

So Esteban continued on his journey until he came to the city of Cíbola. Here he was met by people who refused to allow him to enter the city and who put him in a large house located outside of it, taking away from him everything he carried to trade, turquoises and other things he had obtained from the Indians along the way. They kept him there that night without giving him, or those who came with him, any food or water.

The next morning this Indian was thirsty and left the house to get a drink from a nearby river. From that place he shortly afterward saw Esteban fleeing and people from the city pursuing him, and they killed some of those who came with him. Upon seeing this, this Indian, concealing himself, fled up the river and then crossed over it, reaching the road of the despoblado.

On hearing this news, some of the Indians who were with me began to weep. In view of this wretched news I thought that I should be lost. I feared not so much to lose my life as not to be able to return and report on the greatness of the country, where God, our Lord, can be so well served, His holy faith exalted, and the royal patrimony of his Majesty increased. Withal, I consoled them as best I could and told them that we should not give entire credence to the Indian's story. With many tears, they replied that the Indian would not tell anything except what he had seen.

So I drew aside from the Indians to commend myself to our Lord and to pray Him for guidance in this matter according to His will and to enlighten my heart. Having done this, I rejoined the Indians, and with a knife I cut the strings of the bags in which I carried clothing and articles for trade, for up to then it had not been necessary to do so, and I had not given a thing to any one. I distributed what I carried among all those chiefs. I told them not to be afraid but to accompany me, which they did.

As we were on our way, one day's journey from Cíbola, we met two other Indians of those who had gone with Esteban. They were bloodstained and had many wounds. Upon their arrival, they and those who were with me began such a weeping that they made me cry too, both through pity and fear. The lament was so great that they did not allow me an opportunity to ask them about Esteban, or what had happened to them. I begged them to be quiet so that we might learn what the trouble was. They asked how they could keep still when they knew that of their fathers, sons, and brothers who had gone with Esteban, more than three hundred men were dead. They said that they would no longer dare go to Cíbola as they used to. Nevertheless, I tried my best to calm and overcome their fear, although I was not without need of some one who could quiet my own.

I asked the wounded Indians about Esteban and what had happened. They stood awhile, without uttering a word, weeping, together with those from their pueblos. Finally they told me that when Esteban was within a day's travel of the city of Cíbola, he sent his messengers with a gourd to the ruler of that place, informing him of his visit and of how he was coming to establish peace and to heal them. When the emissaries handed the ruler the gourd and he saw the jingle bells, he became very angry and threw the gourd to the ground, saying, "I know these people, for these jingle bells are not the shape of ours. Tell them to turn back at once, or not one of their men will be spared." Thus he remained very wrathful. The messengers went back very dejectedly, and they hardly dared tell Esteban what had happened to them, although they finally told him. He told them not to fear, that he would go there, for although the inhabitants gave him a bad answer they would receive him well.

So Esteban went ahead with all his people, who must have numbered more than three hundred men, besides many women, and reached the city of Cíbola at sunset. They were not allowed to come into the city, but were placed in a large house, quite a good lodging, which was located outside of the city. Then the natives of Cíbola took away from Esteban everything he carried, saying that it had been so ordered by their lord. "During this whole night," the wounded Indians said, "they did not give us anything to eat or drink. The next morning, when the sun had risen the height of a lance, Esteban went out of the house and some of the chiefs followed him, whereupon many people came out of the city. When Esteban saw them, he began to flee, and we did also. They at once began to shoot arrows at us, wounding us, and we dropped to the ground. Others fell dead upon us, and thus we remained until night, not daring to stir. We heard much shouting in the city, and we saw many men and women on the terraces, watching, but we never saw Esteban again. We believe that they shot him with arrows and also the others who were with him, as no one except ourselves escaped."

Hearing what the Indians said, and in view of the poor conditions for continuing my journey as I desired, I could not help but feel some apprehension for their loss and mine. God is my witness of how much I wished to have some one with whom to take counsel and advice, for I must confess that I did not know what to do. I told them that our Lord would punish Cíbola and that as soon as the emperor should learn of what had taken place he would send many Christians to punish those natives. The Indians would not believe me, because they said that no one could overcome the power of Cíbola. I asked them to calm themselves and not to weep, comforting them with the best words I could command, which would take too long to record here.

Thus I left them and withdrew a stone's throw or two to commend myself to God, in which solace I must have taken an hour and a half. When I returned to them, I found that one of my Indians, whose name was Marcos, and whom I had brought from Mexico, was crying. He said to me: "Father, these people are planning to kill you, because they say that you and Esteban are responsible for the deaths of their relatives, and that not a man or woman among them will be left alive." In order to placate them, I began once more to distribute among them what I had left in clothes and articles for trading. I told them they must realize that if they killed me they would not harm me at all because I would die a Christian and would go to heaven, and those who killed me would suffer for it, because the Christians would come in search of me, and against my wishes they would kill them all.

By these and many other things that I told them they were calmed somewhat, although they still lamented greatly for their people who had been killed. I begged some of them to go to Cíbola to see if any other Indian had escaped, and to gather some information about Esteban, but I could not persuade them to do that. In view of this I told them that, in any event, I was going to see the city of Cíbola, and they told me that no one would accompany me. Finally, seeing me so determined, two of the chiefs said that they would go with me. Accompanied by them and by my own Indians and interpreters, I proceeded on my journey until coming within view of Cíbola, which is situated in a plain, at the base of a round hill.

This pueblo has a fine appearance, the best I have seen in

these regions. The houses are as they had been described to me by the Indians, all of stone, with terraces and flat roofs, as it seemed to me from a hill where I stood to view it. The city is larger than the city of Mexico.[13] At times I was tempted to descend to the pueblo, because I knew I was risking only my life, and this I offered to God the day that I set out on this journey. In the end, realizing my danger, I feared that if I died no information would be obtained concerning this land, which in my opinion is the greatest and best of all that have been discovered.

When I told the chieftains who were with me how well impressed I was with Cíbola, they told me that it was the smallest of the seven cities, and that Totonteac is much larger and better than all the seven, that it has so many houses and people that there is no end to it.

Observing the nature of the city, it seemed to me appropriate to name that land the new kingdom of Saint Francis. And so, with the aid of the Indians, I gathered there a pile of stones, and on top of it I erected a slender and small cross, as I had no materials with which to make a bigger one. I declared that I was erecting that cross and landmark as a sign of possession, in the name of Don Antonio de Mendoza, viceroy and governor of New Spain for the emperor, our lord, in accordance with my instructions. I stated that I was taking possession there of all the seven cities and of the kingdoms of Totonteac, Acus, and Marata; that I was not going to visit them in order to return to give a report of what had been done and seen.

Thus I turned back with much more fear than food. I trav-

13. At this point Ramusio (*Viaggi*, iii, f. 359d) has the following interpolation: "The city is bigger than the city of Temistitán, which has more than twenty thousand houses. The people are almost white. They wear clothes and sleep in beds. For weapons they have bows. They possess many emeralds and other jewels, although they prize none so much as turquoises, with which they decorate the walls and portals of their houses, their garments and their vases, and they use them as money throughout the country. They wear cotton clothes and cattle skins. The latter are considered more valuable and distinguished for clothing. As they possess no other metals, they use vessels of gold and silver, of which they make greater use, and there is greater abundance of it than in Peru. They buy it with turquoises at the province of the Pintados, where it is said that the mines are found in great abundance. I was not able to obtain so detailed information about the other kingdoms."

eled with all possible haste until I met the people who had remained behind. I reached them after marching for two days, and together with them I crossed the despoblado, where I was not so well received now as before, because both men and women were weeping bitterly for their people who had been killed at Cíbola. Being afraid, I took leave quickly of the people of that valley and traveled ten leagues on the first day. Thus I traversed from eight to ten leagues each day without a stop, until I had crossed the second despoblado.

On my way back, and although I was not lacking in fear, I determined to approach the valley[14] where the sierras end, which, as I said previously, I had heard about. There I learned that that valley[15] is inhabited for many days' journeys toward the east. I did not dare to enter it without endangering my person and failing to report what I had seen, and it seemed to me that the Spaniards would first have to come and settle and dominate this other land of the seven cities and kingdoms I have mentioned, and that this valley could then be more easily explored. I only saw, from the opening of the valley,[16] seven fair-sized settlements, somewhat distant, and, below, a very verdant valley with very good soil, from which many smokes rose. I was told that there is much gold there and that the natives make it into vessels, and jewels for the ears, and into little blades with which they wipe away their sweat. These people do not allow those from this region of the valley[17] to trade with them. They could not tell me why.

Here I erected two crosses and took possession of this whole valley and dale[18] in the same manner and order as in the preceding acts of possession, in conformity with my instructions. From there I continued my return trip with all possible haste until coming to the town of San Miguel, in the province of Culuacán, thinking that I would find there Francisco Vázquez de Coronado, governor of New Galicia. As he was not there I continued my journey to the city of Compostela, where I found

14. *Abra.*
15. *Abra.*
16. *Desde la boca de la abra.*
17. *Abra.*
18. *Abra y valle.*

him. From there I immediately reported my arrival to his Excellency, the viceroy of New Spain, and to our father provincial, Fray Antonio de Ciudad Rodrigo, asking for instructions as to what I should do.

I do not record here many details of the journey because they do not pertain to this case. I tell only of what I saw and was told, of the countries I have traversed, and those of which I have been informed. I do this for our father provincial so that he may show it to the fathers of our order, as he deems best, or to the chapter, by whose order I went, so that they may give it to his Excellency, the viceroy of New Spain, at whose request they sent me on this expedition.—FRAY MARCOS DE NIZA, vice commissary. [Rubric.]

LEGALIZATION

In the great city of Temixtitán, Mexico, New Spain, on September 2, 1539, in the presence of his Excellency, Don Antonio de Mendoza, his Majesty's viceroy and governor in this New Spain and president of the royal audiencia and chancellery there established, there being present the very distinguished gentlemen, Licentiate Francisco de Ceínos, his Majesty's judge of the said royal audiencia, and Francisco Vázquez de Coronado, his Majesty's governor of the province of New Galicia, and in the presence of us, Juan Baeza de Herrera, chief notary of the said royal audiencia and of the government of the said New Spain, and Antonio de Turcios, his Majesty's notary of the said royal audiencia, appeared the very reverend father, Fray Marcos de Niza, vice commissary in these regions of the Indies of the ocean sea, a member of the order of Saint Francis, and presented before his Lordship and the said notaries and witnesses above-mentioned these instructions and this relation, signed with his name and sealed with the general seal of the Indies, and which contain nine sheets, including this one which carries our scrolls. He stated, affirmed, and attested that what is contained in the said instructions and relation is true, that what is contained therein has taken place, and that he presents it in order that his Majesty may be informed of the truth of what is reported therein. His Lordship ordered us, the said notaries, to attest it at its end exactly as it was presented and given by the said vice commissary, and to certify it, signed with our names.—Witnesses who were present: the above-mentioned, and Antonio de Almaguer and Fray Martín de Ojacastro, a friar of the same order.[19]

In testimony of which, I, the said Juan Baeza de Herrera, the abovesaid notary, affix here this my scroll, thus †, in testimony of the truth.—JUAN BAEZA DE HERRERA. And I, the aforesaid Antonio de Turcios, abovenamed notary, being present at all the aforesaid affix here this my scroll, thus †, in testimony of the truth.—ANTONIO DE TURCIOS.

19. On September 22, 1539, Fray Marcos again appeared before the viceroy and made a deposition that he had not received any information about the new land that he had explored from Hernando Cortés. This was in regard to the dispute between the viceroy and Cortés as to whether the latter's contract with the king gave him special rights of exploration in the north, a contention vigorously opposed by Viceroy Mendoza. Fray Marcos deposed that he went on the expedition by order of the viceroy and that he followed the Indian guides provided by him. Fray Marcos added that if Cortés had received any report of the "new land," he would not have sent supply ships to Peru. Cortés actually did send two supply ships to Francisco Pizarro in 1535. (Priestley, *The Mexican Nation,* p. 47.) The witnesses to Fray Marcos' deposition were Francisco de Ceínos, Francisco Vázquez de Coronado, Fray Martín de Ojacastro, and two notaries. Fray Marcos' deposition is in A. G. I., *Patronato,* legajo 21.

APPOINTMENT OF CORONADO AS COMMANDER OF THE EXPEDITION TO CIBOLA, JANUARY 6, 1540[1]

I, the King. By order of his Majesty — Cobos, comendador mayor.[2]

————————————

. . . So, considering it conducive to the service of God, our Lord, and our own that this said expedition be carried out in our name, and having confidence that you, Francisco Vázquez de Coronado, our governor and captain general of New Galicia, are a person who would properly and faithfully perform and carry out whatever we may entrust and commend to you, and

1. Translated from a photostatic copy of the original in the Archivo General de las Indias, *Justicia*, legajo 339. There is another copy in legajo 1021. The Spanish text, contributed by A. S. Aiton, has just appeared in the *Hispanic American Historical Review*, xx (1940), pp. 83-87.

Coronado became governor of New Galicia in the fall of 1538, on the death of Licentiate de la Torre, who had succeeded Nuño de Guzmán. When Coronado reached Guadalajara he appointed the regidores of the city, on November 19, and then continued on his way to Compostela. Tello, *Crónica Miscelánea*, p. 303.

Mendoza's action in naming Coronado as leader of the expedition to Cíbola was by virtue of a royal cédula of April 17, 1535, in which the king specifically limited Cortés' claim to exclusive right to further exploration in the north. Cortés based his contention on his appointment as captain general in 1522. The cédula of exemption reads: "I, the king, to Don Antonio de Mendoza, our viceroy and governor of New Spain and president of our royal audiencia and chancellery there.

"Whereas you know that Don Hernando Cortés, Marqués del Valle, has been named captain general of New Spain, although, through the interpretations and limitations added later, he can not discharge this office except by order of our president and judges, and in such cases he is to follow the instructions they may give him, and

"Whereas occasions may occur when it may be desirable to entrust the undertaking to some other persons, we by these presents grant you power and authority so that if an occasion arises when it may be desirable to entrust its execution and fulfillment to some person other than the said Marqués, you may have authority to act accordingly, as president, viceroy, and governor.

"Given in Barcelona, April 17, 1535." Archivo General de Indias, *Justicia*, legajo 1021.

2. Francisco de los Cobos y Molina was comendador mayor, or knight commander, of the order of Santiago in the kingdom of León. He was also secretary to the emperor, Charles V, and held numerous posts of responsibility such as contador mayor of Castile, ensayador mayor of the Indies, secretary of state, and secretary of the supreme council.

that you will take special care in the protection and defense
of the said lands and their natives, by these presents, affirming
and confirming the said appointment made of you, the said
Francisco Vázquez de Coronado, by the said Don Antonio de
Mendoza, our viceroy of New Spain, we appoint you anew as
captain general of the people who now are going, that may
go later, or of any others you may find there, and of the lands
and provinces of Acus and Cíbola, and the seven cities and
the kingdoms and provinces of Matata and Totonteac, and
of all their subjects and dependents; and of the other lands and
provinces that you may discover or that may be discovered
through your industry; that you command all the people who
may go there, whatever their condition or state; that they follow and accept you, the said Francisco Vázquez de Coronado,
as our captain general, and obey you, and respond to and perform your commands, and to respond and appear before you
at your call at the specified times and under the penalties that
you may stipulate and order, which by these presents we impose on them. We grant you power and authority to enforce
these orders on those who may be rebellious or disobedient.
Likewise, we grant you authority to choose and appoint the
captain or captains that may be desirable; that you may dismiss
them and appoint others again whenever you wish and find it
advisable; that you may hear and shall hear all the civil and
criminal litigation which may arise and come up among the
said Spaniards, and among the natives of the lands you travel
through or stay in, and between the said Spaniards and them.
For the hearing and disposal of the said litigations you shall
have power to and may select one, two, or more lieutenants, as
many as you may think convenient or necessary, and these you
may remove and appoint others in their places.

As to the treatment of the native Indians of the lands you
may travel through or stay in, and what you are to do and perform there, we order you to observe and comply to the letter
with what is prescribed in the instructions we have ordered
issued and which are given to persons who go to discover and
pacify new lands, as you are doing. These instructions you are
carrying with you, signed by our said viceroy and the above-

stated secretary. You are not to exceed or go beyond their tenor and contents, under the penalties prescribed in the said instructions.

We command that no impediment or hindrance whatsoever be placed in your way in the discharge and exercise of the office of captain general in the said lands, that every one accept your judgment, and render and have others render you, without any excuse or delay, all the assistance that you may demand from them and that you may need in the performance of the duties of your office. In regard to anything else mentioned in this cédula, we grant you full powers, as the case may require, in everything that is incidental to, dependent upon, or related to it in any way.

Inasmuch as you, Francisco Vázquez de Coronado, are our governor and captain general of the said province of New Galicia and you are going, by our command and in our service, to the discovery and pacification of the said new land and to bring its natives to the knowledge of our holy Catholic faith and to bring the land under our royal crown, by this token we grant you power and authority that, during your absence from the province, you may leave and shall leave in your place a lieutenant or lieutenants, who shall be suitable persons, in the locality or localities where you may wish. And we order that such persons as you may have appointed in New Galicia shall be accepted, respected, and obeyed as lieutenant governors there.

We order that you receive the same salary that we have assigned to you in the order of appointment that was given you for the said office, and that it be disbursed and paid to you; and, since you are going in our service, that you be not deprived at any time of the Indians that have been entrusted or given to you, whether in New Spain or elsewhere.

Likewise, it is our will, and we so order, that the said lands and the others you may pacify and bring to our service as our captain general, you may retain until other arrangements are provided and ordered by us or by our viceroy of New Spain. You are to protect and defend these lands and their natives in our royal name in order that no injury or ill treatment may be inflicted upon them, and in order that no other persons may enter those lands and take possession of or occupy them, saying that the government of the new land belongs to them, until, as has been stated, measures be taken that are most befitting our service.

Issued in the City of Mechuacan, January 6, 1540.—DON ANTONIO DE MENDOZA.

I, the secretary, ANTONIO DE ALMAGUER, had it copied by his command with the approval of the viceroy of New Spain.

Registered—DIEGO AGUNDEZ. By Chancellor GASPAR DE CASTILLA.

MUSTER ROLL OF THE EXPEDITION, FEBRUARY 22, 1540

Testimony Concerning the People, Weapons, and Provisions That Set Out from Compostela in New Spain (When Don Antonio de Mendoza Was its Viceroy), Taken to the Land Newly Discovered by Fray Marcos de Niza, of Which Francisco Vázquez Coronado Was the General.[1]

I, Juan de Cuebas, his Majesty's chief notary of mines and reports in this New Spain, state and certify that at the city of Compostela in New Galicia of New Spain, there being present his Excellency, Don Antonio de Mendoza, his Majesty's viceroy and governor of this New Spain, Gonzalo de Salazar, factor, Peralmyndes Cherino, inspector of the said New Spain, and Cristóbal de Oñate, inspector of the said province, and many other people, a review was held of all those who are going to the land newly discovered by the father provincial, Fray Marcos de Niza, of which Francisco Vázquez de Coronado is going as captain general. This said review was held on February 22, 1540, in the presence of the judge, Licentiate Maldonado, in the following form and manner.[2]

Francisco Vázquez de Coronado, captain general, swore that

1. Translated from a photostatic copy of the original in the Archivo General de Indias, *Guadalajara*, legajo 5. The Spanish text was published by A. S. Aiton in *American Historical Review*, XLIV (1939), pp. 556-570, and his English translation was issued by the William L. Clements Library, *Bulletin No. XXX*, Ann Arbor, 1939.

2. In addition to the soldiers listed in this muster, there were others who went on the expedition. The friars, for example, with their escort left a month in advance of the main body. (See Introduction, pp. 9-12.) There were also the two ships under command of Hernando de Alarcón which were to accompany the expedition by sea but which turned back at the Colorado river when Coronado went inland. Finally we have found the names of a number of additional soldiers in the trial documents and other records of the Coronado expedition. These are given at the end of the muster roll.

he is taking on this expedition in the service of his Majesty twenty-two or twenty-three horses and three or four sets of weapons for bridle and saddle.

Lope de Samaniego,[3] maestre de campo, swore that he is taking sixteen or seventeen horses, two buckskin coats, one coat of mail with its accouterments, some native cuirasses and weapons, since his other belongings were destroyed by fire.

Don Pedro de Tovar,[4] chief ensign, swore that he is taking thirteen horses, one coat of mail, and some cuirasses and other native accouterments and weapons.

Don Lope de Gurrea [Urrea], five horses, native weapons, Castile armor, headpiece, and buckskin coat.

Hernando de Alvarado,[5] captain of artillery, four horses, one coat of mail with sleeves, and native weapons, and other native equipment and arms.

Don Alonso Manrique,[6] three horses, native weapons, Castilian weapons, headpiece, and buckskin coat.

Juan Gallego,[7] coat of mail with breeches, buckskin coat, cross-

3. Samaniego, commander of the arsenal at Mexico, was killed by an arrow near Chiametla shortly after the expedition set out. Buried in the field, his body was later taken to the church at Compostela. See letter of Mendoza to the king, April 17, 1540, note 3, Tello, *Crónica*, p. 328, and A. G. I., *Mexico*, legajo 1089.

4. Tovar was a brother of D. Sancho de Tovar, regidor of Sahagún. Don Pedro was one of the first settlers of Guadalajara with Nuño de Guzmán in 1531 and also one of the founders of Culiacán. At the death of Melchior Díaz, Tovar succeeded him in the encomienda. He was named alcalde mayor of New Galicia in 1549 for a period of two years by Viceroy Mendoza. On his death at Culiacán, he left some papers subsequently used by Castañeda in his history. Tello, *Crónica*, pp. 135, 490-491, 505, 536.

5. Alvarado was a witness for Don García López de Cárdenas. In his testimony of services he says that he came to New Spain with Cortés, and that he went on the Coronado expedition with his own horses and servants, without compensation. He was from Santander, the son of Juan Sánchez de Alvarado and Mencía de Salazar. Tello, *Crónica*, p. 416, says that he was related to the adelantado, Don Pedro de Alvarado. See also A. G. I., *Mexico*, legajo 1064; A. G. I., *Justicia*, legajo 1021, pieza 5, and Icaza, *Diccionario*, no. 1221.

6. Manrique was from Valladolid, the son of Antonio Manrique and Catalina de Aragón. He served on the expedition to Cíbola and in the pacification of New Galicia, after having served with Don Pedro de Mendoza, who sought his fortune in the conquest of the Rio de la Plata. He was a captain and asked for a repartimiento. Icaza, *Diccionario*, no. 1369.

7. Gallego was a witness for López de Cárdenas. He was one of the first settlers of Purificación in 1536. In a petition he said that he was from Coruña, the son of Juan Hernández de Artés and Mayor Rodríguez. He was also a witness at Coronado's residencia. See A. G. I., *Justicia*, legajos 339 and 1021, pieza 5; Tello, *Crónica*, p. 253; Icaza, *Diccionario*, nos. 477 and 1186.

bow and other Castilian and native weapons, and seven horses.

Salinas,[8] son of Andrés de Salinas, resident of Mexico, three horses, one coat of mail, and native weapons including a headpiece.

Rodrigo de Frías,[9] three horses, native weapons, and a buckskin coat.

Francisco de Santillán,[10] two horses and one mare, a buckskin coat, and native weapons.

Andrés do Campo,[11] three horses, native weapons, and a buckskin coat.

Alonso de Velasco, three horses, native weapons, a coat of mail, and a helmet.

Lope Gallego, one horse, one harquebus, and native weapons.

Antón Delgado, two horses, native weapons including a headpiece.

Velasco, one horse with harness, native weapons.

Francisco de Symancas, one horse and native weapons.

Marco Romano, one horse and native weapons.

Juan Pérez, Aragonese, one horse and native weapons.

Francisco Muñoz,[12] one horse and native weapons.

Juan de Peña,[13] one horse and native weapons.

Martín Destepa,[14] one horse and native weapons.

Cristóbal de la Hoz, one horse and native weapons.

Andrés Berrugo, one horse and native weapons.

8. The father, Andrés, said that he and his oldest son went to Cíbola and spent more than one thousand pesos for horses and equipment. Icaza, *Diccionario*, no. 1290.

9. Frías was a witness for Cárdenas. He was from Talavera de la Reina. A. G. I., *Justicia*, legajo 1021, pieza 6.

10. Santillán, given as Francisco de Santillana in C. W. Hackett, *Historical Documents relating to New Mexico, Nueva Vizcaya, and Approaches thereto, to 1773*, Washington, 1923, I, p. 51. Santillán was a blacksmith and veterinarian, but an arrow wound incapacitated him.

11. Campo was a Portuguese. He remained in the new land with Fray Juan de Padilla and went with him to Quivira. See Jaramillo's Narrative.

12. Muñoz, a native of La Granja. He lost his right hand in an accident while firing a gun. Icaza, *Diccionario*, no. 250. See Castañeda, p. 205.

13. Peña, given as Peñas in Icaza, *Diccionario*, no. 752.

14. Alonso Sánchez in his testimony before Judge Tejada accused Estepa of many crimes against the natives. A. G. I., *Justicia*, legajo 1021, pieza 4.

Gómez Román, one horse and native weapons.

Cristóbal Velasco, one horse and native weapons.

Pero Méndez de Sotomayor, one horse and native weapons, two sets.

Gómez Xuárez de Figueroa, four horses, native weapons, a sallet with beaver, and some cuirasses.

Juan Batista de San Vitorees, one coat of mail, one sallet with beaver, a buckskin coat, native weapons, and four horses.

García del Castillo,[15] five horses, one buckskin coat, one of mail, one gauntlet.

Alonso de Canseco, three horses, one coat of mail, one buckskin coat, native weapons.

Melchior Pérez,[16] four horses, one coat of mail, one buckskin coat, native weapons.

Domingo Martín,[17] four horses, one coat of mail, and another of buckskin, one corselet, native weapons.

Lope de la Cadena, two horses, native arms.

Melchior de Robles,[18] two horses, one sallet with beaver, native weapons, one buckskin coat.

Andrés Martín, one horse, native weapons.

Pedro de Ecija, one horse, one simple helmet[19] with beaver, native weapons.

Pedro Linares, two horses, native weapons.

Juan de Ramos, two horses, native weapons.

15. Castillo was a witness for López de Cárdenas. He said that he was from Seville. A. G. I., *Justicia*, legajo 1021, pieza 5.

16. Pérez was a son of Licentiate de la Torre. In the inquiry by Judge Tejada, he gave damaging testimony against López de Cárdenas, accusing him of deceiving the Indians at Arenal with the sign of the cross. He claimed that he had spent more than 2,000 castellanos in the expedition. He was also a witness at Coronado's residencia, and also in 1552 when Coronado was suing to recover some towns. This time Pérez said he had known Coronado for fifteen years. See A. G. I., *Justicia*, legajos 336, 339, and 1021, pieza 4; Icaza, *Diccionario*, no. 1059.

17. Martín was a witness at Judge Tejada's inquiry. He said that he was from Brozas in Castile. A. G. I., *Justicia*, legajo 1021, pieza 4; Icaza, *Diccionario*, no. 37.

18. Robles was a native of Almazán. *Ibid.*, no. 489.

19. The Spanish reads *caxco*, which we have translated "simple helmet." It should be distinguished from *celada*, translated "sallet." The sallet was a form of helmet used in the 16th century.

Pedro de Ledesma,[20] five horses, one coat of armor, one beaver, one sallet, native arms.

Captain Don García López de Cárdenas,[21] twelve horses, three sets of Castilian weapons, two pairs of cuirasses, one coat of mail.

Juan Navarro,[22] five horses, one coat of mail, native weapons, one sallet with beaver.

Alonso del Moral, ensign of this party, two horses, one beaver, one sallet, native weapons.

Rodrigo de Ysla, five horses, native weapons, one coat of armor, and other arms.

Juan López, three horses, native weapons.

Francisco Gómez,[23] two horses, native weapons, one crossbow, and one dagger.

Hernando Botello,[24] one horse, native arms.

Maestre Miguel and his son, three horses, one coat of mail, one doublet of mail, a helmet, and his son had native weapons, one beaver, and a sallet.

Diego Gutiérrez, captain of the cavalry, six horses, one coat of armor, breeches of mail, one buckskin coat, three native weapons.

Juan de Villareal,[25] ensign, six horses, one corselet, one sallet with beaver, one coat of mail, native weapons.

Alonso López,[26] four horses, one sallet with beaver, native weapons.

20. Ledesma, a native of Zamora, was a witness at the inquiry held by Judge Tejada. He was also a character witness for Coronado at his residencia. In 1552 he testified that he had known Coronado for twenty-four years. He married a daughter of Melchior Pérez, the son of Licentiate Diego de la Torre. See A. G. I., *Justicia*, legajos 336, 339, and 1021, pieza 4; Icaza, *Diccionario*, no. 1166.

21. See the testimony of López de Cárdenas, pp. 337-365.

22. Navarro, from Aragon, came to New Spain with Cortés, serving as a crossbowman. Icaza, *Diccionario*, no. 18.

23. *Cf. Ibid.*, no. 1376.

24. Botello, a native of Alcántara. *Ibid.*, no. 1301.

25. Villareal, a native of Agudo and member of the order of Calatrava, said that the army consumed one thousand pesos worth of cattle which he took along on the expedition. He carried messages from Coronado in Cíbola to the viceroy. Later he was a favorable witness in the residencia of Coronado. Judge Tejada held his residencia as alcalde of Guadalajara on September 7, 1544, and sentenced him to pay a fine of thirty pesos. A. G. I., *Justicia*, legajo 339, pieza 1; Icaza, *Diccionario*, no. 548.

26. López, a native of Córdoba. *Ibid.*, no. 144.

Gerónimo de Estrada, two horses, native weapons, one coat of mail, one buckskin coat.

Pero Boo, two horses, native weapons, one buckskin coat.

Francisco de Parada, one horse, native weapons, one buckskin coat.

Gerónimo Hernández, two horses, one buckskin coat, native weapons.

Baltasar de Azebedo, one horse, native weapons.

Miguel Sánchez, one horse and one mare, native weapons.

Alonso Martín Parra, one horse, native weapons.

Juan Gómez de Paradinas,[27] five horses, one coat of armor, one simple helmet, native weapons.

Diego López,[28] captain, alderman of Seville, seven horses, one coat of mail with its trappings, one beaver, native weapons.

Francisco de Castro, two horses, one buckskin coat, native weapons.

Rodrigo de Escobar, one horse, native weapons.

Diego de Morilla, two horses, native weapons.

Nofre Hernández, one horse, native weapons.

Martín Hernández, one horse, native weapons.

Pero Hernández, one horse, native weapons.

Alonso de Aranda, one horse, native weapons.

Gabriel López,[29] two horses, native weapons, beaver and sallet.

Bartolomé Napolitano, three horses, native weapons.

Captain Rodrigo Maldonado,[30] five horses, one coat of mail

27. Paradinas, native of the town of Paradinas and by occupation a tailor. He was for a time alguacil and aposentador (quartermaster) of the army. He brought his wife, María Maldonado, along on the expedition. He was an important witness in Judge Tejada's inquiry. She nursed the sick soldiers, mended their clothes, and performed other good deeds. The name is also written Paladinas. See A. G. I., *Justicia*, legajo 1021, pieza 4; Icaza, *Diccionario*, no. 837.

28. Diego López took part in the conquest of New Galicia with Nuño de Guzmán, and was one of the first settlers of Guadalajara in 1535. He became maese de campo when Cárdenas dislocated an arm and was incapacitated. Tello, *Crónica*, p. 135, and Castañeda, p. 236.

29. Gabriel López claimed that he spent a great deal on the expedition ïo Cíbola. Icaza, *Diccionario*, no. 1103.

30. Maldonado was a native of Guadalajara, Spain; he was a witness for García López de Cárdenas, and also a character witness for Juan Troyano in 1560. Upon his death, his widow almost lost her head, killed some slaves, and was imprisoned. See Baltasar Dorantes de Carranza, *Sumaria Relación de las Cosas de la Nueva España*, Mexico, 1902, p. 217; A. G. I., *Justicia*, legajo 1021, pieza 6; A. G. I., *Mexico*, legajo 206; Icaza, *Diccionario*, no. 127.

with trappings and breeches, one beaver and sallet, native weapons.

Juan de Torquemada, five horses, one coat of armor, one helmet, and native weapons.

Francisco Gutiérrez, two horses, native weapons, one sallet.

Sancho Rodríguez, two horses, native weapons, one buckskin coat.

Alonso de Medina, one horse, native weapons.

Hernando de Barahona, one horse, native weapons.

Leonardo Sánchez, one buckskin coat, helmet, native weapons, one horse.

Cepeda,[31] one horse, native weapons.

Antón Miguel, three horses, native weapons.

Gaspar de Guadalupe, one horse, native weapons.

Hernando de Caso Verde, two horses, native weapons, one buckskin coat, and one *bastidor*.[32]

Don Tristán de Arellano,[33] captain, eight horses, one coat of mail with sleeves and breeches, native weapons, some plate armor, one sallet with beaver, one harquebus, two crossbows, one double-edged sword, three swords and other arms for himself and his followers.

Alonso Pérez,[34] five horses, one coat of armor and one of mail, native weapons.

Juan de Solís Farfán, three horses, native weapons.

Francisco Ródríguez, one horse, native weapons, one sallet.

Jorge Páez, two horses, native weapons.

Miguel de Castro, one horse, native weapons.

31. His name was Juan de Cepeda, a native of Toledo. He became ill at Culiacán, where he remained, but brought dispatches to the viceroy which had been sent from Cíbola. Cepeda claimed that he lost two horses on the expedition. Icaza, *Diccionario*, no. 1321; A. G. I., *Mexico*, legajo 1064.

32. The *bastidor* was some kind of a frame.

33. His full name was Don Tristán de Luna y Arellano. After his return from the expedition to Cíbola, he was entrusted with various important commissions, one of which was his expedition, in 1558, to occupy the Florida coast. See Paso y Troncoso, *Epistolario*, VIII, pp. 256-264; Icaza, *Diccionario*, no. 516; H. I. Priestley, *Tristán de Luna, Conquistador of the Old South*, Glendale, 1936.

34. Pérez was the oldest son of bachiller Alonso Pérez, who came to New Spain with Pánfilo de Narváez. Young Pérez married a daughter of Diego Gutiérrez, captain of the cavalry in the expedition. The bachiller says he spent more than one thousand castellanos in the equipment of his son. Icaza, *Diccionario*, nos. 63 and 244.

Miguel Sánchez de Plasencia, two horses, one buckskin coat, native weapons.

Pedro Nieto, three horses, one coat of mail, native arms.

Don Diego de Guevara,[35] captain, five horses, one buckskin coat, one sallet, native weapons.

Diego Hernández, ensign, three horses, one coat of mail, native weapons.

Pedro Mayoral, four horses, one coat of mail with skirt, one beaver and sallet, native weapons.

Francisco de Olivares,[36] one horse, native weapons.

Cristóbal Gutiérrez, one horse, native weapons.

Andrés Pérez, one horse, native weapons.

Gonzalo de Castilla, three horses, native weapons.

Pedro de Nájera,[37] two horses, one coat of mail, native weapons.

Luis Hernández,[38] two horses, one coat of mail, one gorget, one beaver, native weapons.

Alonso González, ensign, five horses, one coat of mail, one buckskin coat, beaver and sallet, native arms.

Alonso Paradinas, three horses, one coat of mail, one buckskin coat, sallet, beaver, native weapons.

Cristóbal Caballero, two horses, some cuirasses, one helmet with beaver, native weapons.

Pero Hernández, two horses, native weapons, one sallet, one buckskin coat.

Francisco de Ponares,[39] three horses, one buckskin coat, one coat of mail, native weapons.

Antón García, two horses, native weapons.

Pedro Márquez, two horses, native weapons.

Martín Hernández, one horse, one buckskin coat.

Alonso Maldonado, two horses, native weapons.

35. Guevara was a son of the Count of Oñate. In 1547 Viceroy Mendoza appointed him alcalde mayor of New Galicia for a term of two years. In 1553 he engaged in litigation in Mexico to recover property taken from him by the visitador, Ramírez, which he obtained the next year. See Paso y Troncoso, *Epistolario*, VII, pp. 64-126, 189; Tello, *Crónica*, p. 531.

36. Olivares, a native of Béjar, was a witness at Coronado's residencia. A. G. I., *Justicia*, legajo 339; Icaza, *Diccionario*, no. 1214.

37. See Castañeda's narrative, p. 191, note 1.

38. Hernández was killed at San Gerónimo. Tello, *Crónica*, p. 438.

39. Ponares was killed at Mohi. His name is given as Pobares by Castañeda, p. 229, and Tobares by Tello, *Crónica*, p. 423.

Juan Paniagua,[40] two horses, native weapons, one coat of armor, one sallet.

Pedro González, one horse, native weapons.

Antonio Alvarez, one horse, native weapons.

Fernand González,[41] one horse, native weapons.

Manuel Hernández, one horse, native weapons.

Bartolomé del Campo, one horse, native weapons.

Francisco González, two horses, native weapons.

Cristóbal Maldonado,[42] two horses, native weapons.

Juan de Contreras,[43] three horses, native weapons.

Juan Galeras,[44] three horses, one coat of mail, native weapons, a beaver.

Francisco Calderón, four horses, one coat of mail, native weapons.

Velasco de Barrionuevo, three horses, one coat of mail, one buckskin coat, native weapons.

Rodrigo de Barrionuevo, his brother, two horses, head armor, native pieces.

Luis de Vargas,[45] five horses, one coat of mail, head armor, native weapons.

Francisco de Ovando,[46] five horses, one coat of mail, head armor, native weapons.

Fernán González, native weapons, one horse.

40. Paniagua, native of Ecija, wounded by an arrow in one of the battles on the Rio Grande. After the return of the expedition, he settled at Culiacán. See Tello, *Crónica*, p. 423; Mota Padilla, *Historia*, p. 162; Icaza, *Diccionario*, no. 1378.

41. Icaza gives a Hernán Gonzáles, a native of the island of Santo Domingo, who went to Cíbola with Coronado. *Diccionario*, no. 696.

42. Maldonado, native of Burgillos, was with Nuño de Guzmán in the conquest of Jalisco. A. G. I., *Mexico*, legajo 1064; Icaza, *Diccionario*, no. 1038.

43. Contreras was an interpreter at the audiencia of Mexico. He was an important witness in the inquiry held by Judge Tejada. A. G. I., *Justicia*, legajo 1021, pieza 4.

44. Galeras, a native of Almendralejo. He was one of those who tried to descend into the Grand Canyon with Captain Melgosa. He testified for Coronado in 1552 when he was trying to recover the towns taken from him. A. G. I., *Justicia*, legajo 336; Castañeda, p. 216.

45. Vargas testified for García López de Cárdenas. Castañeda gives his name as Luís Ramírez de Vargas. Castañeda, p. 201; A. G. I., *Justicia*, legajo 1021, pieza 5.

46. Ovando, killed at Mohi. See Tello, *Crónica*, p. 423, and Castañeda, *infra*, p. 229.

Fernán Páez,[47] two horses, native arms.

Gaspar de Saldaña,[48] two horses, and armor of the land.

Juan Jaramillo,[49] three horses, native weapons, one corselet.

Juan de Villegas,[50] three horses, one coat of mail, one buckskin coat, native armor, head armor, double thickness.

Pedro de Vargas, two horses, one buckskin coat, native armor and head armor.

Rodrigo de Paz, one horse, native weapons, one buckskin coat.

Sebastián de Soto, two horses, one buckskin coat, native weapons, head armor.

Francisco Gorbalán,[51] two horses, native weapons.

Francisco de Caravajal,[52] two horses, native arms.

Lope de la Cadena, three horses, native weapons.

Pedro de Benavides, three horses, native weapons, one buckskin coat, head armor, one coat of mail.

Cristóbal de Mayorga,[53] two horses, one buckskin coat, native weapons.

Juan de Benavides, two horses, one buckskin coat, native weapons.

Luis de Escobedo, three horses, one coat of mail, one buckskin coat, head armor, native weapons.

Juan de Ribadeneyra, two horses, one buckskin coat, native weapons.

47. Páez was from Villafranca, in Portugal. He testified for García López de Cárdenas. A. G. I., *Justicia,* legajo 1021, pieza 5.

48. Saldaña, a native of Guadalajara, Spain. He testified for García López de Cárdenas. A. G. I., *Justicia,* legajo 1021, pieza 5.

49. See narrative given by Juan Jaramillo, note 1.

50. Villegas was accused of attacking an Indian woman at one of the pueblos near Alcanfor. He was a brother of Pedro de Villegas, regidor of Mexico. See the testimony of Coronado, pp. 330-331, of Cárdenas, p. 351. For further details, see Castañeda, pp. 224-225.

51. Gorbalán, a native of Guadalajara, Spain. He testified for García López de Cárdenas. A. G. I., *Justicia,* legajo 1021, pieza 5.

52. Caravajal, a native of Utrera, was a brother of Hernando de Trejo. He was wounded in the fighting on the Rio Grande. Tello, *Crónica,* p. 424; Icaza, *Diccionario,* no. 865.

53. Mayorga, a native of Benavente, was with Nuño de Guzmán in the conquest of New Galicia. He testified in the inquiry regarding the conduct of the expedition to Cíbola. A. G. I., *Justicia,* legajos 1021 and 116; Icaza, *Diccionario,* no. 1377.

Hernando del Valle,[54] two horses one buckskin coat, native weapons.

Andrés de Miranda, one horse, native arms.

Antonio de Ribera, three horses, native weapons, one buckskin coat, head armor.

García Rodríguez,[55] one horse, native weapons.

Pedro de Urrel, two horses, native weapons, one buckskin coat.

Cristóbal Pérez Dávila, one horse, native weapons.

Luis de Pigredo, one horse, native weapons.

Juan Pérez de Vergara, seven horses, one mule, one coat and breeches of mail, one beaver and sallet, one gauntlet, native weapons, two harquebuses, one crossbow.

Martín de Villaroya, four horses, one coat of mail, native weapons.

Juan de Beteta,[56] one horse, native weapons.

Andrés de Cobarruvias, two horses, native weapons, coat of mail, head armor and beaver.

Miguel de Entrambas Aguas, two horses, sleeves of mail, native weapons.

Diego de Puelles,[57] one horse, native weapons.

Juan de Bustamante, one horse, native arms.

Juan de Vaca, one horse, native weapons.

Gerónimo Ramos, three horses, native weapons.

Florián Bermúdez,[58] two horses, native weapons.

Pedro Alvarez,[59] one horse, native weapons.

Rodrigo de Vera, two horses, native weapons.

Diego de Cerbatos, two horses, one coat and breeches of mail, native weapons.

Rosele Vázquez de Garabel, one horse, native weapons.

54. Valle, a native of Olmedo. He testified for Coronado in 1552, saying that he had known him for fifteen years. At the time he was a resident of Purificación. A. G. I., *Justicia*, legajo 336; Icaza, *Diccionario*, no. 1183.

55. Rodríguez, a native of Alcaraz, was a witness at the inquiry held by Fiscal Benavente. A. G. I., *Justicia*, legajo 1021; Icaza, *Diccionario*, no. 1312.

56. Beteta, a native of Beteta. He testified for García López de Cárdenas. A. G. I., *Justicia*, legajo 1021, pieza 5; Icaza *Diccionario*, no. 1076.

57. Puelles, a native of Miranda de Ebro. Icaza, *Diccionario*, no. 1340.

58. Bermúdez testified for Coronado in 1552 in the litigation to gain possession of some towns. A. G. I., *Justicia*, legajo 336.

59. In regard to Alvarez, see Icaza, *Diccionario*, no. 898.

Juan Franco de Mentre, three horses, one buckskin coat, breeches, native weapons.

Juan Pastor,[60] two horses, native weapons, head armor and beaver.

Rodrigo de Tamarán,[61] three horses, native weapons, one buckskin coat, head armor.

Pascual Bernal de Molina, one horse, one buckskin coat.

Juan Rodríguez de Alanje,[62] one horse, native weapons, and buckskin coat.

Francisco de Temiño,[63] two horses, native arms.

Juan de Gaztaca, one horse, native weapons, one buckskin coat.

Alonso Esteban de Mérida, one horse, native weapons.

Cristóbal de Quesada,[64] three horses, one coat of mail, native weapons.

Lorenzo Alvarez, two horses, native weapons, head armor, one buckskin coat.

Domingo Alonso, five horses, one coat of mail, native weapons, head armor.

Cristóbal de Escobar,[65] two horses, one coat of mail, native weapons, head armor.

Florián de Mazuela, one horse, native weapons.

Pedro Sánchez del Barco Dávila, one horse, native weapons.

Francisco de Alcántara, one horse, native arms.

Juan López de Sayago, three horses, native weapons, one buckskin coat.

Francisco de Padilla, one horse, native weapons.

Pero Martín Cano, two horses, native weapons.

60. Pastor was, in 1552, a resident of San Miguel de Culiacán, and testified for Coronado in his effort to recover the lost towns. A. G. I., *Justicia*, legajo 336.

61. Tamarán, a native of Castañeda. He was a witness at the *residencia* of Coronado. A. G. I., *Justicia*, legajo 339; Icaza, *Diccionario*, no. 1320.

62. Rodríguez was a native of Alanje in Extremadura. Icaza, *Diccionario*, no. 1229.

63. Temiño, a brother of Baltasar Bañuelos, fled from San Gerónimo. Tello, *Crónica*, p. 438; Icaza, *Diccionario*, no. 1279.

64. Quesada, a native of Carmona, in Andalusia. He went to Cíbola, he said, by order of the viceroy to describe what there was in the country, and spent more than one thousand pesos in the enterprise. Icaza, *Diccionario*, no. 1298.

65. Escobar, a native of Aracena. He testified several times at the inquiries concerning the expedition. A. G. I., *Justicia*, legajo 1021, piezas 4 and 6; Icaza, *Diccionario*, no. 640.

Diego de Madrid,[66] three horses, native weapons.

Alonso de Sayavedra, one horse, one buckskin coat, native weapons, and head armor.

Simón García, two horses, one buckskin coat, native weapons

Francisco Gómez, one horse, native weapons.

Luis de la Chica, one horse, native weapons.

Diego Núñez de Garbena, one horse, native arms.

Hernando de Alba,[67] one horse, one buckskin coat, native weapons.

Cristóbal García, one horse, native weapons.

Diego del Castillo, one horse, native weapons.

Juan Rodríguez de Avalos, one horse, native weapons.

Pedro de Ortega, two horses, one buckskin coat, native weapons.

Juan de Céspedes,[68] two horses, native weapons.

Martín Sánchez, two horses, native arms.

Francisco Martín, one horse, native weapons.

Juan Jiménez, two horses, native arms, one buckskin coat.

Pedro de Benavente, one horse, one buckskin coat, native weapons.

Rodrigo de Trujillo, one horse, one buckskin coat, native weapons.

Diego Sánchez de Fromista, two horses, native arms.

Alonso de Valencia, one horse, native weapons.

Bartolomé Serrano, two horses, native weapons, one buckskin coat.

Mathín de Castañeda, four horses, head armor with beaver, native weapons, one coat of mail, one buckskin coat.

Francisco de Valdivieso, two horses, native weapons, one helmet.

Alonso Sánchez[69] and his son, seven horses, native weapons, coats of mail.

66. Diego de Madrid Avendaño, a native of Toledo, held important posts in New Spain. He was a witness for García López de Cárdenas. See A. G. I., *Justicia*, legajo 1021, pieza 5; Dorantes de Carranza, *op. cit.*, p. 277; Icaza, *Diccionario*, no. 620.

67. Alba was a native of Salamanca. Icaza, *Diccionario*, no. 1001.

68. Regarding Céspedes, see Icaza, *Diccionario*, no. 1379.

69. Sánchez, an itinerant shoemaker in Mexico before the expedition, took his wife, Francisca de Hozes, along. Both he and his wife testified in the inquiry conducted by Judge Tejada. See A. G. I., *Justicia*, legajo 1021, pieza 4; Icaza, *Diccionario*, no. 762. See also pp. 111-116 below.

Juan Martín de la Fuente del Maestre, two horses, native weapons.

Cristóbal Hernández Moreno, one horse, native arms.

Gonzalo Vázquez, one horse, native weapons.

Juan Cordero,[70] two horses, native weapons.

Pedro López de Ciudad Real, one horse, native arms.

Sancho Ordóñez,[71] four horses, one coat of mail, native weapons.

Julián de Sámano, two horses, one corselet, one coat of mail, two buckskin coats, native weapons, head armor.

Alonso González, two horses, native weapons.

Hernán Gómez de la Peña,[72] two horses, native weapons, one heavy doublet.

Pero Gerónimo, one horse and lance.

Pero Hernández Calvo, horse and lance.

Diego Núñez de Mirandilla, two horses, one coat of mail.

Francisco Roxo Loro,[73] three horses, native weapons, head armor.

Andrés Hernández de Encina Sola, one horse, native arms.

Miguel de Torres, two horses, native weapons.

Pedro Pascual, two horses, one coat of mail, native weapons.

Aorta, a Portuguese, one horse, native weapons.

Diego de Salamanca, one horse, native weapons.

Gaspar Alvarez, a Portuguese, one horse, native weapons.

Cristóbal Gallego, one horse, native weapons.

Domingo Romero, one horse, one buckskin coat, native weapons.

Pedro Navarro,[74] two horses, one coat of mail, native weapons.

Gonzalo de Arjona, two horses, native weapons.

Juan Fioz,[75] bugler, one horse, one corselet, one buckskin coat, native weapons.

70. Cordero appeared as a character witness for Juan Troyano. A. G. I., *Mexico*, legajo 206.

71. Ordóñez, a native of Alhanje, Extremadura, was one of the first settlers of Puebla. He held the post of corregidor. Icaza, *Diccionario*, no. 949.

72. Gómez, a settler at San Miguel de Culiacán. Icaza, *Diccionario*, no. 1116.

73. Roxo, a native of Sicily, was a resident of Compostela. Icaza, *Diccionario*, no. 1207.

74. Navarro was a native of Estella in Navarre. He testified for García López de Cárdenas. A. G. I., *Justicia*, legajo 1021, pieza 5.

75. Fioz, a native of Worms, upper Germany, and a bugler in the army. He testified for García López de Cárdenas. A. G. I., *Justicia*, legajo 1021, pieza 5.

Hernando Bermejo,[76] four horses, native weapons, one buckskin coat.

INFANTRY

Captain Pablo de Melgossa,[77] not present, because he had not arrived from Mexico.

Lorenzo Ginovés, one harquebus, native weapons.

Francisco de Espinosa,[78] one harquebus, native weapons.

Alonso Ximénez, one harquebus, native weapons.

Juan de Salamanca, one harquebus, native weapons.

Francisco de Godoy, one sword and shield, native weapons.

Juan de Santovaya, a Galician, one harquebus, native weapons.

Juan de Duero, harquebus, sword, dagger, native weapons.

Domingo Ruiz, harquebus, sword, native arms.

Juan Barbero, harquebus, sword, dagger, native weapons.

Diego Díaz de Santo Domingo, sword, shield, native weapons.

Francisco de Vargas, sword, shield, native weapons.

Roque Alvarez, crossbow, sword, buckskin coat.

Rodrigo de Gámez, sword, dagger.

Juan Francés, sword and shield.

Hernán García de Llerena, crossbow, sword, dagger and native weapons.

Juan Martín de la Fuente del Arco, crossbow, buckskin coat, native weapons.

Rodrigo Alvarez de Zafra,[79] crossbow and sword.

Alonso Millero, a Galician, crossbow, sword, native arms.

Andrés Martín, Portuguese, crossbow, sword, native weapons.

Juan de Vallarra, sword, dagger, shield, native weapons.

Antonio de Laredo, crossbow, sword, native weapons.

76. Bermejo was secretary to Coronado and notary for the expedition. Many documents presented by Coronado in his residencia are signed by him. A. G. I., *Justicia*, legajo 539.

77. The clerk added Melgosa's name to the muster roll, although he had not arrived on February 22, 1540. Melgosa was one of those who tried to go down into the Grand Canyon. He was a witness for García López de Cárdenas, but as he had returned to his native Burgos, his deposition was taken there and forwarded to Mexico. A. G. I., *Justicia*, legajo 1021, pieza 5.

78. Could he be the Espinosa who died from eating some poisonous roots as the advance party approached Cíbola? See letter of Coronado to Mendoza, August 3, 1540.

79. Alvarez de Zafra was a witness in Coronado's residencia. A. G. I., *Justicia*, legajo 339.

Juan Bermejo,[80] crossbow, sword, dagger, native weapons.

Miguel Sánchez, crossbow, sword, one horse, native weapons.

Pedro Martín de la Bermeja, crossbow, sword, dagger, native weapons.

Juan Morillo, one horse, sword, shield, native arms.

Alonso Voz de Rivadeo, sword, shield, native weapons.

Pedro de Talavera, sword, shield, sleeves of mail, native weapons.

Martín Alonso de Astorga, sword, native weapons.

Pero Hernández de Guadalajara, harquebus, sword, dagger.

Martín Hernández Chillón, buckskin coat, sword, native arms.

Baltasar de Zamora, sword, shield, native weapons.

Antón Martín, crossbow, sword, native weapons.

Diego de Medina, sword, shield, crossbow, native arms.

Galiveer, buckskin coat, sword, corselet.

Diego de Candia, harquebus, sword, shield.

Miguel Hernández, sword, shield, native weapons.

Jaco de Brujas, sword, harquebus, shield.

Esteban Martín, harquebus, sword, native weapons.

Miguel de Fuenterrabía, two horses, three swords, one shield.

Francisco López, one buckskin coat, one sword, one dagger.

Francisco Górez, one horse, sword, shield.

Gaspar Rodríguez, crossbow, sword, native arms.

Bartolomé de Pedes [Céspedes], sword, dagger, crossbow, native weapons.

Juan Vizcayno, sword, dagger, sword [sic], native weapons.

Pedro de Alcántara, crossbow, sword, native arms.

Gonzalo Yáñez, shield, sword, native weapons.

Pedro Ramos, ensign, harquebus, sword, one horse.

Lázaro, the drummer (atambor), sword, native weapons.

Antón Ruiz, harquebus.

Juan de Celada, harquebus.

Francisco de Villafranca, harquebus, native weapons.

Juan de Plasencia, harquebus, native weapons.

Francisco Gómez, harquebus, helmet, native weapons.

Bartolomé Sánchez, sword, shield.

80. Juan Bermejo testified for Coronado in 1552, saying that he had known him for fifteen years. A. G. I., *Justicia*, legajo 336.

Alonso Hernández, native weapons, shield, sword.

Pedro de Trujillo, harquebus, native weapons.

Miguel de Torres, harquebus, native weapons.

Alonso Alvarez,[81] harquebus, buckskin coat, native weapons.

Francisco Martín, crossbow, sword, native arms.

García de Perea, shield, sword, native weapons.

Diego de Mata, sword, shield.

Gabriel Hernández, sword, shield, native weapons.

There are 552 horses.

These mounted people, in addition to the arms declared, carried lances, swords, and other weapons.

Accordingly there are 230-odd horsemen, in addition to those who are going ahead as an escort for the friars and those who are awaited from Mexico to join this expedition.

The infantry comprised sixty-two men, with the aforesaid weapons, besides other native weapons that were furnished them.

In addition there are the people who are going by sea and by land, sent by the viceroy.

When these said people had been seen, reviewed, and examined by his Lordship, the aforesaid captain general, the maestre de campo, the chief ensign, and the captains and gentlemen mentioned and listed above, came before his Lordship and said that since they had set out with good zeal to join this expedition in the service of God and his Majesty—and that they would endeavor to do their best in the royal service in his royal name—and since this was their desire, they asked his Excellency to permit and command that both they and the rest of the men take a solemn oath, as the case and the trip required, in order that they might more effectively do their duty as faithful vassals and servants of his Majesty, for this is fitting to his royal service.

Forthwith the said captain general, Francisco Vázquez de Coronado, swore by God, Almighty, His holy Mother, and a cross and by the words of the holy gospels, while he placed his

---

81. Alvarez, a native of Villanueva de la Serena. He was Coronado's page at home, and during the expedition he was his guidon. He testified at the inquiry held by Judge Tejada. On August 30, 1544, Judge Tejada fined him twenty gold pesos for quarreling with two other men inside a church. A. G. I., *Justicia*, legajo 1021, pieza 4, and legajo 339, pieza 2; Icaza, *Diccionario*, no. 1206.

right hand physically on a missal held by the reverend father, Fray Francisco de Vitoria, of the order of St. Francis, that, as a good Christian vassal and servant of his Majesty, he would use the said position of captain general, to which he has been appointed by his Lordship in the name of his Majesty for the said expedition, that he would uphold the service of God and his Majesty, would obey and execute his commands and those of the viceroy in his royal name, as a gentleman should do, to the best of his ability and intelligence.

Then the said maestre de campo, chief ensign, captains and gentlemen and other people, all took their oath in the legal manner recorded above, each one in turn placing his right hand on the said cross and book, under which oath each one promised to be obedient to the said Francisco Vázquez de Coronado, their captain general, and to any other captain general that his Majesty or the said viceroy might appoint in his royal name; that they would not desert their captains or companies without his royal command; that they would do all that is expected of them as good captains and vassals of his Majesty. All this took place before his Lordship and the gentlemen and persons mentioned above, and before me the said Juan de Cuebas, notary of mines for their Majesties.

In testimony of this and by order of the said illustrious viceroy of New Spain, I drew up the present list of the said muster roll at the said city of Compostela on February 27, 1540, which is contained in ten pages of writing.

JUAN DE CUEBAS [Rubric]

ADDITIONS TO MUSTER ROLL

Diego de Alcaraz[82]

82. There were two Alcaraz brothers, Diego and Juan, both residents of Culiacán. When Cabeza de Vaca and his companions reached Mexico after their long wanderings over the southwest, they were met by Diego de Alcaraz, who was already acquainted with them. Both brothers were active explorers around Petatlán in 1532, but only Diego, who was killed at San Gerónimo in Sonora when the Indians rose against the Spaniards, accompanied the Coronado expedition. Father Tello often confuses the two brothers in the leadership of San Gerónimo, and his errors are copied by Mota Padilla. In the inquiry held by Judge Tejada, most witnesses blamed Alcaraz for the revolt of the Indians at San Gerónimo. A. G. I., *Justicia*, legajo 1021, pieza 4.

Juan de Arce[83]
Hernando Arias de Saabedra[84]
Pedro de Avila[85]
Alonso de Balderreina[86]
Francisco de Barrionuevo[87]
Benítez (a certain)[88]
Cristóbal Bertao[89]
Tomás Blaque[90]
Lope Caballero[91]
Hernando de la Cadena[92]
Alonso de Castañeda[93]
Cervantes[94]
Francisco de Cornejo[95]

83. Arce, native of Buelna in Santander, was a witness at the residencia of Coronado. A. G. I., *Justicia,* legajo 339; A. G. I., *Mexico,* legajo 1064; Icaza, *Diccionario,* no. 1191.

84. Saabedra was left by Coronado as alcalde mayor at Culiacán. Castañeda, p. 206; Icaza, *Diccionario,* no. 1264.

85. Avila led the rebellion at San Gerónimo and returned to Culiacán. Castañeda, p. 268.

86. Balderreina was a native of Astorga. He was a witness in the inquiry held by Judge Benavente at the request of Fiscal Villalobos. A. G. I., *Justicia,* legajo 1021, pieza 6.

87. Francisco de Barrionuevo, called "a caballero from Granada" by Castañeda, p. 201. Two Barrionuevo brothers, Rodrigo and Velasco, are given in the muster roll. It is possible that Castañeda erred and that there were only two Barrionuevos on the expedition.

88. Benítez was killed at Tiguex. Tello, *Crónica,* p. 424; Mota Padilla, *Historia,* p. 162.

89. Cristóbal Bertao, a native of Bernuel in the province of Rouen. Icaza, *Diccionario,* no. 305.

90. Tomás Blaque (Thomas Blake?), a native of Scotland, was married to Francisca de Rivera. He spent three years with the expedition. Icaza, *Diccionario,* no. 738; G. R. G. Conway, "A Scotsman in America in 1535," *Notes and Queries,* vol. 148, pp. 293-294.

91. Caballero was a native of Lugo. He married a native woman and took her along in the expedition. Icaza, *Diccionario,* no. 987.

92. Cadena, a native of Medellín, was a witness called by Fiscal Benavente. A. G. I., *Justicia,* legajo 1021, pieza 6; Icaza, *Diccionario,* no. 1297.

93. Alonso de Castañeda, a Viscayan, was one of the first settlers of Purificación in 1536. He was wounded at Tiguex. Tello, *Crónica,* pp. 253 and 424; Icaza, *Diccionario,* no. 473. He testified at Colio's residencia. A. G. I., *Justicia,* legajo 339.

94. Cervantes was the man assigned to watch over the Turk. Castañeda, p. 234. Could this be Diego de Cerbatos?

95. Icaza states that Francisco de Cornejo, a native of Salamanca, went "a la tierra Nueva." *Diccionario,* no. 470. He appeared as a witness in Coronado's residencia a number of times. A. G. I., *Justicia,* legajo 339.

Juan de Cuevas[96]
Melchior Díaz[97]
Domingo Fernández[98]
Bartolomé Garrido[99]
Ruy González[100]
Juan Hernández[101]
Gerónimo de Horosco (Orozco) [102]
Francisco de Huerta[103]
Alonso Jiménez[104]
Gonzalo López[105]
Cristóbal Méndez[106]
Gerónimo Mercado de Sotomayor[107]
Mesa[108]
Mondragón[109]

96. Juan de Cuevas, a native of Aranda de Duero, and the son of Licentiate Alonso Cuevas. He married a daughter of Licentiate Téllez. Icaza, *Diccionario*, no. 386.

97. Melchior Díaz, mayor of Culiacán, received Cabeza de Vaca and his companions when they reached that place in 1536. He was an active explorer of the northern territory. When the army reached Culiacán, Díaz joined the expedition there and was made a captain. He discovered the Tizón (Colorado) river when trying to contact Alarcón's ships. Tello, *Crónica*, pp. 306, 327, and 407; Castañeda, *passim*. His daughter received a town from Coronado. Icaza, *Diccionario*, no. 460.

98. Fernández fled from San Gerónimo at the death of Alcaraz. Tello, *Crónica*, p. 438; Mota Padilla, *Historia*, p. 167.

99. Bartolomé Garrido, native of Moguer, went to Cíbola with his arms and horses. Icaza, *Diccionario*, no. 1083.

100. Ruy González, native of Villanueva del Fresno, came to New Spain with Pánfilo de Narváez. He was regidor of Mexico and held other important posts. Icaza, *Diccionario*, no. 52.

101. Juan Hernández, native of Selorio, Asturias. Icaza, *Diccionario*, no. 775.

102. See A. G. I., *Mexico*, legajo 206.

103. Francisco de Huerta, native of Badajoz, sent a son to the new land equipped with horses and arms. Icaza, *Diccionario*, no. 1289.

104. Alonso Jiménez. Icaza, *Diccionario*, no. 1133.

105. López was from Medellín. A. G. I., *Indiferente*, legajo 1208; Icaza, *Diccionario*, no. 734.

106. See A. G. I., *Patronato*, legajo 54.

107. Mercado, a native of Carmona, was a witness for Cárdenas. A. G. I., *Justicia*, legajo 1021, pieza 5; Tello, *Crónica*, p. 492; Icaza gives his name as Gregorio. *Diccionario*, no. 1158.

108. Mesa, a Spaniard wounded by a poisoned arrow. Castañeda, p. 273. There is an Alonso de Mesa in Icaza, *Diccionario*, no. 841, but there is no mention of his going with Coronado.

109. Mondragón led a party of men from Tiguex to explore. He is mentioned by Gaspar de Saldaña in question 18 in his testimony before Fiscal Benavente. A. G. I., *Justicia*, legajo 1021, pieza 6.

Juan Muñoz[110]
Hernando de Orduña[111]
Juan de Orduña[112]
Andrés Orejón[113]
Antón Pérez Buscavida[114]
Riberos, the factor[115]
Alonso Rodríguez Parra[116]
García Rodríguez[117]
Juan Ruiz[118]
Juan Ruiz[119]
Rodrigo Sánchez[120]
Diego Simón (Ximón)[121]
Rodrigo Simón (Ximón)[122]
Juan de Sotomayor[123]
Alonso de Toro[124]

110. Juan Muñoz was sent with Coronado by Miguel de Santiago, who fell ill as the expedition was about to start and was unable to go. Santiago equipped Muñoz with horses and arms, and paid him sixty pesos per year. Muñoz died during the expedition. Icaza, *Diccionario*, no. 1302.

111. Hernando de Orduña, a native of Burgos, was a witness at the inquiry held by Fiscal Benavente. A. G. I., *Justicia*, legajo 1021, pieza 6.

112. Juan de Orduña, native of Toledo, settled at Culiacán on returning from the expedition to Cíbola, on which he lost an eye. Icaza, *Diccionario*, no. 1366.

113. Andrés Orejón, native of Avila. Icaza, *Diccionario*, no. 1314.

114. See A. G. I., *Mexico*, legajo 1064; Icaza, *Diccionario*, no. 1162.

115. See Castañeda, p. 201.

116. Rodríguez was from Coria. Icaza, *Diccionario*, no. 1208; Hackett, *Historical Documents*, I, p. 49.

117. García Rodríguez, a native of Alcázar, took two horses on the expedition. Icaza, *Diccionario*, no. 1312.

118. Juan Ruiz was a native of Agudo, Toledo. He testified for Coronado in his residencia in 1544, and again in 1552 in Coronado's litigation to regain the towns he had lost as a result of the residencia. A. G. I., *Justicia*, legajos 336 and 339; Icaza, *Diccionario*, nos. 1139 and 1304.

119. Juan Ruiz, native of the island of Española, the son of Juan Ruiz, native of Carmona. He married a daughter of Bartolomé Sánchez, another member of the Coronado expedition. This Juan Ruiz is not to be confused with Juan Ruiz, native of Agudo. Icaza, *Diccionario*, no. 1213.

120. Rodrigo Sánchez, a native of Azuaga. Icaza, *Diccionario*, no. 682.

121. Diego Simón was from Moguer. He testified in the inquiry held by Fiscal Benavente. A. G. I., *Justicia*, legajo 1021, pieza 6.

122. Rodrigo Simón, native of Moguer. He testified at the inquiry held by Judge Tejada. A. G. I., *Justicia*, legajo 1021, pieza 4; Icaza, *Diccionario*, no. 176.

123. See Castañeda, p. 201.

124. Alonso de Toro, native of Alcalá de Henares, a resident of Purificación. He was a witness for Coronado in his residencia. Icaza, *Diccionario*, no. 1182; A. G. I., *Justicia*, legajo 339.

Francisco de Torres[125]
Juan Troyano[126]
Cristóbal del Valle[127]
Juan de Vitoria[128]
Juan de Zaldívar[129]

125. Francisco de Torres, a native of Trujillo. Icaza, *Diccionario*, no. 464.
126. Troyano testified at the inquiry held by Judge Tejada. A. G. I., *Justicia*, legajo 1021, pieza 4; *Mexico*, legajos 168 and 206.
127. Cristóbal del Valle, native of Aranda de Duero, took his weapons and horses on the expedition. Icaza, *Diccionario*, no. 1121. He appeared as a witness in the residencia of Coronado. A. G. I., *Justicia*, legajo 339.
128. Vitoria was from Burgos. He was a witness for Cárdenas. A. G. I., *Justicia*, legajo 1021, pieza 5.
129. Juan de Zaldívar, a native of Guadalajara in Spain, was a nephew of Cristóbal de Oñate. When Coronado came to New Galicia in 1538, he appointed Zaldívar as regidor of Compostela. Zaldívar testified in the inquiry held by Judge Tejada that while trying to establish peace with the Indians he received three arrow wounds on his nose and head. In 1544, he was alcalde of Guadalajara in New Galicia and testified in the residencia of Coronado. In A. G. I., *Patronato*, legajo 80, there is found a probanza of Juan de Zaldívar, the husband of Doña Leonor Cortés Montezuma. Several witnesses testified that the Turk was executed in Zaldívar's tent. See A. G. I., *Justicia*, legajo 1021, pieza 4; *Justicia*, legajo 339; Tello, *Crónica*, pp. 268, 303, and 327; Mota Padilla, *Historia*, p. 105.

HEARING ON CHARGES OF DEPOPULATING NEW SPAIN

Report by the Viceroy of New Spain, Don Antonio de Mendoza, Concerning the People Who Are Going to Settle New Galicia with Francisco Vázquez Coronado, its Governor.[1]

At the city of Compostela in New Galicia, New Spain, on February 21, 1540, in the presence of his Excellency, Don Antonio de Mendoza, his Majesty's viceroy and governor in this New Spain, president of the audiencia and royal chancellery established in the city of Mexico, etc. Before me, Juan de León, their Majesties' clerk of the said royal audiencia, Francisco Vázquez de Coronado, governor and captain general of this province and captain general of the land newly discovered by the father provincial, Fray Marcos de Niza, presented a petition to your Lordship, the tenor of which is as follows:

Most illustrious Sir: I, Francisco Vázquez de Coronado, his Majesty's governor of New Galicia, having been appointed by your Lordship as captain general of the newly discovered land, state: Information has reached me that some persons ill disposed toward this expedition, organized by your Lordship in the name of his Majesty, have claimed that many residents of the city of Mexico and this city of Compostela and other cities and towns of New Spain are going on the said expedition at my request and urging; and that for this reason the city of Mexico and New Spain are left with but a few people, which may result in serious difficulties. In order that the truth may be learned concerning the residents of New Spain who are going in my company, who are very few, and who are not going because they were attracted or induced by me but go of their own accord, and since so few men will not be missed in New Spain, I beg and entreat your Lordship to order that a report be made

1. Translated from the copy in Pacheco y Cárdenas, *Documentos de Indias,* XIV, pp. 373-384.

of the matter; there are present here Gonzalo de Salazar and Pero Almidez Cherino, his Majesty's factor and inspector in this New Spain, and other residents of Mexico who will be able to verify the truth of everything and of the report. May your Lordship provide and command what is most suitable to the service of his Majesty and the welfare and protection of the said New Spain.—FRANCISCO VÁZQUEZ DE CORONADO.

Having read this petition, his Excellency ordered that Licentiate Maldonado, judge of their Majesties' royal audiencia, who was present, should draw up this report, and, in order that it be more properly done, make arrangements for the said factor, inspector, regidores, and other persons here present to attend and be present at the examination of the said people when the said review and roll call should be held.

When the appointed day came, Licentiate Maldonado, in view of the petition and the instructions from the viceroy, ordered that Gonzalo de Salazar and Pero Almidez Cherino, his Majesty's factor and inspector in this New Spain, together with Fernando Pérez de Bocanegra, Juan de Xaso, Antonio Serrano de Cardona and Sebastián Bejarano, residents of the city of Mexico, Cristóbal de Oñate, resident of this city and his Majesty's factor in this province, Diego Ordoñez, resident of the city of Los Angeles, Juan Fernández, resident of Purificación, who were present in this city of Compostela, should attend and be present at the roll call that will be held tomorrow in order that they may see and identify the individuals, residents of Mexico and other places in this New Spain, who are going on this expedition, so that upon seeing them they may declare under oath who they are. They were so ordered.

After the aforesaid, at the city of Compostela, by request of the said captain general, on February 26, 1540, Licentiate Maldonado administered the oath to the said Fernando Pérez de Bocanegra and the others, to the said Gonzalo de Salazar and Pero Almidez Cherino, factor and inspector for his Majesty in this New Spain, and to Antonio Serrano de Cardona, regidores of the said city of Mexico, who, after taking oath in due legal manner, testified separately as follows:

Immediately following, in the said city of Compostela, on

February 26, 1540, Cristóbal de Oñate, inspector of this province, after taking his oath in due form, stated what is set forth below:

Witness, Hernand Pérez de Bocanegra, resident of the city of Mexico, brought to testify for this reason, after taking his oath in due form for the purpose of the said report and being asked about the said petition, declared as follows:

This witness was asked if he was present on the previous Sunday at the review and roll call when the people that his Excellency, the viceroy of New Spain, is sending to pacify the land newly discovered by the father provincial, Fray Marcos de Niza, were counted and examined. He answered that it was true, that he was present at the entire roll call, at the counting and examining of the said people in the presence of his Lordship and of many other gentlemen, residents of this New Spain, which was done before a notary, and a list of them drawn up, to which he refers.

This witness was asked, as a resident of the city of Mexico, to state what residents of the city of Mexico and of other places in New Spain were at the roll call and review for the purpose of going to the new land. He declared that, as he has stated, he was present at the roll call and saw and identified the persons going on the expedition, and for further identification he asked to see a copy of the list made of them, which the notary placed before him. Upon seeing and reading the names contained in it, he said that among all those people he did not recognize any residents of Mexico, except Domingo Martín, a married man who at times had resided in Mexico and who had provided him with couriers, and a certain Alonso Sánchez, who used to be a shoemaker and who is taking his wife and one son; also a young man, son of the bachiller,[2] Alonzo Pérez, who arrived a few days ago from Salamanca and who was being sent by his father to the war because of his mischievousness. There were two or three other artisans he had seen working in Mexico, but he did not know whether they were residents of the city. Under the oath he had taken, this witness declared that he did not see in the

2. Now written bachelor. A bachiller was an apprentice for the degree of master in one of the higher faculties, such as law, medicine, or theology.

whole roll call that there was any other resident of Mexico, for this witness has been a resident and inhabitant of Mexico for fourteen years or thereabouts. Exception is to be made of the captain general, Francisco Vázquez de Coronado, and the army master, Lope de Samaniego. He believes and considers it certain that the above-mentioned are going of their own accord like the rest. He said that this is the truth, under his oath, and he signed the statement.—FERNAND PÉREZ DE BOCANEGRA.

Witness, Antonio Serrano de Cardona, resident and regidor of the city of Mexico, a witness introduced and accepted to give information on the foregoing. Upon being asked about the tenor of the said petition, he made the following deposition:

Asked if he was present on the preceding Sunday at the review and roll call held by order of the viceroy, of the people he is sending in the name of his Majesty and in his royal service to the pacification of the land discovered by Fray Marcos de Niza, provincial of the order of St. Francis, by the order of his Lordship, he said that in fact he was present at the entire review and roll call from beginning to end, and that he saw and examined all those who filed past the notary of the royal audiencia and whose names were written down.

He was asked to state, as resident and regidor of the city of Mexico, what residents of the said city and other places he saw in the review of those who are going on this expedition with the said captain general, Francisco Vázquez de Coronado. This witness testified that he did not see in the roll call any residents of Mexico other than Francisco Vázquez de Coronado, the alcaide Lope de Samaniego, army master, and one Alonso Sánchez, who used to be a resident of Mexico, whom he knew to have his home there a long time ago but who then went away as a tradesman seeking his livelihood. He saw likewise one Domingo Martín, who used to live in Mexico, but he has not known him to have a home there for a long time, nor does he believe he has one, because he has not seen him in Mexico. He did not see any other resident in the roll call, nor does he believe that any one else from that city is going on the expedition, because otherwise this witness would have recognized him, as he has been living in Mexico for twenty years, since the city was taken and settled by Christians. He has been a regidor of the city for the last fifteen years and he knows its residents. As for the others, they were the happiest people in this land that he ever saw going on conquests and expeditions. Upon being asked whether those who are going are needed, this witness said he believes and is quite sure that their departure is more beneficial than harmful, that they are not needed, that after these people left Mexico this witness saw the city so full of people that the absence of those who went on the expedition was not noticed. He states that this is the truth, under his oath, and he attached his signature.—ANTONIO SERRANO DE CARDONA.

Witness, Gonzalo de Salazar, his Majesty's factor in this New Spain, resident and regidor of the city of Mexico, a witness presented and accepted for this reason. After taking oath in due form and being asked as to the tenor of the said petition, he testified as follows:

Asked if he had been present on the preceding Sunday at the roll call and general review held of those who are going to the newly discovered land in the service of his Majesty, this witness said he was present at the roll call and review. Asked to state, as factor and resident of the said city, what residents he saw going on the expedition, this witness said that he is one of the persons who has more information on all the people residing there, one who knows most about them.

Under the oath he took he said that he did not see in the whole review any one or any person holding a repartimiento anywhere in New Spain, except the captain general, Francisco Vázquez de Coronado. He recognized only one resident of Mexico, and he had no repartimiento. He did not identify there any other person from Mexico or the whole of New Spain. He held that one of the greatest blessings that had come to this New Spain was the departure of all the young and idle persons who were found in the said city and in all New Spain. He saw that they all went very happy, and that they were the ones who had asked to go on the expedition and did not have to be persuaded. This is the truth, under his oath, and he attached his name thereto.—GONZALO DE SALAZAR.

Witness, Pedro Almides Cherino, his Majesty's inspector in this New Spain, a witness presented and accepted for this reason. After taking oath in due form, he answered as follows: Being asked about the tenor of the said petition and whether this witness was present at the roll call and general review held last Sunday of the people who are going to pacify the newly discovered land in the service of his Majesty, he said that he was present throughout the entire roll call and review.

He was asked, as inspector and resident of the city of Mexico, to state what residents of that city and of other places in New Spain he saw in the review and roll call of the people who were going on the expedition. This witness replied that he did not see in the review any resident, except Francisco Vázquez de Coronado, captain general; the alcaide, Lope de Samaniego, army master; and a certain Alonso Sánchez, who is taking his wife along, and he does not know whether he is a resident. This witness stated that he saw, examined, and inspected most of the people, because, at the time of the roll call, a written report was made of the horses and weapons each one brought; that all the rest of the people were unattached individuals who had come to the country recently in search of a livelihood. He saw also one Domingo Martín, who is absent from Mexico most of the time. In the judgment of this witness, it was very beneficial that those people who were going left Mexico, since they caused the residents more harm than good, for they were mostly idle young gentlemen without any occupation either in Mexico or in their homeland. As far as he could learn they were all going on the expedition to the new land of their own accord and were very happy. In the opinion of this witness, if this said land had not been discovered, most of the people who went there would have returned to Castile or gone to Peru or elsewhere to seek a living. This was the truth, which he swore and signed.—Pero Almidez.

Witness, Serván Bajarano, resident of the city of Mexico, a witness introduced and accepted for that reason. After taking oath in due form he was asked concerning the tenor of the petition, and he made the following statement:

Asked whether this witness was present at the review and roll call of the people going on this expedition in the service of his Majesty to pacify the new land, this witness declared that he was present from beginning to end and that he saw and identified the said people.

This witness was asked, as a resident of the said city, to state what residents from the said city and other cities in New Spain he saw in the review. He declared that he is well informed about all the residents and settlers in Mexico, because he has lived there from the time it was conquered and he grew up among them. In the review he did not recognize any resident except the captain general, Francisco Vázquez de Coronado, who is married and lives in Mexico; Lope de Samaniego, army master, who is not married and whom he believes to be a resident; and Domingo Martín, married, and one Alonso Sánchez, who is taking his wife, and who this witness knows to be a tradesman, and being in narrow straits and unable to make a living, is going to the country to seek his living. He did not see any other resident. This witness is firmly convinced that the city of Mexico and its inhabitants have benefitted by the departure of many of these people, as they were mostly single and dissolute men without anything to do. Most of them were gentlemen and persons who did not have and could not obtain repartimientos of Indians, who had nothing to do but eat and loaf, and who would have had to go to Peru and other places. All of them went of their own accord and very happy. This is the truth, which he swore and signed.—SERVÁN BAJARANO.

Witness, Cristóbal de Oñate, resident of the city of Mexico, and his Majesty's inspector in this province of New Galicia, presented as witness on this account. After taking the oath in due form, he answered the questions as follows:

This witness was asked whether he was present on the preceding Sunday at the general review and roll call of the people who were going on the expedition to the pacification of the new land in the service of his Majesty. He replied that indeed he was present, from the beginning to the end.

He was asked to state, as a resident of the city of Mexico and inspector for this province, what residents of the city of Mexico and of this province he saw in the said review and roll call. This witness declared that he has information about and knows the residents of the city of Mexico and this province, because he has been in this land sixteen years, more or less. In the entire review this witness did not see any residents other than the captain general, Francisco Vázquez de Coronado; the alcaide, Lope de Samaniego; and Domingo Martín, who is leaving a wife in the said city; and one Alonso Sánchez, who is taking his wife on the said expedition. He does not know of any other resident from the city of Mexico who is going, and if any other had been there he would have recognized him. Under the oath he has taken, he declared that no resident of this city of Compostela is going on the expedition. Two residents of Guadalajara are going, one married to an Indian woman, the other a single man. From what this witness saw, all of the people are going of their own accord, without any pressure or violence. On the contrary, it seems to him that many of the young gentlemen and other persons living in the said city and in other parts of this New Spain who are going on the said expedition will do more good than harm by going away, for they were all idle and had no means of support. This is the truth; to which he swore and attached his signature.—CRISTÓBAL DE OÑATE.

Having thus taken and accepted the said depositions from the said witnesses, and his Lordship having examined them, he ordered that, from the original which remains in my possession, a copy be drawn, properly certified, and sent to his Majesty and members of the Council so that he may order what he deems best. By command of his Lordship, I made the said report from the original, today, Friday, February 27, 1540. Witnesses: the secretary, Antonio de Almaguer, and I, the said Joan de León, his Majesty's clerk and also clerk to the royal audiencia of this New Spain located in the city of Mexico. I was present at all of the aforesaid, the reviewing, examining, and administering of oaths to the witnesses, and at the roll call mentioned above. By order of his Lordship I have made a copy of it from the original which remains in my possession, and I have signed it. Accordingly I have added here my scroll—[a scroll follows]. In testimony of the truth.—JOAN DE LEÓN. [Two rubrics.]

INSTRUCTIONS TO ALARCON, 1541

Instructions to Be Observed by Captain Hernando de Alarcón on the Expedition That He Is to Lead to California by Order of Viceroy Don Antonio de Mendoza.[1]

What you, Captain Hernando de Alarcón, are to do on your voyage to the gulf (ancón) where we are sending you is as follows:

First, you are to go to the harbor of Navidad in the province of Colima and there receive the ship named . . . ,[2] which we have designated for your expedition. You are to receive also a large sea-going sloop, which we built for this project, and the provisions, artillery, and munitions that will be delivered to you for this voyage, all of which you are to have recorded in the ship's log by the notary who will accompany you, especially that which is under the management of the skipper and other persons you may put in charge, in order that a good record and account may be kept of everything taken in the ship as well as in the sloop. You are to sign this record jointly with the said notary, and furnish an exact copy of the whole thing to Don Luis de Castilla[3] in order that we may have a record of it here.

Further, you are to enter in the said book the names of the sailors who are to go in the ship and sloop, and the artillery and munitions to go in them. The latter you are to deliver to the artillerymen with proper inventory, instructing them to take good care of it and to have it ready when it should be needed. Take especial care in this matter, as you know what it will mean to you.

1. Translated from the Spanish version in Buckingham Smith, *Colección de vairos documentos para la historia de la Florida*, Madrid, 1857, pp. 1-6. These instructions were for a projected second expedition; the first are not extant.
2. The names of the vessels are given in Alarcón's report of the first expedition. They were the San Pedro and the Santa Catalina. See below, p. 124.
3. Castilla was one of Viceroy Mendoza's right-hand men. See H. R. Wagner, *Spanish Voyages to the Northwest Coast of America*, San Francisco, 1929, p. 56.

Further, you are to make a list of the prominent people taking part in the said expedition. You are to choose the persons you think best for the sloop. Note what arms each one carries, and have this information entered in the book by the said notary and sign it with your name.

I charge you also to honor and respect Fathers Fray Remundo and Fray Antonio de Mena, who are going with you.[4] You are to consult them when it is advisable, as commanded by his Majesty in his instructions, for, besides their being entitled to voicing an opinion as worthy persons, it is proper that it be so done for the service of our Lord.

Further, when our Lord wills that you are ready to sail and begin your voyage to support Francisco Vázquez de Coronado and his people, you shall go to the town of San Miguel, use the sloop there to learn if there is any news of the captain general, Francisco Vázquez de Coronado, and adjust your course according to what you may hear about him, as this is the main purpose for which we are sending you. You are to take one-half of the iron goods found at the said town of San Miguel de Culuacán and deliver this material to the person we put in charge of it at the port of Navidad in order that he may do with it what he may be ordered. If you fail to get news of the said captain at the town of San Miguel de Culuacán, you shall proceed to Puerto de los Puertos. From there on you should land in all possible harbors and places and try to get information of the said general or of Captain Melchior Díaz; the latter set out from the valley of Corazones to explore the coast where you are going. Should you meet Díaz or his men, tell them that you are in search of the general to bring succor. You are to find out what they know about him, and whether there is any way of letting him know about you. If there are means for this, you are to stop at the place that seems most appropriate to you and not go farther until you have established communication with him. To this end you must avail yourself of all possible means, because it is very important that we keep in touch with him by sea and that intercourse be maintained between him and you.

4. These two friars had been with the Ulloa expedition up the coast in 1539. Wagner, *op. cit.*, pp. 12-13.

Should you fail to hear from them in all these harbors and lands, you are to proceed to the Buena Guía river, leaving landmarks and letters at all the harbors on your route, indicating that you have entered that river and that you will continue to follow it as long as possible until obtaining information of the general, for you are in search of him by our command; and if you should fail to hear from him there, you shall send some one to examine the landmarks you have left to learn whether they have been found. If so, the general will know where you are, and if he should be unable to reach you, he can leave information in writing at the posts which may be found by your men, and thus a means of establishing communication with the sea and with you may be established.

When you reach the Buena Guía river, if by this time you have found neither interpreters nor a suitable way of establishing communication with the said general and his people, you are to go up this river in the sloop, and up the estuary that you say extends inland. You are always to inquire and attempt to learn about Cíbola, because, from what he writes to me from there,[5] it would not be possible for them to fail to reach the river or be close to it. In the meantime, if you do not hear from Francisco Vázquez, you should not do anything except to look for him and join him. In this you will render a great service to his Majesty and much pleasure to us through your good work.

When, with the aid of our Lord, you meet the said Francisco Vázquez or his people, you shall deliver or send safely to him the dispatches that you are bringing for him, for I am writing him that since you were the discoverer of the river, and since his people appreciate you and you have served his Majesty in discovering it, he should place you in charge of that region; and that, since you have information of the land farther on, he shall, if necessary, furnish you with more people to add to your forces in order that you may proceed farther on. You are to respect and obey him, do what he orders you, and heed his command.

5. Coronado's first report from the new land was dated at Cíbola, August 3, 1540, and it would seem that this is the letter referred to here. If so, these instructions must have been issued several months later.

In the instructions given to Diego López de Zúñiga,[6] sent as a captain along the coast, there is a clause in which he is asked to take especial care to find out about the people who have gone overland and about those you are taking on the gulf, and if he should obtain any information that would make him think it necessary to join forces with them or with you, he is to do so. These same instructions apply to you, as this is all one and the same undertaking. He also is looking for you, as are those who went to the islands, so you are to do likewise on your part. Whenever possible, you should try to help and aid one another.

The Indians that you are taking with you are to be treated well in order that when they reach their countries they may induce the others to be friendly to you.

You must take particular care that there is no blasphemy of the name of our Lord, His blessed Mother, or the saints; on the contrary, they must be revered. You and your men shall regularly practice the Christian faith and live like Catholics in order that you may not set a bad example to the natives of the land where you may be, but that they may be attracted to friendship and association with you through your virtues and good deeds.

You should see to it that the chiefs of Quicama and Coama are not annoyed or injured in the least, for they welcomed you so graciously before.

Try to be more discreet in your dealings and conversation with the Indians, for it seems that it is necessary to be more circumspect with them than you were the last time.[7]

You must watch very carefully that your people do not do any harm or violence to the Indians, that they do not take anything from them against their will, nor enter their houses without your permission.

Further, you shall try to gain further information of the sea and islands you reported and find out what people inhabit all that region, and through kindness try to learn what there may be in that land. You should find out about this through

6. López de Zúñiga had been sent on an expedition up the coast early in 1541. Viceroy Mendoza's instructions to him, dated April 29, 1541, are translated in Wagner, *op. cit.*, 418-425.

7. These references are to Alarcón's earlier voyage up the coast to establish communication with Coronado.

Indian traders or by any other means you may think better. You are to avoid waging war against the Indians unless you should be forced to it. You shall try to obtain samples of everything in the land.

If you fail to find an interpreter or any trace of the general and his people, and you should think it advisable to send the ship or the sloop to examine the letters and markers you have left farther back or to send us a report of that country, you are authorized, in order to effect the aforesaid, or obtain necessary provisions, to do whatever you deem most desirable, either to keep or send us a dispatch, or send the boat.

Further, should you establish a settlement anywhere it must not be among the Indians, but away from them. You shall command that no Spaniard or other person accompanying you enter the Indian towns or houses except by your express command. Whoever acts contrary to your orders you must punish very severely. Whenever you issue a permit to any one to go there for some necessary thing, it must be a person you know that you can trust not to do something improper. Be sure you observe this command, for it is more important than you can imagine.

You must bear in mind that the main object for which you are sailing is to learn of Captain General Francisco Vázquez de Coronado and his people, to find a way of establishing contact with them by sea, and to discover the port or ports most suitable for this purpose. You must endeavor to do this by all the ways and means possible, both by sea and land. Until you have done this and learned of him, you are not to busy yourself with anything else, nor come back without first notifying us of what you have done and found out in order that we may decide what is most fitting.

As for the articles of trade which we are providing, we command the person in charge of them not to use or trade them except in your presence. You must see to it that these articles are recorded in detail not only in the book carried by the person in charge of these goods, but also in the notary's book, which is under your care in your fleet, and that you, the person in charge of the articles, and the notary sign them both. A detailed record must be kept of what is spent in such transactions and what is obtained in return, entering it all in both books and signing it as indicated above in order to relieve the one in charge from further responsibility. You must see to it that all this is entered very plainly and in detailed manner in order that it may be easily understood.

Further, we have arranged for Francisco Pilo, a merchant, to send one of his agents with merchandise, iron goods, and other supplies for the people who are accompanying you and those who are with the captain general, Francisco Vázquez de Coronado. You are to deliver to him the iron goods that you may take on at Culiacán so that he may dispose of them and use them as his own. The said Pilo is to have these because of other dealings we have with him, and because he is favoring us by venturing his goods; and we must establish a good reputation in order that others may venture their goods. You are to provide good accommodations for the agent and his goods in your ship, treat him well, and allow him freedom to dispose of and sell his goods at will. You must not allow him to suffer any abuse or violence by word or deed from yourself or the people in your company. Whenever he may wish to take his goods ashore, you are to give him every facility and aid. Take care that these goods do not run the risk of being lost, as the loss would fall upon us. As this is a matter that concerns us, we commend it seriously to you. For the documents that may have to be drawn up of what he sells on credit, if there is a royal notary in the fleet you will order him to prepare them, and if there should not be one, you may, if necessary, as captain and chief authority of the fleet, appoint one in the name of his Majesty. I grant you full powers to do so.

Since experience has shown that when crossbows, harquebuses, and other arms and munitions are carried they deteriorate, spoil, and disappear, because special care is not taken of them as they are but supplies, you will order the crossbows, harquebuses, and shields that may be needed for your soldiers and sailors to be delivered to them as their own at moderate prices; to those who receive wages charge the goods to them, and those who do not receive wages, make them responsible for the goods. Whatever else may be taken as supplies you will put in the care of the person that the said Pilo sends, charged to the account between him and Agustín Guerrero, whom we have put in charge of our fleets. The obligations incurred by the persons to whom the said arms may be given and whatever may be handed over to the person delegated by the said Pilo, you will give to Don Luis de Castilla so that it may be sent to the said Agustín Guerrero.[8]

You are to take along certain articles that Doña Beatriz de Estrada is sending to the captain general, her husband. You must order that good care be taken of these and of other articles entrusted to you which you may bring along for some of the soldiers from their friends and relatives.

Dated at the city of Mexico on the last day of May, 1541.

DON ANTONIO DE MENDOZA

By order of their Lordships, Almaguer.

8. Agustín Guerrero was Viceroy Mendoza's major-domo. It was he who represented the viceroy in his negotiations with Alvarado regarding explorations in the Pacific.

REPORT OF ALARCON'S EXPEDITION

Relation of the Navigation and Discovery Undertaken by Captain Hernando de Alarcón by Order of His Excellency, Don Antonio de Mendoza, Viceroy of New Spain, Given at Colima, a Harbor of New Spain.[1]

I

Hernando de Alarcón, after weathering a storm, arrived with his fleet at the harbor of Santiago, and from there at the harbor of Aguayaual. He ran great risks in his attempt to find a gulf, and, on leaving it, he discovered, on the coast, a river with a great current. Entering it and sailing on, he found a large number of armed Indians, with whom he communicated by signs. Fearing some danger, he returned to the ships.

On Sunday, May 9, 1540, I set sail with two boats, one named San Pedro, which was the flagship, and the other, Santa Catalina. We set out toward the port of Santiago de Buena Esperanza.[2] Before we arrived there we met with adverse fortune, and because of this those who were on board the Santa Catalina, becoming unduly frightened, threw overboard nine pieces of artillery, two anchors, a cable, and many other things as indispensable for their undertaking as the ship itself. When we came to the harbor of Santiago, I repaired the damage I

1. Translated from the Italian in Ramusio, *Viaggi*, 1556 edition, III, fols. 363-370. Herrera gives a summarized account of the expedition, but it would seem that he used the original Spanish text. See his *Historia General de los Hechos de los Castellanos*, Madrid, 1730, dec. VI, lib. IX, caps. XIII-XV. An English translation was made by Hakluyt in his *Principal Navigations, Voyages, Traffiques, and Discoveries of the English Nation*, in the section labeled *America*, part III. This report of Alarcón, like all other Spanish documents contained in Hakluyt, was translated from the Italian text in Ramusio. The French translation in Ternaux-Compans, *Voyages, Relations et Mémoires*, Paris, 1838, IX, pp. 299-348, comes likewise from Ramusio, but from the Venice edition of 1606.

2. One of the small ports in the Bahía de Manzanillo. H. R. Wagner, *Spanish Voyages to the Northwest Coast of America*, San Francisco, 1929, pp. 16 and 305.

had suffered, supplied myself with the necessary things, took on board the people who were waiting for me, and set sail for the port of Aguayaval.[3] Upon arriving there I learned that General Francisco Vázquez de Coronado had left with all his forces. So I took over the ship named San Gabriel, which was carrying supplies for the army, and took it with me, following instructions from his Lordship. Then I sailed along the coast without deviating from it, in order to see if I could find any markers, or Indians who would furnish me some information.

In sailing close to shore I was able to discover other harbors, quite good, that had not been seen or found by the boats led by Captain Francisco de Ulloa by order of the Marqués del Valle.[4] Upon reaching the shoals where the aforesaid boats had turned back,[5] it seemed to me and to others that the mainland rose ahead. These shoals were so dangerous and forbidding that it was temerity to venture over them even with small boats.

The pilots and the other men wanted us to do what Captain Ulloa had done. But as your Lordship had commanded me to report on the secret of that gulf, I determined, even at the risk of losing the ships, not to fail under any pretext to reach its end. So I ordered Nicolás Zamorano, chief pilot, and Domingo del Castillo to take a small boat and, with lead in hand, to enter those shoals and see if they could find a channel through which the ships could sail. They thought the ships could sail on, although with great difficulty and danger.

Thus I, together with him, began to follow them over the route they chose. In a short while we found all three of our ships stuck on the sand, so that one could not help the other,

3. Between the Mocorito and Culiacán rivers. Wagner contends that an island existed here in the sixteenth century. It was, he says, the Espiritu Santo island, which had been named San Miguel, or San Cristóbal by Cortés, but in the latter's map it is given as Isla de las Perlas. *Ibid.*, pp. 17 and 305.

4. Ulloa had been sent up the Gulf of California in 1539 by Cortés, who was trying to forestall Mendoza and Coronado. The Ulloa expedition was the first to demonstrate that California was a peninsula and not an island, though this knowledge was soon forgotten. Ulloa's narrative is translated in Wagner, *op. cit.*, pp. 11-50.

5. That is, Ulloa's. One of his ships, the *Trinidad*, was left aground near Bahía de Santa Cruz. *Ibid.*, p. 27.

and the boats could not help either, as the currents were so
strong that it was impossible to approach one another. We
were in such danger that many times the deck of the flagship
was under water. Had it not been for a miraculous rise of the
tide that raised the ship, and, as it were, gave her a chance to
breath again, we should all have drowned. In a similar manner, the other two ships found themselves in great danger,
although as they were smaller and did not draw as much
water they were not in as great danger as ours. With the rise
of the tide the Lord willed that the boats should be afloat again,
and so we sailed ahead. Even though the sailors wanted to turn
back, still I insisted that we sail on and proceed on the voyage
we had started.

We continued ahead with great difficulty, turning our
prows now this way, now that, in trying to find the channel.
God willed that thus we should reach the end of the gulf. Here
we found a mighty river with such a furious current that we
could scarcely sail against it. So I decided to sail up the said
river the best way I could, in two boats, leaving the other with
the ships in care of twenty men. I entered one of the boats
with the treasurer of the fleet, Rodrigo Maldonado,[6] the accountant, Gaspar de Castillejo, and a few pieces of artillery and
some munitions. I began to move up the river and gave orders
to all the men that no one should move or make any sign,
except the man that I should appoint, even if we should meet
Indians.

That very day, which was Thursday, August 26, proceeding
on our voyage by pulling the ropes,[7] we went some six leagues.
The next day, Friday, continuing on our way at about dawn,
I saw some Indians who were going to some huts near the
water. Upon seeing us ten or twelve of them rose, very much
disturbed. At their loud shouting, some others came, totalling
about fifty in number. With great haste they removed what

6. Not to be confused with one of Coronado's captains who bore the
same name.

7. The word in Italian is "alzana," which seems to correspond to the
modern "alzáia," a towing cable. Hakluyt gives the same translation. The
meaning, however, is not very clear, and in places it seems that they used
oars and poles.

they had in their huts and carried it into the brush, many of them running toward the place we were approaching, motioning us to turn back, and making fierce threats, some running on one side, some on the other. Since the Indians were so disturbed I ordered the boat to the middle of the river to reassure the Indians. I rode at anchor and arranged my men to the best of my ability. I commanded that no one should speak or make any sign or motion, nor move from his place, nor become disturbed whatever the Indians did, nor show any warlike attitude. So the Indians came closer to the river to watch us. Slowly I went toward them where the river seemed to be deeper. By this time there had assembled about two hundred and fifty Indians in warlike mood with bows and arrows and some banners like the Indians of New Spain. Seeing that I was nearing the shore, they came toward us with a loud outcry, their bows and arrows ready, and their banners high. I stood at the stern, in company with the interpreter I had brought along, and asked him to speak to them. He did so, but they did not understand him, nor he them, although, seeing that he was one of them, they calmed down. In view of this I drew nearer to the shore, and they, with much shouting, came to keep me from the bank of the river, motioning me not to go farther and placing stakes in the water between us and the shore. The longer I lingered, the larger was the number of Indians in evidence. Looking at them, I began to make signs of peace to them. Taking my sword and shield, I threw them on the deck of the boat and stood up, thus trying to make them understand by this and other signs that I did not seek war with them, and that they should do likewise. Then I took a flag and lowered it and asked my men to sit down. Taking some of the things I carried for trading, I called to the natives and offered to give these articles to them. Withal, no one approached to get them.

Soon they got together, and much talk was heard among them. Suddenly there emerged from among them one bearing a staff, in which certain shells were set, and he entered the water to give it to me. I took it and motioned him to come on board. He did this, and I embraced him and gave him in exchange some beads and other things. When he was back among his people, he looked at them and held a parley. Shortly afterward many of them came toward me, and I signalled them to lower their banners and lay down their arms. This they did at once. Then I motioned that they should put the arms all together in one place and withdraw, which they also did. They asked the Indians who had newly arrived to leave their weapons with the others. Then I asked them to come to me, and to every one who came I gave some article of trade, and treated him kindly. By this time there were so many surrounding me that I did not consider it safe to remain there, and I asked them by signs to withdraw and to stay at a little hill which there was between a plain and the river, and not to come to me more than ten at a time. Right away the oldest among them shouted to them to do so, and then ten or twelve of them came to where I was. Considering myself fairly secure, I decided to go ashore to reassure them. For greater safety, I motioned to them to sit down, which they did, but, seeing that I was followed ashore by ten or twelve of my men, they became disturbed. I motioned to them that we would keep our peace, and that they had nothing to fear. With this they were quieted and sat down again. I came to them and embraced them and gave them a few small articles, commanding my interpreter to speak to them, as I wanted very much to understand their manner of speech, and what they were shouting.

Wishing to learn what kind of food they had, I made signs indicating that I wanted to eat. They brought me some ears of maize and some mesquite bread. They made signs to me that they wanted to see me fire an harquebus. I had one fired, and the Indians all became frightened and ran away, except two or three old men who did not budge in the least but berated the others because they had shown fear. After a talk by one of these old men, they began to get up and lay hold of their weapons. Wishing to placate him, I tried to give him a silken cord of several colors, but he, with great rage, bit his lower lip hard and hit me on the chest with his elbow, and began to talk to his people with greater fury. When I saw that they were raising their banners, I decided to return quietly to my boat, and, as there was a little breeze, I ordered the sail raised, and thus we were able to overcome the very swift current, although my men did not like the idea of sailing farther ahead. In the meantime the Indians followed us along the shore of the river, making signs to me to come ashore and that they would give me things to eat, some of them sucking their fingers; others entered the water with ears of maize to give them to me in the boat.

II

Telling of the habits, weapons, and stature of the Indians discovered. Information of many others with whom, by signs, they traded, obtained food, and were shown marked courtesy.

Thus we traveled two leagues until I came to a canyon where there was a newly made arbor. The natives made signs and shouted to me that I should go thither, pointing with their hands and motioning that there was food there. Seeing that the place was suitable for an ambush, I did not go there but proceeded ahead on my voyage. Shortly afterward more than one thousand Indians armed with bows and arrows came out of that place. Then there appeared many women and children, whom I did not approach, and, as the sun was about to set, I moved to the middle of the river.

These Indians were adorned in different ways. Some had streaks covering their faces almost entirely. Others had their faces half covered, all blackened with soot. Each one was painted according to his fancy. Some wore masks of the same color, shaped like their faces. On their heads they wore a deerskin about two spans in size, worn like a helmet, and on it a small crest with some feathers. The weapons of these natives were bows and arrows of hard wood, and two or three types of maces of wood hardened in the fire. These people were large and well formed, without being fat. They have their noses pierced, and from them hung some pendants, while others wore shells. They have their ears pierced with many holes in which they place beads and shells. All of them, both small and large, wear a multicolored sash about the waist; tied in the middle is a round bundle of feathers which hangs in the back like a tail. Likewise, around the muscles of their arms, they wear a narrow band wound around so many times that it extends the width of a hand. They wear some small blades of deer bones, tied around one arm, with which they wipe their sweat. From the other hang some reed canes. They wear also a sort of bag a span long, tied to their left arm, using it as an arm band for the bow, filled with some seed from which they make a kind of beverage. Their bodies are branded by fire. Their hair is cut in front, and in the back it hangs to the waist. The women go about naked. They wear a large bunch of feathers, painted and glued, tied in front and behind. They wear their hair like the men. There were among these Indians three or four men dressed like women.

Early next day, Saturday, I proceeded on my way up the river, taking out two men for each boat to pull the ropes. At sunrise we heard a great uproar from Indians on both banks of the river. They were armed, although they carried no flag. I thought it desirable to wait for them, both to find out what they wanted and also to see if our interpreter could understand them. In the meantime, when they were across from us, they jumped into the water from both banks of the river with their bows and arrows. When they spoke, our interpreter did not understand them. So I began to motion to them to lay down their weapons as the others had done. Some did so, others did not. Those who put down their weapons, I called to me and gave them some articles of trade. When the others saw this, they, too, laid them down in order to get their share. Judging that I was safe, I went ashore with them and stood in their midst. Realizing that I was not seeking war, they began to give me some shells and beads, and some brought me well-tanned skins, others maize and a cake of the same, poorly ground. There was no one who would not bring something. Before they gave it to me, standing a little distance away, they shouted and made gestures with their bodies and arms, and then they hastened to give me what they brought.

At sunset I put off from shore and moved to the middle of the river. The next day, before daylight, there was heard even a greater outcry from more Indians on both banks of the river who jumped into the water and, swimming, brought me some ears of maize and the cake I have described. I showed them some wheat, beans, and other seeds to see if they had any, but they indicated that they were not acquainted with them. They marveled at everything.

Through signs I learned that what those natives worshipped and revered most was the sun. I gave them to understand that I came from the sun, at which they were very amazed. They stared at me from head to foot, and showed me greater respect then before. When I asked them for food, they brought so much that twice we had to make room for it in the boats.

From then on, whenever they brought something, they first cast some to the sun, then turned to me and gave me the rest. So I was always better served and respected by them, both in pulling the ropes and in being supplied with food. They showed me so much affection that when I was among them they wanted to carry me bodily in their arms to their homes. They did not refuse anything that I requested of them. For my own safety I ordered them not to bear arms in my presence. They were so careful about this that, when any newcomer arrived, they ran to meet him and had him leave his arms far from me. I showed them I was greatly pleased at this. To some of the leaders I gave some pieces of cloth and trifles. If I were to give something to every one, all the goods in New Spain would not suffice. Such was their affection and respect for me that it happened that if perchance an armed newcomer failed to hear the first warning of the one who went to tell him, and he failed to put down his weapons, the natives ran to him and took them away from him by force and smashed them in my presence. Then they took to the ropes so willingly and in such rivalry with one another that it was not necessary to ask them. Had it not been for this help, the current being so swift and the men at the ropes inexperienced, it would have been impossible to navigate up stream against the current.

Seeing that they now understood me in everything and I, too, understood them, I thought I should try to find a way to accomplish a purpose I had in mind. Taking some sticks and paper, I made a few crosses and distributed them among the natives as something I esteemed the most. I kissed them and made signs to the natives that they should honor and prize them highly and wear them around their necks. I told them by signs that it was the symbol of heaven. They took the crosses, kissed and raised them on high, and showed great joy and happiness as they did this. I took them on board and showed much affection for them and gave them some of the small articles I carried. The matter grew to such proportions that there were not enough sticks or papers to make crosses.

In this way I was quite well accompanied on that day, until night came, when I returned to the river and moved to midstream. They asked me for permission to leave, saying that they would return next day with provisions. So gradually they went away until there were only about fifty of them left. These lighted fires across from us and remained there all night calling one another. The day was not yet light when they entered the water, swam to us and asked for the ropes, which we gave them with pleasure. We thanked the Lord for the excellent facilities which He was providing for navigating the river up stream, for the Indians were so numerous that, had they wanted to bar our way, they could have done it easily, even if we had been many more than we were.

III

An Indian, upon hearing the interpreter speak, asked him a few questions regarding the origin of the Spaniards. He told them that the captain was a child of the sun, and that the sun had sent them, and that they should accept him as their lord. They took this Indian on board and he gave much information about the country.

In this way we sailed until Tuesday afternoon, following the same method. I ordered my interpreter to speak to the natives to see if any one could understand him. Observing that one answered him, I ordered the boats to stop. I called the one who understood my interpreter and told the latter not to talk or answer except what I told him. In the meantime I noticed that the said Indian talked to his people heatedly, and all the people began to gather. My interpreter understood that the Indian in the boat was saying that he wanted to know who we were, whence we came, whether we had sprung from the water or the earth or descended from the sky. So asking, he joined a large crowd of people who were astounded at my talking. From time to time this Indian spoke to them in a different language that my interpreter did not understand.

To the one who asked me who we were, I replied that we were Christians who had come from afar to see them. To his question as to who sent me, I answered that I was sent by the sun, pointing out to them the sun as I had done before in order that I should not be caught in falsehood. He asked how the sun could send me when it was high in the sky and never stopped; that for many years past the old men had never seen others like us or heard of them, nor had the sun until then sent any one. I replied that it was true that the sun was high above and never stopped, but that they could see that at sunset and sunrise it came close to the earth where it dwelt; that they could always see it rise in the same place; that the sun had created me in that land where it rose just as it had created many others and sent them to different places; that the sun had sent me now to explore and visit that river and the people living in that region in order that I should talk to them and express my friendship for them, and give them the things they lacked and tell them not to wage wars against one another.

The Indian asked that I explain the reason why the sun had not sent me sooner to stop the wars that had raged among them for a long time, resulting in the killing of many. I answered that the reason was that I was then a child. Then he asked the interpreter if we had taken him by force, or if we had taken him in war, or if he had come by his own will. He replied that he came with us of his own accord and that he enjoyed being with us. Then he again asked why it was that we brought along only him who could understand them and how it was that we did not understand everybody, being children of the sun. I replied that the sun had also created him and had provided him with a language that he might understand the captain and others; that the sun knew perfectly well that they lived here, but that as it was busy with other matters, and I being young, it had not sent me sooner.

Turning suddenly to me, the Indian said: "Come then here and be our lord, and we will serve you." I, considering that it would not please them were I to accept, replied that I did not wish to be their master, but their brother, and to give them whatever I had. He asked me if the sun had created me like the rest; whether I was its relative or son. I answered that I was its son. Then he asked if those who were with me were also children of the sun. I replied that they were not, but that they had, like myself, been created in the same land where I had grown up. Then he spoke in a loud voice and said: "Since you do so much good, and you do not want us to engage in wars and you are a child of the sun, we all want you for our lord and want to serve you always. So we pray you not to go away and leave us." At once he turned to his people and began to tell them that I was a child of the sun, and so they should all accept me as their lord. When the Indians heard this, they were greatly astonished, and came nearer to stare at me. The said Indian asked me still other questions, which I shall not narrate for the sake of brevity.

Thus the day was spent, and as night approached I tried to think of a good way of getting this Indian into the boat with us. As he did not wish to come, the interpreter told him that we would land him on the opposite bank of the river, and under this condition he came on board. I showered him with attentions and gave him the best treatment possible, always reassuring him. When I surmised that he had discarded all misgivings, I thought it opportune to ask him about the country. The first thing I asked him was whether he had ever seen around there men like ourselves or had heard any mention of them. He said he had not, except that he had heard the old men say that very far from their country there were other bearded white men like ourselves, but he knew nothing else. I asked him if he had heard of a place called Cíbola, and a river named Totonteac, but he said no.

Seeing that he could not furnish me any information about Francisco Vázquez or his people, I thought I would inquire of him concerning the things of that country and their ways of living. I began by asking him if they knew there was one God, creator of heaven and earth, or if they had idols. He replied in the negative, but that they esteemed and venerated the sun above all things. They did so because it warmed them and made the seeds germinate; and of all things which they ate they always cast a little into the air to the sun. I asked him next if they had rulers. He answered no, but that they knew there was a mighty lord, but they did not know where he dwelt. I told them He was in heaven and that He was called Jesus Christ. I did not care to dwell on theology with him. I asked him if they had wars and for what cause. He said they had big wars over trifles. Whenever they had no cause for war they would get together and some one of them would say: "Let us go wage war at a certain place," and immediately they would set out with their weapons. I asked him who led the forces, and he said that the oldest and bravest did so. And when the leaders ordered them not to fight any more, they at once abandoned the war. I asked him to tell me what they did with the men they killed in battle. He said that they carved out the hearts of some and ate them, others they burned. He added that had it had not been for my presence at that place, they would have been at war.

Since I had ordered them not to fight but to put down their arms, they would not take them up again until I ordered them to do so, and would not fight any one. Among themselves they said that since I came among them they had overcome their urge for war, and were eager to keep the peace. He complained of some people from across the mountain who waged war on them and killed many of their people. I told him that from then on they need not fear them any more, because I had commanded them to live in peace. Should they fail to do so, I would punish and kill them. He asked how we could kill them, being so few and they so numerous. As it was already late, and as he was getting tired of staying with me, I let him go, and sent him away very happy.

IV

Telling of the Naguachato and other chieftains of those Indians from whom they got many provisions. They induced them to plant the cross in their lands and taught them to worship it. They hear of many people, of their diverse languages, marriage practices, punishment of adultery; their idea of the dead, and the disease that afflicts them.

Early next morning their chieftain, called Naguachato, came and asked me to come ashore as they wanted to give me provisions. As it seemed to me that I was in a safe place, I did it without hesitation. Forthwith there came an old man with maize cakes and some small gourds. Calling me loudly and making many contortions with his body and arms, he came close to me. He made me turn toward these people, and himself turning to them too, he said, "Sagueyca." The entire crowd answered in an outcry, "Hu." He offered the sun a little of everything he had, and a little to me, although later he gave me the rest. He followed the same ceremony with every one of my men. Bringing out the interpreter, I thanked them through him. I told them that as the boats were so small, I could not bring along many things to give them in exchange, but that I would do it when I came back and that if they wanted to come with me to the ships down the river I would give them many things. They replied that they would do it gladly.

Wishing to explain to them through the interpreter the meaning of the emblem of the cross, I asked them to bring me a log, of which I made a large cross. I ordered all my men that after it was made they should adore it and pray our Lord to bestow His grace so that all these people would come to the knowledge of His holy Catholic faith. This being done, I told them, through the interpreter, that I was going to leave them that emblem as a symbol, that I considered them my brothers. I asked them to preserve it carefully until I should come back, and that every morning at sunrise they should all kneel before it. They took it up at once, and, without letting it touch the ground, they erected it amid their houses that all might see it.

I told them to worship it always, as it would preserve them from evil. They asked me how much of it they should bury in the ground, and I showed them. Many accompanied it. Those who stayed asked me how they should put their hands together, and how they should kneel to adore it. They seemed to put their whole heart into learning it.

Then I took the chieftain of the land, and, with him on board my boat, I proceeded on my voyage upstream. On both banks of the river the Indians accompanied me with much affection and helped me by tugging at the ropes and pulling me off the sands when we were aground on them, for in many places we found the river so shallow that there was not enough water for the boats. As we traveled on, the Indians I had left behind came to ask me to teach them to fold their hands when they worshipped the cross. Others wanted me to see whether they did it right, so that I had no moment of repose. Near the opposite bank of the river there was a bigger crowd calling me with great commotion to come and get the provisions they had brought for me. Remembering that they were rivals, I went there, in order not to displease them. An old man met me here as at the previous place. He brought me provisions with like ceremonies and offerings. I wanted to learn something from this man as I had from the preceding one. This one, too, told his people: "This is our lord; you know very well how long ago we heard our forefathers say that there were in the world bearded white people, and we thought them stupid. I and other old men have never seen people like these. If you will not believe it, look at those on this river. Let us then feed them, for they give us of their food. Let us serve willingly this master who is well disposed and who enjoins us from having more wars, and who embraces every one. They have mouth, hands, and eyes as we do, and talk as we do." I gave these people a cross, too, as I had the ones before. I gave them the same talk, to which they listened more attentively, and made greater efforts to learn what I told them.

Proceeding a little farther on we met other people whose language the interpreter did not understand at all. I explained to them by signs also the same ceremony of the adoration of the cross, as I had done to the others.   The chieftain whom I had taken along told me that a little farther up the river I would find people whom my interpreter would understand.   It being already late, some of these people called me in order to give me provisions, and acted exactly as the others, rejoicing and playing to please me.   I wished to know how many people lived along this river.   I was told by the said chief that it was inhabited by twenty-three language groups who lived close to the river, in addition to others not far away; and that besides these twenty-three language groups settled by the river there were others he did not know.   I asked him if each nation lived in one settlement.   He said it did not; that there were some houses scattered in the country.   Each nation had its separate recognized country, and each settlement had considerable people. He showed me a village located on a mountatin, saying it contained a large number of people.   They were evil people who continuously waged war against them.   Having no ruler, and dwelling in that desert place that produced little maize, they came down to the plains to get it in trade for deerskins, in which they were dressed.   They wore long clothes, which they cut with blades and sewed together by means of awls made from deer bones.   They lived in big stone houses.   I asked him if there were any people there from that country.   I found a woman who wore as a dress a sort of blanket that reached from her waist to the ground, made of well-tanned deerskin.   I asked him then if the people who lived on the bank of that river dwelt there permanently or at other places sometimes.   He told me that in summer time they settled here and planted, and that after the harvest they went to live at other houses which they had at the foot of the mountain far from the river.   He told me by signs that the houses were made of logs covered with mud on the outside.   I learned that they built a big round room where they lived all together, men and women.

I asked him if they had women in common, and he answered no; that those who married could have only one wife. I wished to know what marriage ceremonies they had, and he said that when one had a grown daughter, he went among the people and said: "I have a marriageable daughter; is there any man here who wants her?" If there was some one who wanted her, he replied that he did and the marriage was arranged. The father of the one who wanted her brought some presents to give to the girl, and from that moment the marriage was considered performed. They sang and danced, and when night came the parents took them and left them alone at a place where no one might see them. There was no marriage between brother and sister or close relatives. Before marriage the women did not associate or converse with men. They stayed at home and in their places, working. If, perchance, any one had relations with men before she married, her husband abandoned her and moved to another nation. The one who fell in such trangression was considered a bad woman. If, after marriage, a man should be taken in adultery with another woman, they killed him. No one could have more than one wife unless it was in secret. He told me that they burned the dead. The one who became a widow remained unmarried for half or a whole year. As I wanted to know what they believed of the dead, he said they went to the other world but that they endured neither suffering nor bliss.

The main disease which afflicts and kills these people is vomiting blood through the mouth. They have their medicine men who heal them with words and by blowing on the sick. The dress of these people is the same as of the others before. They carry their reed tubes to perfume themselves in the same manner as the people of New Spain use tobacco. Wishing to know if these people had any ruler, I learned that they did not, but that every house chose its own chieftain. These people, in addition to maize, have some gourds and some grain like millet. They possess grindstones, and pots in which they cook the gourds and fine fish which are found in the river. The interpreter would not go beyond this place. He alleged that the people we should meet on our way now were his enemies. So I sent him back, and he was very pleased. It was not long before I saw numerous Indians running toward me, shouting. I stopped to find out what they wanted. They told me that they had erected the cross I gave them in the midst of their houses, as I had told them, but I should know that when the river rose it often flooded up to that place. They wanted me to grant them permission to move it and set it up at some other place that would not be reached by the river. I granted them the permission.

V

Telling how an Indian in that region gave them information of the location of Cíbola, of the type and habits of the people and their rulers, and also of the countries, not far distant, one called Quicama and the other Coana. They were well received by the people of Quicama and others not far away.

Thus sailing on, we came to a place where there were many Indians. There was another interpreter whom I had come on board my boat. As it was cold and my men were wet, I went ashore and ordered a fire built. While we were warming ourselves an Indian arrived, who, touching my arm, pointed to a forest from which I noticed two groups of armed men coming. He pointed out to me how they were coming to attack. Not wishing to open hostilities with any one, I gathered my men in the boats. The Indians who were with us gained the opposite bank of the river by swimming. In the meantime, I asked the Indian who was with me who those people were that were coming out of the forest. He said they were his enemies. These others, upon seeing them, entered the water without uttering a word, in order to go back as they were unarmed. They had not brought their weapons along because they observed my order and wish that they bear no arms.

I asked this interpreter the same questions I had asked the preceding one regarding the things of the country, for I had heard that in some nations men had several wives and in others only one. He told me that he had been in Cíbola, that it was one month's travel from his country. From that place, following a path bordering the river, it could be reached in forty days. He said the only reason why he went was just to see Cíbola, as it was a big place. It had very tall stone houses, three and four stories high, with windows on all sides. It was surrounded by a wall half again as high as a man. The upper and lower parts of these houses were inhabited by people. They used the same type of weapons as the ones we had seen, that is to say: bows, arrows, maces, clubs, and shields. They had a ruler. They were dressed in blankets and cattle skins. Their blankets were painted all around. Their ruler wore a long tunic, tightly tied, and over it other blankets. The women wore very long clothes, were white, and went about completely clad. Every day a large number of Indians stood at the door of their lord to serve him. They wore many blue stones which were dug from some hard rock. These people had only one wife. When their chieftains died they buried all their belongings with them. Also, when these lords ate, many of their people watched them at the table to honor them and see them eat. He said that they ate with napkins, and that they had baths.

Then on Thursday, at break of day, Indians came shouting to the shore of the river. They were more willing to serve. They brought me food, and they performed the same ceremonies for me that the others had done. They had learned who I was. I gave them similar crosses and instructions as to the others. Traveling a little farther on, I came to a country better organized, as all the people obey a single head. Speaking again to the interpreter about the dwellings of the people of Cíbola, he told me that the lord of that country had a dog like the one I had along.

Afterward, when I was about to eat, this interpreter saw plates being carried back and forth. He said that the chieftain at Cíbola had some like them, but that they were green, and that no one had them except the chieftain. The plates, four in all, he had obtained with the dog and other articles from a bearded negro. However, he did not know whence he had come. He had heard that the chieftain ordered him killed. I asked him if he knew of some country near here. He said that he knew of some up the river. Among other people there was the chieftain of a place called Chicama, and another lord of a land called Coama, and that they had many people under their command. After giving me this information, he asked permission to return to his friends.

I proceeded on my voyage from here and, after a day's sail, I came to an abandoned village. Upon entering it there came five hundred Indians with bows and arrows. Among them came the chief Indian, named Naguachato, whom I had left behind. They presented me with some rabbits and yucca. After welcoming them all, as I wanted to go on, I gave them leave to return to their homes. After passing through the desert, a little beyond, we came to some huts where many people led by an old man came out to meet us. They talked in a language that my interpreter understood very readily. The old man said to his people: "Brothers, behold the master. Let us give him of what meat we have, for he is doing good, and he has passed among so many discourteous people in order to visit us." Thus saying, he made an offering to the sun and then to me, in the same fashion as the others had done. These people had some large well-made bags of the fiber of rattan. I understood that this country belonged to the ruler of Quicoma, whose people came here only during the summer to gather the harvest of their planted fields. I met among them one who understood my interpreter very well. So, with much eagerness, I gave these people similar instructions about the cross as I had to the others farther back.

These people had cotton, but they took little interest in cultivating it because there were no persons among them who knew how to weave and make clothes. They asked me how they should erect the cross when they returned to their homes in the mountain. They asked whether it would be proper to build a house around it so that it should not get wet. They wanted to know if they should hang anything from the arms. I told them that they should not; all they needed to do was to erect it at a place where every one might see it, until I came back. They said that they would send more people with me, if perchance we should meet hostile people, that the people I would meet farther up were mean people. However, I refused to accept the offer. Just the same, twenty of them came with me. They warned me as I approached those who were their enemies. I found their sentries watching at the border of their country.

On Saturday morning I met a large body of men sitting under a huge arbor, and some outside. Seeing that they did not get up, I went on my way. When they saw this, an old man rose and said to me: "Sir, why don't you accept food from us when you have accepted it from the others?" I replied that I only accepted what was offered to me; and went only to the people who called me. Without any further question, they brought me abundant provisions, saying that since we did not enter their homes, and we remained on the river night and day, and that I was a child of the sun, they would all accept me as their lord. I motioned them to sit down and called the old man whom my interpreter understood. I asked him whose country that was, and whether its lord was there. He answered that he was. I sent for him, and when he arrived I embraced him and showed great affection for him. Seeing that they were all pleased at my attentions to him, I put a shirt on him and gave him some other trifles. I asked the interpreter to tell this chieftain the same thing we had told the others. Then I gave him a cross, which he took, much pleased, as the others had done. This chieftain accompanied me for a long time, until we were called from the opposite river bank. There was the same old man with numerous people. I gave them another cross, with the same instructions as the others, which was all I could do. Continuing on my way I came to another multitude of people accompanied by the same old man whom my interpreter understood. When I saw their chieftain, who was being pointed out to me, I begged him to come into my boat, which he did readily. So I proceeded on my voyage, always up stream. The old man pointed out the chieftains to me. I always spoke to them with much deference. They all showed much pleasure and spoke many good words about my coming. At night I retired to the middle of the river.

I asked him many questions about the things of the country. I found him as eager to answer as I was to inquire. I asked him about Cíbola, and he said he had been there, that it was something great, and that its ruler was thoroughly obeyed. He said that there were other chieftains in the neighborhood with whom he was continuously at war. I asked him if they had silver or gold, and he, seeing some bells, said that they had some metal of that color. I wanted to know if they obtained it there. He said that they did not, but brought it from a mountain where there was an old woman. I asked him if he had heard of a river named Totonteac. He said he had not, but that he had heard of another very large river in which there were alligators so big that out of their skins they made shields. The people worshipped the sun exactly the same as the ones met farther back. When they offered it the fruits of the soil, they said to it: "Take them, for you have made them grow." They revered it greatly because it warmed them, for, when it did not shine, they were cold. In his conversation, then, he began to complain, saying to me: "I do not know why the sun is with us, for it does not produce any cloth or any one to weave it, nor the things that it gives to many others." He complained because those of that country would not let him enter it and would not give them some of their seed. I told him I would remedy the situation, which pleased him very much.

VI

They obtained information from the Indians as to why the lords of Cíbola killed the Moor who went with Fray Marcos, and many other things; of the old woman named Guatazaca, who lived without food at a lake. Description of an animal with a hide of which they make shields. Fear that they may be identified with the Christians seen at Cíbola, and how they escaped.

On the following day, which was Sunday, it was not yet daylight when the usual shouting began. It came from three or four nations who spent the night by the river waiting for me. They took maize and other grains in their mouths and sprinkled me with them, saying that that was the way they offered sacrifice to the sun. Then they gave me provisions, and among other things, many beans.

I gave these people a cross, as I had given to the others, while the old man told them big things about me and pointed me out to them with his finger, saying to them: "This is our master, a child of the sun." They made me comb my beard and arrange handsomely the clothes I was wearing. Their belief in me was such that they all told me of their past and present troubles and their good or bad disposition toward one another. I asked them why they told me all these affairs of theirs. The old man replied: "You are the lord, and nothing must be concealed from the lord." After these matters, proceeding on my way, I asked him about Cíbola and whether he knew if the people there had ever seen people like us. He answered no, except a negro who wore on his feet and arms some things that tinkled. Your Lordship must remember how this negro who went with Fray Marcos wore bells, and feathers on his ankles and arms, and carried plates of various colors. He arrived there a little more than one year ago. I asked him why they killed him. He replied that the chieftain of Cíbola asked the negro if he had any brothers, and he answered that he had an infinite number, that they had numerous arms, and that they were not very far from there. Upon hearing this, many chieftains assembled and decided to kill him so that he would not reveal their location to his brothers. For this reason they killed him and tore him into many pieces, which were distributed among the chieftains so that they should know that he was dead. He had a dog like mine, which the chieftain had killed a long time afterward.

I asked him if the people of Cíbola had enemies, and he said yes. He told me of fourteen or fifteen chieftains who were at war with them. He said that they had blankets and bows like the people above-mentioned. He told me that up the river I would find people who did not have wars with their neighbors or any one else. He said that they had three or four varieties of trees that produced excellent eating fruit. He said that at a certain lake there lived an old woman whom they served and rendered many offerings. She stayed in a hut there and never ate. He said that at that place they made the things that rattled and that she was given many blankets, feathers, and maize. I asked him what her name was. He said she was named Guatuzaca. He said that in that region there were many chieftains who in life and death had the same customs as those of Cíbola. They had their summer homes made of painted blankets. In the winter they lived in wooden houses two or three stories high. He had seen all these things, except the old woman. I asked him other things, but he would not answer, saying that he was tired of me.

Many Indians standing around me said to one another: "Let

us observe him closely so that we may recognize him when he comes back."

On the following Monday the river was lined with people of the same type. I asked the old man again to tell me how many people there were in that country. He replied that he thought I would soon forget, and forthwith he told me of many chieftains and people, who exceeded two hundred. Speaking of their weapons, he said that some of them carried very large shields made of hide more than two fingers thick. I asked him of what animals they were made. He described for me a very large animal resembling a cow, but more than a span larger, and with broad feet, and forelegs as thick as a man's thigh, the head seven spans long, and the forehead three spans across, eyes as large as fists, horns the length of a man's shin, with sharp points a span long. Its forelegs and hindlegs were more than seven spans long; it had a short but heavy tail. Raising his arms over his head, he said it was still taller than that.

He told me of another old woman who lived on the seacoast. I spent this day distributing crosses to those people the same as I had to the others. My old man went ashore and engaged in conversation with another one who that day had often called to him. Both made many gestures in their talk, waving their arms and pointing to me. I sent my interpreter there to stand near them and listen to what they were saying. After a while I called him back and asked him what they were talking about. He said that the one who made so many gestures was telling the other that at Cíbola there were bearded men like us who said they were Christians. And both maintained that we must all be the same, and that it would be well to kill us in order that the others should not hear of us and come to trouble the natives. He said that the old man told the other: "This one is a son of the sun, and our lord. He is doing good; he will not enter our houses even when we ask him; he does not take anything away from us; he does not seek our women." He added that he said many other things in my praise and behalf. Nevertheless the other one insisted that we must be all one and the same. The old one said: "Let us go to him and ask him if he is a Christian as the others are, or a son of the sun." The old man came to me and said: "You asked me if there were in the country of Cíbola other men like yourselves. At the time I pretended I was amazed and replied that it was not possible. These people assure me that it is true and that two men had been there, had seen them, and said that they carried firearms and swords as you do." I asked him if those people had seen them with their own eyes. He said no, but that some of their companions had seen them. Then he asked me if I was a son of the sun, and I replied that I was. He said that the same was said by the Christians at Cíbola. I replied that it might very well be true. Then they inquired of me what I would do if those Christians at Cíbola came to join me. I told them that they need not fear in the least because if they were children of the sun as they had said, they would be my brothers and would show every one the same courtesy and kindness that I showed. By this I thought they were quite reassured.

VII

Alarcón was told that Cíbola was within ten days' travel, and that there were Christians there fighting the chieftains. Reports of sodomy among the Indians; four youths, dressed as women, devoted to it. Unable to communicate with the people at Cíbola, they return to their ships, following the river.

I asked him, then, how many days' travel away the kingdom of Cíbola was, how far they would say it was from that river. This man replied that it was ten days' distant over uninhabited country. Beyond there he did not reckon, as there were people. At this report I was eager to send news to the general. I consulted with my men, but there was no one who would risk going, although I offered many rewards in the name of your Lordship. Only a Moorish slave volunteered to go, although not very enthusiastically. However, I hoped that the Indians I had been told about would arrive, and so we continued our navigation upstream in the same manner as heretofore.

At this place the old man showed me as something amazing, a son of his dressed as a woman and used as such. I asked him how many such men there were among them. He replied that there were four, and when one died, a search was made for all the pregnant women in the land, and the first boy born was chosen to exercise the function of women. The women dressed them in their clothes, saying that if they were to act as such they should wear their clothes. These men could not have carnal relations with women at all, but they themselves could be used by all marriageable youths of the land. They received no compensation for this work from the people in the region, although they were free to take from any house what they needed for their living.

I noticed also some women who associated brazenly with men. I asked the old man if they were married women. He said no, that they were prostitutes who lived apart from the married women. Through this conversation I asked that the Indians who said they had been at Cíbola be brought to me. He said they were eight days' travel away, but that there was among them one of their companions who had talked with them, as he had met them when they were going to visit the kingdom of Cíbola, and they had told him that he should not go farther, because he would find there other fierce people like us, of the same qualities and features as we, who had fought much with men from Cíbola, for they had killed a Moorish companion of theirs. The Spaniards said to them: "Why did you kill him; what has he done to you; what goods has he taken away from you; what harm did he cause you?" They asked these and similar questions. They added further that these people said they were Christians, and lived in a large house. Many of them had cattle like those of Cíbola. They had also other smaller black animals with wool and horns. Some of them rode swift horses. One day before they left, they did nothing from sunrise to sunset but watch these Christians come. They all lodged where the others were.

These two Indians met two Christians who asked them where they were from. They answered that they were from a distant country and that they had planted fields. Then the Christians gave each one a little cloak, and gave them one to take to their companions. They promised to do so, and then parted.

Upon hearing this I talked again to my men to see if any one would volunteer to go, but I found the same resistance as before and they pointed out greater difficulties. Then I called the old man to see if he would furnish me people to accompany me, and provisions for the desert. He set forth to me many obstacles and risks which I would meet with on that trip. He told me that it was very dangerous to travel there because of a chieftain of Cumana, who was threatening to wage war on them because they had entered his country in pursuit of a deer, and that I should not leave this region without first punishing him.

When I told him that I had to go to Cíbola under any circumstances, he advised me to refrain from going. They expected the said chieftain would come to do them harm, and therefore they would not abandon their land to come with me. It would be better if I put an end to that war for them, then I could go to Cíbola in their company. We argued so much about this matter that we became angry. He would have left the boat in a rage, but I held him back and placated him with kind words, as it was very important to preserve his friendship. But no matter how attentive I was to him, I was unable to change his mind, in which he remained obstinate.

In the meantime I had already sent a man to the ships to tell them of the trip I was contemplating. Then I asked the old man to have this man recalled. Seeing that there was no way to go to Cíbola, and if I remained longer among those people they might find me out, I , too, decided to go in person to inspect the ships, having in mind to leave there some men who had become ill, and come back to the upper part of the river and bring other men along. Telling the old man and the others that I would come back, and leaving them as satisfied as I could, I turned back. They always maintained that I was leaving through fear. I sailed down the river to Cíbola [*sic*].[8] The distance that had taken me fifteen and a half days to travel against the current upstream, I traveled on my way back in two and a half days, so great and swift was the current. So, sailing down stream, many people came to the banks of the river to ask me: "Why are you

---

8. The words "to Cíbola," were omitted in the Hakluyt translation. They do not make sense, but it is possible that the text is faulty.

leaving us, Sir? What displeasure have you experienced? Did you not say that you would always stay among us and be our master? Go back, and if any one in the upper river did you any harm we will accompany you with our army to kill him." They expressed these and other similar words, filled with affection and courtesy.

VIII

Upon returning to the ships the captain named this the Land of the Cross. He ordered that a shrine be constructed to our Lady. He named the river Buena Guía.[9] Then he sailed back. Arriving at Quicana and Coano, the chieftains thereof showed him much courtesy.

When I reached the ships, I found my men all in good condition, although worried on account of my long delay. Because of the swift current, four cables were torn, and they had lost two anchors, which were recovered. Bringing all the ships together, I took them to a sheltered place. I had the San Pedro careened and all the necessary repairs made.

Here I assembled all the people and told them of the information we had about Francisco Vázquez, and that, perhaps, during the sixteen days I spent sailing up the river, he might have heard of me. I was willing to go back up the river and see if we could find means of communicating with him. Although my men were opposed, I ordered all the boats that were not needed in the ships to be made ready. I ordered one of them loaded with goods, trading articles, wheat, and other grains, and also Spanish hens and cocks, and started up the river.

I left orders that in the country named the Cross they should build a shrine or chapel and name it the church of our Lady of Buena Guía. The river should be named Buena Guía, it being the emblem of your Lordship. I took the chief pilot, Nicolás Zamorano, with me so that he might take the latitude. I set out on Tuesday, the fourteenth of September. On Wednesday I came to the first houses of the Indians. They rushed to obstruct my way, thinking it was some other people, because we were

9. The Colorado river.

taking along a fifer and a drummer, and I was dressed differently than when they saw me the first time. When they recognized me, they stopped. However, I could not induce them to become good friends.

I gave them some of the seed I carried and told them how they should plant it.

When I had sailed three leagues, my first interpreter came very joyfully to meet me at the boat. I asked him why he had left me, and he said some of his friends had drawn him away. I accorded him a good reception and treated him well so that he would come with me again, as I realized how valuable he would be at my side. He excused himself, for he had remained here to bring me some parrot feathers, which he gave me. I asked who those people were, and if they had a chief. He said that they did and named for me three or four in addition to the twenty-four or twenty-five he knew, and who had their houses painted on the inside. He said that these people traded with those of Cíbola, and that that kingdom could be reached in two moons. He also told me the names of many other chieftains, and of other people. I have described them in a book of mine, which I shall present to your Excellency in person. But I wanted to hand this summary report to Agustín Guerrero at the port of Colima in order that he might sent it overland to your Excellency. Later, I will amplify it very much.

Continuing on my way I arrived at Quicama, where the Indians came out to welcome me with much rejoicing and with celebrations. They told me their lord awaited me. Upon coming near him, I saw he was surrounded by five or six thousand unarmed men. He separated from them with only two hundred, all carrying provisions, and moved toward me. He walked ahead of them with great authority. By his side walked some who made the people line up, forming a passage for him to pass through. He wore a garment closed in front and back and open on the sides, fastened with buttons worked in chequered black and white. It was made of the fiber of rattan, very fine and well made. When he came to the edge of the water, his attendants took him in their arms and placed him in my boat. I embraced him and gave him a fine reception, showing him all kinds of attentions. This pleased very much his people who were there watching. This chieftain turned to his people and asked them to note my courtesy, that I of my own free will had come among strange people, that they could see how well I acted and with what affection I treated him. They should, therefore, acknowledge me as their lord, wherefore they would all serve me and do whatever I ordered them.

I had him sit down and gave him some sweet preserves to eat. I told the interpreter to thank him in my name for the honor he had done me by coming to call on me. I urged upon him the adoration of the cross, and all the things that I had impressed upon the others, namely, that they live in peace, give up war, and maintain always friendly relations among themselves. He replied that, for a long time, war had been raging between them and their neighbors, but that from then on he would command that food be furnished to all those who passed through his country, and that they be not done any harm. And if any nation came to wage war on them he would tell them that I had ordered that they live in peace. If they did not want peace, he would defend himself. He promised me that he would never engage in war unless others came to attack him.

Then I gave him some trinkets and seeds that I carried, and also some Spanish chickens, which he accepted with the utmost pleasure. When I left I took with me some of his people in order to establish friendly relations between them and the people farther up the river. Here the interpreter said he wanted to go back home. I gave him some presents, and he went away very happy.

On the following day I reached Coano. Seeing me in different clothes, many did not recognize me. But the moment the old man here recognized me, he entered the water, saying: "Sir, here is the man you left with me." He showed up then, very happy. He told me of the many attentions those people had shown him, saying that they vied with one another to see who would take him to his home. He said that their care in joining hands and kneeling before the cross at sunrise was unbelievable. I gave them some seed and thanked them for the good treatment they had accorded my Spaniard. They begged me to leave him there again, which I granted them until the end of my voyage. He remained among them very willingly.

Thus I sailed up the river, taking along the old man. He told me two Indians from Cumana had come to inquire about the Christians, and he told them that he did not know them although he knew one who was a child of the sun.

They had tried to get him to join them to kill me and my men. I asked him to give me two Indians, and to send word to them that we were coming to see them, that I wanted their friendship, but that if they on their part wanted war, I would give them war in a way they would not like. So we traveled among all those people. Some came to ask me why I did not give them a cross as I had to the others, and I gave them one.

IX

They go ashore and see how the people worship the cross which they had given them; they have an Indian paint the things of the country; they send a cross to the chieftain at Cumana; sail down the river again to their ships; the error of Cortés' pilots in locating that coast.

On the following day I decided to go ashore and see some huts. I found many women and children with hands joined and kneeling before the cross I had given them. When I came close to it, I did likewise. The old man proceeded to tell me of many other peoples and countries he knew. When night came I asked the old man to come and spend the night in our boat. He said that he would not come as I would tire him out with questions about so many things. I told him that I would not ask another question other than that he mark on a piece of paper what he knew of that river, and what people lived on both of its banks. He accepted with pleasure. Then he asked me to describe my country in the same way he had done his. In order to please him, I ordered a picture drawn of a few things. The next day I came to some very high mountains among which the river flowed in a narrow canyon. The boats passed with difficulty as there was no one to draw them.

At this place some Indians came to tell me that they were

from Cumana, and that among them there was an enchanter who wanted to know which way we were going. Upon being told that I was coming by the river, he placed some reeds clear across the stream. We passed over them without suffering any of the harm he thought he would cause us.

Thus we traveled until I came to the house of the old man who came with me. I had a very tall cross erected here, on which I carved some letters to indicate that I had come to this place. I did this in order that if people from the general should reach this place they would know of me.

At last, seeing that I could not learn anything of what I wanted to know, I decided to return to the ships. As I was about to leave, two Indians arrived, who through the interpreting of the old man said that they came at my call. They said that they were from Cumana, that their chieftain could not come because his country was so far away, but that I could send him whatever message I wished. I sent him word to try always to remember to be at peace, that I was on my way to visit his country, but could not do so as I had to come down the river, but that I would return later. In the meantime, I asked them to give their master a cross, which they promised to do, and they set out at once to take the cross, with some feathers on it, to him. I tried to learn from these Indians what people lived on the upper river. They told me of many people, and that the river extended much farther up than I had seen, but that they did not know its source, as it originated very far away, and that many other rivers emptied into this river.

Then, early on the following day, I sailed down the river. The next day I arrived at the place where I had left the Spaniard. I talked to him and told him that things had turned out well for me, and that on this and my previous trip I had gone more than thirty leagues inland. The Indians at this place asked me why I was leaving, and when I would come back. I told him that I would come back soon.

As we were sailing down stream, a woman entered the water shouting at us to wait for her. She entered our boat and crouched under a bench, from where we could not make her come out. I learned that she did this because her husband had another wife, by whom he had children. She said that she did not want to be with him any longer since he had another woman. She and an Indian man came with me of their own accord.

Thus I reached my ships. I arranged matters so that we could make our voyage along the coast. We landed frequently and went inland a long ways to see if we could get any news of General Francisco Vázquez and his forces. We got no other information of them than what I had been told up the river.

I bring with me many acts of possession of all that coast. By the river and the latitude I have recorded, I find that the skippers and pilots of the Marqués were wrong in their reckoning, and made an error of two degrees.[10] We have gone more than four degrees farther than they did. I went up the river eighty-five leagues, where I saw and heard what I have related, and also many other things. If your Excellency will grant me permission to come and kiss your hands, I shall give you a long and complete report.

I was fortunate in finding Don Luis de Castilla and Agustín Guerrero at the port of Colima as the schooner of the adelantado was sailing toward me.[11] He was here with his fleet and wanted me to lower my sails. As it seemed unusual to me and not knowing what the situation was in New Spain, I got ready to disobey and to defend myself. At this time Don Luis de Castilla arrived in a boat and talked to me, and I took to the opposite side of the harbor from where the fleet was. I gave him this report. As it was night, I decided to set sail and avoid trouble. This report I brought with me, written in brief form, as I always had in mind to sent it to notify your Excellency as soon as I touched land in this New Spain.

10. All Spanish explorers made errors of this nature as they went northward. It was a common mistake in the sixteenth century and was due primarily to errors in the tables of declination of the sun then in use. *Cf.* Wagner, *op. cit.*, p. 305, note 21.

11. The reference is to the adelantado, Pedro de Alvarado, whose fleet was on the coast and put in at Colima in November, 1540. Don Luis de Castilla and Agustín Guerrero, both close friends of Viceroy Mendoza, were here to protect the interests of their master in any further explorations that might be undertaken by sea. *Cf.* Wagner, *op. cit.*, pp. 55-56.

LETTER OF MENDOZA TO THE KING, APRIL 17, 1540[1]

Holy Cæsarean Catholic Majesty:

On the last of February I wrote to your Majesty from Compostela, giving an account of my arrival there and the departure of Francisco Vázquez with the men whom, in your name, I sent to pacify and settle the newly discovered land. I reported how the alcaide, Lope de Samaniego,[2] was going as maese de campo, he being a reliable, God-fearing, man experienced in matters of this nature, which your Majesty ordered were to be observed. The news since then is that, after crossing the uninhabited country of Culuacán, on nearing Chiametla, the alcaide went out in search of provisions with a few mounted men. And when one of the soldiers with him who had strayed away, called for help, saying that the Indians were killing him, the alcaide rushed to his rescue and was struck by an arrow in one eye, from which he died.

In connection with the fort, considering its bad condition and that it is a poor one, it seems to me that the cost of maintaining it is excessive and that your Majesty could avoid most of this expense. For by appointing a man to take charge of the munitions and the artillery, a gunsmith to keep the latter in condition, and a gunner, and by keeping all of this equipment in the building of the audiencia until the forts are well built, as I have already written to you is being done, none of the rest is needed. Besides, the fort was built for the brigantines, and for no other purpose. And since the lake is so dry at present, the fort can render no service whatever, and for this reason I hold

1. Translated from the text in Pacheco y Cárdenas, *Documentos de Indias*, II, pp. 356-362. It was translated into English by Winship in *Fourteenth Annual Report* of the Bureau of Ethnology, Washington, 1896, pp. 547-551, and reprinted in the Trail Makers edition of this same work in 1904, printed at New York by A. S. Barnes & Co. and in the Grabhorn edition, edited by F. W. Hodge, printed at San Francisco in 1933. There is a French translation in Ternaux-Compans, *Voyages*, IX, pp. 290-298.
2. Samaniego was the governor or commander of the arsenal at Mexico City.

that its maintenance is superfluous. I believe that it will have fallen down before your Majesty's reply can come.[3]

A few days ago I wrote to you telling how I had sent Melchior Díaz, who was in the town of San Miguel de Culuacán, to go with some mounted men and to see if what he might discover conformed to the report of Father Fray Marcos. He left Culuacán on November 17 of last year with fifteen men on horseback. On March 20 of this year I received a letter from him which he sent with Juan de Zaldívar and three other mounted men. He says that, from the time he left Culuacán and crossed the Petatlán river, he was always well received by the Indians. His method was to send a cross as a symbol to the place where he expected to spend the night. The Indians accepted the cross with much veneration and built a house of mats for it, and a short distance from it they prepared quarters for the Spaniards. They drove stakes into the ground for tethering the horses, and there they placed grass and maize in abundance, wherever they had any. It is said that since it was a poor year, Díaz had to endure hunger in many places.

One hundred leagues from Culuacán he began to find the country cold and to meet with heavy frosts. The farther on he went the colder it was. Finally it reached the point where some of the Indians they had along froze, and two Spaniards were in serious danger. In view of this, he decided not to proceed farther until the winter was over, but to send back the men whom I mentioned, with the report of what he had learned of Cíbola and the land farther on. It follows here, copied literally from his letter:

"Now that I have given your Lordship an account of what happened to me on the way, and since it is impossible for me to cross the despoblado extending between here and Cíbola on account of the snow and intense cold, I shall give your Lordship an account of what I have learned regarding Cíbola, which I have verified by persons who have lived there for fifteen to twenty years. I have learned this in many diverse ways, ques-

3. On December 10, 1537, Lope de Samaniego wrote from Mexico City to Charles V, suggesting the removal of the fortress under his command to a better place on the Tacuba road. *Colección de Documentos Inéditos para la Historia de Ibero-América,* recopilados por Sebastián Montoto, Madrid, 1927, I, pp. 85-87.

tioning some Indians together and others separately. They all seem to agree in what I shall now say. Beyond this vast despoblado there are seven villages, a short day's travel from each other. The whole group is called Cíbola. Their houses are built of stone and mud, rudely constructed, in this manner: There is a long wall, and at both ends of this wall some rooms twenty feet square are partitioned off, according to what they say. These rooms are roofed with rough timbers. Most of the houses are entered from the terraces, with ladders to the streets. The houses are three and four stories high. They say that there are few which are two stories high. Each story is more than one estado and one-half high, except the lower one, which must be only a little more than one estado. Ten or twelve adjoining houses are served by one ladder. The inhabitants use the lower stories for service and live in the upper ones. On the ground floor they have some slanted loop-holes as in the fortresses in Spain.

"The Indians say that when the inhabitants are attacked they all withdraw into their houses and fight from there, and that when they go to war they carry shields and wear some skins of the cattle of different colors. They fight with arrows, with small stone maces, they say, and with other weapons, made of wood, that I could not identify. They eat human flesh and keep as slaves those whom they take prisoners in war. There are many native tame chickens. They have plenty of maize, beans, and melons. They keep in their houses some woolly animals resembling large Castilian hounds. These they shear, and with the hair they make colored wigs, which they wear, like the one I am sending your Lordship. They also use this hair in the clothes which they make. The men are of small stature; the women are light and of good appearance. They wear a sort of shirt reaching down to their feet; they part their hair on each side with a number of twists, exposing the ears, from which hang many turquoises, as well as from their necks, wrists, and arms. The dress of the men consists of blankets, and over them hides of the cattle like the one brought by Cabeza de Vaca and Dorantes and which your Lordship must have seen. They wear some sort of coif on their heads. In the summer they wear shoes of skin, painted or colored, and in winter, high buskins of the same type.

"They are unable to give me any information in regard to metals, nor do they say that they have any. They do have turquoises in quantity, although not so many as the father provincial says. They have some small glassy stones like the one I am sending your Lordship, and of which you have seen so many in New Spain. They cultivate the land in the same way as in New Spain, and bear burdens on their heads as in Mexico. The men weave the cloth or spin the cotton. They obtain salt from a lake which is two days' travel from the province of Cíbola. The Indians hold their dances and songs with the aid of some flutes which have holes for the fingers. They make many tunes, singing jointly with those who play. Those who sing clap their hands in the same manner as we do. I saw one of the Indians, who accompanied the negro Esteban and who was a captive there, play, since they had taught him how to do it there. Others were singing, as I said, although not very harmoniously. They say that five or six get together to play, and that the flutes are of different sizes.

"They say that the land is good for maize and beans, that they lack fruit trees and have no knowledge of them. There are very fine forests.[4] The province lacks sufficient water. They do not gather cotton, bringing it from Totonteac. They eat from little flat bowls, as in Mexico. They gather much maize, beans, and other seeds such as sage.[5] They are not familiar with sea fish, nor have they heard of them.

"As to the cattle, there is no other information except that they are found beyond the province of Cíbola. There are numerous wild goats, and they are of the same color as bay horses. Many of them roam around this place where I am located, and although I have asked the Indians if the cattle are like them, they replied that they are not. Of the seven towns, they said that three were very large, the other four not so large. I interpreted their signs to mean that the pueblos were each about three crossbow shots square. And as the Indians

4. The word is *montes,* which usually means wooded hills.
5. The phrase is, "y otras simillas como chia."

describe and represent the houses and their large size, how they are clustered together, and the people in each house, the population must be large.

"We learned that Totonteac lies seven short days from the province of Cíbola, that it is of the same type in houses and people, and that they grow cotton. This I doubt, for I have been told that it is a cold country. They say that there are twelve pueblos, each of which is larger than the largest in Cíbola. They also tell me that there is a pueblo one day's journey from Cíbola, and that they carry on war with each other. The former is affirmed to be larger than any of the others. The houses, people, and ways of trading are similar. I believe that they form a great multitude of people. They are so well known because of their houses and abundant food and turquoises. I have not been able to learn any more than what I have stated, although I brought with me some Indians who have lived there for fifteen and twenty years, as I have said.

"The death of the negro Esteban came about in the manner that Father Fray Marcos must have told your Lordship, and so I shall not tell anything about it here except to say that the people of Cíbola sent word to the people of this pueblo and its environs, telling them that if any Christians should come they should not respect them but kill them, for they were mortal. They were sure of this, they said, because they had the bones of the one who had gone there. If they did not dare to do it they should notify them and they would come and do it themselves. I really believe that it happened thus and that they communicated with the people here, judging by the coldness with which they received us and the mean faces they showed us."

Melchior Díaz says that the people he found along the way have no permanent habitat except those in a small valley located 150 leagues from Culuacán, and which is well settled and has terraced houses. He states that there are many people along the way, but that they are not good for anything unless it be to make Christians of them—as if this were of slight consideration. May your Majesty provide what is best in the service of God and keep in mind the deaths and destruction of people and provinces that have occurred in these Indies. Until today, nothing of what your Majesty has ordered, which was holy and appropriate, has been observed. May you provide friars both for those regions and for these. For I assure you that there is no vestige of Christianity, either much or little, wherever they have not been. The poor people are ready to welcome the friars, and where they flee from us like deer, to the mountains, they come to them. I am saying this as an eyewitness who has seen it very plainly on this trip. I have importuned your Majesty for friars and now can not fail to insist even much more. I would be failing in my duty if I did not do so.

Upon my return to Mexico I shall give your Majesty an account of everything pertaining to these provinces. I could not do it now even if I wanted to because I am very weak as a result of a fever I suffered at Colima; it was very severe although it lasted only six days. By the Lord's will I am well again and I have traveled to this place in Jacona, where I now am.

May our Lord protect the sacred, Cæsarean and Catholic person of your Majesty and prosper and increase your kingdoms and dominions as we, your vassals, desire. From Jacona, April 17, 1540.

The humble servant of Your Holy Majesty, who kisses your royal hands and feet,

Don Antonio de Mendoza

Sacred Cæsarean Catholic Majesty.

LETTER OF CORONADO TO MENDOZA, AUGUST 3, 1540[1]

REPORT GIVEN BY FRANCISCO VÁZQUEZ DE CORO-
NADO, CAPTAIN GENERAL OF THE FORCE THAT
WAS SENT IN THE NAME OF HIS MAJESTY TO THE
NEWLY DISCOVERED COUNTRY, OF WHAT HAP-
PENED ON THE EXPEDITION AFTER APRIL 22 OF
THE PRESENT YEAR, 1540, WHEN HE STARTED
FROM CULIACAN, AND OF WHAT HE FOUND IN THE
COUNTRY THROUGH WHICH HE PASSED.

*Francisco Vázquez starts out from Culiacán with his army, and,
after meeting some hardships on account of bad roads,
reaches the valley of Corazones, where he fails to find any
maize, to procure which he sends [a party] to the valley called
Señora. He receives an account of the important valley of
Corazones, and of its people, and of some islands lying along
the coast.*

On the 22nd of last April, I set out from the province of
Culiacán with part of the army,[2] following the arrangements of
which I wrote to your Lordship. Judging by the outcome, I
feel sure that it was fortunate that I did not employ the whole
of the army in this undertaking, because the hardships have
been so very great and the lack of food such that I do not believe
this enterprise could have been completed before the end of
this year, and even if it should be accomplished, it would be
with a great loss of life. For, as I wrote to your Lordship, I made
the trip from Culiacán in eighty days' travel,[3] during which
the mounted gentlemen in my company and I carried a little

1. Translated from the Italian in Ramusio, *Viaggi*, III, ff. 359-363. There is
an English translation in Hakluyt's *Voyages*, III, pp. 373-380 (ed. 1600), reprinted
in *Old South Leaflet*, general series, no. 20. Translated by Winship in the
Fourteenth Annual Report, pp. 552-565; subsequently reprinted in the Trail
Makers and Grabhorn editions of the Coronado documents. Translated into
French in Ternaux-Compans, *Voyages*, IX, pp. 355-363.
2. This was the select group which went on ahead of the main army. There
were about 75 horsemen and 25 on foot.
3. Winship's translation reads "to Culiacán," but this is an erroneous rendering of the Italian.

food on our backs and on our horses, so that, after leaving this place, we carried no other necessary articles weighing more than a pound. Even then, and although we took all possible care and precautions in the management of the small supply of provisions which we carried, it gave out.

This is no wonder at all, because the road is rough and long, and what with our harquebuses, which had to be carried up the mountains and hills and in crossing the rivers, the greater part of the maize was lost. And since I send your Lordship a drawing of this route, I shall say no more about it here.

Thirty leagues before reaching the place which the father provincial described so well in his report, I sent Melchior Díaz ahead with fifteen horsemen, ordering him to make one day's journey out of two, so that he could examine everything there before I arrived. He traveled through some very rough mountains for four days and did not find anything to live on, nor people, nor information about anything; all he found was two or three poor villages, with twenty or thirty huts each. From the people here he learned that nothing would be found farther on except the continuation of the very rough mountains, entirely uninhabited by people. And, because this was wasted effort, I hesitated to send your Lordship an account of it. The whole company felt displeased at this, that what had been so highly praised and about which the father had told so much, should turn out to be so very different; and they began to believe that all the rest would be of the same sort.

When I noticed this, I tried to encourage them as well as I could, telling them that your Lordship had always thought that this part of the trip would be effort wasted, and that we ought to devote our attention to those Seven Cities and the other provinces about which we had information; that these should be the aim of our enterprise.

With this resolution and purpose, we all marched cheerfully along a very bad trail, where it was impossible to travel without making a new road or clearing the one that was there. This troubled the soldiers not a little, seeing that everything which the friar had reported turned out to be quite the opposite; because, among other things which the father had told and affirmed, was the report that the road would be level and good, and that there was only one small hill, half a league long. And the truth is that there are mountains where, however well the path might be repaired, they could not be crossed without there being great danger of the horses rolling down. And it was so bad that a large number of the animals which your Lordship sent as provisions for the army were lost along this part of the way, on account of the roughness of the rocks. The lambs and wethers lost their hoofs along the way, and I left the greater part of those which I brought from Culiacán at the river of Lachimi[4] because they were unable to travel and in order that they might proceed more slowly. Four horsemen who have just arrived remained with them. They had brought only twenty-four lambs and four wethers; the rest had died from the toil, although they did not travel more than two leagues daily.

At last, on the 26th of May, I reached the valley of Corazones and rested there for several days. From Culiacán to this place I availed myself of nothing but a large supply of corn bread, because I had to leave all the maize, since it was not ripe. In this valley of Corazones we found extensive planted fields and more people than anywhere in the country which we had left behind. There was no eating-corn among them, but as I heard that there was some in another valley called Señora, which I did not wish to disturb by force, I sent Melchior Díaz with goods to exchange for it, so as to give some to the friendly Indians whom we brought with us, and to some who, having lost their animals on the trip, had not been able to carry the provisions which they had taken from Culiacán. By the favor of our Lord, some little maize was obtained by this trading, which relieved the friendly Indians and some Spaniards.

Ten or twelve of the horses had died of exhaustion by the time that we reached this valley of Corazones, because they were unable to stand the strain of carrying heavy burdens and feeding little. For similar reasons some of our negroes and several of the Indians deserted, which was not a slight loss for the expedition.

The natives told me that the valley of Corazones is five

4. The Yaquimi, or Yaqui, river.

days' journey distant from the sea toward the west. I sent to summon Indians from the coast in order to learn about their condition, and while I was waiting for them the horses rested. I stayed there four days, during which time the Indians from the sea came. They told me that, at a distance of two days' journey from the seacoast, there were seven or eight islands, directly opposite from them, well settled with people, but poorly supplied with food, and that the people were savages. They told me that they had seen a ship pass not very far from the land. I do not know whether it was one of those sent to discover the country, or perhaps some Portuguese.

They come to Chichilticale. After resting for two days, they enter a country very poor in provisions and hard to travel for thirty leagues, beyond which they again find pleasant country, and a river called del Lino; they fight against the Indians, being attacked by them; and, having entered the city by their victory, they relieve themselves of the pangs of their hunger.

I set out from Corazones and kept as close to the seacoast as I could judge, but in fact I found myself continually farther from it, so that, when I reached Chichilticale, I found that I was fifteen days' journey distant from the sea, although the father provincial had said that it was only five leagues distant and that he had seen it. We all felt great anxiety and dismay to see that everything was the opposite of what he had told your Lordship. The Indians of Chichilticale say that when they go to the sea for fish, or for anything else that they need, they go across the country, and that it takes them ten days; and this information which I have received from the Indians appears to me to be true. The sea turns toward the west for ten or twelve leagues directly opposite Corazones, where I learned that the ships of your Lordship which had gone in search of the port of Chichilticale, which the father said was at thirty-five degrees, had been seen.

God knows what I have suffered, because I fear that they may have met with some mishap. If they follow the coast, as they said they would, as long as the food lasts which they took with them, of which I left them a supply in Culiacán, and if

they have not been overtaken by some misfortune, I maintain
my trust in God that they will already have discovered something good, for which their delay may be forgiven.

I rested for two days at Chichilticale, and there was good
reason for staying longer, considering how tired the horses
were; but there was no chance to rest further, because the food
was giving out. I entered the borders of the uninhabited region
on Saint John's eve, and, for a change from our past labors, we
found no grass during the first days, but a worse way through
mountains and more dangerous passes than we had experienced
previously. The horses were so exhausted that they could not
stand it, so that in this last desert we lost more horses than
before; and several Indian allies and a Spaniard named Espinosa,
besides two negroes, who died from eating some herbs because
they were out of food.

From this place I sent the maestre de campo, Don García
López de Cárdenas, with fifteen horsemen, a day's march ahead
of me to explore the country and prepare the way, which he
accomplished like the man that he is, justifying the confidence
which your Lordship has placed in him. I am certain that he
did not fail in this task, because, as I have said, the way is very
bad for at least thirty leagues and more, through impassable
mountains. But when we had traversed these thirty leagues,
we found cool rivers, and grass like that of Castile, and especially one kind which is similar to what we call *scaramoio;* we
also found many nut and mulberry trees, but the leaves of the
nut trees are different from those of Spain. There was a considerable amount of flax near the banks of one river, which was
called Rio del Lino on this account.[5]

No Indians were seen during the first day's march, after
which four Indians came out with signs of peace, saying that
they had been sent to that desert place to say that we were
welcome, and that on the next day all the people would meet
us with food. The maestre de campo gave them a cross, telling
them to say to the people in their city that they need not fear,
and that they should have their people remain in their own

5. Hodge suggests that this was probably the Colorado Chiquito.

houses, because I was coming in the name of his Majesty only to defend and help them.

After this was done, Hernando Alvarado came back to tell me that some Indians had come peaceably, and that two of them were waiting for me with the maestre de campo. I went to them and gave them some pater nosters and some little cloaks, telling them to return to their city and tell the people to remain calmly in their houses, and that they need have no fear.

After this I ordered the maestre de campo to go and see if there was any bad passage which the Indians might be able to defend, and to take it and protect it until the next day, when I would come up. He went, and found a very bad place in our way where we might have received much harm. He immediately established himself there with the force which he was conducting. The Indians came that very night to occupy that place so as to defend it, and, finding it taken, they attacked our men. According to what I have been told they attacked like valiant men, although in the end they had to retreat in flight, because the maestre de campo was on the watch and kept his men in good order. The Indians sounded a little trumpet as a sign of retreat, and did no harm to the Spaniards. The maestre de campo sent me notice of this the same night, so that on the next day I started with as good order as I could, for we were in such great need of food that I thought we should all die of hunger if we had to wait another day, especially the Indian allies, since altogether we did not have two bushels of maize, and so I was obliged to hasten forward without delay. The Indians lighted their fires at various places and were answered from a distance, a method of communication as good as we could have devised ourselves. Thus they warned of our coming and where we had arrived.

As soon as I came within sight of this city, I sent the maestre de campo, García López, Fray Daniel, and Fray Luis, and Hernando Bermejo[6] a little way ahead with some horsemen, so that they might find the Indians and tell them that we were not coming to do them any harm, but to defend them in the name

6. Vermizzo, in the Italian. Regarding Fray Daniel, see the Introduction. Hernando Bermejo was the notary of the expedition and Coronado's secretary.

of our lord, the emperor. The requisition, in the form which his Majesty commanded in his instructions, was made intelligible to the people of the country through an interpreter. But they, being a proud people, paid little attention to it, because they thought that, since we were few in number, they would have no difficulty in killing us. They pierced the gown of Fray Luis with an arrow, which, blessed be God, did him no harm.

Meanwhile I arrived with all the rest of the cavalry and footmen and found a large body of Indians on the plain who began to shoot arrows. In obedience to the suggestions of your Lordship and of the marquis,[7] I did not wish that they should be attacked, and enjoined my men, who were begging me for permission, from doing so, telling them that they ought not to molest them, and that the enemy was doing us no harm, and it was not proper to fight such a small number of people. On the other hand, when the Indians saw that we did not move, they took greater courage and grew so bold that they came up almost to the heels of our horses to shoot their arrows. On this account I saw that it was no longer time to hesitate, and, as the priests approved the action, I charged them. There was little to do, because they suddenly took to flight, some running toward the city, which was near and well fortified, and others toward the plain, wherever chance led them.

Some Indians were killed, and others might have been slain if I had allowed them to be pursued. But I saw that there would be little advantage in this, because the Indians who were outside were few, and those who had retired to the city, added to the many who had remained there in the first place, were numerous.

As that was the place where the food was, of which we were in such great need, I assembled my whole force and divided it as seemed to me best for the attack on the city, and surrounded it. As the hunger which we suffered would not permit of any delay, I dismounted with several of these gentlemen and sol-

7. As suggested by previous writers, this is probably a copyist's error for "his Majesty," for in Mexico Cortés was always called the Marquis, and since he was hostile to Mendoza he would not have had anything to do with the Coronado expedition.

diers. I ordered the harquebusiers and crossbowmen to begin the attack and drive back the enemy from the defenses, so that the natives could not injure us. I invested the wall on one side, where I was told that there was a scaling ladder and that there was also a gate. But the crossbowmen soon broke the strings of their crossbows and the musketeers could do nothing, because they had arrived so weak and feeble that they could scarcely stand on their feet.

On this account the people who were on the top for defense were not hindered in the least from doing us whatever injury they were able. As for myself, they knocked me down to the ground twice with countless great stones which they threw down from above, and if I had not been protected by the very good headpiece which I wore, I think that the outcome would have been bad for me. Even then I was picked up from the ground with two small wounds in my face and an arrow in my foot, and with many bruises on my arms and legs, and thus I emerged from the battle, very weak. I think that if Don García López de Cárdenas had not come to my help, like a good cavalier, by placing his own body above mine the second time that they knocked me to the ground, I should have been in much greater danger than I was.[8] But, by the pleasure of God, these Indians surrendered, and their city was taken with the help of our Lord, and a sufficient supply of maize to relieve our needs was found there.[9]

The maestre de campo, Don Pedro de Tovar, Hernando de Alvarado, and Pablo de Melgosa the infantry captain, sustained some bruises, although none of them were wounded. Gómez Xuárez was hit in the arm by an arrow, and one Torres, who lived in Pánuco, in the face by another, and two other footmen received slight arrow wounds. The Indians all directed their attack against me because my armor was gilded and glittering, and on this account I was hurt more than the rest, and not because I had done more or was farther in advance than the

8. Coronado testified in his trial that he was knocked down while trying to scale a ladder to the terrace above. See his testimony, p. 323.

9. The city was the Zuñi pueblo of Hawikuh, twelve miles southwest of the present-day pueblo of Zuñi.

others; for all these gentlemen and soldiers bore themselves well, as was expected of them. I am now well, praised be God, although somewhat sore from the stones. Two or three other soldiers were hurt in the battle which we fought on the plain, and three horses were killed, one belonging to Don García López, another to Villegas, and the third to Don Alonso Manrique. Seven or eight horses were wounded; but now the men, as well as the horses, are healed and well.

Location and condition of the Seven Cities called the kingdom of Cíbola, the sort of people, their customs, and the animals which are found there.

It now remains for me to tell about the Seven Cities, the kingdom and province, of which the father provincial gave your Lordship an account. Not to be too verbose, I can assure you that he has not told the truth in a single thing that he said, but everything is the opposite of what he related, except the name of the cities and the large stone houses. For, although they are not decorated with turquoises, nor made of lime or good bricks, nevertheless they are very good houses, three and four and five stories high, where there are very good homes and good rooms with corridors, and some quite good rooms underground and paved, which are built for winter, and which are something like estufas.[10] Most of the ladders which they have for their houses are movable and portable and are taken up and placed wherever desired. They are made of two pieces of wood, with rungs like ours.

The Seven Cities are seven little villages, all having the kind of houses I have described.[11] They are all within a radius of four leagues. All together they are called the kingdom of Cíbola. Each has its own name, and no single one is called Cíbola, but all together they are called Cíbola. This one which I have called a city I have named Granada, both because it has some similarity to it and in honor of your Lordship. In this one where I am now lodged there are perhaps 200 houses, all sur-

---

10. Spanish for stoves. These were the kivas or ceremonial chambers.
11. According to the studies of Dr. F. W. Hodge, there were only six pueblos here in Coronado's time. See his article, "The Six Cities of Cíbola," in the *New Mexico Historical Review*, I (1926), pp. 478-488.

rounded by a wall, and it seems to me that, together with the others which are not so surrounded, there might be in all 500 hearths.

There is another town near by, which is one of the seven, but somewhat larger than this, and another of the same size as this; the other four are somewhat smaller. I am sending a sketch of them all, and of the route, to your Lordship. The skin on which the painting is made was found here with other skins.

The people of these towns seem to me to be fairly large, and intelligent, although I do not think that they have the judgment and intelligence needed to be able to build these houses in the way in which they are built, for most of them are entirely naked except for the covering of their privy parts. They have painted blankets like the one which I am sending to you. They do not raise cotton, because the country is extremely cold, but they wear blankets, as you may see by the sample which I am sending. It is also true that some cotton thread was found in their houses. They wear the hair on their heads like the Mexicans. They are all well built and comely. I think that they have a quantity of turquoises, which they had removed with the rest of their goods, except the maize, because, when I arrived, I did not find any women here nor any men under fifteen years or over sixty, except two or three old men who remained in command of all the other young men and the warriors. Two points of emerald and some little broken stones, rather poor, which approach the color of garnet, were found in a paper, besides other stone crystals, which I gave to one of my servants to keep until they could be sent to your Lordship. He has lost them, so they tell me.

We found fowl, but only a few, although there are some. The Indians tell me that they do not eat them in any of the seven villages, but that they keep them merely for the sake of procuring the feathers.[12] I do not believe this, because they are very good and larger than those of Mexico.

The climate of this country and the temperature of the air are almost like those of Mexico, because now it is hot and now it rains. I have not yet seen it rain, however, except once when

12. On the basis of his excavations at Hawikuh, Dr. Hodge concluded that turkeys must have been raised for food as well as for feathers.

there fell a little shower with wind, such as often falls in Spain. The snow and the cold are unusually great, according to what the natives of the country say. This may very probably be so, to judge by the nature of the country and the sort of houses they build and the skins and other things which these people have to protect themselves from the cold.

There are no fruits or fruit trees. The country is all level and is nowhere shut in by high mountains, although there are some hills and rough passages. There are not many birds, probably because of the cold and because there are no mountains near. There are not many trees fit for firewood here, although they can bring enough for their needs from a clump of very small junipers[13] four leagues distant. Very good grass was found a quarter of a league away, both for pasturage for our horses and for mowing for making hay, of which we had great need, because our horses were so weak and feeble when they arrived.

The food which they eat in this country consists of maize, of which they have great abundance, beans and game, which they must eat (although they say that they do not), because we found many skins of deer, hares, and rabbits. They make the best tortillas that I have ever seen anywhere, and this is what everybody ordinarily eats. They have the very best arrangement and method for grinding that was ever seen. One of these Indian women here will grind as much as four of the Mexicans do. They have very good salt in crystals, which they bring from a lake a day's journey distant from here.

I have gained no information from them about the North sea or that on the west, nor am I able to tell your Lordship which we are nearest to. I should judge that we are nearer to the western, and 150 leagues is the nearest that it seems to me it can be to there. The North sea must be much farther away.

Your Lordship may thus see how extensive this country is. There are many animals, bears, tigers, lions, porcupines, and

---

13. This word has usually been translated as "cedars," but Dr. E. F. Castetter, of the University of New Mexico department of biology, informs us that there are no real cedars in New Mexico—they are junipers.

some sheep as big as horses, with very large horns and little tails. I have seen some of their horns, the size of which was something amazing. There are wild goats, whose heads I have also seen, and the paws of the bears and the skins of the wild boars. For game they have deer, leopards, and very large roebucks. Everyone thinks that some of them are larger than the animal with which your Lordship favored me, which belonged to Juan Melaz. They inhabit some plains eight days' journey toward the North sea. The natives here have some very well-dressed skins, and they prepare and paint them where they kill the cattle, according to what they tell me.

Describing the nature and location of the kingdoms of Totonteac, Marata, and Acus, wholly different from the account of Fray Marcos; the conference which they had with the Indians of the city of Granada, which they had captured, who had been forewarned of the coming of Christians into their country fifty years before; the account which was obtained from them concerning seven other cities, of which Tucano is the chief, and how he sent to discover them; a present sent to Mendoza of various things found in this country by Vázquez de Coronado.

The kingdom of Totonteac, which the father provincial praised so much, saying that it was something marvelous, and of much richness, and that cloth was made there, is, according to the Indians, a hot lake, on the edge of which there are five or six houses. There used to be some others, but they have been destroyed by war. The kingdom of Marata can not be found, nor do these Indians know anything about it. The kingdom of Acus is a single small city, where they raise cotton, and is called Acucu.[14] I say that this is the town, because Acus, with or without the aspiration, is not a word of this region; and because it seems to me that Acucu may be derived from Acus, I say that it is this town which has been converted into the kingdom of Acus. They tell me that there are some other small kingdoms

14. It is the belief of Dr. Hodge, whose investigations in the Hawikuh area have not been surpassed, that the "hot lake" referred to above was really the salt lake previously mentioned. Totonteac was Tusayán, Acus, or Acuco, was Acoma, while Marata has not been satisfactorily identified. *History of Hawikuh, New Mexico,* p. 43 and *passim.*

not far from this settlement, which are situated on a river, which I have seen, and of which the Indians have told me.

God knows that I wish I had better news to write to your Lordship, but I must tell you the truth, and, as I wrote you from Culiacán, I must inform you of the good as well as of the bad. But you may be assured that if all the riches and treasures of the world had been here, I could not have done more in his Majesty's service and in that of your Lordship than I have done in coming here where you commanded me, carrying, both my companions and myself, our provisions on our backs for 300 leagues, and traveling on foot many days, making our way over hills and rough mountains, besides other hardships which I refrain from mentioning. Nor shall I think of stopping until my death, if it serves his Majesty or your Lordship to have it so.

Three days after I captured this city, some of the Indians who lived here came to make peace. They brought me some turquoises and poor blankets, and I welcomed them in his Majesty's name with the kindest words I could say, making them understand the purpose of my coming to this country, which is, in the name of his Majesty and by the command of your Lordship, that they and all others in this province should become Christians and should accept the true God as their Lord and his Majesty as their king and earthly master. After this they returned to their houses, and suddenly, the next day, they packed up their goods and property, their women and children, and fled to the hills, leaving their towns deserted, with only some few remaining in them. Seeing this, eight or ten days later, when I had recovered from my wounds, I went to the town which I said was larger than this. I found only a few natives there, and I told them that they need not have any fear, and I asked them to summon their lord to me. Although, by what I can find out or observe, none of these towns has any, since I have not seen any principal house by which any superiority over others could be shown.

Later, an old man, who said he was their lord, came with a portion of a blanket made of many pieces, and I talked with him as long as he stayed with me. He said that he would come to see me with the rest of the chiefs of the country, three days later, in order to arrange the relations which should exist between us. He did so, and they brought me some little ragged blankets and some turquoises. They agreed to come down from their strongholds and return to their houses with their wives and children, and that they would become Christians and recognize his Majesty as their king and lord. But they still remain in their strongholds, with their wives and all their property.

I asked them to have a cloth painted for me, with all the animals that they know in that country, and, although they are poor painters, they quickly painted two for us, one of the animals and the other of the birds and fishes. They say that they will bring their children so that our priests may instruct them, and that they desire to know our law. They declare that it was foretold them more than fifty years ago that a people such as we are would come, and from the direction we have come, and that the whole country would be conquered.

So far as I can find out, these Indians worship the water, because they say that it makes the maize grow and sustains their life, and that the only other reason they know is that their ancestors did so.

I have tried in every way to find out from the natives of these pueblos whether they know of any other peoples or provinces or cities. They told me about seven cities which are at a considerable distance, which are like these, except that the houses there are not like these, but are made of earth, and small; and that they raise much cotton there. The first of these four places about which they know is called, they say, Tucano.[15] They could not tell me much about the others. I do not believe that they tell me the truth, because they think that in any case I shall soon have to depart from among them and return home. But they will quickly find that they are deceived in this. I sent Don Pedro de Tovar there with his company and some other horsemen to see it. I would not have dispatched this package to your Lordship until I had learned what he found there if I thought that I could have any news from him within twelve or fifteen days. However, as he will remain away at least thirty, and, considering that this information is of little importance

15. The Hopi pueblos.

and that the cold and the rains are approaching, it seemed to me that I ought to do as your Lordship commanded me in your instructions, which is, that as soon as I arrived here, I should advise you thereof, and this I do, by sending you the plain narrative of what I have seen, which is bad enough, as you may perceive.

I have determined to send men throughout all the surrounding regions in order to find out whether there is anything, and to suffer every extremity rather than give up this enterprise, and to serve his Majesty, if I can find any way in which to do it, and not to be lacking in diligence until your Lordship directs me as to what I ought to do.

We are in great need of pasture, and you should know also that among all those who are here there is not one pound of raisins, nor sugar, nor oil, nor wine, except barely half a quart, which is saved to say mass, since everything has been consumed, and part was lost on the way. Now, you can provide us with what appears best; but, if you are thinking of sending us cattle, you should know that it will be necessary for them to spend at least a year on the road, because they can not come in any other way, nor any quicker. I would have liked to send you, with this dispatch, many samples of the things which they have in this country, but the trip is so long and rough that it is difficult for me to do so. However, I am sending you twelve small blankets, such as the people of this country ordinarily wear, and a garment which seems to me to be very well made. I kept it because it seemed to me to be of very good workmanship and because I do not think that any one else has ever seen in these Indies any work done with a needle, unless it was done since the Spaniards settled here. I am also sending two cloths, painted with the animals which they have in this country, although, as I said, the painting is very poorly done, because the artist did not spend more than one day in painting it. I have seen other paintings on the walls of these houses which have much better proportion and are done much better.

I am sending you a cattle skin, some turquoises, and two

earrings of the same, and fifteen Indian combs,[16] and some boards decorated with these turquoises, and two baskets made of wicker, of which the Indians have a large supply. I also send two rolls, such as the women usually wear on their heads when they bring water from the spring, the same way that they do in Spain. One of these Indian women, with one of these rolls on her head, will carry a jar of water up a ladder without touching it with her hands. And, lastly, I send you samples of the weapons with which the natives of this country fight, a shield, a mallet, and a bow with some arrows, among which there are two with bone points, the like of which have never been seen, according to what these conquerors say.[17]

As far as I can judge, it does not appear to me that there is any hope of getting gold or silver, but I trust in God that, if there is any, we shall get our share of it, and it shall not escape us through any lack of diligence in the search.

I am unable to give your Lordship any certain information about the dress of the women, because the Indians keep them guarded so carefully that I have not seen any, except two old ones. These had on two long shirts reaching down to their feet and open in front, and a girdle, and they are tied together with some cotton strings. I asked the Indians to give me one of those which they wore to send to you, since they were not willing to show me the women. They brought me two blankets, which are these that I am sending, almost painted over.[18] They wear earrings, like the women of Spain, which hang somewhat over their shoulders.

The death of the negro is perfectly certain, because many of the things which he wore have been found, and the Indians say that they killed him here because the Indians of Chichilticale said that he was a bad man, and not like the Christians who never kill women, and he killed them, and because he assaulted

16. The earrings and combs were made of wood inlaid with turquoise. See F. W. Hodge, "Turquois Work of Hawikuh, New Mexico." *Leaflets of the Museum of the American Indian*, no. 2, New York, 1921.

17. These mallets were short war clubs. Dr. Hodge has pointed out that bone arrowpoints were found in the excavation of Hawikuh. "Hawikuh Bonework," *Indian Notes and Monographs*, III, no. 3, New York, 1920.

18. Archaeologists point out that such references to painted blankets probably have reference to embroidered articles.

their women, whom the Indians love better than themselves. Therefore they determined to kill him, but they did not do it in the way that was reported, because they did not kill any of the others who came with him, nor did they wound the lad from the province of Petatlán, who was with him, but they took him and kept him in safe custody until now. When I tried to secure him, they made excuses for not giving him to me, for two or three days, saying that he was dead, and at other times that the Indians of Acucu had taken him away. But when I finally told them that I should be very angry if they did not give him to me, they did so. He is an interpreter; although he can not talk much, he understands very well.

Some gold and silver has been found in this place, which those who know about minerals say is not bad. I have not yet been able to learn from these people where they got it. I perceive that they refuse to tell me the truth in everything, because they think that I shall have to depart from here in a short time, as I have said. But I trust in God that they will not be able to avoid answering much longer.

I beg your Lordship to make a report of the successes of this expedition to his Majesty, because there is nothing more than what I have already said. I shall not do so until it shall please God to grant that we find what we desire.

Our Lord God protect and keep your most illustrious Lordship.

From the province of Cíbola and this city of Granada, the 3rd of August, 1540.

Francisco Vázquez de Coronado kisses the hand of your most illustrious Lordship.

TRASLADO DE LAS NUEVAS

Transcript of the Information and News They Furnished Concerning the Finding of a City, Which They Named Cíbola, Located in the New Land.[1]

His Grace left most of his army at the valley of Culiacán, and with only seventy-five mounted followers and thirty footmen he set out in this direction on Thursday, April 22. The army which remained there was to start out at the end of May. He did not dare to take the whole army along because he received information that all the way to the province of Cíbola, which is 350 long leagues, they would find no provisions of any kind. He ordered that the men he took with him should bring supplies for eighty days. These supplies were carried on horseback, each man taking enough for himself and his followers, at no small labor lest they perish from hunger. And because they explored and opened new trails each day, part of their provisions were lost at the rough passes, rivers, and in the brush. On the whole trip to this province not a single peck of maize was obtained.

His Grace arrived in this province on Wednesday, the 7th of this past July, with all the people with whom he set out from the valley, all well, the Lord be praised, except one Spaniard who died of hunger four days back, and some negroes and Indians who likewise perished from hunger and thirst. The Spaniard was a footman named Espinosa.

So his Grace employed seventy-seven days on the trip here.[2] During this time the Lord knows how frugally we lived, and

1. Translated from Pacheco y Cárdenas, *Documentos de Indias*, XIX, pp. 529-532. Translated in Winship, *Fourteenth Annual Report*, pp. 564-565; reprinted in the Trail Makers and Grabhorn editions. Dr. Hodge has suggested that this anonymous report may have been written by Don García López de Cárdenas, Coronado's chief lieutenant, since the report does not mention the bravery of this officer in defending Coronado when he was struck down. *Journey of Coronado* (1933), p. 100, note 1.
2. That is, from Culiacán.

whether we could have eaten much more than we did on the day when his Grace arrived in this city of Granada, for thus it was named in honor of the viceroy and because some say that it resembles the Albaicín.[3] His people were not received as they should have been, being then all exhausted from the hardships of the trip, of packing and unpacking like muleteers, of not eating as much as they would have liked to, and arriving more in need of a few days' rest than fighting, although there was not a man in the whole army who would not fight if the horses could have helped, but the latter were suffering from the same privations as their masters.

The city had been evacuated by all men over sixty years and under twenty, and by the women and children. All those in the city were warriors who had remained to defend it. Many came out about a crossbow shot, making great threats. The general approached them in person, accompanied by two friars and the maestre de campo, to request them to surrender, as is customary in new lands. Their answer was the large number of arrows which they shot. They wounded Hernando Bermejo's horse, and Father Fray Luis, a former companion of the bishop of Mexico, had the skirt of his frock pierced by an arrow. Seeing this and invoking Santiago, the general attacked them with all his men, whom he had deployed very well. The Indians turned back and thought that they would retire to the city, which was close at hand, but before they reached it they were overtaken and many of them were killed. They killed three horses and wounded seven or eight others.

When the general, my master, reached the city he found that it was protected by a stone wall, and the houses were very tall, of four, five, and even six stories each, with terraces and corridors. As the Indians fortified themselves there and would not allow a man to approach the wall without shooting arrows at him, and as we had nothing to eat unless we took it from them, his Grace decided to enter the city on foot and to surround it by the men on horseback in order that no Indian from the inside might escape. As he stood out among all the others because of his gilded armor and some plumes in his helmet, all the Indians

3. A part of Granada, near the Alhambra.

shot at him, as a marked man. He was felled twice by stones hurled from the terraces. His helmet was dented, and had it not been of such excellent quality I doubt that he would have escaped alive from the place. Withal, our Lord is my witness that he came out on his own feet. He received many stone blows on his head, shoulders, and legs, and received two slight wounds on his face, and an arrow shot in his right foot; nevertheless, his Grace is as hale and hearty as on the day he departed from that city. Your Grace may so certify it to my Lord;[4] and that on July 19 last he went four leagues from this city to inspect a rock,[5] where he was told the Indians of this province were offering resistance. He returned the same day, traveling eight leagues in going and coming.

It has seemed appropriate for me to give your Grace an account of it all, for it is fitting that I, together with your Grace and my Lord, should be the narrator of all that concerns the health of the general, my master. You may, without any hesitation, make it clear that he is quartered in the pueblo and as well and hale as on the day he left the city. For when the Indians saw the determination of his Grace to enter their pueblo, they abandoned it, and they were allowed to leave without threat to their lives. There we found something we prized more than gold or silver, namely, much maize, beans, and chickens larger than those here of New Spain, and salt better and whiter than I have ever seen in my whole life.

4. The Spanish reads: "y asi lo puede V. M. certificar a mi señor;" perhaps the meaning is that "your Grace may assure my lord, the king" of this.

5. Tówayálane, or Corn Mountain, refuge of the Zuñis in times of danger. Hodge, *History of Hawikuh,* pp. 90, 92, 106-107.

DISCOVERY OF TIGUEX BY ALVARADO AND PADILLA

ACCOUNT OF WHAT HERNANDO DE ALVARADO AND FRAY JUAN DE PADILLA DISCOVERED WHILE IN SEARCH OF THE SOUTH SEA.[1]

We set out from Granada toward Coco[2] on Sunday, August 29, 1540, feast day of the beheaded Saint John. After marching two leagues we reached an old building resembling a fortress; a league farther on we found another one, and a little farther on still another. Beyond them we came to an old city, quite large, all in ruins, although a large portion of the wall which must have been six estados high, was still standing. The wall was well built of fine cut stone, with gates and gutters like a Castilian city. Half a league farther on, about a league from the latter,[3] we found the ruins of another city. Its wall must have been very good, about an estado high, built of very large granite stones, and above this of very fine hewn blocks of stone.

Two roads branch out here, one to Chia,[4] the other to Coco. We followed the latter, and reached the said place, which was one of the strongest ever seen, because the city is built on a very high rock. The ascent is so difficult that we repented climbing to the top. The houses are three and four stories high. The people are of the same type as those in the province of Cíbola. They have abundant provisions of maize, beans, and chickens like those of New Spain.

1. Translated from Pacheco y Cárdenas, III, pp. 511-513. Printed in Spanish in Buckingham Smith's *Colección de Varios Documentos para la Historia de la Florida*, Madrid, 1857, pp. 65-66; English translation by Winship in *Fourteenth Annual Report*, pp. 594-595; reprinted in the Trail Makers and Grabhorn editions.

2. Coco, or Acoma. Hodge points out that Alvarado's route lay directly eastward from Hawikuh to Acoma by way of the Ojo Caliente valley, whereas Coronado went by way of Matsaki, farther north. *History of Hawikuh*, p. 42. Hodge adds, however, that "no Zuñi Indian of the present time is known to have taken this trail [Ojo Caliente] through to Acoma."

3. The Spanish original contains this phrase, though it seems that there may be a copyist's error here.

4. Chia was Zia.

From here we went to a fine lake, at which there are trees like those of Castile.[5] From there we marched to a river which we named Nuestra Señora,[6] because we reached it on the eve before her feast day in the month of September. We sent the cross by a guide to the pueblos ahead. On the following day, from twelve pueblos, there came chieftains and people in proper order, those of one pueblo after the other. They marched around the tent, playing a flute, and with an old man for spokesman. In this manner they came inside the tent and presented me with the food, blankets, and skins they had. I gave them some small articles, whereupon they went away.

This Nuestra Señora river flows through a broad valley planted with fields of maize. There are some cottonwood groves. There are twelve pueblos.[7] The houses are of mud, two stories high. The people seem good, more given to farming than to war. They have provisions of maize, beans, melons, and chickens in great abundance. They dress in cotton, cattle skins, and coats made with the feathers from the chickens. They wear their hair short. The old men are the ones who have the most authority among them. We thought they were witches because they said that they could rise to heaven, and other things of the sort. There are in this province seven other pueblos, uninhabited and in ruins, belonging to the Indians who daub their eyes, and about whom the guides told your Lordship. They say that they border on the cattle, and that they have maize and straw houses.[8]

At this place the Indians from the surrounding provinces came to offer me peace. These provinces are the ones your Lordship will note in the report, in which will be found eighty pueblos of the type I have described. Among them there was one located among some banks. It must have twenty districts, and is well worth seeing.[9] The houses have three stories of mud walls and three others of wood or small timbers. On the three

5. Hodge notes that this lake was the one from which the later pueblo of Laguna derived its name.
6. The present Rio Grande.
7. They comprised the Tiguex province, in the vicinity of the modern Albuquerque-Bernalillo area.
8. Hodge points out that the marauders were the warlike Teyas of Texas.
9. The pueblo of Taos.

stories of mud there are three terraces on the outside. We thought this pueblo must have had up to fifteen thousand people. The country is very cold. They do not raise chickens or cotton. They worship the sun and the water. Outside of the pueblo we found dirt mounds, in which they bury their people.

In the places where we erected crosses we taught the natives to worship them, and they offered them their powders[10] and feathers, some even the blankets they were wearing. They did it with such eagerness that some climbed on the backs of others in order to reach the arms of the crosses to put plumes and roses on them. Others brought ladders, and while some held them others climbed up to tie strings in order to fasten the roses and the feathers.

10. Sacred corn meal.

LETTER OF CORONADO TO THE KING

LETTER OF FRANCISCO VÁZQUEZ DE CORONADO TO HIS MAJESTY, GIVING AN ACCOUNT OF THE DISCOVERY OF THE PROVINCE OF TIGUEX. OCTOBER 20, 1541.[1]

Holy Cæsarean Catholic Majesty:

On April 20 of the present year I wrote to your Majesty from this province of Tiguex, in reply to your letter of last year written at Madrid on June 11. I gave you a detailed report and account of this expedition, which the viceroy of New Spain ordered me to make, in the name of your Majesty, to this land that had been discovered by Fray Marcos de Niza, provincial of the order of Saint Francis. I reported on the entire country, on the type of people, as you must have noted by my letters.

While I was engaged in the conquest and pacification of the natives of this province, some Indians, natives of other provinces beyond these, told me that in their lands there were much larger pueblos and better houses than those in this land, that they had lords who governed them, and that they used gold vessels, together with other magnificent things. As I wrote to your Majesty, however, since these accounts were given by Indians and, furthermore, had been obtained by signs, I did not give them credence until I could verify them with my own eyes. Since the information seemed valuable to me, and it was befitting the service of your Majesty that it should be investigated, I decided to go with the men I have here and to see it for myself.

1. Translated from the text in Pacheco y Cárdenas, *Documentos de Indias,* III, pp. 363-369. English translation by Winship in *Fourteenth Annual Report,* pp. 580-583; reprinted in the Trail Makers and Grabhorn editions; reprinted in *American History Leaflet,* no. 13. A French translation is found in Ternaux-Compans, *Voyages,* IX, pp. 355-363. The title in the Muñoz copy is: "Letter of Francisco Vázquez Coronado to the Emperor giving an account of the expedition to the province of Quivira, and of the inaccuracy of what Fray Marcos de Niza has told about the country." The text is exactly the same in both copies.

I set out from this province[2] on the 23rd of last April, going the way the Indians guided me. After traveling nine days I came to some plains, so vast that in my travels I did not reach their end, although I marched over them for more than three hundred leagues. On them I found so many cattle, about which I wrote to your Majesty, that it would be impossible to estimate their number. For in traveling over the plains, there was not a single day, until my return, that I lost sight of them.

After seventeen days of travel, I came upon a ranchería of the Indians who follow these cattle. These natives are called Querechos. They do not cultivate the land, but eat raw meat and drink the blood of the cattle they kill. They dress in the skins of the cattle, with which all the people in this land clothe themselves, and they have very well-constructed tents, made with tanned and greased cowhides, in which they live and which they take along as they follow the cattle. They have dogs which they load to carry their tents, poles, and belongings. These people have the best physique of any I have seen in the Indies. They could not tell me anything about the land to which the guides were taking me.

For five days I went wherever they led me, until we reached some plains as bare of landmarks as if we were surrounded by the sea. Here the guides lost their bearings because there is nowhere a stone, hill, tree, bush, or anything of the sort. There are many excellent pastures with fine grass. While we wandered aimlessly over these plains, some mounted men who went out hunting the cattle met some Indians who were also out hunting and who are enemies of those I met at the previous ranchería. They belong to another nation of people called the Teyas. They paint their bodies and faces and are large people of very fine appearance. They, too, eat raw meat like the Querechos. They live like them and follow the cattle. From them I obtained information concerning the land where the guides were leading me, but their reports did not agree with those I had been given, for these Indians described the houses there as being of straw and hides and not of stone and several stories

2. Of Tiguex.

high, as painted by my guides. Furthermore, the land was poor in maize.

This information caused me considerable worry, and I also suffered greatly from lack of water on finding myself in those endless plains. Many times I drank some which was so bad that it tasted more like slime than water. There the guides confessed that they had not told me the truth regarding the grandeur of the houses, for they were only of straw, but that what they said concerning the large number of people and other things relating to their government was true. The Teyas contradicted this.

In view of this division of opinion among the Indians, and also because many of the people who accompanied me had not eaten anything except meat for several days, for the maize we had taken with us from this province[3] had been exhausted, I decided to go ahead with only thirty horsemen and reach the land, see it, and give a reliable report to you of what was found there. And though it was more than forty days' travel from the place where I met these Teyas to the land where the guides were leading me, and though I realized the hardships and danger I would meet on the journey due to lack of water and maize, I thought it best to go in order to serve your Majesty. I sent the rest of the people I had with me back to this province,[3] under the leadership of Don Tristán de Arellano. For if they had all gone ahead the death of many men could not have been avoided, as water was scarce and there were no other provisions except the food that they got by hunting the cattle.

With only thirty horsemen that I took with me as escort, I traveled forty-two days after leaving the army. During all this time we lived on only the meat of the bulls and cows we killed, at the cost of some horses killed by the cattle, for, as I told your Majesty, the animals are very wild and fierce. We went without water for many days and had to cook our food on cow dung, because there is no other fuel in all these plains, except along the arroyos and rivers, of which there are very few.

After traveling seventy-seven days over these barren lands, our Lord willed that I should arrive in the province called Quivira, to which the guides were taking me. They had pic-

3. Tiguex.

tured it as having stone houses many stories high; not only are
there none of stone, but, on the contrary, they are of straw, and
the people are savage like all I have seen and passed up to this
place. They have no blankets, nor cotton with which to make
them. All they have is the tanned skins of the cattle they kill,
for the herds are near where they live, at quite a large river.
They eat the meat raw like the Querechos and the Teyas. They
are enemies of one another, but they are all people of the same
type. These people of Quivira have the advantage over the
others in their houses and in the growing of maize. In this
province, of which my guides are natives, I was received peacefully.

Although when I set out for the province I was told that I
could not see it all in two months, there are not more than
twenty-five towns, with straw houses, in it, nor any more in all
the rest of the country that I have seen and learned about. They
gave allegiance to your Majesty and placed themselves under
your royal authority. The people are large. I had some Indians
measured and found that they were ten spans tall. The women
are comely, with faces more like Moorish than Indian women.
The natives there gave me a piece of copper that an Indian
chief wore suspended from his neck. I am sending it to the
viceroy of New Spain, for I have not seen any other metal in
this region except this and some copper jingle bells which I am
forwarding to him. I am also sending a small amount of metal
which resembles gold, but I could not find out where it was
obtained, although I believe the Indians who gave it to me got
it from the servants that accompanied me. I can not account for
its presence or its origin otherwise.

As I have been obliged to send captains and soldiers to many
places in this country to find out whether there was anything
by which your Majesty could be served, the diversity of languages spoken in this land and the lack of people who understand them has been a great handicap to me, since the people
in each town speak their own. And although we have searched
with all diligence we have not found or heard of any towns,
except those in these provinces, which do not amount to very
much.

The province of Quivira is 950 leagues from Mexico by the way I came. It is at a latitude of forty degrees. The soil itself is the most suitable that has been found for growing all the products of Spain, for, besides being rich and black, it is well watered by arroyos, springs, and rivers. I found plums[4] like those of Spain, nuts, fine sweet grapes, and mulberries.

As your Majesty has ordered, I have given the best treatment possible to the natives of this province and to others I met on my trip. They have not been injured by me in any way or by those who came with me.

I spent twenty-five days in this province of Quivira both to see and examine the land and also to find out whether there was anything farther on by which your Majesty might be served, because my guides had told me of other provinces beyond this one. The information I gathered was that there was no gold or other metal in all that country. The other provinces of which they told me are nothing more than small pueblos. In many of them they do not farm, neither do they have houses, except some built of skins and reeds. They move about following the cattle.

So the account they gave me was false—given to induce me to go there with all the army, believing that, as the route was so barren and uninhabited and lacking in water, they would take us to a place where we and our horses would starve to death. The guides admitted this much, saying that they had done it on the advice of the natives of these provinces.

Withal, after visiting the land of Quivira and obtaining the information of the region farther on, mentioned above, I returned to this province to look after the force that I had sent there and to send your Majesty a report of the nature of the land, as I had written you that I would do as soon as I had seen it. I have done everything within my power to serve you, as your faithful servant and vassal, and to discover a country where God, our Lord, might be served by extending your royal patrimony. From the moment I arrived in the province of Cíbola, where the viceroy of New Spain had sent me in the

4. Another version of this document in the Archives of the Indies does not mention plums, but says, "I found all the products of Spain . . ."

name of your Majesty, I began to explore this land for two hundred leagues and more around and beyond Cíbola, in view of the fact that nothing was found there of what Fray Marcos had said. The best I have found is this Tiguex river, where I am camping, and the settlements here. They are not suitable for settling, because, besides being four hundred leagues from the North sea, and more than two hundred from the South sea, thus prohibiting all intercourse, the land is so cold, as I have related to your Majesty, that it seems impossible for one to be able to spend the winter here, since there is no firewood or clothing with which the men may keep themselves warm, except the skins that the natives wear, and some cotton blankets, few in number.

I am sending the viceroy of New Spain a report of everything I have seen in the lands that I have traversed. And, since Don García López de Cárdenas, after working diligently and serving your Majesty well in this expedition, is leaving to kiss your hands, he will inform you of everything here as a man who has seen it, and I leave the matter in his hands.

May our Lord protect the sacred Cæsarean Catholic person of your Majesty, increasing your kingdoms and dominions, as we, your faithful servants and vassals, desire. From this province of Tiguex, October 20, 1541.

Your Majesty's humble servant and vassal, who kisses your royal feet and hands,

FRANCISCO VÁZQUEZ DE CORONADO
Sacred Cæsarean Catholic Majesty.

CASTAÑEDA'S HISTORY OF THE EXPEDITION

NARRATIVE OF THE EXPEDITION TO CÍBOLA, UNDER-
TAKEN IN 1540, IN WHICH ARE DESCRIBED ALL
THOSE SETTLEMENTS, CEREMONIES, AND CUS-
TOMS. WRITTEN BY PEDRO DE CASTAÑEDA OF
NÁXERA.[1]

PREFACE

It seems to me, most noble Sir, that the desire to learn and
the eagerness to acquire truthful information concerning matters or events that have taken place in remote regions, and of

---

1. The identity of Pedro de Castañeda de Nájera has long been a puzzling
problem. Undoubtedly the most famous of the chroniclers of the Coronado
expedition, he remains almost unknown, except for the account he wrote of this
venture some years after the return from the Cíbola entrada. The following
facts appear to have some bearing on this question.

We know from Castañeda's own history that he lived at San Miguel de
Culiacán, though he does not explain whether he joined the expedition there or
at Compostela. On his return from the north, however, he left the army at
Culiacán when it passed through his home town.

In the muster roll of the Coronado expedition there appears a Pedro de
Nájera, without any mention as to where he was from. If we turn to Fray
Antonio Tello's *Crónica Miscelánea*, p. 135, we find that he lists the settlers of
San Miguel de Culiacán, and he devotes one special paragraph to "Pobladores
Antiguos," in which he lists five men. They are Don Pedro de Tovar, who
became chief ensign of the Coronado expedition; Diego López, alderman from
Seville, a captain in Coronado's force; Esteban Martín and Juan de Medina, both
from Seville, and Pedro de Nájera, from Baeza. Of these five citizens of Culiacán,
listed as old settlers by Tello, four, all except Medina, went with the Coronado
expedition, two of them as high officers. On checking the muster roll drawn up
at Compostela, we find that these four men appear among those present on that
famous occasion. In other words, these Culiacán settlers did not hesitate to go to
Compostela to enroll among those enlisted in the great enterprise.

With these facts in mind, and remembering that Pedro de Castañeda, the
chronicler, came from Culiacán, it is not hard to identify Pedro de Nájera, the
old settler of Culiacán, and Pedro de Castañeda as one and the same person. Perhaps the Pedro de Castañeda de Nájera family had moved to Baeza, and from
there to the Indies, with the result that Tello records Baeza as his home, whereas
in the Castañeda history we find simply his name on two occasions: once on the
title page, neatly lettered, and again on the title page of the second part. In
each case, the name is written "Pedro de Castañeda de Náxera."

It would really seem strange that a man of as much prominence as Pedro de
Castañeda in the small village of Culiacán, founded in 1531, would not be mentioned in Tello's list of the early settlers.

which there is little knowledge, is an appropriate thing indeed and one that is common in virtuous men. Therefore, I do not reproach some inquisitive persons who, doubtless with good intentions, have often importuned me considerably to explain and clarify for them some doubts generally held regarding specific matters which they had heard took place during events of the expedition to Cíbola, or the new land, which the good viceroy, Don Antonio de Mendoza,[2]—may he be with God in His glory—planned and ordered, and on which he sent Francisco Vázquez de Coronado as captain general.

They are right, indeed, in wanting to learn the truth, for the reason that people very frequently magnify or belittle, without regard to reality, things which they have heard, perhaps from those who were not familiar with them. Matters of importance, they reduce to nothing; and those that are insignificant they convert into such remarkable ones that they appear incredible. This may very well have been caused by the fact that, as the land was not permanently occupied, no one has been willing to spend his time writing about its peculiarities. Wherefore there was lost the information of that which God did not permit—He knows why—that they should enjoy. Indeed, whoever should wish to busy himself writing about what happened in the expedition, as well as what was seen in those lands and the ceremonies and customs of the natives, would have plenty of substance with which to test his mind. And I believe that he would not lack material, which, if presented truthfully, would be so marvelous as to seem incredible.

Furthermore, I believe that some of the stories told are the result of the twenty years and more that have passed since that expedition took place. I say this because some make it an uninhabitable land, others have it bordering on La Florida, others on Greater India, which seems to be no small exaggeration. They may have some basis or cause on which to found their assertions. There are, likewise, those who tell about some very strange animals, while others who went on the expedition affirm that there are no such animals and that they have not been seen.

2. The chief study of Antonio de Mendoza, first viceroy of New Spain, is by A. S. Aiton, Durham, N. C., 1927.

Others differ as to the location of the provinces, and even as to the matter of customs and dress, attributing to one people what pertains to others. All of this has been the chief cause that moved me, most noble Sir, although late, to the desire of writing a brief general account for all those who are by nature inquisitive, and also to save myself the time of which I am deprived through inquiries. In it will be found things difficult to believe, indeed. All of which, or most of them, I have seen with my own eyes; others I have learned through reliable information, obtained from the natives themselves.

Realizing as I do that this little work of mine would be valueless in itself or lack acceptance unless it were favored and protected by a person whose authority would check the boldness of those who, without any consideration, give free rein to their wagging tongues, and knowing, as I do, under what great obligation I have always been and am to your Lordship, I humbly beg, as a true vassal and servant, that this little work be received under your protection.

The book is divided into three parts so that it may be better understood. The first will tell of the discovery of the new land and the force or army that was organized, of the entire expedition, and the captains who went with it. The second will describe the locations of the pueblos and provinces that were found, their ceremonies and customs, and the animals, fruits, and vegetation, and in what parts of the land they are found. The third will narrate the return of the army and the reasons for the abandonment of the land, although they were not valid, since this is the best place from which to explore the interior of the land in these western regions, as will be seen, and as has been made clear since that time. Finally there will be related some of the remarkable things that were observed and the route by which one may return more easily to discover what we did not see, which was the best. And it would not be a bad plan to enter the country by way of the land sought by Marqués del Valle, Don Fernando Cortés, under the Western Star, and which cost him not a few fleets.

May the Lord grant me His grace so that, with my limited understanding and small ability, I may, while telling the truth, please the learned and discriminating reader with this, my little work, if it be accepted by your Lordship. For my aim is not to gain fame as a good writer or rhetorician, but simply to strive to give a truthful account and to render your Lordship this small service. You will, I hope, receive this as from a faithful servant and soldier who was present there. Although not in polished style, I write what took place, what was heard, experienced, seen, and discussed.

I have always noticed, and it is a fact, that often when we have something valuable in our possession and handle it freely, we do not esteem or appreciate it in all its worth, as we would if we could realize how much we would miss it if we were to lose it. Thus we gradually belittle its value, but once we have lost it and we miss its benefits we feel it in our heart and are forever moody, thinking of ways and means to retrieve it. This, it seems to me, happened to all or most of those who went on that expedition, which Francisco Vázquez Coronado led in search of the Seven Cities, in the year of our Savior, Jesus Christ, 1540. For although they did not obtain the riches of which they had been told, they found the means to discover them and the beginning of a good land to settle in and from which to proceed onward. And since, after they returned here from the land which they had conquered and abandoned, time has made clear to them the location and nature of the region they reached, and the beginning of a fine land they had in their grasp, their hearts bemoan the fact that they lost such an opportune occasion. Since it is a fact that men see more at a bullfight when they climb on top of the fence than when they walk around in the bull-ring, now that they are outside and realize and appreciate the localities and resources amid which they had been, and seeing now that they can no longer enjoy or recover them, their time wasted, they rejoice in telling what they saw, even realizing how much they lost, especially those who today are as poor as when they first went there, and who have worked constantly, spending their time to no benefit. I say this because I believe that some of those who came from there would today be glad if they could go back and try to recover what they lost. Others would now enjoy knowing the reason why the land was discovered. And since I offered to narrate the story, I shall start at the beginning, which is as follows.

FIRST PART

CHAPTER I

Which tells how information was obtained about the first settlement of the Seven Cities, and how Nuño de Guzmán organized a force to discover it.

In the year 1530, when Nuño de Guzmán was president of New Spain,[1] he had under his authority an Indian whom the Spaniards called Tejo, from the valley or valleys of Oxitipar. This Indian said that he was the son of a trader who was dead and declared that when he was very small his father used to go into the interior of the land to trade rich-colored plumes, used for feather crests, and in exchange brought back large quantities of gold and silver, which abound in that land; Tejo said that he went with his father once or twice, and saw very large pueblos, so large that he would compare them with Mexico city and its surroundings. He had seen, he related, seven very large pueblos, in which there were streets lined with silver-smiths' shops. To reach these pueblos from his land required forty days' travel over entirely deserted country, bare of vegetation except for some plants about one span high. The direction he went, he said, was to the north, through the country between the two seas.

Upon obtaining this information, Nuño de Guzmán assembled almost four hundred Spaniards and twenty thousand friendly Indians of New Spain. As he was then in Mexico, he crossed the Tarasca, which is the land of Mechuacán, in order to find the region which the Indian said would be found upon crossing the country toward the North sea. There they would come upon the land they were seeking, which they were already calling the Seven Cities. Since Tejo had said that it would be found after forty days' travel, they thought that they would cross the land upon traveling two hundred leagues.

1. For an account of his rule, see José López-Portillo y Weber, *La Conquista de la Nueva Galicia*, Mexico, 1935, p. 80 *et seq.*

Leaving out some incidents that happened on this journey, as soon as they reached the province of Culiacán, which was the most remote region of his government, now the new kingdom of Galicia, they wanted to cross the country. They met with great difficulties because the range of the sierra sloping down to the sea is so abrupt that, however hard they tried, it was impossible to find a pass in that locality. On account of this the whole army tarried so long in that land of Culiacán that influential men in the party, who had repartimientos in Mexico, changed their minds and every day wanted to turn back.

Aside from this, Nuño de Guzmán learned of the arrival from Spain of the Marqués del Valle, Don Fernando Cortés, with a new title and with great honors and powers. And as Nuño de Guzmán, during the time he was president, had been his bitter rival and had done much damage to his estates and those of his friends, he feared that Don Fernando Cortés might try to pay him back with similar or worse deeds. So he decided to found the villa of Culiacán and return with the rest of the people, having accomplished nothing else on the expedition.* On his return he settled Xalisco, which is the city of Compostela, and Tonalá, called Guadalajara. This is now the new kingdom of Galicia. The guide they took along, called Tejo, died about this time. So the names of these Seven Cities, which have not been discovered, remain unknown, and the search for them continues to this day.

Chapter II

How Francisco Vázquez Coronado came to be governor, and the second report given by Cabeza de Vaca.

Eight years after Nuño de Guzmán made this expedition, he was arrested by a judge of residencia named Licentiate Diego de la Torre, who came from Spain with full powers to hold his residencia.[1] Later this judge died, at the time the government of New Galicia was under the care of the good Don Antonio de Mendoza, viceroy of New Spain. The latter appointed as gov-

* Culiacán, founded in 1531, long remained the most northerly Spanish outpost on the west coast of Mexico.
1. See Coronado's letter of December 15, 1538, note 2.

ernor of that land, Francisco Vázquez de Coronado,[2] a gentleman from Salamanca, who at that time had married, at Mexico city, a daughter of Alonso de Estrada. He had been treasurer and governor of Mexico and was generally believed to be the son of the Catholic king, Don Ferdinand, which many affirm to be true. What I have to say is that at the time Francisco Vázquez was appointed governor he was holding the office of visitor general of New Spain. This brought him in touch and in friendly relations with many prominent persons who later accompanied him on the expedition he led.

It happened that, at this time, there arrived in Mexico three Spaniards, Cabeza de Vaca, Dorantes, and Castillo Maldonado, and a negro, who had been shipwrecked in the fleet sent to Florida under Pánfilo de Narváez. They came by way of Culiacán, after crossing the country from sea to sea, as any one may learn from a report which Cabeza de Vaca himself addressed to Prince Philip, who is now king of Spain and our lord.[3] They told the good Don Antonio de Mendoza how, through the lands they had traversed, they obtained interpreters and important information regarding powerful pueblos with houses four or five stories high, and other things quite different from what turned out to be the truth. The good viceroy communicated all this to the new governor. This caused him to hasten in bringing the visita he was holding to a close and to return to his government. He took with him the negro who had arrived and three friars of the order of Saint Francis. One of them was named Fray Marcos de Niza, a theologian and priest; the other, Fray Daniel, a lay brother; and the third, Fray Antonio de Santa María.[4]

As soon as he arrived in the province of Culiacán, he at once sent the above-mentioned friars and the negro, named Esteban, in search of that land. Fray Marcos de Niza was chosen to go

2. See *ibid.*, note 2.

3. For a full discussion of Cabeza de Vaca's narrative, first printed at Zamora in 1542, see H. R. Wagner, *The Spanish Southwest, 1542-1794*, I, pp. 29-50. The latest contribution on Cabeza de Vaca is Cleve Hollenbeck, *Alvar Núñez Cabeza de Vaca; the journey and route of the first European to cross the continent of North America, 1534-1536*, Glendale, 1940.

4. Compare the Report of Fray Marcos, p. 63. His companion was Fray Onorato.

to examine this land because he had been in Peru at the time when Don Pedro de Alvarado went there overland. After the said friars and the negro Esteban set out, it seems that the negro fell from the good graces of the friars because he took along the women that were given to him, and collected turquoises, and accumulated everything. Besides, the Indians of the settlements they crossed got along better with the negro, since they had seen him before. For this reason he was sent ahead to discover and pacify the land so that when the others arrived all they would have to do would be to listen and make a report of what they were searching for.

CHAPTER III

How they killed the negro Esteban at Cíbola, and how Fray Marcos returned in flight.

When Esteban got away from the said friars, he craved to gain honor and fame in everything and to be credited with the boldness and daring of discovering, all by himself, those terraced pueblos, so famed throughout the land. Accompanied by the people who followed him, he tried to cross the uninhabited regions between Cíbola and the inhabited area. He had traveled so far ahead of the friars that when they reached Chichilticale, which is the beginning of the despoblado, he was already at Cíbola, a distance of eighty leagues of despoblado. From Culiacán to the beginning of the despoblado it is 220 leagues, and with 80 through the despoblado this makes 300, perhaps ten more or less.

I say, then, that when the negro Esteban reached Cíbola, he arrived there laden with a large number of turquoises and with some pretty women, which the natives had given him. The gifts were carried by Indians who accompanied and followed him through every settlement he crossed, believing that, by going under his protection, they could traverse the whole country without any danger. But as the people of that land were more intelligent than those who followed Esteban, they lodged him at a lodging house which they had outside of the pueblo, and the oldest and those in authority listened to his words and tried to learn the reason for his coming to that land.

When they were well informed, they held councils for three days. As the negro had told them that farther back two white men, sent by a great lord, were coming, that they were learned in the things of heaven, and that they were coming to instruct them in divine matters, the Indians thought he must have been a spy or guide of some nations that wanted to come and conquer them. They thought it was nonsense for him to say that the people in the land whence he came were white, when he was black, and that he had been sent by them. So they went to him, and because, after some talk, he asked them for turquoises and women, they considered this an affront and determined to kill him. So they did, without killing any one of those who came with him. They took a few boys, and the others, who must have been some sixty people, they allowed to return to their lands unmolested. As these who were now returning were fleeing in fright, they chanced to see and meet the friars in the despoblado, sixty leagues from Cíbola, and gave them the sad news. The friars were seized with such fear that, not trusting these people who had accompanied the negro, they opened their bags and distributed everything they had among them, keeping only the vestments for saying mass. From there they turned back without seeing more land than what the Indians had told them of. On the contrary, they were traveling by forced marches, with their habits up to their waists.

Chapter IV

How the good Don Antonio de Mendoza organized the expedition for the discovery of Cíbola.

After sending Fray Marcos de Niza and his party to the aforementioned exploration, Francisco Vázquez Coronado remained in Culiacán attending to matters pertaining to his government. He received a reliable report of a province named Topira, which touched Culiacán on the north, and he set forth at once with a few conquistadores and some of his allies to discover it. His trip produced few results because it was extremely difficult to cross the mountain ranges, and they soon found that the information they had received was untruthful; nor did they find any signs of good lands. So he turned back.

On his return he found the friars, who had just returned. They told so many glowing tales of what the negro Esteban had discovered and what they had heard from the Indians, together with other news of the South sea, of islands of which they had heard, and of other riches, that the governor, without further delay, left at once for Mexico city, taking Fray Marcos along to give a report of the matter to the viceroy. The friar magnified things by refusing to talk to any one, except under great mystery and secrecy, to some particular individuals.

As soon as they reached Mexico city and met Don Antonio de Mendoza, it was at once publicized that the Seven Cities, which Nuño de Guzmán had sought, had now been found, and they began to organize an expedition and to recruit people to go and conquer them. The good viceroy managed everything so well with the friars of the order of Saint Francis that they appointed Fray Marcos to the office of provincial. The result was that from the pulpits of this order there emanated so many tales of great wonders that in a few days there were recruited more than three hundred Spaniards and some eight hundred Indians of New Spain. Among the Spaniards there were men of great distinction, such a large number that I doubt whether there were ever assembled in the Indies so many noble people in such a small group of three hundred men. The captain general of them all was Francisco Vázquez Coronado, governor of New Galicia, as he had been the author of it all.

The good viceroy, Don Antonio, did all this because at that time Francisco Vázquez was the person closest to him at court and he considered him clear-minded, able, and of good judgment, in addition to being the caballero that he was. He should have paid more attention and regard to the rank to which he had been elevated and to the commission entrusted him than to the estate he was leaving in New Spain, or at least to the honor he had won and was to win by having such caballeros under his command. However, it did not turn out that way for him, as will be seen further on at the end of this work. Neither did he know how to preserve his position nor the government he held.

CHAPTER V

Which tells about those who went to Cíbola as captains.

The viceroy, Don Antonio de Mendoza, had already seen the very noble people he had assembled and how openly and willingly they all offered themselves to him. Knowing their personal worth, he should have liked to appoint each one of them as leader of an army, but, as their number was small, he could not carry out his wishes. Thus he selected the leaders and captains he thought best, for since he had ordered everything, no one would disobey his command as he was so respected and loved. After they had all learned who was to be their general, he appointed as chief ensign, Don Pedro de Tovar, a young caballero, son of Don Fernando de Tovar, escort and chief majordomo of Queen Juana, our natural sovereign—may she be in heaven. As maestre de campo he chose Lope de Samaniego, commander of the arsenal at Mexico, a caballero most competent for the position.

Selected as captains were Don Tristán de Arellano, Don Pedro de Guevara, son of Don Juan de Guevara and nephew of the Count of Oñate; Don García López de Cárdenas; Don Rodrigo Maldonado, brother-in-law of the Duque del Infantado; Diego López, alderman of Seville; Diego Gutiérrez, in charge of the cavalry. All the other caballeros went under the banner of the general, as befitting distinguished persons. Some of them became captains later and were continued in the service by order of the viceroy, and others by General Francisco Vázquez. I shall name a few of those whom I happen to remember. They were Francisco de Barrionuevo, a caballero from Granada; Juan de Zaldívar, Francisco de Ovando, Juan Gallego, and Melchior Díaz, a former alcalde mayor and captain of Culiacán, who, although he was not a caballero, deserved the appointment he held.

Other caballeros who distinguished themselves were Don Alonso Manrique de Lara; Don Lope de Urrea, an Aragonese caballero; Gómez Suárez de Figueroa; Luis Ramírez de Vargas; Juan de Sotomayor; Francisco Gorbalán; the factor, Riberos; and other caballeros, men of great worth, whom I do not now remember. As captain of infantry went Pablo de Melgosa, from Burgos, and of artillery, Hernando de Alvarado, a caballero from Santander. I repeat that after such a long time I have forgotten many worthy hidalgos whom I should have named so that one might see and understand that I am right when I say that there had gathered for this expedition the most brilliant company ever assembled in the Indies to go in search of new lands. But they were unfortunate in having a captain who was leaving in New Spain estates and a young wife, a noble and generous lady, which were no small incentives for what he did later.

CHAPTER VI

How all the companies assembled at Compostela and set out in order on the journey.

When the viceroy, Don Antonio de Mendoza, had done and ordered what we have narrated, after selecting the company leaders or captains, he distributed forthwith some aid from the treasury of his Majesty to the most needy soldiers. And as it seemed to him that if the army traveled together from Mexico the soldiers might do some damage to the lands of their allies, he ordered that they assemble in the city of Compostela, capital of the new kingdom of Galicia, 110 leagues from Mexico. From there they were to commence the expedition in orderly fashion.

There is no need to relate what happened on this trip, but finally they all assembled in Compostela on the day of Shrovetide of the year 1541 [1540]. When the viceroy got all the people out of Mexico, he ordered Pedro de Alarcón[1] to sail with two boats that were in the harbor of Navidad, on the southern coast, to the port of Jalisco to take on board the personal belongings that the soldiers might be unable to carry. He was to follow the army along the coast, because, according to information received, it was thought that the army would have to travel along the sea coast, and that in the rivers we would find

1. This was Hernando de Alarcón. See H. R. Wagner, *California Voyages, 1539-1541*, San Francisco, 1925, pp. 82-84. Mendoza's instructions to Alarcón and the latter's report are translated above, pp. 117-155.

harbors, where the boats would always be able to contact the army. This later proved to be false, and as a result all the personal belongings were lost, or, to be more accurate, were lost by their owners, as will be told later.

Thus, after arranging and dispatching everything, the viceroy set out for Compostela, accompanied by many caballeros and prominent men. He spent New Year's day of 1541 [1540] at Pásquaro, which is the seat of the bishopric of Mechuacán. From there, amid much joy, pleasure, and fine receptions, he crossed the whole land of New Spain to Compostela, which is a distance of 110 leagues, as I have stated. There he found all the people assembled, well cared for and lodged by Cristóbal de Oñate, who at that time was in charge of the government of New Galicia;[2] he had maintained it and was captain of all that land when Francisco Vázquez became governor. The viceroy arrived, to the rejoicing of every one, and held a review of the people who were going and found all those we have mentioned. He distributed the captainships.[3] This done, on the following day, after mass, the viceroy delivered a short but very eloquent address to all, both soldiers and leaders. He reminded them of the allegiance they owed their general, explaining to them the benefits that might result from carrying out the expedition, not only for the conversion of the natives, but for those who conquered the land, and for the service of his Majesty; and he reminded them of the obligation that the king had assumed to help and favor them at all times. This finished, he received, upon the gospels in a missal, the oaths of all in general, both leaders and soldiers, all in proper order. They swore that they would follow their general and would obey and do on that expedition all that was commanded them. This they afterward fulfilled faithfully, as will be shown. After this, on the following day, the army set out with flags unfurled, and the viceroy, Don Antonio, accompanied them for two days. Then

2. For the Oñate family, see Beatrice Quijada Cornish, "The Ancestry and Family of Juan de Oñate," in *The Pacific Ocean in History*, ed. by H. M. Stephens and H. E. Bolton, New York, 1917, pp. 452-464; and G. P. Hammond, *Don Juan de Oñate and the Founding of New Mexico*, Santa Fe, 1927.

3. See the muster roll, pp. 87-108.

he took leave and returned to New Spain, accompanied by his friends.

CHAPTER VII

How the army reached Chiametla, how the maestre de campo was killed, and what else happened until they arrived at Culiacán.

After the viceroy, Don Antonio, left, the army continued on its way. As all had to carry their belongings on horseback and not every one knew how to pack them, and as the horses were fat and rested when they started out, there was considerable difficulty and trouble during the first days of travel. Many discarded numerous valuable articles or gave them away as gifts to any one who would take them, in order to save loading them. At last necessity, which is a good teacher, in time made the men skillful. One could see many gentlemen acting as muleteers, and whoever belittled this occupation was not considered a man. With these hardships, which at that time they considered serious, the army reached Chiametla, where it had to remain for a few days on account of the shortage of food and supplies.

During this time the maestre de campo, Lope de Samaniego, with a number of men, went in search of food. At a pueblo, as he carelessly entered a brushy place in pursuit of hostile Indians, he was struck in one eye by an arrow which pierced his brain, and, as a result, he died on the spot. Five or six other men were hit by arrows. Upon his death Diego López, alderman of Seville, took charge of the party and sent word to the general, who placed guards to watch over the pueblo and the supplies. Samaniego's death caused great apprehension when the army learned of it. He was buried. Several sorties were made, on which they brought in food and a few native prisoners. They hanged those who were thought to belong to the place where the maestre de campo was killed.

It seems that at the time when General Francisco Vázquez left Culiacán with Fray Marcos to give the viceroy, Don Antonio de Mendoza, the information already mentioned, he had arranged that Captain Melchior Díaz and Juan de Zaldívar, with a dozen good men, should leave Culiacán and search for what Fray Marcos had seen and heard about. They set out and went as far as Chichilticale, which is the beginning of the despoblado, 220 leagues from Culiacán. They did not find anything worthwhile, and turned back, arriving at Chiametla at the time when the army was about to leave there. They reported to the general, but no matter how secretly they talked, the bad news soon spread. Some remarks circulated which, although they had been gilded, did not fail to reveal the truth. Fray Marcos de Niza, noticing the misgivings of some, tried to clear away these clouds, assuring them that what they would see would be fine, and that he had been there and would lead the army to a land where they could fill their hands with wealth. With this they were calmed and seemed well satisfied.

From there the army marched until it reached Culiacán, making a few excursions into hostile territory to gather supplies. They were two leagues from the town of Culiacán on the day before Easter. The inhabitants came out to meet their governor, and they begged him not to enter the town until the day after Easter.

Chapter VIII

How the army entered the town of Culiacán, the reception it was accorded, and what else transpired until its departure.

On the day after Easter, the army set out early in the morning to enter the town, and on entering a cleared field found the people of the town, some of our soldiers among them, drawn up in military order by companies, on foot and horse, with mounted artillery consisting of seven bronze pieces, as if to defend the town. Our army, in similar array, began a sham battle with them. So the townsmen gradually gave ground, after the artillery on both sides had been fired, in such a manner that the town was taken by force of arms. It was a joyful demonstration and reception, although not so for the artilleryman whose hand was shot off because he gave the order to fire before he had completely drawn out the ramrod.

After taking the town the soldiers were at once well quartered and lodged by the residents. They took all the caballeros and distinguished persons of the army, all of whom were very honorable men, into their own homes, although quarters for all had been arranged outside of the town. Some of the residents were not badly remunerated for this hospitality, because as their guests were all richly attired and since from this place they were to transport provisions on their animals, they had of necessity to discard their accouterments, and many preferred to give them to their hosts rather than trust them to the fortunes of the sea by placing them on the boats that followed the army along the coast to take on the baggage, as has been stated.

When all had arrived and had been properly lodged in the town, the general, by command of Viceroy Don Antonio appointed there Fernandarias de Saavedra, uncle of Hernandarias de Saavedra, Count of Castellar, a former alguacil mayor of Seville, as his lieutenant and captain in this town. The army rested here a few days, since the residents that year had gathered abundant food supplies, and they shared them generously with the people in our army, especially each one with his guests. Thus not only was there plenty to use there but also to take along, so that at the time of departure more than 600 laden animals set out, as well as our allies and servants, who totaled more than 1,000 persons.

After fifteen days the general arranged to go ahead with about fifty mounted men and a few footmen and most of the allies, leaving the army to follow him within fifteen days. He appointed Don Tristán de Arellano as his lieutenant.[1]

During this time, before the general started out, there occurred an amusing incident, which I shall narrate. It happened that a young soldier named Trujillo pretended that he had seen a vision while bathing in the river. Feigning to be under the vision's spell, he was brought before the general. He said that the devil had told him that if he would kill the general he could marry Doña Beatriz, his wife, and that he would give him great treasures. He told other very amusing things, from which Fray Marcos de Niza took some sermons, making out that the devil, being jealous of the benefits that would result from that expedition, wanted to disrupt it by these means. The story did not end here, for the friars who accompanied the expedition

1. See the Muster Roll, note 33.

also wrote about it to their convents, which caused many fables on the subject to be told from the pulpits in Mexico.

The general ordered Trujillo to remain in that town and not to go on the expedition, which was precisely what the soldier sought when he planned the trick, as was learned later. The general set out with the people already mentioned and continued on his journey. The army followed later, as will be narrated.

CHAPTER IX

How the army set out from Culiacán; how the general reached Cíbola, and the army Señora, and what else took place.

As has been stated, the general set out from the valley of Culiacán on his journey, lightly equipped. He took along the friars, since none of them wished to remain with the army.[1] On the third day a friar named Fray Antonio Victoria broke a leg. This friar, one ordained to officiate at mass, was taken back in order to be attended to; later he accompanied the army, which was of no slight consolation to all. The general and his men crossed the land without encountering any opposition. They found everything peaceful, because the Indians knew Fray Marcos and some of those who had accompanied Captain Melchior Díaz when he and Juan de Zaldívar had gone out to explore.

When the general crossed the settled region and reached Chichilticale, where the despoblado began, and they could not see anything of any account, he could not help but feel some disappointment, because, although the reports of what lay ahead were alluring, no one had seen it except the Indians who had accompanied the negro, and they had already been caught in several lies. The men were all disillusioned to see that the famous Chichilticale turned out to be a roofless ruined house, although it appeared that formerly, at the time when it was inhabited, it must have been a fortress. One could easily tell that it had been built by strange people, orderly and warlike, from afar. This house was built of red mud.

From here they proceeded over the despoblado and after

1. See the Introduction, pp. 9-12.

fifteen days, at a distance of eight leagues from Cíbola, arrived at a river which, because its water was muddy and red, they called Red River.[2] In this stream they found barbels like those in Spain. Here it was that they saw the first Indians in that land —two of them—who fled and went to warn the others. On the night of the following day, two leagues from the pueblo, the Indians began shouting from a safe place, and although the men were forewarned some were so confused that more than one put his saddle on backward. This happened only to beginners, as the veterans quickly mounted their horses and rode out over the field. The Indians, well acquainted with the land, fled, for none could be found.

On the following day, in good formation, the soldiers entered the inhabited land. When they got within sight of the first pueblo, which was Cíbola, the curses that some hurled at Fray Marcos were such that God forbid they may befall him.

It is a small, rocky pueblo, all crumpled up, there being many farm settlements in New Spain that look better from afar. It is a pueblo of three or four stories and has some 200 warriors. The houses are small, have little space and no patios, for one patio serves a whole section. The people of the district had gathered there, for this is a province comprising seven pueblos, some of which are by far larger and stronger pueblos than Cíbola. These people waited in the open within sight of the pueblo, drawn up in squadrons. As they refused to accept peace in response to the requisitions which the Spaniards made through interpreters, but, on the contrary appeared warlike, the Spaniards gave the "Santiago, after them,"[3] and they were quickly routed. Then the soldiers proceeded to take the pueblo, which was no easy task; for, as the entrance was narrow and winding, the general was struck to the ground by a large stone as they were entering and he would have been killed had it not been for Don García López de Cárdenas and Hernando de Alvarado, who threw themselves upon him and carried him away, receiving a good many blows from the stones.[4] However,

2. Rio Bermejo.
3. The ancient Spanish battle cry was, "Santiago! Cierra España!" Translated, it reads: "St. James! Spain! Close on them!"
4. Compare the testimony of Coronado and Cárdenas, pp. 323 and 345.

as nothing could resist the first onrush of the Spaniards, in less than one hour they entered and conquered the pueblo. Here they found provisions, of which there was the greatest need. After that the whole province submitted peacefully.

The army, which had remained in charge of Don Tristán de Arellano, set out following the route of the general. They were all burdened with provisions, their lances on their shoulders, and all on foot in order that the horses could be loaded. After considerable labor they reached, by stages, a province which Cabeza de Vaca had named Corazones, because there the natives had offered him many hearts of animals. Without delay Arellano proceeded to establish a town there, naming it San Hierónimo de los Corazones, and began at once to settle it. Later, seeing that it could not be maintained, he moved it to a valley called Persona—I mean Señora—and the Spaniards called it Señora, and so I shall call it from now on. From there he marched down the river to the seacoast in search of the harbor in order to find out about the ships, but he did not find them.

Don Rodrigo Maldonado, who was in charge of the search for the boats, brought along back an Indian so large and tall that the biggest man in the army did not come up to his chest. It was said that, on the coast, there were other Indians still taller. There the army rested during the rainy season, and afterward it went to the town of Señora, for in that locality there were provisions that would enable them to wait for orders from the general.

During the middle of October, Captains Melchior Díaz and Juan Gallego arrived from Cíbola. Juan Gallego was going to New Spain and Melchior Díaz was to remain in the new town of Corazones, as captain of the people who should stay there, in order that he might go in search of the boats along that coast.

Chapter X

How the army set out from the town of Señora, leaving it settled, and how it reached Cíbola, and what happened on the way to Melchior Díaz while he was in search of the ships, and how he discovered the Tizón [Firebrand] river.

Immediately upon the arrival of Melchior Díaz and Juan Gallego at the town of Señora, the departure of the army for Cíbola was announced, and also that Melchior Díaz was to remain as captain in the town of Señora with eighty men, and that Juan Gallego was going to New Spain with a message for the viceroy. He was accompanied by Fray Marcos, who did not consider it safe to remain at Cíbola, seeing that his report had proved false in every respect. For they had not found the kingdoms he had told about, neither populous cities, nor the riches of gold and precious stones that had been broadcast, nor brocades, nor other things that were mentioned from the pulpits.

After this announcement was made, the people who were to remain were named, the others loaded up with provisions, and in proper order they were on their way to Cíbola by the middle of September to join their general. Don Tristán de Arellano remained in this new town of Señora with the least reliable people, and thus, from that time on, riots and disturbances were never lacking. For as soon as the army had left, Captain Melchior Díaz took twenty-five picked men and set out with guides in search of the seacoast between north and west, leaving as his lieutenant a certain Diego de Alcaraz, a man unfit to have people under his command. After traveling some 150 leagues Díaz came to a province inhabited by people like giants, exceedingly tall and muscular. They were, however, naked and lived in huts of long straw built underground like caves, with only the straw rising above the ground. They entered these at one end, without stooping, and came out at the opposite end. More than one hundred persons, large and small, slept in one hut. When transporting burdens they carried on their heads more than three and four hundred pounds. It once happened that when our men wanted to bring a log for the fire and six of them could not carry it, one of the Indians picked it up in his arms, put it on his head all by himself, and carried it quite easily.

These Indians eat corn bread, as large as the big loaves of Castile, baked by the heat of ashes. When they travel about from place to place they carry, on account of the intense cold, a firebrand with which they warm their hands and body by changing it from one hand to another from time to time. For this reason the large river that flows through that land is called Tizón [Firebrand] river. It is a mighty stream, more than two leagues across at the mouth. At that place it was half a league across. There the captain learned, through the interpreter, that the ships of Alarcón had come up the river from the sea to a point within three days' travel from there. When Díaz's party reached the place where the boats had come, which was more than fifteen leagues up the river from the mouth of the bay, they found written on a tree: "Alarcón came this far; there are letters at the foot of this tree." They dug up the letters and from them they learned how long the ships had waited for news from the army and that Alarcón had returned to New Spain from there with the boats because he could not proceed any farther, for that sea was a gulf which extends toward the Island of the Marquis, which is called California. They reported that California was not an island, but a point of the mainland on the other side of that gulf.

In view of this Captain Díaz returned up the river without seeing the sea. He wanted to find a fording place in order to cross to the other shore and follow it. After marching five or six days they thought that they could cross it on rafts. For this purpose they called together many natives of the land. These natives were planning to attack our men and were looking for an opportune occasion. When they saw that our men wanted to cross the river, they rushed to build the rafts with much diligence and speed. Thus they hoped to catch them on the water and drown them, or find them divided so that they could not support and aid one another.

During this time, while the rafts were being built, a soldier who had gone foraging in the country saw a large number of armed men cross a mountain. They were waiting for our men to cross the river. He reported this, and an Indian was locked up secretly in order to learn the truth from him. As they tortured him he told of the whole plan the Indians had arranged for the moment when the soldiers should cross. Their plan was that when some had crossed the river, others being on the river, and while others were waiting to cross over, the natives on the rafts were to try to drown those they were taking across and the other Indians were to attack on both banks. If they had had as much discretion and courage as they had power and strength, they would have succeeded in their scheme. After learning of their plans the captain ordered that the Indian who had confessed the plot should be killed in secret, and they tossed him into the river that night with a heavy weight in order that the Indians should not know that they were suspected. The next day, sensing that our men suspected them, they came in a warlike mood, shooting showers of arrows. However, as the horsemen began to overtake them and the lances cut them down mercilessly and the harquebusiers also were taking fine shots, they had to abandon the field and take to the mountains, until not a man was to be seen. The captain came back there and the men crossed safely, the Indian allies and the Spaniards crossing on the rafts by turns, and the horses swimming alongside.

We shall leave them here on their journey and tell of the army that was traveling to Cíbola.[1] As it was marching in orderly manner and the general had left everything at peace,[2] they found the natives cheerful and submissive everywhere, and without fear. In a province named Vacapan there were large quantities of prickly pears, of which the natives made large amounts of preserves. They brought much of this preserve as a present, and when the people of the army ate of it they all became drowsy with headaches and fever, so that the Indians could have done great harm to them if they had wished. This illness lasted intermittently for twenty-four hours. Then marching from there they reached Chichilticale. One day's travel from there, the advance guard saw a flock of sheep pass by. I saw them and followed them. They were large of body, had abundant long hair, and had very thick long horns. When they run they raise their heads and rest their horns on their backs. They are fleet in rough country, so we could not overtake them and had to let them go.

After going through the despoblado for three days, the

1. To join Coronado who had gone on ahead with the advance party.
2. In the land through which he had passed.

army found, at the bank of a river down in some deep canyons, a horn, which the general, after examining it, had left there in order that those in the army might see it. It was a fathom long and as thick at the base as a man's thigh. By its shape it looked more like the horn of a buck than of any other animal. It was worth seeing.

Proceeding ahead, when the army was already a day's journey from Cíbola, there arose in the afternoon a bitter cold whirlwind, followed by a heavy snowfall, which brought considerable hardship to the Indian servants. The army marched until it came to some rocky caves, which were reached well in the night. Great fear was felt for the welfare of the allies, for as they were from New Spain and most of them from warm lands, they felt that day's cold very much, so much in fact that on the following day there was plenty to do taking care of them and carrying them on horseback while the soldiers walked. With this labor the army reached Cíbola, where the general awaited them with lodgings. There the army was again brought together, although some captains and men who had gone to explore other provinces were missing.

CHAPTER XI

How Don Pedro de Tovar discovered Tusayán, or Tutahaco,[1] and Don García López de Cárdenas saw the Tizón [Firebrand] river, and what else transpired.

While the aforesaid events were taking place, General Francisco Vázquez, who was resting peacefully at Cíbola, tried to learn from the natives what provinces belonged to that district. He also wanted them to tell their friends and neighbors about the coming of the Christians to their land, to inform them that they wanted nothing from them except to be their friends and to learn of good lands where to settle, and that the Indians should come to see them and communicate with them. The natives immediately carried this message to those localities that had communication and commerce with them. They also told of a province composed of seven pueblos

1. Tusayán and Tutahaco were not the same. See p. 220, note 1.

of the same quality as their own, although they had some disagreement with them and were not on good terms with them. This province is called Tusayán, distant 25 leagues from Cíbola. The pueblos are built in terraces, and there are warlike people among the inhabitants.

The general had sent Don Pedro de Tovar with seventeen mounted men and three or four footmen to these towns. With them went Fray Juan de Padilla, a Franciscan friar who had been a warrior in his youth. When they arrived, they entered the land so quietly that they were not observed by any one. The reason was that there were no towns or settlements between the various provinces, and the people did not leave their pueblos beyond their estates, especially at that time, for they had heard that Cíbola had been conquered by very fierce men who rode animals that ate people. To those who had never seen horses, this news was so wonderful that it astonished them. Consequently our men, arrived at night, were able to conceal themselves at the bottom of the gully of the town and remain there, listening to the natives talk in their homes.

When morning came, however, they were discovered. The natives formed their ranks and set out after them, well armed with arrows, shields, and wooden maces. They came in wing formation without confusion. There was opportunity for the interpreters to talk to them and to make the requisition for peace upon them, since they were an intelligent people; but withal, they drew lines, requesting that our men should not cross those lines toward their pueblos, but that they should be orderly. Some did cross these lines in places while parleying with them. This lasted so long that one of the Indians lost control of himself and struck one of the horses a blow with a mace over the checks of the bridle. Fray Juan, angry at the time being wasted on them, said to the captain: "Indeed, I do not know what we have come here for." Seeing this, the Spaniards gave the cry of "Santiago" and attacked so suddenly that they knocked down many Indians, who were soon routed and fleeing to the pueblo; some did not have that chance since the people rushed out of their pueblos quickly, offering peace and presents. Our men were ordered to fall back and not to do any more harm.

The captain and his men looked for a place near the pueblo to establish their camp. There they found—I mean, they alighted—when the people came peacefully, saying that they came to offer obedience for the whole province, that they wanted to be friends, and that they should accept the gift they brought. It consisted of some cotton clothes, although a small quantity, since cotton was not found in that land.[2] They presented a few dressed hides and quantities of flour, piñon nuts,[3] corn, and native fowl. Later they brought a few turquoises, although not many. On that day the natives of the land assembled and came to offer their obedience. They offered their towns openly, permitting the soldiers to go there in order to buy, sell, and trade.

The province is governed like Cíbola, by an assembly of the oldest men. They have their chosen governor and captains. Here information was obtained of a large river and that several days down the river there were people with very large bodies.

As Don Pedro de Tovar had no other commission, he returned from Tusayán and gave his report to the general. The latter at once dispatched Don García López de Cárdenas there with about twelve men to explore this river. When he reached Tusayán he was well received and lodged by the natives. They provided him with guides to proceed on his journey. They set out from there laden with provisions, because they had to travel over some uninhabited land before coming to settlements, which the Indians said were more than twenty days away. Accordingly when they had marched for twenty days they came to the gorges of the river, from the edge of which it looked as if the opposite side must have been more than three or four leagues away by air. This region was high and covered with low and twisted pine trees; it was extremely cold, being open to the north, so that, although this was the warm season, no one could live in this canyon because of the cold.

2. Castañeda was mistaken in respect to the cultivation of cotton among the Hopi. Espejo was given numerous cotton articles here. See *Expedition into New Mexico made by Antonio de Espejo, 1582-1583*, George P. Hammond and Agapito Rey, Quivira Society, I, Los Angeles, 1929.
3. The word is piñol. In other cases it is written piñoles and piñones.

The men spent three days looking for a way down to the river; from the top it looked as if the water were a fathom across. But, according to the information supplied by the Indians, it must have been half a league wide. The descent was almost impossible, but, after these three days, at a place which seemed less difficult, Captain Melgosa, a certain Juan Galeras, and another companion, being the most agile, began to go down. They continued descending within view of those on top until they lost sight of them, as they could not be seen from the top. They returned about four o'clock in the afternoon, as they could not reach the bottom because of the many obstacles they met, for what from the top seemed easy, was not so; on the contrary, it was rough and difficult. They said that they had gone down one-third of the distance and that, from the point they had reached, the river seemed very large, and that, from what they saw, the width given by the Indians was correct. From the top they could make out, apart from the canyon, some small boulders which seemed to be as high as a man. Those who went down and who reached them swore that they were taller than the great tower of Seville.

The party did not continue farther up the canyon of the river because of the lack of water. Up to that time they had gone one or two leagues inland in search of water every afternoon. When they had traveled four additional days the guides said that it was impossible to go on because no water would be found for three or four days, that when they themselves traveled through that land they took along women who brought water in gourds, that in those trips they buried the gourds of water for the return trip, and that they traveled in one day a distance that took us two days.

This was the Tizón river, much closer to its source than where Melchior Díaz and his men had crossed it. These Indians were of the same type, as it appeared later. From there Cárdenas and his men turned back, as that trip brought no other results. On the way they saw a waterfall which came down a rock. They learned from the guides that some clusters which hung like fine crystals were salt. They went thither and gathered quantities of it which they brought and distributed when they returned to Cíbola. Here they rendered their general a written report of what they had seen, since a certain Pedro de Sotomayor, who was chronicler of the army, had accompanied Don García López.* They left the pueblos of that province in peace and never visited them again, nor did they seek or make attempts to locate other settlements in that region.

CHAPTER XII

How people from Cicuye came to Cíbola to see the Christians, and how Hernando de Alvarado went to see the cattle.

While they were engaged in these discoveries there came to Cíbola some Indians from a pueblo of the province in the interior called Cicuye, distant seventy leagues to the east.[1] Among them came a chieftain whom our men called "Bigotes," because he had long mustaches. He was a young man, tall, well built, and robust in appearance. He told the general they came to serve him in response to the appeal that they should offer themselves as friends and that, if the Spaniards planned to visit their land, they should consider them as their friends. The Indians gave them some presents of dressed skins, shields, and headpieces. All this was accepted with much affection. The general gave them glassware, pearl beads, and jingle bells, which they prized very highly as something they had never seen before.

The natives gave information of the cattle. They were made out to be cattle by the picture which one of the Indians had painted on his body, since this could not be determined from the skins, because the hair was so woolly and tangled that one could not tell what the animals were.

The general ordered Hernando de Alvarado and twenty men to go with the Indians and gave him a commission for eighty days, after which he was to come back and report on

---

* This report has not come to light.

1. On the pueblo of Pecos, see A. F. Bandelier, "Report on the Ruins of the Pueblo of Pecos," *Papers of the Archaeological Institute of America*, Boston, 1881; A. V. Kidder, *An Introduction to the Study of Southwestern Archaeology with a preliminary account of the excavations at Pecos*, New Haven, 1924; also his, *The Artifacts of Pecos*, New Haven, 1932; E. A. Hooton, *The Indians of Pecos Pueblo*, New Haven, 1930.

what they had found.[2] Captain Alvarado set out on the expedition and after five days' travel he came to a pueblo called Acuco, built on a rock.[3] It contained some two hundred warriors—robbers who were feared throughout the land. The pueblo was extremely strong because it was built above the entrance to the rock, which was hewn sheer on all sides and so high that it would require a good musket to land a ball on top. There was only one way to go up, a stairway made by hand. This started at a place where the path sloped to the ground. This stairway was wide and had some two hundred steps leading up to the top. Then there was another narrow one, built against the wall, with about one hundred steps. At the top of this it was necessary to climb up the rocky stairway about three times the height of a man by placing one's toes in the holes in the rock and likewise the hands. At the top there was a protecting wall of large and small stones so that, without exposing themselves, the inhabitants could hurl so many down that no army, however powerful, could reach the top. At the top there was space for planting and growing a large amount of maize. There were cisterns to store snow and water.

These people came down to the valley in a warlike mood, and no amount of entreaties was of any avail with them. They drew lines and tried to prevent our men from crossing them. But, as they saw that they were pressed, they soon gave up the field, I mean, they accepted peace before any harm was done them. They made their peace ceremonies by approaching the horses, taking their sweat, and anointing themselves with it, making crosses with the fingers of their hands. However, their most reliable peace pact consists in crossing their hands, and this peace they keep inviolable. They presented a large number of turkey cocks with very large wattles, much bread, dressed deerskins, piñon nuts, flour, and maize.

2. See the report of Alvarado, pp. 182-184.
3. The pueblo of Acoma, a few miles south of Highway 66 between Albuquerque and Grants. It still occupies its ancient site on top of the rock described by Castañeda. See Mary K. Sedgwick, *Acoma, the Sky City*, Cambridge, 1926.

Three days' travel farther on Alvarado and his men arrived at a province named Triguex.[4] The Indians all came out peacefully, seeing that men who were feared in all those provinces were coming with Bigotes. Alvarado sent word to the general from there, asking him to come to spend the winter in that land. The general was highly pleased to learn that the country was improving.

Five days farther on Alvarado reached Cicuye, a very strong pueblo four stories high. The people came out to meet him and their captain with demonstrations of joy and took him into the pueblo with drums and flageolets, similar to fifes, of which they had many. They presented the Spaniards with quantities of clothing and turquoises, which are found in abundance in that region.

Here the soldiers rested for a few days. They took as interpreter an Indian slave, a native of the farthest interior of the land extending from there to Florida, which is the region discovered by Don Hernando de Soto. This Indian, whom they named the Turk because he looked like one, told of large towns, which he should not have done.[5] Hernando de Alvarado took him along as a guide, to the cattle. The Turk told so many and such great tales about the riches of gold and silver found in his land that the Spaniards did not care to look for the cattle, and as soon as they saw a few they turned back to report the rich news to the general.

In the meantime the general had sent Don García López de Cárdenas with some men to Tiguex to prepare winter quarters and lodging there for the army that had arrived from Señora. When Hernando de Alvarado arrived in Tiguex, on his return from Cicuye, he found Don García López de Cárdenas, and it was not necessary that he should proceed farther. And as the natives had to provide quarters for the Spaniards, they found themselves compelled to abandon a pueblo and seek lodging

4. The ancient Tiguex province, inhabited by the Tigua Indians, extended along the valley of the Rio Grande in the vicinity of the modern Albuquerque-Bernalillo area.

5. The Turk was from the kingdom called Quivira, which played a large part in the subsequent history of the expedition.

for themselves in the other pueblos of their friends.* They did not take along any belongings but their persons and clothing.

In this locality information was obtained of numerous pueblos toward the north, and I believe it would have been far better to travel in that direction than to follow the Turk, who was the cause of all the misfortunes that ensued.

CHAPTER XIII

How the general with a few men went to Tutahaco; he left the army with Don Tristán, who took it to Tiguex.

All these afore-mentioned events had taken place when Don Tristán de Arellano arrived at Cíbola from Señora. Immediately upon his arrival, the general, having received information of a province of eight pueblos, took thirty of the most rested men and went to see it, intending to come back by way of Tiguex. He had experienced guides.

He left instructions that when the people had rested for twenty days, Don Tristán de Arellano was to leave with the army straight for Tiguex. Then he continued on his way. On one occasion it happened that, from the time they left their stopping place until noon of the third day when they came within sight of a snow-covered mountain where they had gone in search of water, neither they nor their horses had had anything to drink. The Indian servants likewise could not stand it on account of the intense cold. After an eight-days' journey, they reached Tutahaco, although with difficulty, where they learned that down the river were other pueblos.[1] The people came out peacefully. The pueblos are terraced like those of Tiguex, and the people wore similar clothes.

* Winter quarters were established at the pueblo of Alcanfor or Coofor. See testimony of Coronado and Cárdenas, pp. 329 and 347.

1. Regarding this province of Tutahaco, there has long been considerable speculation. Dr. Hodge writes: "This province has always been a historical puzzle. Coronado probably reached the Rio Grande about Isleta, and it is also likely that the pueblos in this vicinity formed the province of Tutahaco, for Castañeda speaks of other pueblos down the Rio Grande, which evidently were the Piro settlements. On the other hand, Tutahaco may have included the Tigua and Piro pueblos east of the Rio Grande, which were inhabited until the seventh decade of the 17th century, when the Apache forced their abandonment." *Journey of Coronado*, 1933, p. 26, note 1.

The general went on from there, visiting the whole province up the river until he reached Tiguex, where he found Hernando de Alvarado and the Turk. He rejoiced greatly at the good tidings, for the Turk claimed that in his land there was a river, flowing through plains, which was two leagues wide, with fish as large as horses and a great number of very large canoes with sails, carrying more than twenty oarsmen on each side. The nobles, he said, traveled in the stern, seated under canopies, and at the prow there was a large golden eagle. He stated further that the lord of that land took his siesta under a large tree from which hung numerous golden jingle bells, and he was pleased as they played in the wind. He added that the common table service of all was generally of wrought silver, and that the pitchers, dishes, and bowls were made of gold. He called gold *acochis*. At first he was believed on account of the directness with which he told his story and also because, when they showed him jewels made of tin, he smelled them and said that it was not gold, that he knew gold and silver very well, and that he cared little for other metals.

The general sent Hernando de Alvarado back to Cicuye to demand some gold bracelets, which, the Turk said, the natives had taken from him at the time they had seized him. Alvarado went thither and the people of the pueblo received him in a friendly way. When he asked for the bracelets they denied in all possible ways that they had them, saying that the Turk was lying and deceiving them. When Captain Alvarado saw that there was no other recourse he managed to get Captain Bigotes and the governor to come to his tent. Upon their arrival he arrested them and put them in chains. The men in the pueblo came out to fight, shooting arrows and berating Hernando de Alvarado, saying that he had broken his word and friendship. Hernando de Alvarado took them to the general at Tiguex, where they were kept prisoners for more than six months.[2] This was the beginning of the distrust the Indians had from then on for the word of peace which was given them, as will be seen by what happened next.

2. The treatment of Bigotes and the Turk by the Spaniards was aired in the trials of Coronado and Cárdenas. See below, pp. 319-336, 337-365.

CHAPTER XIV

*How the army left Cíbola for Tiguex, and what happened to it
on the way on account of snow.*

We have already related how, upon leaving Cíbola, the
general instructed Don Tristán de Arellano to follow him
within twenty days. This he did, seeing that his men were now
rested and supplied with provisions and anxious to go in search
of their general. He set out with his army for Tiguex. The
first day they stopped at the largest and most beautiful pueblo
in that province.[1] This pueblo alone has houses seven stories
high. These are private houses which serve as fortresses in
the pueblo. They are superior to the others, and rise like
towers at the top, being provided with embrasures and loop-
holes for defending the roofs, for as the pueblos have no
streets and the roofs are of the same height and common to
all, the terraces have to be conquered first, and these larger
houses are their protection.

It began to snow while we were there and our people
sought shelter under the pueblo's eaves, which project like
balconies, supported by wooden pillars beneath. These balconies are often reached by climbing ladders to them, for
there are no doors in the lower part.

When it stopped snowing the army continued on its way
from there. As the season was well advanced, for it was the
beginning of December, in the ten days that the army tarried
there it snowed every afternoon and nearly every night, so that,
in order to prepare lodging, wherever they camped they had
to clear away a cubit of snow. Moreover, no roads were visible,
although the guides, knowing the land, led us by their sense
of direction. Throughout the land are junipers and pines with
which we lighted big fires, succeeding, with the heat and smoke,
in clearing a yard or two of the ground around the fire. The
snow that was falling was a dry snow, for even if half an estado

1. The pueblo of Matsaki, near the northwestern base of Tówayálane, or
Corn Mountain, about fifteen miles from Hawikuh. This pueblo was at a convenient distance from Hawikuh, and it was also the last Zuñi pueblo that the
expedition could have seen in proceeding up the Zuñi valley from Hawikuh on
the way to the Rio Grande. Hodge, *History of Hawikuh*, p. 42.

fell, it did not wet the equipment, and by shaking the latter the snow fell off and the bundles remained clean. As the snow fell during the night, it covered the baggage and the soldiers in their beds, in such a way that, if some one should come suddenly upon the camp, he would see nothing but heaps of snow, and the horses. Even though the snow were half an estado deep, one could stand it, and it rather warmed those who were under it.

The army passed the great rock of Acoma.[2] As it was at peace, the people entertained us well, giving us provisions and birds, although, as I have already said, the people there are few. Many soldiers climbed to the top to see the pueblo. They found it very difficult to climb the steps in the rock, not being used to them. The natives, on the contrary, go up and down so freely that they carry loads of provisions, and the women carry water, and they do not seem to touch the walls with their hands. Our men had to hand their weapons to one another when they tried to make the climb.

From here they went to Tiguex where they were well received and lodged. There they learned the good news of the Turk, which brought no little rejoicing, as it helped to lighten the hardships, although, when the army arrived we found that land or province up in arms, for causes that were sufficient and not at all slight, as will be told. Our men had already burned a pueblo the day before the army arrived and were returning to their quarters.[3]

CHAPTER XV

Why Tiguex revolted, and the punishment inflicted upon its people without any one of them being to blame.

We have already told how the general arrived at Tiguex, where he found Don García López de Cárdenas and Hernando

2. From Matsaki, the Spaniards went "up the Zuñi River, past the present summer village of Piscado (Heshotatsinakwin) to El Morro or Inscription Rock, . . . across the pine-clad Zuñi mountains, through Guadalupe or Zuñi Pass to El Gallo, where the town of San Rafael now is and where the first Fort Wingate was established, thence to the site of McCarthy station and Acoma." Hodge, *Journey of Coronado*, 1933, p. 28, note 2.

3. See the story in the testimony of Cárdenas, pp. 352-358.

de Alvarado; how he sent the latter back to Cicuye, and how Alvarado brought Captain Bigotes and the governor of the pueblo as prisoners. The latter was an old man. The people at Tiguex did not feel well about these arrests. This ill feeling was aggravated by the general's desire to gather some clothing to distribute among the soldiers. For this purpose he sent for an Indian chief of Tiguex with whom we were already acquainted and with whom we were on good terms. Our men named him Juan Alemán because they said he had some resemblance to a certain Juan Alemán living in Mexico.[1] The general spoke with him, asking him to furnish three hundred or more pieces of clothing which he needed to distribute to his men. He replied that it was not in his power to do this, but in that of the governors'; that they had to discuss the matter among the pueblos; and that the Spaniards had to ask this individually from each pueblo. The general ordered it thus and provided that certain chosen men who were with him should go to ask for it. As there were twelve pueblos, some were to go on one side of the river and some on the other. As all this was unexpected, the natives were not given time to discuss or consult about the matter. As soon as a Spaniard came to the pueblo, he demanded the supplies at once, and they had to give them, because he had to go on to the next one. With all this there was nothing the natives could do except take off their own cloaks and hand them over until the number that the Spaniards asked for was reached. Some of the soldiers who went along with these collectors, when the latter gave them some blankets or skins that they did not consider good enough, if they saw an Indian with a better one, they exchanged it with him without any consideration or respect, and without inquiring about the importance of the person they despoiled. The Indians resented this very much.[2]

In addition to what has been narrated, an outstanding person, whose name I shall omit to spare his honor, left the pueblo

1. John, the German, a man with a long history. He had been to Florida before coming to New Spain, where he was appointed to a corregimiento. Hackett, *Documents relating to New Mexico*, I, pp. 32-33.

2. See the testimony of Coronado and Cárdenas, pp. 329-330, 351.

where the camp was and went to another one a league distant, and on seeing a beautiful woman in the pueblo, he called her husband down below and asked him to hold his horse by the bridle while he went up; and, as the pueblo was entered from the top, the Indian thought that he was going to some other place. While the native was detained there, some commotion took place, the man came back, took his horse, and rode away. When the Indian climbed to the upper part, he learned that he had ravished or had attempted to ravish his wife. Accompanied by other prominent persons in the pueblo, he came to complain, saying a man had outraged his wife, and told them how it had taken place. The general ordered all the soldiers and persons in his company to appear before him, but the Indian could not identify the man, either because he had changed clothes or for some other reason. But he said he would recognize the horse because he had held it by the rein. He was led through the stalls, and when he saw a blossom-colored horse covered with a blanket, he said that the owner of that horse was the man. The owner denied it, saying that the Indian had not recognized him, and perhaps he was mistaken also in the horse. In the end he went away without getting any redress for what he had demanded.[3]

On another day an Indian from the army who was guarding the horses came bleeding and wounded, saying that the Indians of the land had killed one companion and were driving the horses before them to their pueblos. The soldiers went to round up the horses, many of which were found missing, including seven mules belonging to the general.[4]

One day Don García López de Cárdenas went to visit the pueblos and to get an interpreter from them. He found the pueblos inclosed by a palisade and heard a great shouting inside, with horses running around as in a bull ring and the Indians shooting arrows at them. The natives were all up in arms. Cárdenas could do nothing because they refused to come out into the field, and as the pueblos are strong they could not

3. Both Coronado and Cárdenas were questioned in regard to this incident. The soldier in question was Juan de Villegas.

4. This incident is mentioned by Cárdenas at his trial. See below, p. 348.

be harmed. The general ordered Don García López de Cárdenas to go at once with the rest of the force and surround a pueblo. This was the pueblo where the greatest damage had been done and where the incident of the Indian woman had taken place.

The general went ahead, accompanied by many captains, such as Juan de Zaldívar, Barrionuevo, Diego López, and Melgosa. They caught the Indians so unawares that they soon took possession of the high terraces, but at great risk because the defenders wounded many of our men with arrows which they shot from the inside of their houses. In much danger our men remained on the top during the day, the night, and part of the following day, taking good shots with crossbows and harque-buses. Down on the ground the mounted men, together with many Indian allies from New Spain, built some heavy smudge fires in the basements, into which they had broken holes, so that the Indians were forced to sue for peace. Pablo de Melgosa and Diego López, the alderman from Seville, happened to be in that place and they answered their signs for peace by similar ones, which consisted of making a cross. The natives soon laid down their arms and surrendered at their mercy. They were taken to the tent of Don García, who, as was affirmed, did not know of the peace and thought that they were surrendering of their own accord, as defeated men.

As the general had ordered them not to take any one alive, in order to impose a punishment that would intimidate the others, Don García at once ordered that two hundred stakes be driven into the ground to burn them alive. There was no one who could tell him of the peace which had been agreed upon, as the soldiers did not know about it either, and those who had arranged the terms of peace kept silent, believing it was none of their business. Thus when the enemies saw that their comrades were being tied and that the Spaniards had started to burn them, about one hundred who were in the tent began to offer resistance and defend themselves with what they found about them and with stakes which they rushed out to seize. Our foot-men rushed the tent on all sides with sword thrusts that forced the natives to abandon it, and then the mounted men fell upon them; as the ground was level, none escaped alive except a few who had remained concealed in the pueblo and who fled that night.[5] These spread the news throughout the land, telling how the peace that was granted them had not been kept. This resulted in great harm later. After this incident, and as it snowed on them, the Spaniards abandoned the pueblo and returned to their quarters at the time when the army arrived from Cíbola.[6]

CHAPTER XVI

How Tiguex was besieged and taken, and what else happened during the siege.

As I have said already, when they had just conquered that pueblo it began to snow in that land, and it snowed so much for two months that the Spaniards could do nothing except go over the trails and tell the natives to come peacefully and that they would be pardoned, giving them all sorts of assurances. To this the Indians replied that they would not trust those who did not know how to keep the word they had pledged and reminded them that they were still holding Bigotes a prisoner and that, at the burned pueblo, they had not kept the peace.

One of those who went to make these requests was Don García López de Cárdenas, who had set out with some thirty men one day. He went to Tiguex to talk with Juan Alemán, and although they were at war the Indians came to talk with him. They told him that if he wanted to talk with them he should dismount and they would approach him on foot to discuss peace. They asked that the mounted men withdraw and said that they would withdraw their people. Juan Alemán and another chieftain of the pueblo drew near the Spaniard, and all was done as they requested. When he was close to them, they said that they bore no weapons and that he should remove his. Don García López did so in order to reassure them further, being eager to make peace with them. When he came close to them, Juan Alemán embraced him while two other Indians who accom-

5. The attack on this pueblo played a large part in the trials of Coronado and Cárdenas, but Castañeda's figures were evidently exaggerated. From the testimony in the trials it would seem that the total number of prisoners was about eighty. See below, pp. 334-335 and 355-358.
6. Their quarters had been established at the pueblo of Alcanfor. See testimony of Coronado and Cárdenas, pp. 329 and 347.

panied him drew two maces, which they had concealed behind their backs, and struck him two blows over the helmet so that they nearly stunned him. Two mounted soldiers who had not withdrawn, although they had been ordered to do so, were close at hand and they attacked so quickly that they wrested Cárdenas from the hands of the natives, although they could not harm the enemy because they had shelter near at hand and because of heavy showers of arrows that soon fell upon them. The horse of one of them was pierced through the nose. The other mounted men came in a rush and got their captain out of difficulty, but without being able to do any harm to the enemy. On the other hand, many of our men came out badly wounded. Thus they withdrew, a few staying to give battle.

Don García López de Cárdenas went with a part of the force to another pueblo located one-half league farther on, because most of the people of these pueblos had taken refuge in these two places. But they paid no attention to the requisitions for peace made upon them, nor would they grant it; on the contrary, they shot arrows from the terraces with much shouting. Don García López returned to the company that had remained to oppose the pueblo of Tiguex.

Then the warriors of the pueblo came out in large numbers. Our men, half checking the horses, pretended that they were running away, and as a result they drew the enemy into the plain, where they turned upon them in such a way that they struck down some of the most prominent among them. The others took shelter in the pueblo, at the top of it. Thus the captain returned to quarters.

Immediately after this the general gave the order to lay siege to the pueblo.[1] He set out one day with his men, in good array and with a few hand-ladders. Upon his arrival he established camp close to the pueblo, and shortly afterward attacked; but the enemy had been getting ready for many days and had so many stones to hurl on our men that they stretched many on the ground. They wounded close to one hundred men with

1. From the testimony of Coronado we learn that this was the pueblo of Moho, or Mohi, and that Coronado himself was in command during the attack. Coronado testified that the Indians killed Captain Ovando "and four or five other soldiers at Mohi." See below, p. 333.

arrows, of whom some died later because of the inefficient care of a poor surgeon who was with the army. The siege lasted fifty days. During this time the Spaniards attacked several times. What troubled the Indians most was their lack of water. Within the pueblo they dug a very deep well, but they were unable to obtain water; on the contrary, it caved in while they were digging, killing thirty persons. Of the besieged, two hundred men died in the various attacks. One day when there was a vigorous fight they killed Francisco de Ovando on our side, captain and maestre de campo during the time when Don García López was away on his explorations, and a certain Francisco de Pobares, a fine gentleman. They dragged Francisco de Ovando into the pueblo, as our men were unable to rescue him. This was very much regretted, as he was a distinguished person and besides very honorable, gracious, and unusually well liked.

One day, before the pueblo was finally taken, the Indians asked for a conference. When their request became known, they said that as they had learned that we did not harm women and children, they wanted to give us theirs, because they were exhausting their water. We were unable to induce them to make peace. They insisted that we would not keep our word. So they delivered about one hundred persons, consisting of women and children, as no more would leave the pueblo. While they delivered them, our men remained on their horses in formation before the pueblo. Don Lope de Urrea was on horseback, without helmet, receiving the boys and girls in his arms. When they ceased bringing more, Don Lope urged them to make peace, offering them all sorts of promises of security. They warned him to draw back, for they did not want to trust people who did not keep their friendship or the word they gave. As he would not withdraw, an Indian came out armed with a bow and arrow and threatened to kill him, saying that he would shoot if he did not go away. However much the other Spaniards shouted for Don Lope to put on his head armor, he refused, saying that the natives would not harm him while he remained there. When the Indian saw that he would not go away, he shot an arrow, which landed at the foot of Don Lope's horse. Putting another arrow in his bow, he told him to leave or he would shoot to kill. Don Lope put on his helmet and slowly rejoined the other riders without being harmed by the Indians. When they saw he was in a safe place they began to shout and howl and to send a shower of arrows. The general did not wish to fight them on that day because he wanted to see if he could find a way to make peace with them, to which they never consented.

Fifteen days later the Indians decided to abandon the pueblo during the night, and they did so. Placing their women in the middle they set out during the first quarter of the watch. During that quarter forty mounted men were on guard. When the men in the barracks of Don Rodrigo Maldonado sounded the alarm, the enemy fell upon them, killing a Spaniard and a horse and wounding others. However, they were repulsed, a good many of them being killed. They fell back to the river, which was high and extremely cold, and as the men from the camp quickly rushed to attack, few of the enemy escaped death or injury. In the morning the army crossed the river and found many wounded Indians who had collapsed because of the intense cold. They brought them back to heal them and make servants of them. Thus ended the siege, and the pueblo was conquered, although there were a few who had remained in the pueblo and who resisted in one of the sections, but they were overcome in a few days.

The other large pueblo had been conquered in a siege by the two captains, Don Diego de Guevara and Juan de Zaldívar.[2] Early one morning when the Spaniards were going to make an ambush in order to apprehend certain warriors who used to come out every morning to make a display to frighten our army in some way, the spies who were on duty to watch the approach of the Indians saw that the natives were leaving and going to the country. The soldiers left the ambush and went to the pueblo and, seeing the Indians in flight, they pursued and killed many of them. As news of this was sent back, some of the men in the army came and sacked the pueblo. They apprehended

2. Coronado testified that only two pueblos offered resistance, Arenal and Moho (or Mohi). He stated that López de Cárdenas was in command at the taking of the former, and he himself at the siege of the latter. See below, p. 332.

all the people found there, comprising about one hundred women and children. This siege was completed by the end of March, 1542 [1541]. Other things happened during this time, which I could have related, but which I have omitted so as not to break the thread of the narrative, but we must tell them now, as it is fitting that they should be known in order to understand what follows.

CHAPTER XVII

How the messengers from the valley of Señora reached the army, and how Captain Melchior Díaz died on the expedition to the Tizón river.

We have already told how Captain Melchior Díaz had crossed the Tizón river on rafts in order to continue the exploration of that coast. Well, shortly after the siege ended, some messengers arrived at the camp from the town of San Hierónimo with letters from Diego de Alarcón,[1] who had remained there to replace Melchior Díaz. They brought information that Melchior Díaz had died while carrying out the mission entrusted to him, and his men had returned without finding what they had gone to look for. It happened in the following manner:

After they had crossed the river they went ahead in search of the coast, which in that region turned south or southeast, for that arm of the sea extends straight to the north and the river, flowing from north to south, empties into the head of the gulf. While they were traveling in this direction, they encountered some beds of burning lava. No one could cross them, as it would be like going into the sea to drown. The ground which the Spaniards walked on resounded like a kettle-drum, as if there were lakes underneath. It was amazing to see the cinders boil in some places, for it looked like something infernal. They turned away from this place because it seemed to be dangerous, and also because of the lack of water.

One day a greyhound belonging to a soldier took a notion to chase some sheep, which they had brought along for food, and as Melchior Díaz saw it, he started in pursuit, throwing his lance at the dog on the run. The lance stuck in the ground, and

---

1. This was Diego de Alcaraz.

not being able to stop his horse the rider ran upon it in such a way that the lance pierced his groin, tearing his bladder. In view of this the soldiers turned back, carrying their captain. In addition to this, they had to fight daily skirmishes with the Indians, who were in revolt. Díaz lived about twenty days. His men endured many hardships, until he died, in their desire to bring him back. They returned in good order without losing a man. When they were through the most difficult part and had reached Señora, Alcaraz dispatched the messengers already mentioned. He informed the general of the outcome of the exploration and how some soldiers had become restless and had tried to cause some disturbances. He had sentenced two of them to be hanged, but they escaped.

Because of this the general sent Don Pedro de Tovar to that town[2] to select a few people and also to accompany the messengers he was sending to the viceroy, Don Antonio de Mendoza, with reports of what had transpired and of the promising information furnished by the Turk.

Don Pedro de Tovar left, and upon his arrival there he found that the natives of the province had killed a soldier with a poisoned arrow. He had only a small wound on one hand. On account of this several soldiers had gone out and had been ill received by the Indians. Don Pedro de Tovar sent Diego de Alcaraz with a small force to apprehend the native leaders and principal men of a pueblo called Valle de los Vellacos located on a prominence. Upon arriving there Diego de Alcaraz arrested them. Holding them prisoners, he deemed it appropriate to release them if they furnished some thread, clothing, and other things which the soldiers needed. When the Indians found themselves free they rose in arms. The soldiers attacked them, but as they were fortified and had poison they killed some Spaniards and wounded others, who died later as they were retreating to the town. If the soldiers had not taken along allies from Corazones, they would have fared still worse. They retreated to the town, leaving behind seventeen soldiers dead from the poison. They died in terrible agony from small wounds, their flesh rotting in an unbearable stench. When Don Pedro

2. In Señora.

de Tovar saw the result of the skirmish, thinking they would not be safe in that town, he moved it forty leagues farther toward Cíbola, to the Valle del Suya. We shall leave them there in order to relate what happened to the general with the army after the siege of Tiguex.

Chapter XVIII

How the general tried to leave the land pacified in order to go in search of Quivira, where, the Turk said, the real riches began.

During the siege of Tiguex the general decided to go to Cicuye. He took along the governor to set him free, promising that when he went to Quivira he would free Bigotes and leave him in his pueblo. When the general reached Cicuye he was peacefully received and entered the pueblo with a few soldiers. The natives welcomed their governor with much affection and rejoicing. After visiting the pueblo and talking to the natives, the general returned to his army, leaving Cicuye pacified and in hopes of recovering Bigotes, their captain.

At the end of the siege, as we have already stated, the general sent a captain to Chia,[1] a fine pueblo with a large population, which had sent messages offering submission. It was situated four leagues west of the river. They found the pueblo quiet and left in its care four bronze cannons which were in bad condition. In addition six men went to Quirix, a province containing seven pueblos.[2] At the first pueblo, which must have contained one hundred residents, the people ran away, not daring to wait for our men. The latter ran to intercept them and brought them back, fully protected, to their pueblo and homes. From there the Spaniards sent word to the other pueblos in order to restore their confidence. Thus the whole region was gradually reassured.

Meanwhile the river was thawing and it became possible to cross it to facilitate the journey. However, the twelve pueblos

1. Zia, in the Jemez valley.
2. These were the pueblos a short distance up the Rio Grande, Santo Domingo, Santa Ana, San Felipe, Cochití. See F. W. Hodge, *Handbook of American Indians,* Keresan Family.

of Tiguex were never resettled as long as the army remained in
that region, no matter what assurances were given them.

As the ice in the river was thawing, after being frozen for
almost four months, during which it was possible to cross over
the ice on horseback, the departure for Quivira was arranged.
There, the Turk said, gold and silver would be found, but not
so much as at Arehe and Los Guaes.[3] There were already some
men in the army who distrusted the Turk, because a Spaniard
named Cervantes, assigned to guard him during the siege, swore
under oath that he had seen the Turk talk to the devil in an olla
filled with water, and that, held under lock and key without
being able to communicate with any one, the Turk had asked
the guard what Christians had been killed by the people of
Tiguex. He replied that they had not killed any one, but the
Turk retorted: "You are lying, for they have killed five Christians, including a captain." And Cervantes, seeing that he was
telling the truth, admitted it in order to find out who had told
him. The Turk said that he knew it already and that he needed
no one to tell it to him. For this reason Cervantes spied on him
and found him talking to the devil in the olla, as I have stated.

In the meantime a review was held before leaving Tiguex.
At this time Indians arrived from Cíbola to see the general. The
latter ordered that they be well treated by the Spaniards who
might return from Señora with Don Pedro de Tovar. He gave
them letters for Don Pedro in which he instructed him as to
what he was to do and how he was to join the army, and that he
would find letters under the crosses on the route which the army
was to follow.

The army left Tiguex on May 5,[4] going by way of Cicuye,
which, as I have told, is twenty-five days—I mean leagues—distant from there. They took Bigotes along, and when they
reached Cicuye, Francisco Vázquez gave the Indians back their
captain, who was already free under guard. The pueblo rejoiced very much at his return. The inhabitants were friendly
and furnished provisions. Bigotes and the governor gave the

3. These two groups have been identified as the Pawnee and Kansas. Hodge
in J. V. Brower, *Harahey*, St. Paul, 1899, p. 129.
4. April 23, according to Coronado's letter of October 20, 1541.

general a young boy named Xabe, a native of Quivira, so that he might get information from him about the land. This boy said that there was gold and silver there but not in the quantities stated by the Turk. On the way the Turk, who went along as guide, reaffirmed what he had said, and thus they set out from there.*

CHAPTER XIX

How they set out in search of Quivira, and what befell them on the way.

The army departed from Cicuye, leaving the pueblo at peace and to all appearances pleased and under obligation to maintain their friendship, as the Spaniards had returned their governor and captain to them. They traveled in the direction of the plains, which are on the other side of the mountain range. After four days' march they came to a deep river carrying a large volume of water flowing from the direction of Cicuye. The general named it the Cicuye river.[1] They stopped here in order to build a bridge for crossing it. This was completed in four days with all diligence and quickness. Once finished, the entire army and livestock crossed over the bridge. Ten days later they came to some rancherías of a nomadic people, called Querechos around there.[2] Cattle had been sighted two days before.

These people live in tents made of dressed skins of the cattle. They follow the cattle to provision themselves with meat. Although they saw our army, they did not move away or disturb themselves in the least. On the contrary, they came out of their tents to scrutinize us. Then they spoke to the advance guard and asked what the army was. The general spoke to them, but as the Indians had already spoken to the Turk, who came with the advance guard, they agreed with him in everything he said. These people were so skillful in the use of signs that it seemed as if they spoke. They made everything so clear that an inter-

* From Cicuye.
1. The Pecos river. The crossing seems to have been in the Santa Rosa-Puerto de Luna region.
2. These Querechos were the plains Apache. The Spaniards were along the New Mexico-Texas border.

preter was not necessary. They said that by going down in the direction in which the sun rises there was a very large river, that the army could travel along its bank through continuous settlements for ninety days, going from one settlement to another. They said that the first settlement was called Haxa,[3] that the river was more than one league wide, and that there were many canoes. These Indians left this place the following day, with droves of dogs carrying their belongings.

Two days later when the army was still traveling in the direction it had taken when it left the settlement, which was between north and east, rather toward the north, other Querechos were seen on their ranches. There were seen also such large numbers of cattle that it now seems incredible. These Indians gave lavish reports of settlements, all east of our present location.

Here Don García López broke an arm, and a man got lost. He went out hunting and could not find his way back to the camp, because this land is very level. The Turk said that Haxa was one or two days away.

The general sent Captain Diego López ahead with ten companions, lightly equipped. He traced his direction toward the rising sun by means of a sea-compass, for he instructed him to travel with all speed for two days, to find Haxa, and to rejoin the army. On the following day López and his men set out in this direction, and they came upon so many cattle that those who went in the advance guard found a large number of bulls in front of them. As the animals were running away and jostling against one another, they came to a barranca, and so many cattle fell into it that it was filled and the other cattle crossed over them. The men on horseback who followed them fell on top of the cattle, not knowing what had happened. Three of the horses that fell, disappeared, with their saddles and bridles, among the cattle, and were never recovered.

The general, believing Diego López should be back by now, sent six men to go up a small river, and an equal number to go downstream, to look for traces of his horses at the source and

3. Haxa, perhaps identical with the Aiish. See Hodge in J. V. Brower, *Harahey*, St. Paul, 1899, p. 63.

mouth of the river. No tracks could be found on the fields because the grass rises up again after being trampled on. They found by chance the tracks, showing which way the party had gone. On the way back some Indians from the army who had gone out in search of fruit a good league from the place where the tracks were found, discovered López and his men, and thus they marched down the river to the camp. They told the general that in the twenty leagues they had marched they saw nothing but cattle and sky.

There was in the army another painted Indian, a native of Quivira, named Sopete.[4] This Indian persisted in saying that the Turk was lying, and for this reason no one paid any attention to the former. And although on this occasion he also said that the Querechos had talked with him, Ysopete was not believed.

From here the general sent Don Rodrigo Maldonado ahead with his company; he traveled four days and came to a large barranca like those of Colima. At its bottom he found a large ranchería with people. Cabeza de Vaca and Dorantes had passed this way. Here the natives presented Don Rodrigo with a heap of dressed skins and other things, and a tent as big and tall as a house. He ordered that it be kept as it was until the army came. He sent some men to go and guide the army there so that it would not get lost, although the men had already been placing markers of bones and cow-dung, and by these means the army was already following the advance guard.

The general arrived with his army, and on seeing such a quantity of skins he thought he would distribute them among his people, and he ordered that guards be placed to watch them. But as the men arrived and saw that the general was sending some particular individuals to the guards with instructions to give them some skins, and they were selecting them, angered at this unjust distribution, the soldiers laid hands on the hides and in less than a quarter of an hour there was nothing left but the bare ground.

The natives who saw what was going on also lent a hand to

4. Generally written Ysopete. He was a Wichita Indian from the province of Quivira. *Ibid.*, pp. 68-72.

the job. The women and some men who remained cried because they thought the army would not take anything, but would merely say a blessing over the goods as Cabeza de Vaca and Dorantes had done when they passed that way.[5] At this place there was seen an Indian woman as white as if she were from Castile, except that her chin was painted like that of a Barbary Moorish woman. In general they all adorn themselves in that fashion there and they decorate their eyes.

CHAPTER XX

How large hailstones fell on the army; how another barranca was discovered, and how the army was divided there into two parts.

While the army was resting in this ravine we have mentioned, a violent whirlwind arose one afternoon. It began to hail, and in a short time such an amount of hailstones fell, as large as bowls and even larger, and as thick as rain drops, that in places they covered the ground to a depth of two and three and even more spans. One abandoned his horse, what I mean is that there was not a horse that did not get loose except two or three which were held by negroes covered with helmets and shields. All the others were swept away until they ran into the barranca. Some climbed to places from which they were brought down with great difficulty. If the storm which caught them in the barranca had found them on the level plain the army would have been in great danger of losing its horses, for many would never have been recovered. The hailstones destroyed many tents and dented many headpieces. Many horses were bruised, and all the pottery and gourds of the army were broken. This caused great inconvenience, because pottery is not made in that locality, nor are gourds found there. They do not cultivate maize either, nor do they eat bread, but they eat either raw or badly roasted meat and fruits.

The general sent out exploring parties from there. After

5. Various critics have made much of this reference to Cabeza de Vaca, but it is quite possible that Castañeda added it for effect. In the lengthy trials of Coronado and Cárdenas, in which many witnesses were heard, there is not a single reference to Cabeza de Vaca or his companions.

four days they came to other rancherías resembling *alixares*.[1] This was a densely populated country. It produced abundant frijoles, plums like those of Castile, and wild grapes. These pueblos of rancherías extended for a three days' journey. It was called Cona. From this place a few Teyas,[2] for so those people were called, accompanied the army. They traveled with their packs of dogs, their women and children, to the last of the rancherías, where they furnished guides to proceed beyond. From here the army went to a deep barranca. They did not let these guides talk to the Turk, as the former did not corroborate the information that the Spaniards had heard before, to the effect that Quivira was to the north; the guides said that we would not find a good route; accordingly we began to believe Ysopete.

Thus the army reached the last barranca, which extended a league from bank to bank. A small river flowed at the bottom, and there was a small valley covered with trees, and with plenty of grapes, mulberries, and rose bushes. This is a fruit found in France and which is used to make verjuice. In this barranca we found it ripe. There were nuts, and also chickens of the variety found in New Spain, and quantities of plums like those of Castile. During this trip we saw a Teya shoot an arrow through both shoulders of a bull. It would have been a good feat for an harquebus. These natives are intelligent people. The women are well treated, and through modesty they cover their whole body. They wear shoes and buskins of dressed skins. The women wear blankets over their short underskirts, all of skins, with sleeves tied at the shoulders. They wear a sort of short tunic over their underskirts, with small fringes reaching to the middle of the thigh.

The army rested many days at this barranca in order to explore the country. They had traveled thirty-seven days of

1. *Alexeres,* in the margin.
2. "There is no question that the *Teyas* of Coronado and the *Tejas* or *Texas* of later times were the same; but as the term was applied collectively to perhaps all the Caddoan tribes of the present Texas region as well as specifically to the Céni or Asine and to the Ioni, it is not possible to tell what Indians the name, as applied by Castañeda, included." Hodge, in Brower, *op. cit.,* p. 64. *Cf.* H. H. Bancroft, *North Mexican States and Texas,* San Francisco, 1884, I, p. 391.

from six to seven leagues each to this point. A man had been detailed to make the calculations and even to count the steps. They said that the distance to the settlements was 250 leagues. General Francisco Vázquez realized, and now felt sure, that until this time they had been deceived in their travels by the Turk, and knew that the army lacked provisions, and that there was no place in that region where they could be procured. He called a meeting of all the captains and ensigns to decide what they thought should be done. The agreement reached by all was that the general, with thirty mounted men and half a dozen footmen, should go in search of Quivira, and that Don Tristán de Arellano should take the army back to Tiguex. When the people in the army heard of this, knowing now the decision reached, they begged the general not to leave them, but to take them along, for they all wanted to die with him rather than go back. This was of no avail, although the general promised them that he would send them messengers within a week to say whether or not it was advisable to follow him. Thus he set out, taking along the guides and Ysopete. The Turk went along in chains.

CHAPTER XXI

How the army returned to Tiguex, and how the general reached Quivira.

The general set out from the barranca, led by the guides furnished him by the Teyas. He appointed the alderman of Seville, Diego López, as his maestre de campo and took along the people who seemed to him the most reliable and who possessed the best horses. The army remained behind with some hope that perhaps the general would send for them. They once more sent a petition to him by two horsemen traveling lightly and in relays.

The general arrived—I mean his guides ran away in the first days' travel—and Diego López had to return to the army for guides and with orders for the army to return to Tiguex to seek provisions and to wait for the general. López was given other guides by the Teyas, furnished voluntarily. The army waited for its messengers and remained at that place for fifteen days, getting provisions of dried cattle meat to take along. It was reckoned that they had killed five hundred bulls in these fifteen days. It was unbelievable that there were so many of them there without cows.

During this time many of the men who went hunting got lost and were unable to return to the camp for two or three days. They wandered from place to place without knowing how to find their way back, even though they could hardly miss the lower or upper ends of the barranca in which the camp was located. Every night upon making the check to find if any one was missing, the soldiers fired their artillery, blew their horns, beat their drums, and lit great bonfires. Some of the hunters were so far away and had strayed so much that all these things profited them little, although they helped others. The best method for them to find their way was to go back to the place where they had slaughtered the cattle and to march in one direction and then in another until they came to the barranca or until they met some one who could direct them. It must be remarked that since the land is so level, when they had wandered aimlessly until noon, following the game, they had to remain by their kill, without straying, until the sun began to go down in order to learn which direction they then had to take to get back to their starting point. This could be done only by experienced men; those who were not so had to put themselves under the guidance of others.

The general followed his guides until he reached Quivira. This journey required forty-eight days because of the great deviation toward Florida which they had made. Francisco Vázquez and his men were peacefully received. They asked the Turk through the guides why he had lied to them and guided them so perversely. He replied that his country was in that region, that the people of Cicuye had asked him to take the Spaniards out there and lead them astray on the plains. Thus, through lack of provisions, their horses would die and they themselves would become so feeble that, upon their return, the people of Cicuye could kill them easily and so obtain revenge for what the Spaniards had done to them. This, the Turk said, was the reason that he had misdirected them, believing that they would not know how to hunt or survive without maize. As to gold, he declared that he did not know where there was any. He said this like one in despair, feeling angry that they had believed Ysopete and that he had guided them better than himself. The men, fearing that he might give some information that would bring harm to them, garrotted him.[1] Ysopete was pleased at this, because the Turk had always said that Ysopete was a scoundrel who did not know what he was talking about. They had always prevented him from talking to anyone. No gold or silver was found among these people, nor information of any. The chieftain wore a copper plate about his neck and he esteemed it highly.

The messengers that the army had sent to the general came back, as I have said. And as they brought no other word than what the alderman of Seville had said, the army was soon on its way back to the Teyas from the barranca. Here they sought guides to take them over a more direct route. The Indians furnished them willingly. Being people who travel continuously in that land, following the cattle, they are very familiar with it. Their method of guiding was as follows: early in the morning they watched where the sun rose, then, going in the direction they wanted to take they shot an arrow, and before coming to it they shot another over it, and in this manner they traveled the whole day until they reached some water where they were to stop for the night. By this method, what had taken them thirty-seven days to travel they now covered on their return in twenty-five, hunting cattle on their way. Along this route they found many salt lakes, for salt abounds there. One could see salt slabs on the water larger than tables and four or five fingers thick. Two or three spans under the water there was granulated salt more tasty than that of the slabs, which was somewhat bitter. It was crystalline salt.

1. The execution of the Turk was thoroughly aired in the trial, and three witnesses gave definite explanations of how it happened. Alonso Sánchez testified that the Indian was choked to death by Francisco Martín, a meat cutter, by order of Captain Diego López. Domingo Martín averred that he was garrotted at Tabas in Quivira. Juan Contreras testified that he carried the message from Coronado to Diego López that the Turk be executed in secret. He added that the Indian was strangled with a rope by a soldier named Pérez in the tent of Zaldívar. Archivo General de Indias, *Justicia*, legajo 1021, pieza 4.

In those plains there were large numbers of some animals resembling squirrels, and many of their holes. On its return the army arrived at the Cicuye river more than thirty leagues below the town—I mean below the bridge which had been built on the trip out. We marched upstream along its bank; almost everywhere it contained bushes with fruit which tasted like muscatel grapes. They grow on light branches an estado high and have leaves resembling parsley. There were unripe grapes, much wine and marjoram. The guides said that this river joins the Tiguex more than twenty days' travel from there, and that it flows to the east again. It is believed that it empties into the mighty Espíritu Santo which Don Hernando de Soto's men discovered in Florida.[2]

During this trip a painted[3] Indian woman ran away from Juan de Zaldívar. She fled down the barrancas when she recognized the land, for she was a slave at Tiguex where they had obtained her. This Indian woman had come into the possession of some Spaniards from Florida, who had penetrated as far as that region in their explorations. I heard our men say when they returned to New Spain that the Indian woman told them that she had fled from others nine days before, and that she named the captains. Thus we are led to believe that we were not far from the region they discovered, although it was affirmed that we were more than two hundred leagues inland at that time. It is calculated that the land at that place must be more than six hundred leagues across from sea to sea.

Thus, as I have said, the army went up the river until it reached the pueblo of Cicuye. They found it unfriendly, for the inhabitants would not come out peacefully or furnish any aid in provisions. From there the Spaniards continued to Tiguex, where some natives had gone back to settle and had then fled again on account of fear.

2. This was the Mississippi river.
3. The Spanish word is *labrada*, which could also mean tattooed or decorated. Other terms used are *pintados, rayados,* and *embijados,* ordinarily rendered as painted. It is thought this term applied to the Jumano Indians. See, F. V. Scholes, *Some Aspects of the Jumano Problem* in *Carnegie Institution Publication 523*, Washington, 1940, pp. 274-275. Cited from author's proofs which Dr. Scholes kindly sent us. See also *infra*, pp. 67, 238.

CHAPTER XXII

How the general returned from Quivira, and how other explorations were made to the north.

Soon after Don Tristán de Arellano reached Tiguex in the middle of July, 1542 [1541], he ordered that provisions be gathered for the approaching winter. He sent Captain Francisco de Barrionuevo with some men up the river toward the north. He found two provinces, one of which was called Hemes, containing seven pueblos,[1] and the other Yuque-Yunque.[2] The pueblos of Hemes came out peacefully and furnished provisions. Those of Yuque-Yunque abandoned two very beautiful pueblos which were on opposite sides of the river, while the army was establishing camp, and went to the sierra where they had four very strong pueblos which could not be reached by the horses because of the craggy land. In these two pueblos were found abundant provisions and beautiful glazed pottery of many decorations and shapes. Our men also found many ollas filled with a select shiny metal with which the Indians glazed their pottery. This was an indication that silver mines would be found in that land if they were sought.

Twenty leagues farther up the river there was a large and powerful river—I mean pueblo—called Braba, and which our men named Valladolid.[3] The river flowed through the center of it, and the river was spanned by wooden bridges built with very large and heavy square pine timbers. At this pueblo there were seen the largest and finest estufas that had been found in all that land. They had twelve pillars, each one two arms' length around and two estados high. This pueblo had been visited by Hernando de Alvarado when he discovered Cicuye. This land is very high and extremely cold. The river was deep

1. The Jemez group of pueblos in the Jemez valley.
2. A Tewa pueblo on the site of Chamita at the junction of the Chama and the Rio Grande and opposite San Juan pueblo in northern New Mexico. This became the first Spanish capital in New Mexico when Oñate and his colonists arrived in 1598. See G. P. Hammond, *Don Juan de Oñate and the Founding of New Mexico.*
3. This was Taos, named Valladolid after an important town in Spain. Presumably the name Braba came from the Spanish *bravo, brava,* meaning brave or fearless. It could also apply to the pueblo's abrupt scenic background.

and had a swift current, without any ford. Captain Barrionuevo turned back from here, leaving all those provinces at peace.

Another captain marched down the river in search of those settlements which the people of Tutahaco said were located a few days' journeys from there. This captain went down eighty leagues and found four pueblos, which he left in peace. Then he traveled until he found that the river disappeared underground like the Guadiana in Extremadura. He did not go farther on, where the Indians said it reappeared as a large stream, because his commission was limited to eighty leagues.

When this captain got back—and the time when the captain general was to return from Quivira was about to expire and as he had not come—Don Tristán chose forty men, and, leaving the army in the care of Francisco Barrionuevo, he set out in search of the general. When he arrived at Cicuye the people of the pueblo came out to fight. This caused the Spaniards to tarry four days to inflict some punishment on them, as was done, because a few shots fired into the pueblo killed some of their people. They would not come out into the open because, on the first day, two of their prominent men were killed.

In the meantime, news arrived announcing the coming of the general. For this reason, too, Don Tristán had to wait there to protect that pass. When the general arrived he was received with great rejoicing by all. Xabe, the young Indian furnished to the general by the people of Cicuye when he set out in search of Quivira, was with Don Tristán de Arellano. When he learned that the general was coming back, making demonstrations of joy, he exclaimed, "Now that the general is coming back you will see that there is gold and silver in Quivira, although not so much as the Turk pretended." But when the general arrived and Xabe saw that they had not found anything, he was sad and dejected, claiming that there was some. He made many believe that it was so, since the general had not gone inland. He had not dared to do so because it was densely populated and he did not feel that his force was strong enough. He turned back with the intention of leading his men there after the rainy season, for it was raining already, it being the early part of August. With good guides and traveling lightly, it took him forty days to make his way back. When the army left Tiguex the Turk asked why they loaded their horses with so much provisions, saying that they would get tired and not be able to load so much gold and silver later, which showed plainly the deceit.

After the general arrived at Cicuye with his men he set out, at once, for Tiguex, leaving the pueblo much more calm, since the people came readily to speak to him in a peaceful way. Arriving at Tiguex he tried to establish winter quarters there, planning to go back[4] with the whole army. He said he had reports of large settlements and mighty rivers, and that the country was very much like Spain in fruits, vegetation, and climate. They were not satisfied to think that there was no gold; on the contrary, they were of the belief that it was to be found inland, because, although the natives said there was none, they knew what it was and they had a name for it, calling it *acochis*. With this we bring to a close this first part, and we shall try to give a description of the provinces.

SECOND PART

In which we discuss the provinces and terraced pueblos, their rituals and customs, compiled by Pedro de Castañeda, inhabitant of the city of Náxara.

Laus Deo

It does not seem to me that the reader will be satisfied with what he has seen and understood of what I have related about the expedition, although from it one may easily understand the discrepancy in the information, for after reporting such fabulous treasures it seems perplexing not to find any sign or vestige of them. Instead of settlements there were found great deserts, and instead of populous cities nothing but pueblos with two hundred residents, the largest one containing between eight hundred and one thousand. I do not know whether or not this will furnish them matter to reflect on and consider the uncertainties of this life.

To satisfy them I will give a detailed narrative of all the

4. To Quivira.

inhabited territory that was seen and discovered on the expedition, together with some of the native customs and ceremonies, based on what we were able to learn from them. I shall state, also, the location of every province in order that thus one may later be able to understand the position of Florida, in what region greater India is situated, and how this land of New Spain is part of a continuous continent with Peru, as well as with greater India or China. There is no strait in this region to divide it. On the contrary, the land is so wide that it makes possible the existence of such vast uninhabited areas as there are between the two seas. For the northern coast above Florida turns to the Bacallaos (Cod) and then extends to Norway; the southern coast turns to the west, forming the other point to the south, almost like an arch which extends toward India. As a result the lands which extend along the mountain ranges on both coasts draw so far apart from one another that they leave in the center extensive but uninhabitable plains which abound in cattle and many other animals of various species. However, there are no snakes, for these plains are bare of mountains, but they contain all sorts of game and fowl, as will be told later.

I shall not tell about the return of the army to New Spain until the reader may see how little justification there was for this. We shall begin with a description of the villa of Culiacán and note the difference between that region and the Cíbola country, explaining why the former is settled by Spaniards and the latter is not, when it ought to be the opposite, inasmuch as the Spaniards are Christians; for in the Cíbola country there is the intelligence of men, while in the other the barbarism of animals dominates, even surpassing that of beasts.

CHAPTER I

Concerning the province of Culiacán, its ceremonies and customs.

Culiacán is the most remote region of the new kingdom of Galicia. It was the first area settled by Nuño de Guzmán when he conquered this kingdom. It is 210 leagues west of Mexico. There are, in this province, three main languages in addition to other dialects derived from them. The first language is that of the Tahus, who were the best and the most intelligent people, the ones who are at present more civilized and have acquired the most light of the faith. They used to worship the devil and offer him presents of their belongings and riches, such as clothing and turquoises. They did not eat human flesh nor did they practice human sacrifices. They used to breed very large snakes, which they worshipped.

There were among them men dressed as women, who married other men and served them as women. They used to canonize, with great solemnity, the women who wanted to remain unmarried in a great ritual or dance at which all the dignitaries of the district gathered. They took such persons out to dance naked, and when they had all danced with her, they placed her in a hut which had been fittingly decorated for the occasion. The women adorned her with clothes and bracelets of fine turquoises. Then the dignitaries came in to make use of her one at a time, and after them all the others who cared to. From then on she was not to deny herself to any one, as she was paid a certain established amount for the service. And even though she might take a husband later on, she was not thereby free to deny herself to any one who offered her pay.

These Indians' greatest festivals are their market days. One custom among them was that when women got married their husbands bought them from their parents and relatives at a high price. Then the husband took her to a dignitary, whom they respected as a priest, and he would deflower her and find out whether she was a virgin. If she was not, her parents were to return to her husband all he had paid for her, and he was free to decide whether he wanted to take her as a wife or let her be canonized. Sometimes the natives held great drinking orgies.

The second language is that of the Pacaxes. These are the people who inhabit the lands between the plains and the mountains. They are more savage people. Some eat human flesh, particularly those who dwell at the foot of the mountains. They are inveterate sodomites. They take many wives, even though these are sisters. They worship carved stones and are great wizards and sorcerers.

The third language is that of the Acaxes. These people have a considerable portion of their land in the mountains and throughout the cordillera. Thus they go out to hunt men as well as deer. They all eat human flesh, and he who has the most human bones and skulls hanging around his hut is the most feared and respected. These Indians live in groups in very rough country, avoiding the plains. Between their settlements there must be a gully in between so that they can converse across it, but can not easily cross it. Five hundred men will gather at a single call. On the slightest pretext they kill and eat one another. They were difficult to subdue because of the roughness of their land, which is very great.

Many rich silver mines have been found in this land. They do not run very deep, so soon become exhausted. On the coast of this province there begins the gulf which extends north to the sea and inland 250 leagues and ends at the mouth of the Tizón river. One point of this land lies to the east; the point to the west is California. The width from point to point, as I have heard from men who sailed this gulf, is thirty leagues, for, having lost sight of land on one side, they begin to see the other. They say the gulf is 150 leagues wide from shore to shore. Moreover, from the Tizón river the coast turns to the south, forming an arch as far as California, where it turns to the west, forming the headland which formerly was thought to be an island. It is a low and sandy land, inhabited by savage, bestial, naked people who eat their own excrement, and where men and women couple like animals, the female placing herself publicly on all fours.

CHAPTER II

Regarding the province of Petlatlán and all the inhabited region as far as Chichilticale.

Petlatlán is a settlement of houses, covered with a sort of mats made of reed grass, grouped into pueblos extending along a river from the sierras to the sea. The people are of the type and ceremonies of the Tahues Culhacaneses. There are many sodomites among them. They have a large population and a territory of other pueblos in the mountain ranges. These people differ somewhat in language from the Tahues, but they understand one another. It was named Petlatlán because the houses were built with *petates*.[1] This type of houses extends in that region for 240 leagues and more, the distance from Petlatlán to the beginning of the despoblado of Cíbola. The land forms a frontier for the obvious reason that from there on there are no trees except pines, nor fruits except prickly pears, mesquite, and pitahayas. The distance from Petlatlán to Culiacán is twenty leagues, and 130 from Petlatlán to the valley of Señora. In between there are many rivers settled by people of the same type, such as the Sinaloa, Boyomo, Teocomo, Yaquimi,[2] and other smaller ones. There is also Corazones, which belongs to us, down the valley of Señora.

Señora is a river and valley thickly settled with comely people. The women wear skirts of dressed deerskins and small tunics reaching to their waists. In the morning the dignitaries of the pueblos stand on some terraces which they have for that purpose and remain there for one hour, calling like town criers, instructing the people in what they are to do. They have their temples in small houses, into which they drive numerous arrows, making them look like porcupines on the outside. They do this when war is about to break out. Around this province, toward the sierras, there are large settlements forming separate small provinces. They are composed of ten or twelve pueblos. Seven or eight of them whose names I know are Comu, Patrico, Mochil, Agua, Arispa, and Vallecillo. There are others which we did not visit.

From Señora to the valley of Suya there is a distance of forty leagues. In this valley was founded the town of San Hierónimo, where later the natives revolted and killed some of the people settled there, as will be told farther on in the Third Part. Round about this valley there are many pueblos. The people are of the type of those of Señora. They have the same dress, language, ceremonies, and customs and all else found up to

1. Mats. They are still widely used in this region of Mexico.
2. Castañeda's Petlatlán was the Sinaloa river; his Sinoloa, the Fuerte; his Boyomo, the Mayo; his Teocomo, the Cocoraqui; his Yaquimi, the Yaqui; his Señora, the Sonora.

the despoblado of Chichilticale. The women paint their chins and eyes like Moorish women from Barbary. The men are inveterate sodomites. They drink the juice of the pitahaya, a fruit of big thistles[3] which opens like the pomegranate. They become stupefied with this drink. They make preserves of prickly pears in great amounts. It keeps in its own juice in large quantities without additional sugar. They make mesquite bread, in loaves resembling cheeses, which keeps for a whole year. There are native melons in this land, so large that one person has all he can do to carry one of them. The natives cut them into pieces and dry them in the sun. They taste like dried figs. When cooked they are very good and sweet. When so cured they will keep a whole year.

Royal eagles were seen in this land. The native dignitaries have them as an emblem of power. No fowl of any sort were seen in any of these pueblos except in the valley of Suya, where chickens like those of Castile were found. We could not understand how they had passed through so much hostile territory, for the natives are ever at war with one another. Between Suya and Chichilticale there are many rams and mountain goats with very large bodies and horns. Some Spaniards maintained they had seen flocks of more than one hundred head. They are so fleet that they quickly disappear.

The land changes again at Chichilticale and the thorny trees disappear. The reason is that since the gulf extends as far as that place and the coast turns, so also the ridge of the sierra turns. Here one comes to cross the ridge and it breaks to pass into the plains of the land.

CHAPTER III

Describing Chichilticale and the despoblado of Cíbola, its customs, ceremonies, and other things.

Chichilticale received its name because the friars found in this region a house formerly inhabited by people who broke away from Cíbola. It was built of brown or red earth. The

3. "Que es fruta de Cardones." This may refer to the fruit of the giant cactus which resembles the pitahaya.

house was large and showed clearly that it used to be a fortress. It must have been despoiled by the natives of the region, the most barbarous people thus far encountered. They live by hunting, and in rancherías, without permanent settlements. Most of the region is uninhabited. There are large pine forests and pine nuts in abundance. The pines that were found are squatty and have long branches upward of two or three estados in height. There are oak trees bearing sweet acorns, and *fanonas* which produce a fruit like that from which coriander preserves are made. When dried the fruit is very sweet, like sugar. In some springs watercress was found, and there are also vines, pennyroyal, and wild marjoram. In the rivers of this despoblado there are barbels and picones[1] as in Spain. Gray lions were seen from the beginning of the despoblado. The land rises gradually until one reaches Cíbola, which is eighty leagues by the northern route. To get there from Culiacán we marched with the north on our left.

Cíbola is composed of seven pueblos, the largest of which is called Mazaque. The houses, as a rule, are three and four stories high, but at Mazaque there are houses of four and seven stories. The natives here are intelligent people. They cover the privy and immodest parts of their bodies with clothes resembling table napkins, with fringes and a tassel at each corner, tying them around the hips. They wear cloaks made with feathers and rabbit skins, and cotton blankets. The women wear blankets wrapped tightly around their bodies, and fastened or tied over the left shoulder, drawing the right arm over them. They also wear well-fashioned cloaks of dressed skins, and gather their hair over their ears in two wheels that look like coif puffs.

This land is a valley between sierras that rise like boulders. The Indians plant in holes, and the corn does not grow tall, but each stalk bears three and four large and heavy ears with 800 grains each, a thing never seen in these regions. There are in this province numerous bears, lions, wild cats, and otters. There are very fine turquoises, although not in the quantity

1. Dr. Hodge suggests that the barbels and picones were catfish and Gila trout.

claimed. The natives gather and store piñon nuts for the year. A man has only one wife. There are estufas in the pueblos, in which they gather to take counsel, and which are located in the patios or plazas. They have no rulers as in New Spain, but are governed by the counsel of their oldest men. They have their priests, whom they call papas, who preach to them. These priests are the old men, who mount the high terrace of the pueblo in the morning as the sun rises, and from there, like town criers, preach to the people, who all listen in silence, seated along the corridors. The priests tell the people how they should live. I believe they give them some commandments to observe, because there is no drunkenness, sodomy, or human sacrifice among them, nor do they eat human flesh, or steal. They work in common in the pueblo, and the estufas are for all, but it is considered sacrilegious for the women to enter them to sleep. As an emblem of peace, they make the sign of the cross. These people burn their dead, casting with them into the fire the tools the deceased used in their occupations.

Tusayán lies twenty leagues away between north and west. It is a province with seven pueblos of the same type, dress, ceremonies, and customs as those of Cíbola. In these two provinces, comprising fourteen pueblos, there must be about three or four thousand men. The distance to Tiguex is forty leagues or more by the northern route. On the way there is found the rock of Acuco, which we described in the First Part.

Chapter IV

How the people of Tiguex live, as well as those of the province of Tiguex and its environs.

Tiguex is a province of twelve pueblos, on the banks of a large and mighty river. Some pueblos are on one bank, some on the other. It is a spacious valley two leagues wide. To the east there is a snow-covered sierra, very high and rough.[1] At its

1. The province of Tiguex was in the Albuquerque-Bernalillo area. In the Coronado and Cárdenas trials, the witnesses did not agree wholly as to the number of pueblos but their figures ranged from 12 to 15. The sierra was the Sandía ridge east of Bernalillo and Albuquerque, a range often snow-covered during the winter months.

foot, on the other side, there are seven pueblos, four in the plain and three sheltered on the slope of the sierra.

Seven leagues to the north there is Quirix, with seven pueblos.[2] Forty leagues to the northeast there is the province of Hemes, with seven pueblos.[3] To the north or east, four leagues away, is found Acha.[4] To the southeast there is Tutahaco, a province comprising eight pueblos.[5] All these pueblos have, in general, the same ceremonies and customs, although some have practices among them not observed elsewhere. They are governed by the counsel of their elders.[6] They build their pueblo houses in common. The women mix the plaster and erect the walls; the men bring the timbers and set them in place. They have no lime, but they mix a mortar made with charcoal ash and dirt, which is almost as good as if it were made with lime. For although the houses are four stories high, their walls are built only half a yard thick. The people gather large amounts of brush and reeds, set fire to it, and when it is between charcoal and ash, they throw in a large amount of water and dirt and mix it, then make round balls with it, which they use as stones when dry. They set them with this same mixture, so that it becomes like a mortar.[7]

The unmarried young men serve the pueblo in general. They bring the firewood that is needed and stack it up in the patios of the pueblos, from where the women take it to their homes. These young men live in the estufas, which are located in the patios of the pueblo. They are built underground, either square or round, with pine columns. Some have been seen having twelve pillars, four to the cell, two fathoms thick; the common ones had three or four columns. The floors are paved with large smooth slabs like the baths in Europe. In the interior there is a fireplace like the binnacle of a boat where they burn a handful of brush with which they keep up the heat. They can

2. Quirix is the Queres, or Keres. See above, p. 233.

3. In the Jemez valley, but the distance and direction are obviously wrong.

4. Acha, identified by Hodge with Picuris.

5. Tutahaco, see *ante*, p. 220, note 1.

6. See Elsie Clews Parsons, *Pueblo Indian Religion*, Chicago, 1939, 2 vols.

7. The practice of molding mud into adobe bricks was first introduced by the Spaniards.

remain inside the estufa as in a bath. The top is even with the ground. We saw some so large that they could be used for a game of ball.

When some one wishes to marry he must have the permission of the rulers. The man must spin and weave a blanket and place it before the woman. She covers herself with it and becomes his wife. The houses are for the women, the estufas for the men. If a man repudiates his wife he must come to the estufa. It is punishable for the women to sleep in the estufas or to enter them for any other purpose than to bring food to their husbands or sons. The men spin and weave; the women take care of the children and prepare the food. The land is so fertile that they need to cultivate only once a year, just for planting, for the snow falls and covers the fields, and the maize grows under the snow. In one year they harvest enough for seven years. There are numerous cranes, geese, crows, and thrushes which feed on the planted fields. With all this, when, in the following year, they proceed to plant again, they find the fields covered with maize, which they had not been able to gather fully.

There were in these provinces large numbers of native hens and cocks with gills.[8] These, if not dressed or cut open, could be kept for sixty days after death without giving any smell. This was true also of human beings. And they could be kept even longer during the winter. The towns are free from filth because the inhabitants go outside to discharge excrement, and they urinate in earthen jars, which they empty outside the pueblo.

Their houses are well separated and extremely clean in the places where they cook and where they grind flour. They do this in a separate place or room in which there is a grinding place with three stones set in mortar. Three women come in, each going to her stone. One crushes the maize, the next grinds it, and the third grinds it finer. Before they come inside the door they remove their shoes, tie up their hair and cover it, and shake their clothes. While they are grinding, a man sits at the door playing a flageolet, and the women move their stones, keeping time with the music, and all three sing together. They grind a large amount at one time. All their bread is made with

8. Not chickens, but turkeys.

flour, mixed with hot water, in the shape of wafers. They gather large quantities of herbs, which they dry and keep for their cooking throughout the year. There are no edible fruits in this land, except pine nuts. The natives have their own preachers. No sodomy was observed among them nor the sacrificing or eating of human flesh. They are not a cruel people, as was shown at Tiguex, where Francisco de Ovando remained dead for some forty days. When the pueblo was at last taken the Spaniards found his body whole, among the native dead, without any other injury than the wound from which he died. He was as white as snow, without any bad smell.*

From one of our Indians who had been a captive among these people for a year, I learned some details of their customs. In particular I asked him why the young women went about naked in that province when it was so cold; he answered that the maidens had to go about that way until they took a husband and that as soon as they had relations with a man they covered themselves. In that region the men wore jackets of dressed deerskin and over them their robes. Throughout these provinces one finds pottery glazed with alcohol, and jugs of such elaborate designs and shapes that it was surprising.

CHAPTER V

Regarding Cicuye and the surrounding pueblos; how some people came to conquer that land.

We have already explained that the people of Tiguex and all the provinces located on the banks of that river are similar in type, nature, and customs, and it will not be necessary to give any details about them. I wish to tell only about the location of Cicuye and some abandoned pueblos which lie in this region, on the direct road that the army followed to get there. I will tell also of others, located across the snowy sierra of Tiguex, which also lie away from the river in that region.

Cicuye is a pueblo containing about 500 warriors.[1] It is feared throughout that land. It is square, perched on a rock

---

* This was Ovando, killed at the pueblo of Mohi. *Cf.* above, pp. 228-229.
1. See above, p. 217, note 1.

in the center of a vast patio or plaza, with its estufas. The houses are all alike, four stories high. One can walk on the roofs over the whole pueblo, there being no streets to prevent this. The second terrace is all surrounded with lanes which enable one to circle the whole pueblo. These lanes are like balconies which project out, and under which one may find shelter. The houses have no doors on the ground floor. The inhabitants use movable ladders to climb to the corridors, which are on the inner side of the pueblos. They enter them that way, as the doors of the houses open into the corridors on this terrace. The corridors are used as streets. The houses facing the open country are back to back with those on the patio, and in time of war they are entered through the interior ones. The pueblo is surrounded by a low stone wall. Inside there is a water spring, which can be diverted from them.[2] The people of this town pride themselves because no one has been able to subjugate them, while they dominate the pueblos they wish. The inhabitants [of Cicuye] are of the same type and have the same customs as those in the other pueblos. The maidens here also go about naked until they take a husband. For they say that if they do anything wrong it will soon be noticed and so they will not do it. They need not feel ashamed, either, that they go about as they were born.

Between Cicuye and the province of Quirix there is a small, strong pueblo, which the Spaniards named Ximena,[3] and another pueblo, almost deserted, for only one of its sections is inhabited. This pueblo must have been large, to judge by its site, and it seemed to have been destroyed recently. This was called the town of the silos, because big maize silos were found in it.

Farther on there was another large pueblo completely destroyed and leveled. The patios were covered with numerous stone balls as large as jugs of one arroba. It looked as if the stones had been hurled from catapults or guns with which an

2. Bandelier, "A Visit to the Aboriginal Ruins in the Valley of the Rio Pecos," *Papers of the Archaeological Institute of America,* American series, I, p. 89.
3. The Tano pueblo of Galisteo.

enemy had destroyed the pueblo. All that we could find out about it was that some sixteen years before some people called Teyas had come in large numbers to that land and had destroyed those pueblos. They besieged Cicuye but could not take it because it was strong. Before leaving the land they made friends with all. They must have been powerful people who must have had war machines to batter down the pueblos. The natives of Cicuye could not tell from which way the invaders had come except to point to the north. As a rule these people call the Teyas brave people, just as the Mexicans refer to the Chichimecas or Teules.[4] The Teyas whom the army met, although they were brave, were known by the people of the towns as their friends. The Teyas often go to the latter's pueblos to spend the winter, finding shelter under the eaves, as the inhabitants do not dare to allow them inside. Evidently they do not trust them, although they accept them as friends and have dealings with them. At night the visitors do not stay in the pueblo, but outside under the eaves. The pueblos keep watch at night with bugles and calls, as in the fortresses in Spain.

There are seven other pueblos by the side of this road in the direction of the snowy sierra. One of them had been partly destroyed by the aforesaid people, who live under the jurisdiction of Cicuye. Cicuye is located in a small valley between sierras and mountains covered with big pines. There is a brook which abounds in excellent trout and otters. Big bears and fine falcons multiply in this region.

CHAPTER VI

Which lists the number of terraced pueblos visited in the settlements, and their population.

It seems to me that before I proceed to tell about the plains of the cattle and of the native ranches and settlements, it would be well to know how large the settled area was, where the terraced houses, clustered into pueblos, were seen, and what expanse of land they occupied. I say that Cíbola is the first.

Cíbola, seven pueblos.

4. *Teul,* Aztec word meaning brave.

Tusayán, seven pueblos.

The rock of Acuco, one.

Tiguex, twelve pueblos.

Tutahaco, eight pueblos.

These pueblos were down the river.

Quirix, seven pueblos.

On the sierra nevada, seven pueblos.

Ximena, three pueblos.

Cicuye, one pueblo.

Hemes, seven pueblos.

Aguas Calientes, three pueblos.[1]

Yuque-Yunque, in the sierra, six pueblos.

Valladolid, called Brava, one pueblo.

Chia, one pueblo.

They make a total of sixty-six pueblos. It seems that Tiguex is the heart of the pueblos; Valladolid is the farthest up the river to the northeast. The four pueblos down the river are to the southeast, where the river turns to the east. From the most distant point reached down the river to the farthest place up stream, in which extent all the settlements are located, there is a distance of 130 leagues, ten more or less. All these pueblos, counting those on side trips, total sixty-six, as I have stated. All combined must contain about 20,000 men. This can be easily estimated by the population of the pueblos, for between them there are no villages or houses, but, on the contrary, the land is all uninhabited. Thus it is clear that as the natives are small in number and so different in customs, government, and way of living from all the nations that have been visited and explored in this region of the west, they must have come from that region of greater India, the coast of which lies on the west of this land. They may have come down through this region, crossing the cordilleras, and marching down the river and settling where it seemed most suitable to them. Then as they increased in numbers they extended their settlements until they came to the end of the river, for this disappears under ground, its course being toward Florida. It descends from the northeast, where the Spaniards obtained further information of the pueblos, but the

---

1. Aguas Calientes doubtless refers to the pueblos in the San Diego canyon.

general had ceased following the Turk who gave the reports. If those sierras where the river rises had been crossed, I believe that valuable information would have been gathered and one would have reached the lands from which these natives came. For, according to the location, they are the beginning of greater India, although these are remote, unexplored, and unknown regions, for, according to the coastline, the region between Norway and China is very far inland. At the center the distance from sea to sea is very great, as shown by the direction of the coasts, not only from what Captain Villalobos[2] had discovered by sailing this sea to the west in search of China, but also from what may be discovered on the North sea toward the Bacallao, which is up the Florida coast toward Norway.

Returning to my original purpose, I will say that in the distance of seventy leagues in the breadth of that inhabited land, and in 130 leagues along the Tiguex river, no other towns or peoples were seen or found than the ones already mentioned. There are not one but many repartimientos in New Spain containing a larger number of people. In many of the pueblos, there were found silver ores, which the natives used to glaze and to paint their pottery.

CHAPTER VII

Dealing with the plains that were crossed, the cattle, and the people who live in the plains.

We have already told of the terraced settlements, which, it seems, were located in the center of the cordillera, in the most level and spacious portion of it, for it is 150 leagues across to the plains located between the two mountain ranges. I refer to the one along the North sea and the one on the South sea, which on this coast could be more properly called West sea. This cordillera is the one at the South sea. Thus to better understand how the settlements I am describing extend along the middle of the cordillera, I will state that from Chichilticale, which is the beginning of this stretch, to Cíbola, there is a dis-

2. For a discussion of the Villalobos expedition to the Philippines, see H. R. Wagner, *Spanish Voyages to the Northwest Coast of America*, San Francisco, 1929, pp. 98 *et seq.* The bibliography of this enterprise is in *ibid.*, p. 340.

tance of eighty leagues. From Cíbola, which is the first pueblo, to Cicuye, which is the last one on the way across, is seventy leagues; from Cicuye to the beginning of the plains it is thirty leagues. Perhaps we did not cross them directly but at an angle so that the land seemed more extensive than if it had been crossed at the center. The latter route might have been more difficult and rough. One can not determine this very clearly because of the bend which the cordillera makes along the coast of the gulf of the Tizón river.

Now we shall describe the plains, a vast level area of land more than 400 leagues wide in that part between the two cordilleras. The one was crossed by Francisco Vázquez Coronado on his way to the South sea, the other by the men of Don Fernando de Soto when coming from Florida to the North sea. What we saw of these plains was all uninhabited. The opposite cordillera could not be seen, nor a hill or mountain as much as three estados high, although we traveled 250 leagues over them. Occasionally there were found some ponds, round like plates, a stone's throw wide, or larger. Some contained fresh water, others salt. In these ponds some tall grass grows. Away from them it is all very short, a span long and less. The land is the shape of a ball, for wherever a man stands he is surrounded by the sky at the distance of a crossbow shot. There are no trees except along the rivers which there are in some barrancas. These rivers are so concealed that one does not see them until he is at their edge. They are of dead earth,[1] with approaches made by the cattle in order to reach the water which flows quite deep.

As I told in the First Part, over these plains there roam natives following the cattle, hunting and dressing skins to take to the pueblos to sell in winter, since they go to spend the winter there, each group to the nearest place. Some go to the pueblos of Cicuye, others to Quivira, and others toward Florida to the settlements located in the direction of that region and port. These peoples, called Querechos and Teyas, gave reports of large settlements. From what was seen of these natives and of others which they said lived in other sections, they are by far more numerous than those of the pueblos, better proportioned,

1. Son de tierra muerta.

greater warriors, and more feared. They go about like nomads with their tents and with packs of dogs harnessed with little pads, pack-saddles, and girths. When the dogs' loads slip to the side they howl for some one to come and straighten them.

These people eat raw meat and drink blood, but do not eat human flesh. They are gentle people, not cruel, and are faithful in their friendship. They are very skillful in the use of signs. They dry their meat in the sun, slicing it in thin sheets. When it is dry they grind it, like flour, for storage and for making mash to eat. When they put a handful in an olla it soon fills it, as the mash swells a great deal. They cook it with fat, which they always try to have with them. When these Indians kill a cow they clean a large intestine and fill it with blood and put it around their necks to drink when they are thirsty. After they cut open the belly of the cow they squeeze out the chewed grass and drink the juice, which remains on top, saying that it contains the substance of the stomach. They cut open the cow at the back and pull off the skin at the joints, using a flint the size of a finger, tied to a small stick, doing this as handily as if they used a fine large tool. They sharpen the flints on their own teeth. It is remarkable to see how quickly they do it.

In these plains there are numerous wolves, with white hair, which follow the cattle. The deer are white spotted and have long hair. When they are killed, their skin can be pulled off easily by hand while warm; they look like skinned pigs. Hares, which are very plentiful, run about so stupidly that the mounted men kill them with their lances. This is because the hares are used to running among the cattle. They run away from men on foot.

CHAPTER VIII

About Quivira, its location, and the information obtained concerning it.

Quivira is situated west of those barrancas in the midst of the land, somewhat close to the coastal cordillera. For up to Quivira the country is flat, and there one commences to see some sierras. The country is well settled. From the very border of the land it was noticed that it is very similar to that of Spain in its vegetation and fruits. One finds plums like those of Castile, grapes, nuts, mulberries, rye grass, oats, pennyroyal, wild marjoram, and flax in large quantities, but the natives do not utilize this as they do not know its uses. The people are almost of the same type and dress as the Teyas. Their pueblos are similar to those in New Spain. The houses are round, without any enclosure. They have some terraces resembling barbacoas,[1] under the roofs of which the inhabitants sleep and keep their belongings. The roofs are of straw.[2]

There are in the neighborhood other provinces settled by numerous people. There remained here in this province a friar named Fray Juan de Padilla and also a Spanish-Portuguese, a negro, a mestizo, and some Indians from the province of Capothan in New Spain. The friar was killed because he wanted to go to the province of Gaus, whose inhabitants were their enemies. The Spaniard escaped, riding a mare, and finally reached New Spain, coming by way of Pánuco. The Indians from New Spain who were with the friar buried him with the consent of the murderers and then fled, following the Spaniard until they overtook him. This Spaniard was a Portuguese whose name was Campo.

The great Spiritu Santo river that had been discovered by Don Fernando de Soto in the land of Florida flows from this region. It runs through a province called Arache, according to information which was considered reliable, though its sources were not seen, because it was said that they come from very far, from the land of the southern cordillera, where it empties into the plains and, crossing the flat lands, cuts through the northern cordillera and comes out at the place where it was sailed by Don Fernando de Soto's men. This is more than three hundred leagues from where it empties into the sea. On account of this and its many tributaries, it becomes so mighty

1. Barbacoas were lacustrine dwellings of the natives of Antilles, built on piles or posts. This same term is used by Balboa to describe the native houses at Panama. See I. B. Richman, *The Spanish Conquerors*, New Haven, 1921, p. 73. For a more complete description of these houses visited by Coronado, see Jaramillo's narrative, below, p. 305.

2. Ethnologists say that this is further proof that Quivira was the land occupied by the Wichita Indians in Kansas, for they lived in grass houses.

when it reaches the sea that they lost sight of the land, and the water was still fresh.

Quivira was the most remote land seen, and of which I can now give a description or narrative. It behooves me now to go back to my account of the army, which I left at Tiguex, resting for the winter, waiting to proceed or return to the search of these settlements of Quivira. This was not done, finally, because the Lord willed that these discoveries should wait for other peoples, and that those of us who went thither should be satisfied with telling that we were the first to discover it and gain information of it, just as Hercules made known the place where Julius Cæsar was to found Seville or Híspales.[3]

May it please the Almighty God to determine everything. For it is plain that had it been His will neither Francisco Vázquez would have returned to New Spain without cause or justification, nor would Don Fernando de Soto's men have failed to settle such a fine land as they had found, so extensive and so well populated, especially as they had received news of our army, as they had.

THIRD PART

Which deals with what happened to Francisco Vázquez Coronado while in winter quarters, and how he abandoned the expedition and returned to New Spain.

Laus Deo

Chapter I

How Don Pedro de Tovar arrived with men from Señora, and Don García López de Cárdenas left for New Spain.

At the close of the First Part of this book we told how Francisco Vázquez Coronado, on returning from Quivira, had ordered that winter quarters be prepared at Tiguex, in order to return with all his army, after the passing of the winter, to discover all those settlements. During this time Don Pedro de Tovar, who, as we have said, had gone to bring some people

3. Híspales, ancient name for Seville.

from the town of San Hierónimo, arrived with his men.[1] And, indeed, considering the fact that he needed good people to follow his general to the land of the Indian called the Turk, he did not take along the rebellious or troublesome men, but the most experienced and best soldiers, the most trusted men he could find. They reached Tiguex, and although they found the army there they were not very pleased because they had come with their noses high in the air, thinking they would find the general in the rich land of the Indian called the Turk. They consoled themselves with the hope of the return trip they were to make, and they lived in great satisfaction and joy in anticipation of this expedition and that the army would soon leave for Quivira.

Don Pedro de Tovar brought letters from New Spain, both from the viceroy, Don Antonio de Mendoza, and from private individuals. One of these letters was for Don García López de Cárdenas, in which he was notified of the death of his older brother. He was asked to return in order to go to Spain to take possession of his inheritance. So he obtained permission and left Tiguex with some other persons who had permission to go and retire to their homes. Many others would have liked to go, but they did not do so in order not to appear weak-kneed.

In the meantime the general tried to pacify some neighboring pueblos that were restless, and to invite the people of Tiguex to make peace. He tried also to obtain some native clothing, because the soldiers were already naked and in a wretched condition. They were plagued with lice, and they were unable to kill them or get rid of them.

General Francisco Vázquez Coronado had been, among his captains and soldiers, the most beloved and best obeyed leader who had ever ventured forth in the Indies. But as necessity knows no law, and as the captains who gathered the clothing distributed it badly, taking the best for themselves and their friends and servants, leaving the discards to be distributed among the soldiers, some ill feeling and bad words soon developed. This situation arose partly on account of what has been

1. See above, p. 232.

said and partly because the soldiers saw that some prominent men were spared from labor and sentry duty and fared better in the distribution of clothes and provisions. The fact that there was nothing in Quivira to induce them to return to that land was responsible in no small degree for what happened later, as will be seen.

CHAPTER II

How the general fell, and how the return to New Spain was arranged.

When winter had passed, the march to Quivira was announced and the men began to provide themselves with the necessary things. As nothing in this world depends on the plans of men but on the will of Almighty God, it was His design that our desires should not be fulfilled. It happened that on a holiday the general rode out on horseback as he often did, to find recreation. Riding a spirited horse, he raced by the side of Captain Don Rodrigo Maldonado. His servants had used a new girth, which, because of being kept so long, must have been rotten. It burst during the race, and the general fell on the side where Don Rodrigo rode, and on passing over him the horse struck him on the head with a hoof. As a result Francisco Vázquez was on the point of death and his recovery was long and uncertain.

During this time when the general was in bed, Don García López de Cárdenas, who had set out for New Spain, returned in flight from Suya. He had found the town abandoned and the people, horses, and cattle dead. He arrived at Tiguex, and when they learned the sad news they did not dare to transmit it to the general, because of his condition, until he was well. Then, when he was able to get up, he was informed, and it affected him so much that he had a relapse, which may have induced him to make the decision he did, as was later believed. It happened that when he found himself in this state of affairs, he remembered that at Salamanca a mathematical friend of his had told him that he would find himself in strange lands, that he would become mighty and powerful, and that he was to suffer a fall from which he would be unable to recover. This thought of death made him desire to go back to die near his wife and children. Furthermore, as the physician and surgeon who attended him was a newsmonger, he learned from him of the grumblings among the soldiers, so he plotted secretly and underhandedly with some caballeros of his own views and brought about the return to New Spain by discussions and gatherings among the soldiers. This led to the holding of consultations and to their presenting the general, through their ensigns, with petitions signed by all the soldiers. As they had discussed this whole matter in detail, it was not necessary to waste much time, for many were already inclined to return.

When they presented this petition, the general pretended that he would not consent to it unless it was confirmed by all the caballeros and captains in a signed statement. As some were in on the secret they granted it readily and even induced the others to do likewise. Thus they expressed their opinion that they should return to New Spain since they had not found any wealth nor had any settled area been discovered where repartimientos could be provided for the whole army. And as soon as the general had the signatures, the return to New Spain was announced.

But as nothing can remain secret, the double-dealing became known and many caballeros who had been deceived and outdone tried by all means to retrieve their signatures from the general. He guarded them so closely that he did not leave his chamber, pretending that his ailment was much more serious, placing guards about himself and his room, and at night about the upper story where he slept. Despite all of this they stole his coffer from him, and it was said that they did not find the signatures in it because he kept them in his mattress. Others said that they had recovered them. They asked the general to give them sixty chosen men, and they would remain there and hold the country until the viceroy should send them reinforcements or recall them. Another suggestion was that the general should leave the army but pick out sixty men to go back with him.

But the soldiers would not remain there under any circumstances. In the first place they had already set their prow for New Spain, and in the second place they clearly foresaw the discord that would arise over who should rule. The caballeros—we do not know whether it was because they had sworn loyalty or because they believed the soldiers would not support them—although hurt, had to accept and put up with the decision. From then on, however, they did not obey the general as they formerly had, and he was disliked by them. He catered to the soldiers and flattered them. This produced the results he sought, namely, the return of the entire army.

CHAPTER III

How Suya rose in rebellion, and how the settlers contributed to it.

In the preceding chapter we have already told how Don García López de Cárdenas returned in flight from Suya when he found the land in revolt, telling how and why that town was abandoned, which happened as I shall relate.[1] It turned out that since only worthless people, turbulent and seditious men, were left in the town, although some honorable men were left in administrative posts and for governing the others, the wickedness of the scoundrels got the upper hand. Every day they held gatherings and schemed, saying that they had been sold out and would not be employed to advantage, since that region was being entered through another section of New Spain better situated than that one. This was not so because they were on an almost direct route. With all this a certain group, choosing as their leader one Pedro de Avila, rebelled and returned to Culiacán, leaving Captain Diego de Alcaraz with a few sick people in the town of San Hierónimo. There were no able men left to follow them or to entreat them to turn back.

---

1. Diego de Alcaraz had been left in charge of San Hierónimo, also called Corazones, on the death of Melchior Díaz. When he got into trouble with the people of this region and lost a considerable number of men from the poison used by the Indians, the settlement was moved farther north, to Suya, said to be 40 leagues nearer toward Cíbola, but retaining the name of San Gerónimo de los Corazones. It was apparently in the vicinity of the modern town of Bacoachi. *Cf.* Sauer, "The Road to Cíbola," *op. cit.,* pp. 34-35.

On their way some of their people were killed in some pueblos. Finally they reached Culiacán, where Hernando Arias de Sayabendra detained them with promises, as he was awaiting Juan Gallego, who was to arrive there with men from New Spain and who would take them back. Some, fearing what would happen to them, fled during the night to New Spain.

Diego de Alcaraz, now ill, who had been left[2] with a few people, could not maintain himself there even if he had wanted to because of the deadly poison used in that region by the natives. The latter, knowing the weakness of the Spaniards, no longer submitted to the same treatment as before.

Some gold veins had already been discovered before this. But, being located in warring country and of little possibility, they were not worked. During this confusion the Spaniards never relaxed their watches, but were more cautious than ordinarily.

The town was situated near a small river. One night, unexpectedly, they saw unusual and inexplicable fires. This caused them to redouble their watches. But, as they did not hear anything throughout the night, toward morning they relaxed their vigilance and the enemy entered the town so quietly that they were not noticed until they began to plunder and murder. Some people who had time, fled to the plain and in so doing the captain was mortally wounded. After some Spaniards had reorganized with a few horses, they turned on the enemy and rescued some people, although not many. The enemy departed with their booty and without suffering any harm, having killed three Spaniards, many servants, and more than twenty horses.

The surviving Spaniards on that day set out on foot and without horses on their way to Culiacán, keeping away from the roads and without any provisions until they reached Corazones. Here the Indians, like the faithful friends they have always been, helped them with provisions. From there, after enduring untold hardships, they reached Culiacán. Here the alcalde mayor, Hernandarias de Saavedra, received them and

2. At Suya.

lodged them to the best of his ability until Juan Gallego arrived with the reinforcements he was bringing in order to push on in search of the army. He was not a little worried that that pass had been abandoned, believing that the army was in the rich land described by the Indian whom they called the Turk because he looked like one.

CHAPTER IV

How Fray Juan de Padilla and Fray Luis remained in the country and the army got ready to return to Mexico.

Now when General Francisco Vázquez saw that all was calm and that his plans had turned out according to his desires, he ordered every one to be ready to start the return to New Spain in the early part of April, 1543 [1542].

When a certain Fray Juan de Padilla, a friar of the minorite order, with authority to say mass, and another lay brother, Fray Luis, saw this, they told the general that they wanted to remain in that land. Fray Juan de Padilla chose Quivira, as it seemed to him that his teachings would bear fruit there; Fray Luis went to Cicuye. For this reason, since it was Lent, he preached for the occasion, on a Sunday, the sermon about the Father of the Multitudes, basing his text on the authority of Holy Scripture. His aim in remaining was to convert those peoples and bring them to the faith; and as they had permission, although this was not necessary, the general provided them with an escort to accompany them to Cicuye, where Fray Luis remained, and Fray Juan continued to Quivira. He took along the Portuguese we have already mentioned, the negro, the mestizo, and Indians from New Spain, together with the guides who had accompanied the general. Within a short time of his arrival there he was murdered, as we have told in Part Two, chapter VIII. Thus we may believe he died a martyr, for his zeal was holy and sincere.[1]

Fray Luis remained at Cicuye. Nothing has been learned

---

1. Mota Padilla says that after Fray Juan had carried on missionary work among the Indians for some time, they shot him with arrows, for not all would accept his teachings. *Historia de la Conquista de la Provincia de la Nueva-Galicia,* Mexico, 1870, p. 168. The same in Tello, *Crónica,* p. 489.

of him to this day, although, before the army left Tiguex, when some men took him a certain number of sheep for him to keep, they met him accompanied by people. He was going to visit other pueblos which were fifteen or twenty leagues from Cicuye. This gave rise to no little hope that he was in the good graces of the pueblo, and his teachings would be fruitful. Nevertheless, he complained that the old men were deserting him and he believed they would end by killing him. As for myself I believe that, as he was a man of good and saintly life, our Lord would protect him and would grant him grace to convert some of those people, and upon his demise he would leave some one to maintain them in the faith. There is no reason to believe otherwise, since the people around there are pious and in no way cruel. On the contrary, they are faithful friends and opposed to cruelty. They keep their word and are loyal to their friends.

After the friars left, the general, fearing that the taking of natives from that land to New Spain might result in harm, ordered the soldiers who had natives in their service to let them go freely to their pueblos or wherever they wished. In my opinion he erred in this, for it would have been better if they had been taught among the Christians.

The general was now joyful and happy when the designated date came. Every one being equipped with the necessary things for the journey, the army left Tiguex for Cíbola, but an incident worthy of notice happened on this trip. It was that although the horses started out well broken to toil, fat and beautiful, in the ten days that it took to reach Cíbola over thirty of them died. There was not a day on which two, three, and even more did not die. Later, until reaching Culiacán, a large number of them died, a thing that had not happened on the whole expedition.

When the army came to Cíbola it was reassembled for the march through the despoblado, because Cíbola marked the end of the settled region of that land. That whole land was left pacified and calm, some of our Indian allies remaining among them.

CHAPTER V

How the army left the settled country and marched to Culiacán, and what befell it on the way.

Leaving now astern, we may say, the settlements that had been discovered in the new land, which were, as I have said, the seven towns of Cíbola, the first to be seen and the last to be left behind, the army set out over the despoblado. For two or three days the natives never ceased to follow the rear guard of the army to pick up any baggage or Indian servants, for although they remained at peace and they had been good and faithful friends, still, when they saw that we were abandoning the land, they rejoiced at keeping some of our people. However, it is believed that it was not to harm them, as was learned from some who refused to go with them, although they had been importuned and asked by them. Still they kept some people, and others remained of their own accord. As a result there must be fine interpreters there at present.

The despoblado was traversed without incident. Juan Gallego met the army on the second day out of Chichilticale. He was coming from New Spain with necessary reinforcements of men and supplies for the army, thinking that he would find it in the land of the Indian called the Turk.

When Juan Gallego saw that the army was turning back, the first word he uttered was not, "I am glad you are coming back." Nor did he regret it either, for, after speaking to the general when they came to the army, I mean its quarters, there was not lacking some restlessness among the men on account of that new aid. The reinforcements had endured considerable hardship to reach that place, having had daily skirmishes with the Indians of that region who were in revolt, as we have already told. There were some discussions and schemes to establish a settlement somewhere around there and send a report to the viceroy, informing him of what was taking place. The soldiers who were returning from the new land would not agree to anything except to return to New Spain. On account of this nothing came of the plans advanced in these discussions. And although there were some disturbances, in the end the men calmed down.

There came with Juan Gallego some of those who had revolted and abandoned the town of Corazones. They were protected and guaranteed by his word, and even if the general had wanted to impose some punishment, his authority was slight, for he was now disobeyed and little respected. From there on he began to be afraid again; and, pretending that he was ill, he surrounded himself with guards. At some places there were outbreaks by the Indians, and some horses wounded and killed. This continued until we arrived at Batuco,[1] where friendly Indians from the valley of Corazones came out to meet the army. They came to meet the general like the good friends they had always been. Thus they had treated all the Spaniards who had come through their land, furnishing them with needed supplies, and even with men when necessary. So they had always been well treated and rewarded by our men on this expedition.

We discovered that quince juice was a good remedy against the poison of this locality. For, at a pass a few days before reaching the valley of Señora, the hostile Indians wounded a Spaniard named Mesa, and although it was a deadly wound infected with fresh poison and it was more than two hours before he was attended to, he did not die, thanks to the juice. Nevertheless the portion infected by the poison rotted away and the flesh dropped off, leaving the bones and tendons bare, with a pestilential stench. The wound was on the wrist and the poison had reached his shoulder before he recovered, and all this portion was left without flesh.

1. Hodge observes, *Journey of Coronado,* 1933, p. 70, note 1, "There were two Opata settlements of this name, the one here evidently referred to being on the Rio Moctezuma, about 22 miles east of Ures, site of the first Corazones. It became the seat of the Jesuit Mission of Santa María in 1620. If this is the Batuco mentioned by Castañeda, it would seem that instead of retracing his journey down the Rio Sonora, he followed the Rio Moctezuma evidently on account of the hostility of the Opata at Suya (Corazones) in the Sonora valley."

To this may now be added the statement of López de Cárdenas regarding the return route, indicating that the expedition retraced its steps down the Sonora valley. "The general and the whole army set out on their way to Mexico. They passed through Corazones on their way to San Miguel. At various passes some Indians attacked them and wounded several Spaniards." See below, p. 363.

The army traveled without taking time to rest, for by now provisions were running low, and as these regions were in revolt there was no way of obtaining food supplies. The army marched until it reached Petlatlán, making a few forays across the country in search of provisions. Petlatlán belongs to the province of Culiacán, and for this reason it was at peace, although since then some changes have taken place. The army rested there for a few days in order to get provisions. After leaving this place with greater haste than on previous occasions, it managed to traverse the thirty leagues to the valley of Culiacán. Here the men were again received as people whose leader was badly injured.

CHAPTER VI

How the general left Culiacán in order to give the viceroy an account of the army he had entrusted to him.

It seems that, upon reaching the valley of Culiacán, the hardships of this expedition came to an end, first because the general was governor there and second because they were in the land of the Christians. And so some began to square accounts because of the superiority and authority which their captains had exercised over them, and even some captains under the command of the general did likewise. Each one now conducted his own affairs in his own way, so much so that when the general went to a pueblo ten leagues away, many people or most of them remained at the valley to rest. Some were determined not to follow him. The general well realized that he could no longer constrain them by force, even though his governorship gave him new authority. He chose to find a better way. This consisted in sending all his captains to gather provisions and meat from the supplies in some pueblos, which, as governor, were under his jurisdiction. He pretended to be ill and stayed in bed in order that those who wanted to conduct business dealings with him could speak to him and he to them more freely and without hindrance or observation. He did not neglect to send for some citizen friends of his, begging and urging them to speak to the soldiers and persuade them to accompany him on his way from there back to New Spain, and to tell them that he would recommend them to the viceroy, Don Antonio de Mendoza, and that he himself, in his government, would favor those who might wish to settle there.

When the general had arranged matters, he set out with his army during bad weather. It was the beginning of the rainy season, the day of St. John.[1] During this time it rains heavily, and the rivers of that uninhabited region which they had to cross to reach Compostela are numerous and very dangerous. They are infested with big and fierce alligators. While the army was camped by one of these rivers, a soldier who tried to cross from one side to the other was carried away within sight of all by an alligator, and they were unable to rescue him.

The general continued on his way, leaving everywhere people who would not follow him. He arrived in Mexico with less than one hundred men to report to the viceroy, Don Antonio de Mendoza, and was not well received by him, although he presented his excuses. From then on Francisco Vázquez lost reputation and retained only for a short time the governorship of New Galicia that had been entrusted to him, for the viceroy assumed the administration of it until the audiencia was established there, by which it is governed to this day. And this was the end of these discoveries and of the expedition that was made to the new land.

There remains now for us to explain how the army could have entered the land by a more direct route. However, I may say that there is no short cut without its handicap. And what one knows beforehand is always better because then men take appropriate measures for the eventualities and needs which they know they will encounter and which they have experienced before. We will tell now of the location of Quivira, which was the route followed by the army. We will likewise speak of the location of greater India, which was what the army was supposed to be in search of when it set out in that direction. Since Villalobos has now discovered this coast of the South sea, which turns toward the west, it is clear and obvious that, since we were in the north, we should have traveled to the west and not to the east as we did.

1. June 24.

With this we shall dispose of this matter and bring this treatise to a close, having mentioned some noteworthy things which I did not describe in order to deal more fully with them in the following two chapters.

Chapter VII

Concerning the incidents that happened to Captain Juan Gallego in the revolted land when he came with reinforcements.

One might well complain that, in the preceding chapter, I have passed over in silence the exploits of Captain Juan Gallego and the twenty companions who went with him. We shall tell them in this chapter in order that those who, in the future, may read and talk about them may have a reliable author on whom to depend, an author who does not write fables, like some things we read now-a-days in books of chivalry. Were it not for the fables of enchantments with which they are laden, there are events that have happened recently in these parts to our Spaniards in conquests and clashes with the natives that surpass, as deeds of amazement, not only the aforesaid books but even the ones written about the twelve peers of France. Taking into consideration the deadly strength that the authors of ancient times attribute to those heroes and the brilliant and resplendent arms with which they bedeck them, and considering the small stature of men in our times and the limited and poor weapons in these parts, the remarkable deeds performed with such weapons by our men at the present time are very amazing, more so than those narrated of the ancients, for they, too, fought against naked savages as our men do against the Indians. Among the latter there are not lacking brave and valiant men and accurate archers. We have seen them bring down birds on the wing, and shoot hares while running in pursuit of them.

I have stated all this so that some things which we consider to be fabulous may be accepted as real, for every day in our own times we see greater events, just as in the future men will marvel at the exploits of Don Fernando Cortés, who with 300 men dared to penetrate into the heart of New Spain, where there was such a great number of people as Mexico contains, and with 500 Spaniards complete its conquest and domination in two years, a most amazing feat. The deeds of Don Pedro de Alvarado in the conquest of Guatemala, of Montejo in Tabasco, the conquest of the continent, and of Peru, are all deeds that should compel me to omit and pass over in silence what I want to narrate now. But since I am bound to give an account of the incidents of this expedition, I wish to bring out the things which I am going to narrate presently as well as what I have told before.

Captain Juan Gallego reached the town of Culiacán with very few people. There he enlisted as many men as he could of those who had run away from the town of Corazones, or rather from Suya. All together he had twenty-two men, with whom he traveled throughout that inhabited land. He traveled 200 leagues over unfriendly country and among people in revolt, people who formerly were on friendly terms with the Spaniards. Almost daily he had clashes with the enemy.

His method of travel was to leave the baggage behind with two-thirds of his people, while he always led the advance guard with six or seven Spaniards, and without any of the allies they had along. This advance guard forced its way into the pueblos, killing, destroying, and applying the torch, and falling upon the enemy so suddenly, with such swiftness and vigor, that they did not give them time to assemble or plan any resistance. Thus they became so feared that there was not a pueblo that dared to oppose them. On the contrary the natives fled from them as from a powerful army; in fact, Gallego traveled for ten days entirely through inhabited country without an hour of rest, and all this was done with seven companions. When the baggage arrived with the rest of the men, the latter found nothing to do other than to plunder, since the advance guard had already killed or apprehended the people they had been able to lay hands on; the others had fled.

Since the Spaniards did not halt anywhere, even when the pueblos farther on were forewarned, they fell upon the inhabitants so swiftly that they gave them no time to organize. This was especially true in the region of the town of Corazones, where Gallego killed and hanged a large number of people in punishment for their rebellion. With all this he did not lose a man nor was any one wounded, except one, who, while despoiling a dying Indian, was struck by the latter on the eyelid and the skin broken. As the arrow was poisoned he would have died had he not been given some quince juice. As it was, he lost his eye. These deeds were such that the soldiers will remember them as long as they live. This will be particularly true of four or five friendly Indians who left Corazones with them. They were so amazed that they thought the Spaniards more divine than human. And if our army had not met Gallego's men, as it did, they would have gone to the land of the Indian called the Turk, for which they were headed. And they would have reached there without great risk, such was Gallego's good order and management, and so well were the men trained and experienced in war. Some of them remained at this town of Culiacán, where I am now writing this chronicle and report. Here both they and I, and the others who remained in this province, have never lacked trouble in pacifying and holding this land, apprehending rebels and falling into poverty and privation. This is especially true now since the land is poorer and more overrun than ever before.

CHAPTER VIII

In which are told some unusual things that were seen on the plains, with a description of the bulls.

It was not without some mystery that, in the Second Part of this book, chapter seven, which tells of the plains, I suppressed and concealed the things that I shall relate in this special chapter. Here they will be brought together, for they were outstanding things not seen anywhere else. I dare to set them down in writing because I am writing at a time when many of the men are still living who saw them all and who will vouch for my story.

Who could believe that although one thousand horses, five hundred of our cattle, more than five thousand rams and sheep, and more than 1500 persons, including allies and servants, marched over those plains, they left no more traces when they got through than if no one had passed over, so that it became necessary to stack up piles of bones and dung of the cattle at various distances in order that the rear guard could follow the army and not get lost. Although the grass was short, when it was trampled it stood up again as clean and straight as before.

Another thing that they found on the south side of a salt lake was a large heap of cattle bones a crossbow shot in length or very close to it. In places it was nearly two estados high and three or more fathoms wide. The bones were found at a place where there are no people who could have gathered them. From this the Spaniards figured that these bones must have been piled up by the waves produced by the high north winds in the lake. They must have been the bones of cattle that died in the lake, not being able to get out because of being old or feeble. What was astounding was the number of cattle that must have been required to produce all those bones.

I want to tell, also, about the appearance of the bulls, which is likewise remarkable. At first there was not a horse that did not run away on seeing them, for their faces are short and narrow between the eyes, the forehead two spans wide. Their eyes bulge on the sides, so that, when they run, they can see those who follow them. They are bearded like very large he-goats. When they run they carry their heads low, their beards touching the ground. From the middle of the body back they are covered with very woolly hair like that of fine sheep. From the belly to the front they have very heavy hair like the mane of a wild lion. They have a hump larger than that of a camel. Their horns, which show a little through the hair, are short and heavy. During May they shed the hair on the rear half of their body and look exactly like lions. To remove this hair they lean against some small trees found in some small barrancas and rub against them until they shed their wool as a snake sheds its skin. They have short tails with a small bunch of hair at the end. When they run they carry their tails erect like the scorpion. One peculiar thing about them is that when they are calves they are reddish like ours, and with time, as they become older, they change in color and appearance. Furthermore, all the bulls slaughtered were found to have their left ears slit, while these are whole when they are calves. The reason for this we were unable to discover. Excellent garments could be made from their fine wool, although not colored ones, as the wool itself is dark red.

Another remarkable observation was that the bulls roam without the cows in such large herds that there was no one who could count them. They move so far away from the cows that the distance from the place where we began to see them to where we saw cows was over forty leagues. The land where they roamed was so level and bare that, wherever one looked at them, one could see the sky between their legs. Consequently at a distance they looked like cleared pine trunks with the crowns joining at the top. When a bull stood alone it resembled four such pines. And however close one was to them, one could not see the ground on the other side when looking across their backs. This was because the earth was so round, for, wherever a man stood, it seemed as if he were on the top and saw the sky around him within a crossbow shot. No matter how small an object was placed in front of him, it deprived him of the view of the land.

Other things were seen, but not being of such importance I do not describe or mention them. However, we should not fail to mention the great respect that the Indians have for the symbol of the cross in some places in these tall pueblos. At Acuco, by a spring down in the valley, they have a cross two spans high and the thickness of a finger. It was made of wood and had a base one yard square around which were many small sticks adorned with plumes and many withered flowers torn into small pieces.

At a tomb outside the pueblo of Tutahaco, where it seemed that some one had been buried recently, there was another cross at the head. It was made of two small sticks tied together with cotton thread, and there were many dry and crumbled flowers. I say that in my opinion they have gained, in some way or other, some light of the cross of Christ, our Redeemer. This may have come by way of India, whence these natives came.

CHAPTER IX

Which deals with the route taken by the army and how a more direct one could be found if we were to go back to that land.

I very much wish that I now had some knowledge of cosmography or geometry to make clear what I want to say. This would have enabled me to appraise and evaluate the advantage that might accrue to any one who should ever again leave New Spain in search of that land and go there through the interior of the land instead of following the route taken by the army. However, relying on the favor of the Lord, I shall state what I understand, explaining it to the best of my ability.

I believe it is already known that the Portuguese Campo was the soldier who escaped alive when the Indians of Quivira killed Fray Juan de Padilla. He reached New Spain by way of Pánuco, having traveled over the plains until he crossed the cordillera of the North sea, keeping always to his left the land discovered by Don Hernando de Soto. This man never saw the Espíritu Santo river. After crossing the North sea cordillera, he came upon Pánuco, so that if he had not started to search for the North sea he would have come to the limits of the land of Zacatecas, of which there is information now.

To go back in search of Quivira the above route would be far better and more direct, for in New Spain, to serve as guides, are some of those who came with the Portuguese, although I believe it would be better and shorter to go by way of the land of the Guachichules, always keeping close to the South sea cordillera, since it is more inhabited and there would be more provisions. To engulf oneself in the plains would mean to get lost on account of their great vastness and the scarcity of food in the land, although it is true that after reaching the cattle no such privation would follow. This applies only if going in search of Quivira and of those pueblos mentioned by the Indian whom they called Turk, and not if following the round-about way taken by the army of Francisco Vázquez Coronado. For they went 110 leagues west of Mexico, and then to the northeast one hundred leagues, and to the north 250, and all this brought them only to the barrancas where the cattle were. And although they traveled 850 leagues they were not more than 400 leagues from Mexico by a direct route. If one wishes to go to Tiguex in order to turn west from there in search of India, one should follow the route taken by the army, because, even though one might wish to take a different route, there is none. It is hindered by the arm of the sea that enters this coast inland toward the north. This might be overcome by building a fleet that would cross this gulf and land at the island of the negroes. From there the land in the interior could be entered by crossing the cordillera in search of the country whence the people of Tiguex came, or other similar peoples. As for trying to enter by way of Florida and the North sea, we have already seen and learned that all the expeditions that came through there have been unfortunate failures. Furthermore, this land is full of swamps, is rough and sterile, and the worst country that the sun shines upon. This is true unless they land beyond the Espíritu Santo river, as was done by Don Hernando de Soto.

Just the same I still hold that, even at the cost of much hardship, it is better to go by way of land already traveled and where the watering places are known. It would be easier to carry the necessary things in larger quantities.

The most essential thing in new lands is horses. They instill the greatest fear in the enemy and make the Indians respect the leaders of the army. Artillery is also much feared in places where they are not acquainted with its use. In the case of pueblos like the ones discovered by Francisco Vázquez, a good piece of heavy artillery to batter them down would be useful, but he had only some little machines and no skilled men who could build a catapult or some other war machine to put fear into the natives, which is very essential.

I say, then, that with the knowledge we now have of the directions along this coast of the South sea sailed by the ships exploring this western portion, and what we know of the North sea toward Norway, which is up the Florida coast, whoever should now enter to explore by the same route that Francisco Vázquez did, will easily know, upon reaching the land of Cíbola or Tiguex, which way to go to locate the land that was sought by the Marqués del Valle, Don Hernando Cortés. They would likewise know the trend made by the gulf of the Tizón river and choose the proper direction.

This will suffice to bring our narrative to a close. In all other matters, may the Almighty Lord of all things, God Omnipotent, who knows how and when these lands are to be discovered, determine for whom this good fortune is preserved.

LAUS DEO
The copying was completed in Seville, on Saturday, October 26, 1596.

RELACION DEL SUCESO

RELATION OF THE EVENTS ON THE EXPEDITION THAT FRANCISCO VÁZQUEZ MADE TO THE DISCOVERY OF CÍBOLA.[1]

When the army arrived in the valley of Culiacán, Francisco Vázquez divided it because of the unfavorable report obtained in regard to Cíbola and because the provisions along the way were scarce, according to Melchior Díaz, who returned at that time after traversing it. Francisco Vázquez took eighty men with horses, twenty-five footmen, and a portion of the artillery and set out from Culiacán, leaving the rest of the people under the command of Don Tristán de Arellano, with instructions to follow within twenty days, and to proceed to the valley of Corazones and wait there for the general's letter, which would be sent after he had reached Cíbola and had seen what it was like, and he did so. This valley of Corazones is 150 leagues from the valley of Culiacán and an equal distance from Cíbola.

The entire route up to within fifty leagues of Cíbola is inhabited, although in some places at a distance from the road. The people are all of the same type, because their houses are all of mats, some of them with low terraces. The inhabitants all have maize, although not in great abundance, and in some places little of it; they also have melons and beans. The best portion of all this inhabited territory is a valley named Señora, which is ten leagues beyond Corazones, where a town was later established. They have some cotton; for the most part they use deerskins to clothe themselves.

1. Translated from a photostatic copy of the original in the Archivo General de Indias, *Patronato*, legajo 20. In the original the date is given as 1531, obviously a copyist's error for 1541. Printed in Buckingham Smith's *Colección de Varios Documentos*, pp. 147-154, from a copy made by Muñoz, and also in Pacheco y Cárdenas, *Documentos de Indias*, XIV, pp. 318-329, from a copy found in the Archives of the Indies at Seville. This printing has numerous bad readings. Translated by Winship in *Fourteenth Annual Report* of the Bureau of Ethnology, pp. 572-579, and in the Trail Makers and Grabhorn editions, 1904 and 1933, respectively.

Francisco Vázquez passed by all this because the crops were small. There was no maize anywhere along the way, except at this valley of Señora, where they obtained a little; this was in addition to what we brought from Culiacán, where we procured a supply for eighty days. We arrived in Cíbola after seventy-three days,[2] although after much hardship and the loss of many horses and the death of some Indians. These troubles were doubled when we saw Cíbola, even though we found considerable maize there. All along the way we found the natives peaceful.

The day we reached the first pueblo some of the people came out to attack us, while the others remained fortified in the pueblo. We could not make peace with them, however much we sought peace, so we were compelled to fight, killing some of them. The others withdrew to the pueblo, which was at once surrounded and attacked in order to enter it. However, we were forced to withdraw on account of the great damage that they caused us from the terraces.

We began to attack them from the outside with the artillery and harquebuses. They capitulated that afternoon. Francisco Vázquez was badly bruised from some stones, and I am sure that he would have been there yet had it not been for the maese de campo, Don García López de Cárdenas, who rescued him. After surrendering the pueblo, the Indians abandoned it and left for the other pueblos, and as they left their houses to us we took lodging in them.

Father Fray Marcos understood or gave the impression that the area and region in which the seven pueblos are located was one single pueblo, which he called Cíbola. This whole settlement and district is called Cíbola. The pueblos consist of three hundred, two hundred, and one hundred and fifty houses each. In some pueblos the houses are all clustered together, although in others they are divided into two or three sections, but for the most part they are all together. In the center there are patios, within which are estufas for the winter, and outside the pueblo are estufas for the summer. The houses are two and three stories high; the walls are of stone and mud, and some of

2. From Culiacán.

mud. The pueblos in many places are fortresses for the Indians. The houses are too good, especially for these people, who are like animals and have no order at all except in their houses.

Their food consists mostly of maize, beans, melons, and some Mexican chickens. The latter they raise more for their feathers than for food, because they make quilts of them, since they have no cotton. They wear blankets of henequen[3] and deerskins, and some of skins of the cattle.

They hold their rituals and sacrifices before some idols, but what they worship most is water, to which they offer painted sticks, plumes, and powders of yellow flowers, this usually at the springs. They also offer some turquoises which they have, although they are of little worth.

From the valley of Culiacán to Cíbola, two routes extend over the two hundred and forty leagues. Up to thirty-four and one-half degrees the route is north, and from there to Cíbola, which is at almost thirty-seven degrees, the route is northeast.

Upon inquiring of the natives of Cíbola through an interpreter regarding the country farther on, they said that there were settlements to the west. Francisco Vázquez at once sent Don Pedro de Tovar to explore. He found seven other pueblos, called the province of Tuzán,[4] thirty-five leagues to the west. The pueblos are somewhat larger than those of Cíbola. In other respects, in food and everything else, they are alike, except that at Tuzán they raise cotton.

While Don Pedro de Tovar had gone to see this region, Francisco Vázquez dispatched messengers to the viceroy with a report of what had taken place up to that point.[5] At the same time he sent orders with them for Don Tristán, who, as I have said, was at Corazones, to establish a town in the valley of Señora and to proceed to Cíbola. This he did, leaving there eighty mounted men, all those who had but one horse and who were the least dependable people. He left Melchior Díaz with them as their captain and alcalde mayor, for it had been so ordered by Francisco Vázquez.

3. That is, yucca.
4. The Hopi pueblos. This is the Tusayán of Castañeda, see p. 213.
5. This was Coronado's letter of August 3, 1540. See above, p. 162.

Don Tristán instructed Díaz to take half of his men from there and explore to the west. He did so, traveling one hundred and fifty leagues until he came to the river which had been entered from the sea by Hernando de Alarcón, who had named it Buenaguia. The settlements and people along this route are almost like those of Corazones, except at the river and its region, where the people are more comely and have more maize. However, the houses in which they live are shacks and resemble pigsties, being almost underground. The roofs are of straw and made without any skill. This river, it is claimed, is large. Díaz's party reached it thirty leagues from the coast. These leagues and thirty more Alarcón had sailed from the sea with his boats two months before they arrived. At that place this river flows from north to south.

Melchior Díaz continued for five or six days to the west, but turned back because he did not find water or grass, but many sand dunes. On the way back he had some skirmishes at the river district, because the natives wanted to waylay them while they were crossing the river. During this return, Melchior Díaz died from an accident. He killed himself when hurling a lance at a dog.

When Don Pedro de Tovar returned and gave an account of those pueblos, the general at once sent Don García López de Cárdenas, maestre de campo, over the same route by which Don Pedro had come, for the purpose of going west beyond that province of Tuzán. He allotted him eighty days for the round trip of exploration. He went beyond Tuzán with native guides who said that there were settlements ahead, although quite far. After going fifty leagues west from Tuzán, and eighty from Cíbola, he came to the canyon of a river where it was utterly impossible to find a way down, either for horses or on foot, except at a very difficult descent where it was almost two leagues down. The canyon was so lined with rock that one could hardly see the river, although it is said to be as large or much larger than the one at Seville. From the top it looked like an arroyo. Although the men sought diligently in many places for a crossing, none was found.[6]

6. The famous Grand Canyon of the Colorado.

Here they spent a good number of days, suffering from lack of water which they could not obtain even though they had the river before their eyes. For this reason Don García López was compelled to go back until they found some. This river flows from the northeast and turns south southwest, so it can not fail to be the one reached by Melchior Díaz.

Four days after Francisco Vázquez sent Don García López on this discovery, he sent Hernando de Alvarado to explore the route to the east. He set out, and thirty leagues from Cíbola he found a rock with a pueblo on top, the greatest stronghold ever seen in the world. The natives call it Acuco in their language, and Father Fray Marcos called it the kingdom of Hacus.[7] They came down to meet us peacefully, although they could have spared themselves the trouble and stayed on their rock and we would not have been able to trouble them in the least. They gave us cotton blankets, cattle and deer skins, turquoises, chickens, and some of the rest of their food, which is the same as at Cíbola.

Twenty leagues east of this rock we found a well-settled river, flowing from north to south.[8] Along it there must be seventy pueblos altogether, counting the large and small, a few more or less. They are of the same type as those of Cíbola, except that they are almost all of well-built mud walls. Their food is exactly the same. These natives grow cotton—I mean those living near the river—which the others do not. There was plenty of maize here. These people have no markets.

These settlements extend more than fifty leagues from north to south along this river, some pueblos being fifteen or twenty leagues apart. This river originates at the limits of the settlement north of the slopes of the sierras, where there is a large pueblo, different from the others. It is called Yuraba.[9] It is established as follows: It contains eighteen sections, each occupying as much ground as two lots. The houses are built very close together. They are five or six stories high, three built of

7. The people of Acoma call themselves Akómé, their pueblo Ako. The Zuñi name of Acoma is Hákukia, and of its people, Hákukwe. See Hodge, *Handbook.*

8. The Rio Grande.

9. The pueblo of Taos.

mud walls and two or three of wood frame. They become narrower as they rise. On the outside on top of the mud walls each house has its small wooden corridor, one above the other, extending all around. The natives of this pueblo, being in the sierras, do not grow cotton or raise chickens. They wear only cattle and deer skins. This pueblo has more people than any other in all that land. We reckoned that it must have numbered fifteen thousand souls.

Of the other type of pueblos there is one which is larger than them all, very strong, called Cicuique.[10] Its houses are four and five stories high. It has eight large patios, each one with its corridor. There are fine houses in it. They do not either plant cotton or raise chickens, because it is fifteen leagues east of the river, close to the plains where the cattle roam.

Alvarado, after making a report of this river to Francisco Vázquez, went on to these plains. At the beginning of the plains he found a small river running southeast. Within four days he came upon the cattle, which are the most monstrous beasts ever seen or read about. He followed this river for one hundred leagues, finding more cattle every day. We availed ourselves of them, although with danger to the horses at first, until we gained experience. There are such quantities of them that I do not know what to compare them with, unless it be with the fish in the sea. For both on this journey as well as on the one made later by the whole army to Quivira, there were so many that we often traveled among them. Should we have wished to go some other way we could not have done it, because the fields were covered with them. Their meat is as good as that of the cattle of Castile, and some said that it was even better.

The bulls are large and fierce, although they do not attack very often. However, they have mean horns and they thrust and rush well. They killed several of our horses and wounded many. We found that the best weapon for killing them was a spear for hurling at them, and the harquebus when they are standing still.

Upon returning from these plains to the river named

10. Pecos.

Tiguex, Alvarado found the maestre de campo, Don García López de Cárdenas, preparing quarters for the whole army which was coming there. It soon arrived, and, although all the population had met Hernando de Alvarado in a friendly way, when the whole army arrived some of them revolted, particularly twelve pueblos that were close together. One night they killed forty of our horses and mules that were loose in the field. They fortified themselves in their pueblos, whereupon we attacked them, first of all, Don García López, who caught and executed many of them. When the others saw this they abandoned their pueblos, except two, one of them the strongest of all, which the army besieged for two months. And although, soon after besieging it, we entered it one day and took a portion of the terrace we were forced to withdraw because so many were wounded and it was so hazardous to maintain ourselves there. In spite of the fact that at this time we succeeded in entering it again, in the end we could not take all of it. For this reason we besieged it during all this time, and finally we conquered it through thirst. They held out so long because it snowed twice when they were on the verge of capitulating. Finally we conquered them and many were killed because they tried to get out at night.[11]

From some Indians found at this pueblo of Cicuique, Francisco Vázquez obtained information that, had it been true, would have led to the richest prize found in the Indies. The Indian who furnished this report and information was from a pueblo he called Harale,[12] three hundred leagues east of this river. He expressed himself so well that it seemed as if what he was saying were true and that he had seen it. Later it looked as if the devil had spoken through him. Francisco Vázquez and all of us believed him. Nevertheless the general was advised by some gentlemen not to mobilize the whole army, but to send a captain out first to find out what there was to it. He would not do that; on the contrary he decided to take the whole army. He

11. Compare the account given by Castañeda, and especially the versions of Coronado and Cárdenas when they were brought to trial and accused of these crimes.

12. Harahey, identified with the Pawnee of Nebraska. See Hodge's study in Brower's, *Harahey*, pp. 127-129.

even sent Don Pedro de Tovar to Corazones for half of the people who were at that town.

Thus he set out with the entire army, and, after marching one hundred and fifty leagues, one hundred to the east and fifty to the south,[13] the Indian was found untrue in what he had said in regard to settlements there and maize with which to go farther on. Examining the other two guides again as to how that happened, one of them admitted that what the Indian said was false, except that the province called Quivira existed, that there was maize, and houses of straw, but that they were very far away because we had been led away from the route. In view of this and the small supply of provisions on hand, Francisco Vázquez, with the agreement of the captains, decided to go ahead with thirty of the best and well-equipped men, and to send the army back to the river. So it was done at once.

Two days before this it happened that the horse of Don García López fell, and he dislocated an arm, as a result of which he was very ill. On account of this, Don Tristán de Arellano led the army back to the river. On the way they endured great hardships, because most of them had nothing to eat but meat, and it made many sick. Enormous numbers of cows and bulls were killed. There were days when sixty and seventy head were brought to the camp. Every day it was necessary to go hunting. As a result of this and of not eating maize in all this time, the horses fared very badly.

After Francisco Vázquez set out over the plains in search of Quivira, induced more by the information we had obtained at the river than the credence we gave to the guide here, traveling many days by the needle, God was pleased that in thirty days we should come to the Quivira river.[14] It is reached thirty leagues before coming to the settlement of the same name. In our march through the valley we met many natives of Quivira who were out hunting.

At Quivira there is a bestial people without any organization in their houses or anything else. The houses are of straw,

13. This is given as "southeast," in Buckingham Smith's Muñoz copy.
14. Identified as the Arkansas in central Kansas. See Hodge in Brower, *op. cit.*

like Tarascan ranchos. In some towns as many as two hundred houses are clustered together. The natives have maize, beans, and calabashes. They do not have cotton or chickens, nor do they bake bread in comales,[15] but under ashes.

Francisco Vázquez marched twenty-five leagues through this settlement, where he inquired about the country ahead. They said that the plains came to an end, and that down the river there were people who did not plant, but who lived by hunting. They told also of two other large pueblos, one called Taraque and the other Arae.[16] The Taraques have straw houses; the Araes some of straw and the rest of hides. Copper was found here, and they said that it existed farther on; near this pueblo of Arae, according to what the Indian told us, there was more of it, to judge by the good signs he made about it. Here we found no more news or signs of it.

Francisco Vázquez returned from here to the Tiguex river, where he found the army. We came back by a more direct route, because, on the way out, we traveled three hundred and thirty leagues, and, on the way back, we covered not more than two hundred.[17]

Quivira is at forty degrees, and the river at thirty-six. Traveling in these plains is like traveling at sea, since there are no roads other than the cattle trails. Since the land is so level, without a mountain or hill, it was dangerous to travel alone or become separated from the army, for, on losing sight of it, one was lost. Thus we lost one man, and others, while out hunting, were lost three or four days.

In these plains, among the cattle, two types of people were found; one group was called Querechos and the other Teyas. They are well built, and are painted; they are enemies of each other. They have no settlement or occupation other than to follow the cattle, of which they kill as many as they want. They tan the skins, with which they clothe themselves and build their

15. Flat earthenware pan for cooking maize cake.

16. Taraque was evidently a Wichita settlement. Arae was identical with Harahey. See Hodge in Brower, *op. cit.,* pp. 68 *et seq.*

17. It is generally assumed that this return route of Coronado approximated the later Santa Fe trail.

tents. They eat the meat of the cattle, sometimes raw, and they also drink the blood when thirsty.

Their tents are in the shape of pavilions. They set them up by means of poles which they carry for the purpose. After driving them in the ground they tie them together at the top. When they move from place to place they carry them by means of dogs, of which they have many. They load the dogs with their tents, poles, and other things. They make use of them, as I said, because the land is very level. The dogs drag the poles. What these people worship most is the sun. The hides of their tents are dressed on both sides, free from hair. The cattle and deer skins that they do not need, and the meat dried in the sun, they trade for maize and blankets to the natives at the river.

When Francisco Vázquez arrived at the river where the army was, Don Pedro de Tovar soon came with half of the men from Corazones, and Don García López de Cárdenas left for Mexico. Besides being badly injured in his arm, he had permission from the viceroy to leave on account of the death of his brother. With him went ten or twelve sick men, there being not one among them who was able to fight. He arrived at the town of the Spaniards and found it burned and two Spaniards and also many Indians and horses killed. On account of this he returned to the river,[18] escaping from the Indians through good fortune and diligence. The cause of the disaster was that after Don Pedro went away, leaving forty men there, half of them revolted and fled. The Indians, remembering the bad treatment they had received, fell upon them one night and overpowered them, both because of their carelessness and weakness. They fled to Culiacán.

In the meantime, Francisco Vázquez fell from a horse while racing and was very sick for many days. When the winter was over he was determined, regardless of any statement to the contrary, to turn back, and he did so. He longed for this more than anything else. Thus we returned together as far as Culiacán. From there each one went wherever he pleased. Francisco Vázquez came here to Mexico to report to the viceroy, who did not

18. Tiguex, to warn Coronado and to accompany the main army on its return shortly thereafter.

rejoice at his return, although at first he dissimulated. He was glad that Father Fray Juan de Padilla had remained there. He had gone to Quivira, together with a Spaniard and a negro; and Fray Luis, a very saintly lay brother, had remained at Cicuique.

At this river we spent two intensely cold winters, with snow and heavy frosts. It was so cold that the river froze one night and continued so for more than a month, and the loaded horses crossed over on the ice. The reason that these pueblos are settled as they are is believed to be due to the intense cold, although it is due in part also to the wars they wage against each other.

This is what was seen and heard in all that land, which is very sterile in fruits and trees. Quivira is a better land, with many savannas and not so cold, although it is farther north.

JARAMILLO'S NARRATIVE

Narrative Given by Captain Juan Jaramillo of His Journey to the New Land in New Spain and to the Discovery of Cíbola Under General Francisco Vázquez Coronado.[1]

We set out from Mexico straight for Compostela, the land being inhabited and at peace all the way. The route was to the west, and the distance one hundred and twelve leagues. From there we continued to Culiacán, about eighty leagues distant. It is a well-known and much-used road, because there is in the said valley of Culiacán, a town inhabited by Spaniards, with a repartimiento under the jurisdiction of Compostela. The route to this town and back is to the northwest.

The sixty mounted men who accompanied the general set out from here, having learned that the way was uninhabited and almost all of it without provisions. He left his army behind and, with the above-mentioned party, went to explore the route and to provide information for those who were following. We

1. Translated from a photostatic copy of the original in the Archivo General de Indias, *Patronato*, legajo 20. Printed in Buckingham Smith's *Colección de Varios Documentos*, pp. 154-163; in Pacheco y Cárdenas, *Documentos de Indias*, XIV, pp. 304-317. This text has numerous bad readings. Translated by Winship in *Fourteenth Annual Report*, pp. 584-593; reprinted in The Trail Makers and Grabhorn editions. Translated into French in Ternaux-Compans, *Voyages*, IX, pp. 364-382.

Juan de Jaramillo is listed in the muster roll as bringing three horses and native weapons. He was a native of Villanueva de Balcarrota in Castile, son of Gómes Méndez and Ana de Toro. Icaza, *Diccionario*, no. 867.

Visitador Tello de Sandoval, in question XXIV, accused Viceroy Mendoza of conspiring with Luis de Quesada to marry a daughter of Juan de Jaramillo against her will and the will of her father. C. Pérez Bustamante, *Don Antonio de Mendoza*, p. 178. Another daughter of Jaramillo was married to Don Luis López de Mendoza. Icaza, *Diccionario*, No. 210.

In connection with the promulgation of the "New Laws" of 1542, regulating the exploitation of the Indians, the Council of the Indies ordered an inquiry into the number of Indians held by Juan de Jaramillo and other persons. A. G. I., *Indiferente*, legajo 737; also Pacheco y Cárdenas, XVI, p. 389.

Jaramillo testified for García López de Cárdenas during the inquiry made by Licentiate Tejada concerning the conduct of the expedition. A. G. I., *Justicia*, legajo 1021, pieza 6.

continued on this route, although with a few deviations, until we crossed a mountain range, which I knew to be over three hundred leagues from here in New Spain. We named this pass Chichilte-calli, for we heard from some Indians whom we met farther back that it was called by this name.

Upon leaving the said valley of Culiacán, we came to a river called Petlatlán,[2] which must be about four days' journeys distant. We found these Indians friendly, and they gave us a small amount of food to eat. From here we traveled to another river called Cinaloa.[3] There must have been about three days' journeys between these two rivers. At this place the general sent ten of us with horses to travel lightly by forced marches until we came to the Arroyo de los Cedros, and from there to enter an opening[4] in the sierras on the right side of the road, and to see the sierras and what there was behind them. If we needed more days than we were allowed, he would wait for us at the said Arroyo de los Cedros. Thus it was done, and all that we found there was some poor Indians settled in a few valleys in the manner of rancherías. The land was sterile. The distance from the river to this arroyo must be an additional five days' travel.

From here we proceeded to the river called Yaquemí,[5] which must be distant about three days' travel more. From here we marched by a dry arroyo, and we continued on our way three more days, although the dry arroyo extended only for one league, and we came to another arroyo where there were some Indians settled. They had straw shacks, and fields planted with maize, beans, and calabashes. On leaving this place we went to the arroyo and pueblo called Corazones, so named by Dorantes, Cabeza de Vaca, Castillo, and the negro, Estebanillo. They gave it this name because they were given, as a customary present, hearts of animals and birds to eat.

The distance to this pueblo of Corazones must be about two days. There is an irrigation arroyo here, and the climate is

2. The modern Sinaloa.
3. Evidently the Fuerte.
4. The Spanish word is *abra*.
5. That is, Jaramillo is now referring to the main army, not to the reconnaissance party of ten men. The Yaquemí refers to the Yaqui.

warm. Their houses consist of huts. After setting up the poles in the shape of ovens, although much larger, they cover them with mats. For their food they have maize, beans, and calabashes, in abundance, I believe. They dress in deerskins.

As this place seemed to be a suitable one, an order was issued to establish a town here with some of the Spaniards who were coming in the rear. They lived here almost until the expedition failed. There is poison in this region, and, judging by what we saw of it and its effects, it is the worst that one could find. From what we have learned, it was obtained from the sap of a small tree like the lentisk, which grows among broken shale and in sterile soil.

From here, passing a sort of small gateway, very close to this arroyo, we went to another valley made by this same arroyo. It is called Señora. It is also irrigated and has more Indians than the others, and the settlements and food are of the same type. This valley must extend about six or seven leagues, more or less. These Indians, at first, were friendly, but not later; on the contrary, they and those they could assemble around there became our bitter enemies. They possess poison, with which they killed several Christians. They have sierras on both sides that are not very productive.

From here we continued in general along the said arroyo, crossing its meanderings, to another Indian settlement called Ispa.[6] It must be one day's journey from the confines of the last one. These people are of the same customs as the preceding ones. One goes from here in four days over a despoblado to another arroyo, which we understood was called Nexpa.[7] Some poor Indians came out to meet the general, bringing presents of little value, such as roasted maguey leaves and pitahayas. We continued down this arroyo for two days; leaving the arroyo we went to the right in two days' travel to the foot of the cordillera, where we learned that it was called Chichilticalli. Crossing the cordillera, we went to a deep arroyo and ravine where we found water and grass for the horses.[8]

6. The name was crossed out in the original; it could be Arispa, the modern Arispe. *Cf.* Bandelier, *Gilded Man,* p. 175.

7. The San Pedro.

8. This river must have been the Gila.

From this last arroyo of Nexpa that I have mentioned we turned almost to the northeast, it seems to me. Following this same route we went from here, in three days, I believe, to a river which we named San Juan,[9] as we reached it on St. John's day. On leaving this place we went over somewhat hilly country to another river,[10] and from there more to the north to the river we named Las Balsas, since we used some rafts for crossing it because it was swollen. It seems to me that it took us two days to go from one river to the other. I say this since it is so long ago since we traveled there that I might be mistaken in regard to some day's journey, but not about the other things. From here we went to another arroyo which we called La Barranca.[11] The distance between them is two short days' travel, and the direction is almost northeast.

From here we went to another river which we named Rio Frio,[12] because its water was cold, reaching it in a day's travel. Then from here we continued through a pine forest, almost at the end of which we found a spring and a cool little arroyo. This took about another day's travel. At this place on this arroyo a Spaniard named Espinosa and two other persons died as a result of some plants they ate because of their great privation.

From here, in two days and in the same direction, but not so much to the northeast, we went to another arroyo which we named Bermejo.[13] Here we saw one or two Indians whom we later thought belonged to the first settlement of Cíbola. In a march of two days we went from here to the said pueblo, the first one of Cíbola. The houses have terraces, and the walls are built of stone and mud. At this place they killed Estebanillo, the negro who had come with Dorantes from Florida, and who was returning here with Fray Marcos de Niza.

There are in this province of Cíbola five small pueblos, including this one. They all have terraces and are built of stone and mud, as I have stated. It is a cold country, as is evidenced

9. The Gila Bonita, according to Hodge.
10. Identified by Hodge as the Salado.
11. Perhaps an upper branch of the Colorado Chiquito, says Hodge.
12. The Colorado Chiquito itself, says Hodge.
13. The Zuñi river.

by their houses and estufas. They have sufficient provisions of maize, beans, and calabashes for their needs. These pueblos are one league and more apart, forming a circuit of about six leagues. The soil is somewhat sandy and not very well covered with grass. The woods found around there consist for the most part of savins.

The dress of the Indians consists of deerskins, extremely well tanned. They already have some tanned skins of the cattle with which they cover themselves. These are like rugs and very warm. They possess square cotton blankets of different sizes, about a yard and a half long. The Indian women wear them over their shoulders as do gypsies, with the ends tied around the waist with a sash of the same cotton.

A little to the northeast of this first pueblo of Cíbola, to the left, a little less than five days' travel, there is a province called Tuçayán. It contains seven pueblos with terraces, with as good or even better food than these others, and with even better houses. They, too, have skins of cattle and deer, and the cotton blankets I have mentioned.

All the springs, rivers, and arroyos that we have found as far as Cíbola, and I do not know but that those one or two days beyond also, flow to the South sea, and those farther on from there flow to the North sea.[14]

From this first pueblo of Cíbola, as I have said, we went to another one[15] of the same group which was about a short day's journey away, on the road to Tihuex; there must be nine days' journeys, of the ones we normally travel, from this town of Cíbola to the Tiguex river. Midway, I do not know whether one day more or less, there is a pueblo of earth and cut rock in a very strong place. It is called Tutahaco.[16] All these Indians, except those at the first pueblo of Cíbola, received us well.

At the Tiguex river, there are along it, in a distance of about twenty leagues, fifteen pueblos, all of terraced houses of earth like mud walls, and not of stone. Away from it in other arroyos

14. This reference is to the Continental Divide, which is just east of the Zuñi country.

15. The pueblo of Matsaki.

16. Tutahaco is here confused with Acoma. The former was farther to the east.

which join this one, there are other pueblos. Three of them were, for Indian pueblos, quite worth seeing, particularly one called Chia, another Uraba, and another Cicuique.[17] Uraba and Cicuique have many tall houses two stories high. All of the other pueblos and these have maize, beans, calabashes, skins, and some feather quilts which they make by twisting the feathers and fastening them with thread, forming a smooth weave with which they make the blankets to keep themselves warm. All the pueblos have estufas underground, well protected, although not very elaborate. The natives grow and gather very small amounts of cotton, with which they weave the blankets that I have told about.

This river comes approximately from the northwest, flowing to the southeast, demonstrating the fact, which is certain, that it empties into the North sea.

After leaving this settlement and river,[18] we passed two other pueblos whose names I do not know, and in four days we came to Cicuique, which I have already mentioned. This route was to the northeast.

From here we proceeded in three days to another river which we Spaniards called Cicuique. If I remember correctly, it seems to me that to reach this river, at the point where we crossed it, we went somewhat more to the northeast.[19] Upon crossing it we turned more to the left, which must be more to the northeast, and we began to enter the plains where the cattle roam. Nevertheless we did not find any cattle for more than four or five days, after which we began to see bulls, for there are large numbers of them. Continuing in the same direction for two or three days, and meeting bulls, we then found ourselves in the midst of an immense herd of cows, calves, and bulls, all together.

At the beginning of the plains of the cattle we met some Indians, called Querechos by the people of the terraced houses. They did not live in houses, but carried some poles with them which they put together at their camping places in order to

17. These three pueblos were Zia, Taos, and Pecos.
18. The main camp on the Tiguex river.
19. It is usually assumed that Jaramillo is mistaken here and that the army went southeast down the Pecos river. See Hodge's discussion of this point in Brower, *Harahey,* p. 60.

make a sort of shack which they used as houses. They fasten these poles at the top and spread them at the base, covering the whole thing with cattle hides which they carry along. These tents they used as homes, as I have said. From what we have learned about these Indians, they satisfy all their human needs from the cattle, for from them they obtain their food, clothes, and footwear. They are men who wander from place to place as it suits them.

We traveled in the said direction some eight or ten days along the waters found in the cattle country. From here on the Indian guided us, the one who had told us of Quivira and Arahe, and of this being a rich country abounding in gold, and other things. He and the other guide were from this land I have mentioned and to which we were going. These two Indians were found at the terraced pueblos. It seems that as the said Indian was anxious to get back to his land, he extended himself to tell stories that we found to be untrue. I do not know whether it was for that reason, or because he had been advised to lead us elsewhere by taking a different road, although there is none anywhere around here, unless it be the cattle paths. We realized, also, that he had guided us away from the route we were to follow, and had led us over the plains as he did in order that we would exhaust our food, and without it, both we and our horses would become weak. Then, whether we wanted to turn back with him or go ahead, we would not be able to offer any opposition to whatever they wanted to do with us. Finally, from the time when, as I have said, we left this ranchería of Querechos and entered the plains, he drew us farther to the east, until we found ourselves in dire straits owing to lack of food. The other Indian, a companion of his and from his land, seeing that he was not taking us the way we should go, for we had never followed his advice but that of the Turk, as he was called, dropped to the ground and indicated by signs that he would rather have his head cut off than go that way, and that it was not our route either.

I believe that we traveled in this direction for twenty days or more, at the end of which we came to another ranchería of Indians having the same type of houses and ways as the ones farther back. Among them there was an old blind and bearded Indian who gave us to understand by signs that, many days before, he had seen four others of our people near there and closer to New Spain. Thus we understood and assumed them to be Dorantes, Cabeza de Vaca, and the ones I have mentioned.[20]

In this ranchería the general, seeing our troubles, ordered a meeting of the captains and persons whose advice he used to seek, in order that we might compare our counsel with his. We all agreed that, to save itself, the entire army should go back to its point of departure in search of food and that thirty picked and mounted men should go in search of what the Indian had told about. We agreed to this decision. We marched all together for a day to an arroyo flowing between some barrancas in which there were good meadows. Here we were to select the ones who were to go ahead, and to send back the rest.

At this point we asked the Indian we called Isopete, companion of the said Turk, to tell us the truth and to lead us to the land we were seeking. He said he would do so, and that it was not as the Turk had told us. The things he had told us and given us to understand at Tiguex were amazing indeed, in regard both to gold and the ways of obtaining it, to buildings, the inhabitants' customs and trade, and many other things, which I omit as too prolix. All of this had moved us to go in search of it, at the advice of the friars and of all those who offered it. As a reward for guiding us, Isopete asked that we leave him in the land, as it was his country, and also that the Turk should not go along, because the latter quarreled with him and annoyed him in everything he wanted to do in our behalf.

The general granted him all this, in so far as it was to our advantage, and said that he wanted to be the first of the thirty, and so he was. We assembled to make the selections and leave the others behind.

Turning always to the north from here, we continued on our way for more than thirty days, or close to thirty days of travel, although the marches were not long, without ever lack-

20. According to Hodge, this may have been a Jumano Indian who had seen Cabeza de Vaca and companions farther to the south.

ing water in all these days. We traveled always among the cattle, some days seeing larger numbers than others, depending on the watering places we came to. So on the feast day of Saints Peter and Paul we came to a river that we found there, below Quivira.[21] Upon reaching this river the Indian recognized it and said that it was the one and that the settlements were down the stream. We crossed it at that place and followed it downstream along the opposite north bank, turning our route to the northeast.

After traveling for three days we met some Indians who were out hunting, killing cattle to take meat to their pueblo, which was about three or four days from us, farther down. Here where we met the Indians and they saw us, they became alarmed and began to shout and run away. Some of them even had their women along. The Indian Isopete began to call to them in their own language, and thus they approached us without signs of fear. When both they and we had come to a halt, the general showed the Indian Turk there. We had always kept him concealed among our rear guard, and whenever we came to a lodging place we managed it in such a way that he would not be noticed by the other Indian called Isopete. This was done to give the latter the satisfaction he had asked for. Seeing the good appearance of the land, and indeed it was fine, not only this among the cattle but also that farther back and from here on, Isopete received some satisfaction.

Here the general wrote a letter to the governor of Harahey and Quivira, believing that he was a Christian from the shipwrecked fleets of Florida. The form of government and society that the Indian had described to us made us believe so. Once the Indians left for their homes, which were at the distance mentioned, we, too, proceeded by our regular journeys until we reached the settlements. We found them along streams, which, although not carrying much water, were good and had fine banks; they flowed into the larger one I have mentioned. They were, if I remember well, six or seven pueblos, removed from

21. Hodge believes that Coronado reached the Arkansas river near Ford, Ford county, Kansas, and continued downstream to Greatbend, Barton county. Consult his discussion of this point in Brower, *op. cit., passim*, and in the *Journey of Coronado*, San Francisco, 1933, p. 112, note 21.

one another. We traveled for four or five days among them, since it was understood to be uninhabited between the two arroyos. We came to what they said was the remotest region of Quivira, to which they took us, saying that it was of much importance, expressing it to us by the word *teucarea*.[22]

This river carried more water and was more settled than the others. We asked if there was anything else farther on. The Indians replied there was nothing beyond Quivira, except Arahey, with the same customs, settlements, and size as the former.

The general sent for the chief of these settlements and the other Indians who, they said, lived at Arahe. He appeared with some two hundred men, all naked, and with bows. They wore —I do not know what—over their heads, and had their privy parts somewhat covered. The chief was a huge Indian, with large body, and limbs in proportion.

Taking note of the ideas of various people, the general asked them what we should do, remembering that we had left the army behind and that we were here. So, as it seemed to all that it was almost the beginning of winter, for, if I remember correctly, it was past the middle of August, and as there were so few of us to establish winter quarters there, and because of the scantiness of our provisions, the uncertainty as to the welfare of the army which had remained behind, and so that winter might not obstruct the roads with snow and make the rivers impassable, and knowing also the experiences of the other people left behind, we all concluded that his Lordship should turn back in search of them, and, upon finding them, learn of their situation, spend the winter there, and, at the beginning of summer, return to that land to explore and cultivate it.

This place, as I have said, was the last place reached by us. The Turk, realizing that he had lied to us, called on all these people to fall upon us some night and kill us. We found it out and took precautions. He was garrotted that night, so he never saw the dawn.

In view of the agreement we had reached, we marched back —I do not know whether two or three days—to a place where we

22. This last phrase is omitted in the Pacheco y Cárdenas copy.

got provisions of shucked ears of green maize and dry maize for our return. At this place the general erected a cross, at the foot of which some letters were cut with a chisel, saying that Francisco Vázquez de Coronado, general of the army, had reached this place.

This country has a fine appearance, the like of which I have never seen anywhere in our Spain, Italy, or part of France, nor indeed in other lands where I have traveled in the service of his Majesty. It is not a hilly country, but one with mesas, plains, and charming rivers with fine waters, and it pleased me, indeed. I am of the belief that it will be very productive for all sorts of commodities. As for the cattle, we have the proof that large numbers exist there, as large as any one could imagine. We found Castilian plums, a variety that are not wholly red but blending from red to somewhat black and green. The tree and the fruit are surely Castilian, the latter of excellent taste.

In the cattle country we found a sort of flax growing wild in small clumps separated one from another. As the cattle do not eat it, it remains there with its little heads and blue flowers. Although small, it is excellent, a sumach native like ours in Spain. At some arroyos there are grapes of fairly good taste, considering that they are not cultivated.

The houses of the Indians there were of straw, differing in size and shape from those around here, most of them round, the straw hanging to the ground like a wall. Superimposed on the outside they had a sort of chapel or sentry box with a doorway where the Indians were seen either seated or lying down.

Isopete was left here at the place where the cross was erected, and five or six Indians were taken from these pueblos to guide and lead us to the terraced houses. Thus they took us back over the same route we had come as far as the point where I have said we came upon the Saints Peter and Paul river. Here they abandoned our previous route, and, taking off to the right, they led us by watering places and among the cattle and over good road, although there is no good road anywhere unless it be the paths of the cattle, as I have said. Finally we came to the region, and recognized it, where, as I said at the beginning, we had found the ranchería where the Turk took us away from the route we should have followed.

Thus, omitting further details, we arrived in Tiguex, where we found the rest of the army. Here the general fell from his horse while racing and hurt his head. As a result he showed a mean disposition and plotted the return. Although ten or twelve of us pleaded with him, we were unable to dissuade him. So, when the return was arranged, the Franciscan friars who were with us, one ordained and the other a lay brother, were already prepared, and had the authority from their provincial, to remain.

The ordained friar was named Fray Juan de Padilla, and the lay brother, Fray Luis de Escalona. Fray Luis wanted to remain at the terraced houses, saying that with a chisel and an adze which he still had he would erect crosses in those pueblos and would baptize the children that he might find on the verge of death and send them to heaven. For this purpose he desired no other company than a young slave of mine named Cristóbal for his comfort. He said that Cristóbal would soon learn the local language if the natives would only help him. The friar did so much to obtain him that I could not refuse him, and thus no more has been heard of the boy. The fact that this friar remained in that locality was, I believe, the cause for the staying of some Indians from here and two negroes, one of them, named Sebastián, belonging to me, and the other to Melchior Pérez, son of Licentiate de la Torre. This negro was married and had a wife and children. I remember also that several Indians remained at Quivira, one of them a Tarascan from my company named Andrés.

Fray Juan de Padilla insisted on returning to Quivira and sought to obtain the Indians I have said that we had brought as guides. They were given to him and he took them, and, in addition, a Portuguese and a free negro interpreter, who went as a tertiary and became a Franciscan friar. He took also a mestizo and two Indians from Capotean[23] and near there, I believe, whom he had reared and was taking along, wearing the habits of friars. He took sheep, mules, one horse, and church ornaments

23. Probably Capotlán.

and other trifles. I do not know whether it was on account of these or for some other reason, but it seems that they killed him. It was done by the messengers or the very Indians he brought back from Tiguex, in payment of the good deeds he had done for them.

After his death, the said Portuguese and one of the Indians whom I said he took along in the garments of a friar, or both of them, I believe, ran away. I say this because they got back to this land of New Spain by a different and shorter way than the one I have described. They came out at the valleys of Pánico.[24]

I gave information of this to Gonzalo Solís de Meras and to Isidro de Solís, for it seems to me an important matter, according to what you tell me, and I understood that his Majesty had ordered your Lordship to inquire about and explore a way to join that land with this one. It might also happen that this Indian Sebastián, during his stay at Quivira, has learned of the locality and the surrounding lands, has reports also of the sea, the way he came, what there is along the route, and the number of days' travel it takes to get here.

Thus, surely, if your Lordship can reach Quivira and Arahe from your present place I believe you will be able to bring many people from New Spain to settle it without any hesitance, in view of the fine appearance and reports of the land.

24. Pánuco, on the Gulf of Mexico. The two Indians in friars' habits were the oblates Lucas and Sebastián. See Introduction, p. 10.

RELACION POSTRERA DE CIBOLA

THIS IS THE LATEST ACCOUNT OF CÍBOLA, AND OF MORE THAN FOUR HUNDRED LEAGUES.[1]

It is more than three hundred leagues from Culiacán to Cíbola, and little of the way is inhabited. There are very few people, the land is sterile, and the roads are wretched. The people go about entirely naked, except the women, who, from the waist down, wear white dressed deerskins which reach to their feet like skirts. Their houses are built of reed mats, and are round and small, a man being hardly able to stand up inside. The place where they are settled and where they have their planted fields has sandy soil. They grow maize, although not much, and beans and calabashes; they also live on game: rabbits, hares, and deer. They do not offer sacrifices. This is true from Culhuacán to Cíbola.

Cíbola is a pueblo of about two hundred houses, which are two, three, four, and five stories high. Their walls are a span thick. The timbers used in their construction are round, as thick as a wrist; the roofs are built of small reeds with the leaves on, on top of which they add well-packed dirt; the walls are built of dirt and mud;[2] the house doors are like the scuttles of ships. The houses are built compact and adjoining one another. In front of them there are some estufas built of adobe, in which the natives shelter themselves from cold in winter, for it is extremely cold; it snows six months of the year.

Some of the people wear cotton and maguey[3] blankets, and dressed deerskins. They wear boots made of these skins that

1. Translated from a photostatic copy of the Spanish text, which is now preserved in the University of Texas Library. The document was formerly in the possession of Joaquín García Icazbalceta. Translated by Winship, *Fourteenth Annual Report*, pp. 569-571; reprinted in the Trail Makers and Grabhorn editions of the Coronado documents.

2. According to the investigations of F. W. Hodge, the Cíbola houses were of stone, plastered inside and out with adobe mortar.

3. Yucca. The maguey grows farther south.

come to above their knees. They also make blankets of hare and rabbit skins, with which they keep warm. The women wear maguey blankets reaching to their feet and wear their clothes tight around the waist. They have their hair rolled above their ears like small wheels. These natives grow maize, beans, and calabashes, which is all they need for subsistence, as they are not very numerous. The land they cultivate is all sandy. The water is brackish; the land is very dry. They possess some chickens, although not many. They have no knowledge of fish.

In this province of Cíbola there are seven pueblos within a distance of five leagues. The largest one must have 200 houses; two others have 200, and the rest sixty, fifty, and thirty houses.

It is sixty leagues from Cíbola to the river and province of Tibex [Tiguex]. The first pueblo is forty leagues from Cíbola, and it is called Acuco. This pueblo is situated on the top of a very strong rock. It must contain about 200 houses, built similar to Cíbola, which has a different language. It is twenty leagues from there to the Tiguex river. This river is almost as wide as the one at Seville, although not so deep. It flows through level land; its water is fine; it has some fish; it rises in the north.

The one who makes the foregoing statement saw twelve pueblos within a certain region of the river; others claim to have seen more up the river. Down the river the pueblos are all small, except two which must have about 200 houses. These houses have very strong walls made of mud and sand. The walls are a span thick. The houses are two and three stories high. Their woodwork is like that of the houses of Cíbola.[4] The natives have their estufas as at Cíbola. The land is extremely cold, and the river freezes so hard that laden animals cross over it, and carts could cross also. The natives plant maize, beans, and calabashes, enough for their needs, and they possess some chickens, which they keep to make blankets with their feathers. They grow some cotton, although not much. They wear cotton blankets and shoes of hides as at Cíbola. They are people who know how to defend themselves from their very houses, and they are not inclined to leave them. The land is all sandy.

4. This probably refers to the ceilings and roofs.

Four days' journey from the province and river of Tiguex the Spaniards found four pueblos. The first must have thirty houses; the second was a large pueblo destroyed by war; the third had about thirty-five houses, all inhabited. These three pueblos are similar in every respect to those on the river. The fourth is a large pueblo situated between mountains, and is called Cicuic. It had some fifty houses with terraces like those of Cíbola, and the walls are of dirt and mud like those of Cíbola. The inhabitants have abundant maize, beans, calabashes, and some chickens.

At a distance of four days' travel from this pueblo, the Spaniards came to some land as level as the sea. In these plains there is such a multitude of cattle that they are beyond counting. These cattle are like those of Castile, and some larger. They have small humps on their backs, and are more reddish in color, blending into black. Their hair, over a span long, hangs down between their horns, ears, and chin, and from the neck and shoulders like a mane, and down from the knees. The rest of their bodies is covered with short wool like sheep. Their meat is fine and tender and very fat.

Traveling many days over these plains the Spaniards came to an inhabited ranchería with about two hundred houses. The houses were made of tanned cattle skins, white, and built like pavilions or tents. These Indians live or sustain themselves entirely from the cattle, for they neither grow nor harvest maize. With the skins they build their houses; with the skins they clothe and shoe themselves; from the skins they make ropes and also obtain wool. With the sinews they make thread, with which they sew their clothes and also their tents. From the bones they shape awls. The dung they use for firewood, since there is no other fuel in that land. The bladders they use as jugs and drinking containers. They sustain themselves on their meat, eating it slightly roasted and heated over the dung. Some they eat raw; taking it in their teeth, they pull with one hand, and in the other they hold a large flint knife and cut off mouthfuls. Thus they swallow it, half chewed, like birds. They eat raw fat without warming it. They drink the blood just as it comes out of the cattle. Sometimes they drink it later, raw and cold. They have no other food.

These people have dogs similar to those of this land, except that they are somewhat larger. They load these dogs like beasts of burden and make light pack-saddles for them like our pack-saddles, cinching them with leather straps. The dogs go about with sores on their backs like pack animals. When the Indians go hunting they load them with provisions. When these Indians move—for they have no permanent residence anywhere, since they follow the cattle to find food—these dogs carry their homes for them. In addition to what they carry on their backs, they carry the poles for the tents, dragging them fastened to their saddles. The load may be from thirty-five to fifty pounds, depending on the dog.

From Cíbola to these plains where the Spaniards came it must be thirty leagues, and perhaps more. The plains extend ahead—we do not know how far. Captain Francisco Vázquez traveled ahead over these plains with thirty mounted men, and Fray Juan de Padilla accompanied him. The rest of the people went back to the settlement by the river to await Francisco Vázquez, for so he had commanded. It is not known whether he has returned.

The land is so level that the men get lost when they draw half a league away. This happened to a man on horseback who got lost and never returned, and also to two horses, with harnesses and bridles, that were never again found. No tracks are left over the places which are traveled. On account of this they must leave land marks of cow dung along the way they follow in order to find their way back, for there are no stones or anything else.

The Venetian, Marco Polo, in chapter xv of his treatise, says that he has seen these same cows, with the same kind of hump. In the same chapter he speaks also of rams the size of horses.

The Venetian, Nicolas, told the Florentine, Micer Pogio, in the second book, toward the end, that in Ethiopia there are oxen with humps like camels, and with horns three cubits long.

They throw their horns back over their spine, and one of these horns will hold a pitcher of wine.

In chapter 134, Marco Polo says that in the land of the Tartars, toward the north, there are dogs the size of donkeys, more or less. They hitch them to a sort of cart and enter very marshy land, a real quagmire, where other animals would not be able to enter without drowning. For this reason they use dogs.

LICENTIATE TEJADA'S COMMISSIONS

Tejada's Commission to Investigate the Cruelties on the Expedition to Cíbola, September 7, 1543.[1]

Don Carlos, by divine clemency, emperor, etc.

To you, Licentiate Tejada,[2] judge of our royal audiencia of New Spain, greetings and peace:

Know you that it has been reported to us that in the expedition which Francisco Vázquez de Coronado made to the province of Cíbola, he and the Spaniards who went with him committed, both in going and returning, great cruelties against the natives of the lands through which they passed, killing large numbers of them and committing other acts and injustices to the detriment of the service of God and ours.

As it is our desire to provide the punishment due, we have examined the matter in our Council of the Indies, and, relying on your rectitude, loyalty, and conscientiousness, and trusting that you are a person who would carry out properly, faithfully,

1. Translated from a photostatic copy in A. G. I., *Justicia*, legajo 1021, pieza 4. This document and those that follow have been selected from the voluminous testimony in the Coronado and Cárdenas trials as most appropriate in throwing new light on the history of the expedition. Much new information appears in the records of these trials, but especially do they shed new light on many matters related by Castañeda and other ancient chroniclers with reference to the Coronado expedition.

2. As visitador and juez de residencia in New Galicia, Licentiate Lorenzo de Tejada was efficient and just. He was a judge of the audiencia of Mexico for many years, returning to Spain in 1552 to attend to personal matters. The ecclesiastical cabildo, in a letter signed by nine church dignitaries addressed to the Council of the Indies from Mexico on January 26, 1552, expressed regret at his leaving. See Francisco del Paso y Troncoso, *Epistolario de Nueva España*, VI, Mexico, 1939, p. 132.

Tejada accused the visitador, Tello de Sandoval, of being prejudiced and influenced by Cortés, whereupon the visitador retaliated by charging the judge with abusing the Indians, forcing them to trade land for considerations of little value. Consult C. Pérez Bustamante, *Don Antonio de Mendoza*, p. 105, and A. S. Aiton and A. Rey, "Coronado's Testimony in the Viceroy Mendoza Residencia," in *New Mexico Historical Review*, XII (1937), pp. 317-318.

Some idea of the measures taken by Judge Tejada for the good administration of New Galicia may be gathered from his own correspondence. See Paso y Troncoso, *op. cit.*, IV, nos. 238 and 244.

and diligently whatever commission we may give you, it was agreed that we should entrust and commission it to you, as we do entrust and commission it to you through our appointment. Wherefore we order you to obtain information and to find out, both in the province of Galicia and in the city of Mexico and in any other place where you may deem it desirable, how and what took place in the above affair. You are commissioned to investigate any cruelties, unusual executions, and robberies that were perpetrated by the said Francisco Vázquez and the Spaniards who went and returned with him from the said province of Cíbola; who and what individuals did it and by whose order; and who rendered counsel, favor, and aid in such matters.

When you have completed the said inquiry and established the truth, you may arrest physically those against whom charges may be preferred. You will hear their testimony and forward it to the said royal audiencia of New Spain, together with the report you may prepare, adding the testimony that they may offer, in order that everything may appear in it and that justice may be done. This investigation you may hold wherever you may happen to be, both in the said province of Galicia, where we are sending you as our juez de residencia, and in any other place. The report, as has been stated, you will forward to our president and judges, and we commanded them to accept the accused whom you may thus send to them, and also the judicial inquiry and proceedings you may have instituted against them in accordance with the laws of these kingdoms, and the ordinances and decrees issued by the Catholic kings and the emperor, my lord, for the good treatment of the Indians.

We order the parties who may be concerned with the above business, and any other person whom you may wish to question and investigate in order to learn the truth in regard to the aforesaid matters, to answer your requisitions and summons and to make their statements and depositions within the time limits and under the penalties that you, in our name, may prescribe or order imposed on them. These penalties we hereby impose and accept as imposed, and we authorize you to execute them on those who may be rebellious or disobedient. If, to carry out and fulfill the aforesaid, you should need support and aid, we hereby command all the councils, judges, aldermen, caballeros, squires, officials, and leading men in all the cities, towns, and villages both in the province of Galicia and in the other provinces of New Spain, to render it to you and to order that it be given, under the penalties which you, in our name, may impose on them, which we hereby impose and accept as imposed on them and consider them as guilty if they should act contrary to these orders. To this effect and to execute them on their persons and estates, and in anything else that concerns this investigation, we grant you full powers, with all their implications.

Given at Valladolid on September 7, 1543. I, THE PRINCE.

I, JUAN DE SÁMANO, secretary to the Cæsarean and Catholic Majesties, had it written by order of his Highness. Registered, OCHOA DE LUYANDO; by Chancellor BLAS DE SAAVEDRA. LICENTIATE GUTIERRE VELÁZQUEZ, LICENTIATE SALMERÓN.

APPOINTMENT OF LICENTIATE TEJADA AS JUDGE OF RESIDENCIA FOR NEW GALICIA.[1]

Don Carlos, by divine grace, emperor, etc.

To you, Licentiate Lorenzo de Tejada, our judge of the audiencia and royal chancellery in New Spain, greetings:

In order that you may know that, due to some matters concerning our service and the enforcement of justice, it is our pleasure and will to order the holding of the residencia of Francisco Vázquez de Coronado, our governor of the province of New Galicia, and his alcaldes mayores and officials for the time that they have been in office and administered our justice there, having confidence that you are a person who will discharge this commission, and anything else that we may entrust to you, with the fidelity, diligence, and care befitting our service and the administration of justice and the general welfare of the said province of New Galicia and its residents and settlers, it is our will and pleasure to charge and entrust this

1. Translated from a photostatic copy in A. G. I., *Justicia*, legajo 339, pieza 4.

commission to you. By this letter we do so appoint and commission you. Wherefore we order you, upon receiving this our commission, to go to the said province of New Galicia, assume the staffs of our authority, and hold the residencia of the said Francisco Vázquez de Coronado and the said alcaldes mayores and other officials, for a period of forty days, and impose justice on those who may be proved guilty. You are to impose sentence in each case according to justice and what has been prescribed in the decrees and ordinances of the Catholic kings, our parents and grandparents—may they be in heaven—and according to those issued by us.

We command the said Francisco Vázquez and his alcaldes mayores and officials and lieutenants to answer this said residencia before you, at the place where you establish quarters. They must remain in such locality for the duration of this residencia under the penalties specified in the laws and decrees that have been issued in this connection in these kingdoms.

Further, we order you to investigate and determine through your commission how and in what manner the said Francisco Vázquez and his alcaldes mayores and officials have discharged their duties and administered our justice, especially in what concerns public offenses, and in what manner they have observed the laws, decrees, and instructions issued by the Catholic kings, our parents and grandparents, and by us, promulgated and decreed for these regions, and in what manner they have enforced and protected our authority, rights, prestige, and royal patrimony.

If you should find them guilty on any charge as a result of the secret investigation, you are to call in the parties and establish the truth; and, having established the truth, you are to administer justice in the whole matter. This being done and the forty days having passed, without any delay and with all diligence and care, you are to send the matter to us, in order that we may be informed quickly of the state of affairs in that province. Also, you are to gather information of the manner in which the said Francisco Vázquez and his alcaldes mayores and officials have used, interpreted, and dealt with the matters pertaining to the service of God, our Lord, especially in what concerns the conversion of the natives of the said province of New Galicia and in matters pertaining to our service, not only in the administration of our justice but also in the care and integrity of our finances and the welfare of the said province and its settlers. Likewise, whatever fines have been imposed against any councils or private persons, you are to collect from them the portion that belongs to our treasury and exchequer, and deliver it to our treasurer in the said province of New Galicia or to his authorized representative.

Likewise, you are to investigate in what manner the regidores, majordomos, clerks of councils, and other officials of the cities, towns, and villages of the said province of New Galicia have observed and discharged the duties of their offices since they have been appointed by us, whether they have disobeyed and acted contrary to the laws promulgated by the Cortes of Toledo and contrary to what has been decreed and ordered by the said Catholic kings.

If you should find them guilty on any charge through this secret hearing, you are to give them a copy of the charges and hear their testimony. Having ascertained the truth in every detail, you are to decide what is just. Through you, we, by this letter, suspend the said Francisco Vázquez de Coronado and his alcaldes mayores and officials from their posts and offices, and we order you, the said Licentiate Tejada, to take charge of the business and affairs now entrusted to the said Francisco Vázquez and his alcaldes mayores and lieutenants. You are to take over the litigations in the state in which you find them. And, in conformity with the tenor and spirit of the ordinances and decrees that were given to them, you are to administer justice as if these commissions had been addressed to you. To this end and to hold the said residencia and carry out and execute our justice, and in whatever else has been stated, we grant you full power, with all its implications.

When the days of the said residencia have expired, you are to leave, in the said province of New Galicia, the rods of justice in the hands of the alcaldes ordinarios of the towns there, until we or our audiencia shall make other provisions. Then you are to come back. We order that you take an additional forty days in going from the audiencia[2] to the said province to hold the said residencia. We command that you receive for each one of the said forty days a salary of two ducats to reimburse you for the expenses you may incur in the journey, in addition to the salary that you receive as judge. These two ducats, for each one of the said eighty days, we order to be paid to you by our treasurer in the said province of New Galicia from any funds in his possession. He is to obtain your receipt of payment, and we order that with this receipt and this letter they be accepted and credited to his account.

Given at Valladolid, September 7, 1543. I, the Prince.

I, Juan de Sámano, secretary to his Majesty, had this written by order of his Highness. Endorsed by Doctor Bernal, Licentiate Gutierre Velázquez, and Licentiate Salmerón. Registered —Ochoa de Luyando; By Chancellor Blas de Sayavedra.

2. The audiencia of Mexico in Mexico city.

CORONADO'S TESTIMONY CONCERNING THE EXPEDITION

Testimony of Francisco Vázquez de Coronado On the Management of the Expedition, September 3, 1544.[1]

At the city of Guadalajara, September 3, 1544, Licentiate Tejada, judge of the royal audiencia of New Spain, visitador and juez de residencia for New Galicia, ordered Francisco Vázquez de Coronado, former governor of this province, to appear before him. He administered the oath to him in due legal form in the name of God and Holy Mary and on a crucifix on which he placed his right hand. He swore to tell and explain the truth of everything he knew and that might be asked of him. Under this oath he was asked the following questions:

This witness was asked whether he had been named general of the entire army for the discovery and conquest of the new land of Cíbola, and what captains, maese de campo, and ensign went with the army, and who appointed them.

Francisco Vázquez declared that the viceroy of New Spain sent him as general of all the people and forces that were to go and who went to the discovery and conquest of the new land and province of Cíbola and anything else that should be found. In the same manner the viceroy appointed the alcaide, Lope de Samaniego, as maese de campo and Don Pedro de Tovar as chief ensign. The other captains that set out from the city of Compostela were appointed by this witness with the approval of the viceroy. They were Don Rodrigo Maldonado, Don Diego de Guevara, Don Tristán de Arellano, Don García López de Cárdenas, Diego López, alderman of Seville, as captains of the cavalry. He also gave the maese de campo and the chief ensign companies of cavalrymen. Hernando de Alvarado was named

1. Translated from a photostatic copy of the original in the Archivo General de Indias, *Justicia*, legajo 1021, pieza 4.

captain of the artillery, and Pablos de Melgosa of the infantry. On account of the death of the alcaide, Lope de Samaniego, this witness appointed Don García López de Cárdenas to replace him as maese de campo. Upon consulting with the viceroy, he approved the choice.

When they came to the town of San Miguel, located in the province of Culiacán, this witness considered it very inconvenient to travel with the entire army, on account of the information that had been obtained regarding the scarcity of provisions. For this reason he took with him about eighty horsemen, more or less, and the maese de campo, Don García López, to go ahead and explore and see what there was to be found. He left the rest of the army at the said town of San Miguel under the command of Don Tristán de Arellano, with instructions as to what he should do. He named Velasco de Barrionuevo as maese de campo. He left orders that in case Juan de Zaldívar,[2] who had come back from the said province of Cíbola and was going to report to the viceroy of what he had seen in the land, should again wish to serve his Majesty in the expedition, they should draw a certain number of men from each company and form a captaincy and give it to him as a captain he had so named.

With these arrangements and plans, this witness set out with the horsemen he has mentioned and some infantry under Pablos de Melgosa. Upon reaching Cíbola and seeing that it was not what had been claimed, he ordered Melchior Díaz to go back to the valley of Corazones, to stop there and settle, and to try to bring the natives to the obedience of his Majesty and to the knowledge of God, our Lord. He also appointed him alcalde mayor of the town which he ordered him to establish there. And, taking some of the horsemen of those who had been left with Don Tristán, and leaving that place[3] settled and peace-

2. Zaldívar and Melchior Díaz had been sent north on November 17, 1539, after the return of Fray Marcos and before Coronado's force started its journey to the new land. They returned the next spring; Viceroy Mendoza reported that on March 20, 1540, he received a letter from Melchior Díaz, brought him by Juan de Zaldívar, giving an account of their reconnaissance. Letter of Mendoza to the king, April 17, 1540.

3. The town was San Gerónimo in the Sonora valley.

ful, Melchior Díaz was to set out through that region in search of the South sea, following instructions he had in his possession.

Francisco Vázquez was asked whether, in the pueblos and provinces through which he and the rest of the army passed from the town of San Miguel to the province of Cíbola, the natives received them peacefully, submitted to the obedience of his Majesty, and gave them of the provisions they had and accorded them a good reception, or whether they met them with force.

He said that all of the pueblos through which he passed between the town of Culiacán and the province of Cíbola met them in a friendly manner and accorded them a good reception. Wherever they had provisions to spare, they gave them to him. This witness always arranged that some men from the army should go ahead, carrying a cross as a sign of peace and to assure the natives that no harm would be done them. This witness gave the Indians some articles of barter that the viceroy had provided him for this purpose, and other things, whereby they were very pleased.

Francisco Vázquez was asked whether any cruelties, offenses, or abuses were perpetrated on the persons or properties of the Indians of the valley of Corazones and Señora, and on the other pueblos through which they passed, and whether he punished those who did it or winked at such deeds.

He replied that he did not know that any person in the said army had committed any cruelty, ill treatment, or harm to the natives of the said pueblos or their properties, because he kept the army so orderly and disciplined that no one dared get out of hand or disobey him. When any Indians accompanying the army entered any planted field, he punished them harshly in the presence of the natives. On account of the edict he issued, no one, either Spaniard or Indian, dared enter the houses of the natives. The army always camped outside of the pueblos in order to avoid the trouble that soldiers usually cause.

Francisco Vázquez was asked whether, upon reaching Cíbola, the province received him peacefully, or whether it offered resistance, and whether he summoned them as is ordered by his Majesty.

He said that on approaching Cíbola, he sent Don Pedro de Tovar and Melchior Díaz[4] to bring him some Indians from among a group that were near a lake, and that they should not harm them, in order to get information from them and an interpreter. They brought two or three of them. This witness explained to them through an interpreter whom he brought from the valley of Corazones that he had come in the name of his Majesty to place them under his dominion and to bring them to the knowledge of God; that they should become Christians, and that no harm would be done them in their persons or properties, provided they submitted peacefully to the obedience of his Majesty. With them he sent two Mexican Indians bearing a cross in their hands as an emblem of peace.

When this witness came within three leagues of Cíbola, where he was told that the pueblo and province were up in arms and would not come to meet them peacefully, he sent Don García López with about twenty or thirty men on horseback to examine a pass among some rocks that seemed difficult and where the army might suffer great harm from the natives. He was to clear it, spend the night there, and notify him of what should take place. And, Don García López having gone and camped at the said pass, during the early hours of the morning the natives fell upon his force and wounded some horses with arrows. They would have done greater damage had it not been that he was on the alert.

This witness, when he learned of it and when it became day, marched with his army and joined Don García López. Arriving within view of Cíbola, he noticed many smokes rising in different places around it, and saw some Indians in warlike array blowing a horn. He sent Don García López and Fray Luis with some men on horseback, and Hernando Bermejo, notary, to read to them the summons prescribed by his Majesty. As they advanced to carry out the aforesaid, this witness decided he wanted to be present. Taking a few mounted men and some articles to trade, and ordering the army to follow, he overtook and joined Don García López and the friar.

4. Melchior Díaz did not return to the Sonora valley till after the soldiers had entered Cíbola.

Some three hundred Indians with bows, arrows, and shields approached the place where this witness and the others were. Although he summoned the Indians to peace three times and explained to them the object of his coming through the interpreter, whom he had sent to talk to them, they never consented to submit peacefully nor to render obedience to his Majesty, nor did they cease shooting arrows at the Spaniards. Seeing that the Indians were wounding the horses and that they had hit Fray Luis with an arrow, he ordered them to be attacked. They turned their backs and ran into the pueblo, where they fortified themselves.[5] This witness ordered that they be summoned anew, asking them to submit peacefully, giving them assurances that no harm would be caused them and that they would be well treated. Seeing that they would not grant it and that they continued shooting arrows at them from above, and particularly because the army was suffering from hunger, he ordered that they be attacked.

As this witness entered through a narrow street of the said pueblo, the Indians, with the numerous stones they hurled at him from above, knocked him down twice from a ladder by which he tried to climb to the terraces. From this place he was removed as dead by Don García López and the soldiers. He escaped with three wounds on his face, an arrow wound in one leg, and his whole body bruised. They placed him in a tent where he remained unconscious for a long time. When he recovered consciousness, they told him that the pueblo had been taken and that quantities of provisions were found there. This witness and the other soldiers entered the said pueblo and took possession of it.[6]

Francisco Vázquez was asked whether, after taking and entering the pueblo, this witness or any of the captains and soldiers committed any cruelties, killings, or abuses on the Indian men and women they found there and who surrendered.

He said that they did not. On the contrary, he ordered that

5. The pueblo of Hawikuh, first of the Zuñi pueblos to the south.
6. The date was July 7. See Traslado de las Nuevas, above, p. 179. Coronado had left Culiacán on April 22. See his own letter of August 3, 1540, to the viceroy, p. 162.

all of them be well treated, especially the women and children, and he forbade any one to touch them under severe penalties. He sent for some of the chieftains and explained to them through the interpreter that they had done wrong in not coming to render obedience peacefully, as they had been asked and summoned, but that he would forgive them if they would render obedience. If any of them wished to remain there with their women and children, they would be accorded every good treatment, and he would leave them their belongings and houses undisturbed, and the wounded would be cared for. They replied that they realized they had done wrong, and that they wanted to go to the pueblo of Maçaque in order to return from there with the other neighboring pueblos to render obedience, for there were people from all those pueblos in the pueblo that the Spaniards had taken.

Next day, or within two days, the chieftain of Maçaque and those of the other pueblos came with presents of deer and cattle skins, henequen blankets,[7] some turquoises, and a few bows and arrows. This witness gave them some of the barter articles that he had. With this they went away very pleased, after rendering obedience to his Majesty and saying that they wanted to serve him and become Christians.

Francisco Vázquez was asked whether, while they remained at the pueblo of Cíbola, the Indian chieftains of the province from the pueblo of Cicuique came to render their obedience to his Majesty and to offer themselves to the said general as friends, inviting the Spaniards to visit their pueblo.

He said that among the above-mentioned there came three Indian chiefs, one of whom was called Cacique and another Xabe. He observed that while they were in the said pueblo of Cíbola there came three or four Indians from the pueblo of Cicuique. One he named Bigotes, but he does not remember the names of the others or whether those named Cacique and Xabe were among them. They told him they had learned that strange people, bold men who punished those who resisted them and gave good treatment to those who submitted, had come to

7. Not henequen, but yucca. See Relación Postrera de Cíbola, above, p. 308, note 3.

make their acquaintance and be their friends. This witness thanked them and told them that he came in the name of his Majesty to bring them to his obedience, and in order that they might know God and become Christians; that they should do so and would be well treated by them and would have them as their friends.

After having ordered that lodgings be provided for them and that they be accorded good treatment and after giving them some articles of barter, within two or three days he told them that he wanted to send Captain Hernando de Alvarado with some horsemen to notify them of his coming, to explain the reason why his Majesty had sent him to their provinces and neighboring pueblos, and to explore what there was beyond. The Indians said that they were pleased at this, and they asked that the Spaniards go by way of their pueblo, where they would be well received and be furnished with provisions and guides. He knows that Hernando de Alvarado went with twenty mounted men, and he learned that, at the pueblo of Cicuique, they accorded him a fine reception. They had the other pueblos along the way come out to meet them peaceably and bring them provisions and food. As the Spaniards wanted to travel farther on, the natives gave them two Indians as guides, one of whom they named the Turk and the other Isopete.

Francisco Vázquez was asked if, after Captain Hernando de Alvarado traveled farther on, he returned to the pueblo of Cicuique and was again well received there and presented with certain skins, blankets, and other things, which he sent to this witness at Cíbola, where he was.

He replied that he knew that Captain Hernando de Alvarado returned with his men by way of Cicuique, where he was well received. He does not know whether it was from this pueblo or from Uraba[8] that he sent some skins and blankets to this witness at the pueblo of Cíbola, where he was. He heard that they had been given to him, and that he had sent them, not on his way back, but on his journey out.

Francisco Vázquez was asked whether he knew that Captain

8. Uraba has been identified with Taos. It is the same as Yuraba in the Relación del Suceso, and the Braba of Castañeda.

Hernando de Alvarado took the Indian chief named Bigotes and the Indian called Cacique from the pueblo of Cicuique by deceit, saying that he needed them to guide and show him through certain pueblos.

This witness said that he heard that Captain Hernando de Alvarado brought along the said Indians named Bigotes and Cacique, and also the Indians named Turk and Isopete. He told him that matters at Cicuique remained in good order, except that he thought he had found the Indian named Bigotes ill disposed and somewhat dishonest in his conduct.

Francisco Vázquez was asked if he knew that, after Hernando de Alvarado left Cicuique, he put chains and collars on the said Cacique and Bigotes and in this manner brought them into camp, where this witness was, because the Indian named Bigotes would not hand over to him a gold bracelet and other jewels that the Indian named the Turk said he had, and also because he would not tell where he had obtained them, nor show them the rich country described by the Turk. This is what he told this witness and that it was for these reasons that he had put them in chains and collars.

He stated that Hernando de Alvarado told this witness that he had put these and other chains on the said Indian Bigotes because he felt that he was trying to help the Indian Turk escape, and that if the latter went back he would get the country to revolt. He remembers that Alvarado kept him in chains, and this witness saw him with the others at the camp where he was. At the time, Alvarado did not say that he had put him in chains on account of the reasons stated in the question, but for the ones this witness has set forth.

He remembers that the first night this witness arrived at the pueblo of Coofor in Tiguex,[9] where the headquarters had been established, the said Indian named the Turk came with Hernando de Alvarado to see this witness. Among other things that he related was the statement that at the pueblo of Cicuique

9. Called Alcanfor by López de Cárdenas. This pueblo served as the headquarters for the expedition during the two years it remained on the Rio Grande. Tello recorded the name as Coofer and Coofort (*Crónica*, pp. 414-415, 436-437), and Mota Padilla, as Coofer (*Historia*, p. 160).

there was a bracelet and other gold pieces which he had brought from Quivira, and that the Indian Bigotes had ordered them hidden, and if this witness should allow him to go back without Bigotes he would go and bring them.

Francisco Vázquez was asked if, upon learning what is stated in the preceding questions, he ordered the dogs unleashed on the Indian Bigotes to force him to tell about the bracelet and jewels, and how many times the dogs were set on him, and who did it.

He said that Fray Juan de Padilla told this witness that it was very important to the service of his Majesty that the truth about the rich country mentioned by the Turk be learned, that this could be found out from Bigotes, who, the Turk claimed, had the gold bracelet and jewels. This witness replied that Padilla, as a man who had talked more to Bigotes, since he had accompanied the said Hernando de Alvarado,[10] would understand him better, and he should take hold of him and try to learn the truth. Fray Juan de Padilla replied that Hernando de Alvarado understood him better, and if Francisco Vázquez wished, they would both try to find out.[11]

This witness agreed that they do so. Father Fray Juan said that he questioned Bigotes, and he denied everything. A few days later, seeing that Bigotes had an arm bandaged, this witness asked what had happened to that Indian, and he was told that a dog had bitten him. Later, when this witness returned to this province,[12] he learned that, as the Indian denied what he was asked, Don Pedro de Tovar, since he would not confess, told him to tell the truth or the dog that was loose around there would bite him. As he would not confess, Don Pedro called the dog and it bit him.[13]

Francisco Vázquez was asked if the tent of Hernando de

10. Here we have evidence that Fray Juan de Padilla accompanied Alvarado to Pecos. See below, pp. 328-329, and above, pp. 182-184.

11. Castañeda tells about the gold bracelet, but he makes no mention whatever of any dogs being set upon Bigotes or the other Indians. See also the testimony of López de Cárdenas, pp. 350-352.

12. New Galicia.

13. At the trial the testimony of the witnesses was that the dogs belonged to Don Pedro de Tovar, but Alvarado was charged with setting them on Bigotes.

Alvarado and the place where the dogs were set on the Indian named Bigotes were in the same camp and pueblo where this witness was lodged and whether they were close to his lodging.

He said that the lodging of Hernando de Alvarado was close to that of this witness, and that he had heard that they had not set the dog on him in the said lodging but had taken him out into the field to ask him what this witness has stated.

Francisco Vázquez was asked if this witness had not also seen that the Indian Bigotes had been bitten in the legs, and whether any one had told him that same night or day when it happened that they had unleashed the dogs on Bigotes because he would not confess what the Indian, Turk, claimed.

He said that, as he has stated, he did not remember having learned in the said camp or province that dogs had been unleashed on the Indian named Bigotes, nor having seen any wounds on him other than the one on his arm or leg.

Francisco Vázquez was asked if he knew that certain Indians from the pueblo of Cicuique were sent to this witness to ask for the Indian named Bigotes and the others from the said pueblo he held prisoners, and that they told him that he was repaying badly the good treatment they had accorded the Spaniards, and the friendship and obedience they had offered, but that he always refused to have the prisoners released to them.

He said that they never came to ask for such a thing. On the contrary, Bigotes and Cacique, after the aforesaid had taken place, told him that they and those of their pueblo were enemies of those of Tiguex, and that they were short of land, of which there was an abundance in the province of Tiguex, and they asked him to give them a pueblo there in order that they might settle it with their people, and that they would come and help him in the war.

Francisco Vázquez was asked if the province and pueblos of Tiguex approached this witness to offer peace and obedience in the name of his Majesty, and whether they welcomed the Spaniards and the army in their land and pueblos and presented them with skins, blankets, fowl, and other necessary provisions, and accorded them fine treatment.

He said that as Hernando de Alvarado and Fray Juan de

Padilla traveled through the said province together with the other Spaniards they had taken along, the pueblos there came to meet them peaceably and furnished them with maize, hens [turkeys], blankets, skins, and whatever they had, in trade for what Hernando de Alvarado and Fray Juan de Padilla gave them. The natives received them well, without making any signs of war or offering any resistance.

Fray Juan de Padilla wrote to him at Cíbola,[14] where this witness was, saying that on the bank of a river in that province there were very good pastures, and that it seemed to him that he should establish camp at that place. He sent Don García López, with Indians from Cíbola and allies to go and establish camp and prepare quarters at the place indicated by the said Fray Juan. The Indians at the pueblo of Coofor, seeing that the said Don García López wanted to put up houses, told him not to build them as they would vacate that pueblo for him and go to other neighboring ones where they had friends and relatives. Thus they evacuated the pueblo and the Spaniards established themselves in it.

This witness was asked if he sent some persons, and who they were, to the pueblos of the said province to gather skins and blankets to clothe the people, and hens [turkeys] to feed them, and some feather quilts, and who thus, by his command, gathered the said blankets, skins, quilts, fowl, maize, and necessary provisions at the said pueblos and brought them to the one where they were quartered.

He said that a certain number of Spaniards, soldiers, and Indian allies complained to this witness that they were naked and dying from cold and asked him to order some clothing gathered from the surrounding pueblos with which they might protect themselves and not perish from cold. Seeing their distress, this witness ordered Don García López to take some articles of trade and to try to obtain through them at the pueblo of Xia some quilts, skins, and blankets to clothe and relieve the people. So he knows that they went and brought a certain

14. From this statement it would seem that the report usually attributed to Hernando de Alvarado, above, pp. 182-184, was in fact written by Fray Juan de Padilla.

number of blankets, skins, and quilts, not as many as the people needed, because the natives did not give them to him. This clothing, which they obtained by means of trading the articles which the viceroy had ordered them to bring for the purpose of trading with the Indians, was distributed among the people most in need.

Francisco Vázquez was asked if he knew or had heard that the said clothing, fowl, and provisions had been taken from the houses against the will of the Indians and that the gathering of these had caused annoyance and commotion.

He said that he did not know of such a thing. On the contrary, he was told that the said Indians gave everything willingly in exchange for the said articles of barter. He believes that this was the case, as Don García López is a good Christian and a gentleman.[15]

Francisco Vázquez was asked whether he knew also that when they went to gather the said clothing, skins, quilts, and provisions one Villegas, a soldier of the said army, took an Indian woman by force and had carnal relations with her against her will, and that this incident and the taking of the said clothing from their houses against their will caused the Indians to become very incensed and wrought up. He was asked whether he knew or heard of it and whether he punished it.[16]

He said that he never heard of such a thing, because if he had he would have punished it in keeping with an edict he had issued. Upon returning to this province he heard it told that the said Villegas had violated the said Indian woman. The other contents of the question he said he did not know anything about.[17]

He was asked whether he knew that the natives of not only the said pueblo of Cicuique but also the province of Tiguex rose and rebelled because of the imprisonment and dog-biting of the Indian named Bigotes, the violence done by Villegas,

15. See Castañeda, p. 224.
16. *Ibid.*, pp. 224-225.
17. Joan de Contreras, Coronado's chief equerry, testified that this was Juan de Villegas, a brother of Pedro de Villegas, a regidor of Mexico, for which reason he was not punished. A. G. I., *Justicia*, legajo 1021, pieza 4.

and the taking of clothing and provisions from the pueblo against the will of the natives, and that it was thus publicly stated that they rose and rebelled on account of the aforesaid causes and other cruelties and abuses.

He replied that, as he has said and declared, he never knew anything about what is contained in the question. He does not believe, either, that they rose on account of the aforesaid causes, because, after the gathering of the clothing, the natives from the pueblo of Chia came to the camp and talked to this witness, and brought him hens [turkeys] and other provisions and offered to aid him. He knows, likewise, that the natives of the pueblo of Cicique did not rebel because of the imprisonment or on account of what is set forth in the question, because, after the aforesaid had taken place and the province of Tiguex had revolted, this witness went to the pueblo of Cicuique to seek their aid, bringing with him Bigotes and Cacique, and they welcomed him in their pueblo and accorded him a fine reception. He entered the pueblo accompanied only by Don Lope de Urrea and Fray Juan de Padilla, although he did not stay in the pueblo overnight. They refused to grant him the favor he was asking of them, excusing themselves by saying that they were busy with their plantings, but that if he insisted they would abandon everything they were doing. As he saw that they did not volunteer willingly he did not try further to urge it on them. On the contrary, he told them that he was grateful to them and that if he needed them he would let them know.

Francisco Vázquez was asked, since the said pueblo of Cicuique and the province of Tiguex came of their own accord to render obedience and to offer themselves as friends—and, as he said, they were not accorded any ill treatment—why it was, then, that the natives rose and rebelled.

This witness said that he did not know the reason, other than, being at peace and without having given them any cause that this witness knows of, they revolted, and one morning some thirty or fifty horses, more or less, of those loose in the fields, and also two Mexicans who were in charge of them, were found dead or shot with arrows.[18]

18. See Castañeda, p. 225, and testimony of Cárdenas, p. 347.

Francisco Vázquez was asked in how many pueblos of the province of Tiguex the natives withdrew and fortified themselves, and how many of these pueblos were abandoned and desolated.

He said that the natives gathered and resisted in only two pueblos, and that nine or ten others in the province were abandoned and desolated.

He was asked why, if these ten pueblos were abandoned and offered no resistance, they were burned and destroyed, and whether it was done by orders of this witness or if he knew who did it or ordered it done.

This witness said that he did not order the burning or destruction of the said pueblos, nor does he know exactly what captain burned or destroyed them, but he believes that, because of the intense cold prevailing and being far from the woods and camped in the open, the soldiers must have burned the wood [of the pueblo houses] to get some relief. He does not know whether they demolished only the walls or whether the pueblos were completely destroyed.

This witness was asked if he had ordered Don Rodrigo Maldonado to burn and destroy the first of the said pueblos or any one of them.

This witness said that he sent Don Rodrigo Maldonado to one of the said pueblos that had been abandoned, which was said to be the strongest, and to take out all of the provisions found in it. He does not remember that he ordered him to burn or destroy it. If he so ordered, it must have been to prevent the Indians who had left it, and other pueblos, from returning and fortifying themselves there. When he was in camp he saw smoke rising from the said pueblos, and, asking what it was, he was told that one of the said pueblos had been set on fire. He never knew what captain had burned it or who ordered it burned.

He was asked if the camp of this witness was near one of the two pueblos that the Indians had fortified, and how far it was from the abandoned pueblos that were burned and destroyed.

He said some were half a league, and others one, two, and three from the camp.

He was asked if, before laying siege to the said pueblos and attacking them, he summoned them to submit peacefully and said that he would pardon them and cause them no harm.

This witness said that, in view of the revolt of the said Indians, he called to his quarters Fray Juan de Padilla and Fray Antonio de Castilblanco,[19] and the officials of his Majesty, consulting them as to what should be done. Fray Juan de Padilla said that it was not permissible for them to kill anyone, but that he would approve and consider appropriate whatever the general should do. Fray Antonio gave a like answer. All agreed that war should be waged against them.

Thus decided, this witness sent Diego López, alderman of Seville, to the pueblo called Arenal to tell the natives of all the evil they had done, and that if they had revolted on account of some offense or abuse committed against them by any soldiers they should say so and he would do them justice in their presence. He said that they should render obedience to his Majesty once more and he would pardon them. With this same purpose he sent Don Rodrigo Maldonado to the pueblo of Moho,[20] which was the other fortified one. At both places the Indians tried to kill the Spaniards through trickery. Seeing that they were in revolt and that if they left those at war behind them it would be dangerous to go ahead, the Spaniards besieged and attacked them, with great risk to the army because, at the first attack on the pueblo that was besieged by Don García López,[21] they wounded more than forty Spaniards and Indian allies. And at the one named Mohi, which was besieged by this witness, they wounded many soldiers and killed Francisco de Ovando, a captain, and four or five other soldiers.[22] In the end, although the siege was long and exhausting, the defenders were overcome and pacified.

He was asked how many Indians were bitten by dogs and burned at the pueblo which this witness laid siege to, by whose order it was done, and whether this witness heard of it.

19. Regarding Father Castilblanco, see Introduction, p. 12.
20. Also written Mohi. These two pueblos, Arenal and Mohi, were evidently close to Alcanfor. They were the scenes of the chief battles in the province of Tiguex between the Spaniards and the pueblo Indians.
21. The pueblo of Arenal.
22. See Castañeda's version, p. 229.

This witness replied that he did not order any Indian burned or dogs unleashed on him, nor did he know that such a thing had been done. All he learned was that while he was ill in his tent, some Indians of the said pueblo who had been captured during the war and were imprisoned, were set free, and that a dog chased and bit them, but no one died, nor does he know that anyone set the dogs on them. When the Indians were brought back he ordered them released again so that they could go wherever they wished.

Francisco Vázquez was asked if he saw or heard that the Indians who, through hunger or thirst, left the pueblo without weapons and without offering resistance were lanced and the dogs set on the trail to overtake and hunt them down.

He said that he did not know anything about what is set forth in this question. Those who left and came into the power of this witness, he accorded very good treatment. He ordered that they be returned to the pueblo in order that they might tell the others to surrender and that they would be pardoned.

He was asked if, after the Indians were attacked and part of the terraces taken at the pueblo of Arenal, which was besieged by Don García López de Cárdenas, the natives who had not yet been conquered made signs to the said Don García López that if he guaranteed their lives they would surrender peacefully. Don García López promised and assured them by signs that he would, and thus some eighty persons left the said pueblo without any weapons and Don García López ordered them taken and placed in his tent at the camp.[23]

This witness said that he heard that after the attack some Indians had left the said pueblo unarmed and peaceful and that Don García López ordered them taken and placed in his tent.

Francisco Vázquez was asked if the said Don García López had notified this witness that he was holding the said Indians in his tent and had asked what he should do with them, and whether this witness sent him word by Contreras, his stable man, not to burn them until the arrival of the Indians named Turk and Isopete in order that they might witness it and spread

23. Castañeda says that about two hundred prisoners were taken.

the report in their countries of the justice that was meted out to those who rebelled.

He said that he denied what is set forth in the question. What happened was that Don García López sent word to this witness that the pueblo had been entered but that there were still some houses containing Indian men and women to be taken, and he wanted to know if this witness wanted him to go ahead and wage war on the others who were in revolt. He sent him orders not to raise the siege of the said pueblo until it was completely subjugated. Further, this witness told him that he was coming to examine the situation at the pueblo, and on his way they met at the pueblo of Alameda.[24]

Francisco Vázquez was asked whether he knew, saw, or heard that Don García López ordered and burned at the stake some forty or fifty Indians of the ones he had imprisoned in the tent.

He replied that he had never heard that Don García López had burned any Indians at the said siege, nor had any such information ever reached him that he remembers.

Francisco Vázquez was asked whether he knew that the said Don García López, and the soldiers by his command, speared and stabbed to death thirty or forty other Indians who were held in the tent.

He stated that he had heard that the Indians in the tent had revolted and offered resistance and that some of them had been killed.

Francisco Vázquez was asked whether, during the said burnings at the stake and stabbings in the said tent, the Indians named Turk and Isopete were at the camp of Don García López, whether they witnessed the aforesaid, and whether this witness sent them to the said camp.

He replied that he did not remember anything of what is set forth in this question.

24. It is a curious coincidence that there is still a place called Alameda in the immediate vicinity of the Spanish headquarters of 1540-1542. Since Alameda is a common name and there are still many cottonwoods in this area, it would be strange if the Alameda of 1540 were identical with the site that now bears this name, a village eight miles north of Albuquerque, though that would not be impossible.

Francisco Vázquez was asked whether he ordered the killing of the Indian named Turk, for what reason, who killed him, whether this witness was present or if he was in the camp where he was strangled.

This witness said that when he went to the province of Quivira with a number of his men, he took along the Indians named Turk and Isopete. In the last pueblo of the said province where this witness was there was a scarcity of maize, and, inquiring as to the reason why the natives did not furnish it to them, he was told that it was because the Indian called the Turk had told them not to give the general any maize, that, if they did not provide it, the horses would soon die; that they should keep an eye on certain of the best horses in order to kill them, for once the horses were dead then they could kill the Christians. Upon hearing this, Francisco Vázquez ordered Diego López, maese de campo, that he should have the Turk executed upon verifying this information. He also told him to ask the Turk why he had arranged the plot and why he had deceived and led them astray. The maese de campo, upon learning that the Turk was plotting their death, ordered him killed. This took place at the camp where this witness was.[25]

This is the truth of what he knows about this matter, in keeping with the oath he has taken.

This statement and testimony was read to him immediately after he had finished giving it. He confirmed it, and it was signed by him and the said judge.

FRANCISCO VÁZQUEZ DE CORONADO
LICENTIATE TEJADA

25. See Castañeda, p. 242, note 1.

TESTIMONY OF LOPEZ DE CARDENAS

THE COUNCIL. YEAR OF 1551. HIS MAJESTY'S FIS-
CAL VS. DON GARCÍA RAMÍREZ DE CÁRDENAS,
RESIDENT OF MADRID, CONCERNING CHARGES
BROUGHT AGAINST HIM FOR THE EXCESSES HE
COMMITTED WHILE HE WAS MAESTRE DE CAMPO
OF THE EXPEDITION TO CÍBOLA, AN EXPEDITION
THAT WAS MADE IN NEW SPAIN.[1] SECRETARY
SÁMANO.

Don Carlos, Emperor by divine grace, etc.

To you, Licentiate Gaspar de Jaem and Licentiate Ruiz de Monjaraz, lieutenants of our governor of the province on the mainland named Castilla del Oro, and to you, Asensio de Xáuregui, official secretary of the council of the city of Nombre de Dios, to each one and any of you, in what concerns you, greetings and peace. Know ye that Hernán González de Párraga, resident at present in this capital, brought before us in our Council of the Indies a petition of accusation of the following tenor:

> Accusation against Don García López de
> Cárdenas by Licentiate Villalobos, your
> Fiscal, in the Council of the Indies.

Respectful Sirs:

To the best of my ability, and as it is my duty, I bring criminal charges against Don García López de Cárdenas, resident of this city of Madrid. I state that at the time when our most holy father, Paul III, was pontiff of the church of God, our Lord, and your Highness ruled these your kingdoms of the Indies and the islands of the Indies and over the mainland of the ocean sea, that in one and many days of the months of the preceding years of 1541, 1542, and 1543, during a certain ex-

---

1. Translated from a photostatic copy of the original in the Archives of the Indies, *Justicia*, legajo 1021, pieza 1.

pedition that Francisco Vázquez Coronado made in New Spain of the said Indies, in particular from the city of Mexico to the province of Cíbola, the above-mentioned Don García López, accused by me, served as maestre de campo of the people who went on the said expedition.

On this journey, both on the way forth and back, the said defendant and the Spaniards whom he took in his company perpetrated robberies, burnings, cruelties, and many other offenses against the native Indians of the lands through which they passed, killing a large number of them, taking their women by force and against their will and that of their husbands and parents, lying with them carnally. He apprehended other Indians, unleashing vicious dogs to attack them, taking by force the food and clothing they had to maintain their lives. He drove the Indians from their homes when they had received him peacefully and had given him willing of what they had. They inflicted upon the said Indians much bad treatment, wherefore by necessity, in order to defend themselves against them, the Indians revolted. The defendant and the Spaniards and soldiers that he brought with him besieged the said Indians and attacked and fought them by fire and sword.

In this war the Spaniards burned twelve or thirteen pueblos belonging to the said Indians. And the Indians, being placed in a precarious position by this attack, asked safeguards from their adversary to surrender peacefully. This safeguard the defendant granted them, even with the sign of the cross, and said that if they would submit peacefully, they would suffer no harm in their persons or property. In view of this safeguard, the Indians came out of their pueblo and placed themselves in the hands of their adversary. Thus, more than eighty of the leading Indians placed themselves in the hands of the said defendant, and the others, who remained in the pueblo, gave up the said place and houses so that the Spaniards could enter, as they did, in peace and safety. When the said Indians had delivered themselves into his hands through his assurance of safeguards, the said defendant broke his promise and did not keep it. On the contrary, he acted against it. He arrested the said Indians and took them as prisoners to his tent. Taking out more than thirty of them in order to burn them, he tied each one to a stake and burned them alive there in the fire. When the other Indians who were prisoners in the tent saw that the said promises of security were not kept, but on the contrary the Indians were being burned, they tried to get out of the tent in which they were kept prisoners and there the said adversary had them all killed by lance and sword thrusts.

This was all through greed of getting gold and silver and because he had heard that a leading Indian cacique named Bigotes, who was friendly and had provided them with very good lodgings, wore a gold bracelet and other jeweled ornaments of gold and silver. And because two other friendly Indian chieftains, one named the Turk and the other Ysopete, did not give him gold or silver nor take him where gold and silver could be found, he killed them.

The said defendant caused and perpetrated many other bad abuses, injuries, and cruelties against the Indians. For this reason the said Indians rebelled and ceased to be friendly and peaceful, and the discovery, pacification, and settling of the land was abandoned, and the propagation of our holy Catholic faith hindered, whereby God, our Lord, and your Highness were very poorly served. Your royal patrimony missed the opportunity to obtain more than five hundred thousand ducats in gold and silver and other things.

Wherefore the said defendant ought to be severely punished in his person and estates. I beg and entreat your Highness for an order to proceed against the said Don García López de Cárdenas. In view of the above, there must be imposed on him the greatest and most severe penalties, which, because of the aforesaid, should be executed against his person and property, in order that it may serve as a punishment for him, an example or warning to others, and a credit to your royal office. I beg you for all that is needed and that you order the said defendant sentenced so that he be pressed to pay and restore to your royal patrimony and treasury up to the sum of five hundred thousand ducats, on account of the aforesaid damages and losses which he caused you through his misdeeds. This is the amount at which I appraise and reckon the said damages and costs, subject to your royal appraisal and moderation.

I swear to God in proper form that in the aforesaid I do not say maliciously anything except what has occurred, or ask for anything except to obtain complete fulfillment of the justice that I seek. In proof of the abovesaid, I introduce the present investigation made by Licentiate Tejada, judge of your royal audiencia in New Spain, through your royal commission. It is signed by PEDRO DE REQUENA, your clerk of the said royal audiencia, before whom it was done. [Rubric]

Madrid, January 7, 1546. Licentiate Villalobos, Fiscal, presented this petition in the Council of the Indies of their Majesties.

The gentlemen of the Council ordered that the relator bring the report. [Rubric]

In the city of Madrid, February 19, 1546, the members of the royal Council of the Indies of his Majesty ordered that Licentiate Cianca go to the fortress in the town of Pinto, and before Jorge Vázquez, his Majesty's notary, take the deposition of Don Gárcia López de Cárdenas, who is imprisoned there by order of his Highness and the members of the said Council. He is to take this deposition from him based on the accusation brought against him by the fiscal and the report which he is to give him. For this purpose they said that they gave him full powers in the name of his Majesty. And if necessary, they ordered the said Don García López to make his deposition before the said Licentiate Cianca without offering any excuses in the case, under penalty of a fine of one thousand gold castellanos for the treasury of his Majesty.[2]

OCHOA DE LUYANDO

2. Don García López de Cárdenas, who came to the Indies in 1535, was, like Coronado and many other caballeros there, a second son without fortune or future in Spain. While in New Mexico with the Coronado expedition he received news of his oldest brother's death and of his own inheritance, and when the expedition returned to Mexico in the summer of 1542, Don García sailed for Spain and there assumed the headship of the family estate, changing his name to García Ramírez de Cárdenas.

Don García's wife was Doña Ana de Mendoza, daughter of the Count of Coruña, Don Lorenzo de Mendoza, member of one of Spain's most influential

DEPOSITION OF DON GARCÍA BEFORE LICENTIATE CIANCA

In the town of **Pinto**, February 20, 1546, Licentiate Andrés de Cianca, before me, the present secretary, stated that he had come here to the said town by order of the members of the royal Council of the Indies of his Majesty to take the deposition of Don García López de Cárdenas, a prisoner by their command in the fortress of the said town. To carry out and execute what he had been charged, he went to the said fortress and ordered the said Don García López de Cárdenas to appear before him. He took and received, in due legal form, his oath and promise to tell the truth, which he swore. Under oath, he asked him the following questions.

Asked what his name was, he answered that in the Indies he was called Don García López de Cárdenas, but since he returned to Spain, he inherited his father's estate and is called Don García Ramírez.

---

families, and by his marriage the conquistador became a distant relative of Don Antonio de Mendoza, viceroy of Mexico.

Judge Lorenzo Tejada's investigation of the conduct of the Coronado expedition, completed on March 11, 1545, resulted in the formulation of serious charges against Don García, who had been the expedition's maestre de campo, or chief officer. When the papers forwarded by Judge Tejada to Spain reached the Council of the Indies, Don García was immediately imprisoned in the fortress of Pinto. Fiscal Villalobos of the Council filed criminal charges against him on January 7, 1546, and on February 20 of the same year Licentiate Andrés Cianca visited the prison to take his deposition. As both the accused and the fiscal ordered new testimony drawn up in Mexico, the case was a long-drawn-out affair and was not completed until July of 1551.

During these six long years of litigation, Don García remained in jail. His attorney, Sebastián Rodríguez, tried every scheme to obtain the release of his client on bail, but to no avail. Cash bond of 25,000 ducats, imposing lists of wealthy and prominent bondsmen, failed to move the Council of the Indies. Nor did appeals for a twelve-day permit to visit his dying father-in-law, the Count of Coruña, who was seriously ill at Guadalajara, prove any more successful. All petitions, whether elaborate or simple, brought from the Council the terse answer, "no ha lugar"—denied.

Finally, on December 20, 1549, the judges passed sentence, ordering Don García to serve thirty months in Orán, Africa. He appealed the sentence and petitioned to have the place of servitude changed to Navarre. But when, on July 17, 1551, the sentence, reaffirmed in amended form, ordered him to serve a year in the province of Navarre, he said that the climate of that region was injurious to his health. He finally paid his fine and served his year's sentence at Vélez, Málaga, actually being imprisoned seven years, counting the six he spent in jail during the trial. This information was gleaned from documents contained in A. G. I., *Justicia,* legajo 1021, comprising several thousand sheets.

Asked if he had been in the Indies of the ocean sea, in the provinces called New Spain, he replied that he had. Asked how long ago it was since he went from these kingdoms of Spain to the Indies, he said that he went to the Indies in the same year that his Majesty embarked for Tunis.[3]

Asked how long he had resided in the Indies, and in what regions and places, he said he had been on the mainland, in the provinces of Santa Marta[4] and Cuba. This witness spent the first year there, more or less, and from the said island of Cuba he passed on to New Spain, to the city of Mexico, where he remained for a year, more or less, ill, without being able to do anything. At the end of the said year Don Antonio de Mendoza, viceroy of New Spain, ordered him to go to the province of Guaxaca, to appraise it with Bishop Zárate[5] and to keep the Indians at peace among themselves, and to investigate the litigations which there might be between them and the Spaniards. He spent three years in this appointment, and another year and a half, more or less, in other commissions for the viceroy and royal audiencia of Mexico.

Don García Ramírez was asked to state and declare under the charge and oath he had taken whether at the time that Francisco Vázquez Coronado went as general to the discovery of Cíbola, which is in these Indies, this witness went with him and what office he held.

He replied that at the time Francisco Vázquez was chosen general, this witness was not in the city of Mexico, but was engaged in one of the above-mentioned commissions. He said that at the time this witness came to Mexico he found the said Francisco Vázquez ready to start on the said expedition, and

3. Charles V made his great attack on Tunis in 1535, the fleet leaving Barcelona on June 14. R. B. Merriman, *The Rise of the Spanish Empire*, III, p. 309 *et seq.*

4. Santa Marta, founded in 1525 by Rodrigo de Bastidas, near the Magdalena river in modern Colombia.

5. Juan de Zumárraga was consecrated as first bishop of Mexico at Valladolid, Spain, on April 27, 1533. His urgings resulted in a royal cédula, issued in February, 1534, that New Spain be divided into four bishoprics. They are known as Mexico, Michoacán, Tlascala, and Oaxaca. The see of Oaxaca was given to the Dominican, Juan López de Zárate, a licentiate in canonical law and doctor of theology. Bancroft, *History of Mexico*, II, pp. 386-392.

that he went with him by order of and with the consent of the viceroy as captain of some mounted men. During the said expedition and journey, before they reached the province of Cuyuacán,[6] the Indians of the said province killed a certain Lope de Samaniego, maestre de campo of the said army. Because of the death of the aforesaid Samaniego, General Francisco Vázquez appointed this witness as maestre de campo of the army. He accepted and went in this capacity, exercising the office until they came to the plains where they discovered the cattle.

Don García Ramírez was asked to state and declare in what entradas and skirmishes he took part from the time he was appointed maestre de campo until he resigned.

He replied that, from the said province of Cuyuacán, Francisco Vázquez went on in search of Cíbola with sixty horsemen, more or less. The rest of the people he left in the said province under the command of Don Tristán de Arellano. This witness was one of those who went with Francisco Vázquez as far as the said province of Cíbola. Until they came to within three or four leagues of the said Cíbola, they did not have any encounters with the Indians.

Upon reaching that place, this deponent was ahead with eight or ten soldiers on horseback and noticed some Indians on top of a hill. This witness advanced alone to the place where the said Indians were, making signs of peace to them, and giving them presents of the things he carried to trade. With this, some of the said Indians came down and took the articles that this witness gave them. He shook hands with them and remained at peace with the said Indians, and he gave them a cross and told them by signs to go to the pueblo[7] and tell those who were there that they were coming peacefully and that they wanted to be their friends. With this the said Indians went to the pueblo, and this witness remained there to await Francisco Vázquez and the others who were with him.

At this very place where he met the Indians, the soldiers camped for the night, awaiting the said Indians, while this

6. Cuyuacán, generally written Culiacán.
7. This was Hawikuh.

witness with a few men set about to guard a bad pass, because if the Indians should come with hostile intent the Spaniards would not let them pass. At midnight many Indians attacked this witness and those who were with him at the said pass. Because of the Indians' cries and shouting and the arrows that they shot at them, the horses which this witness and the other men had became frightened and ran away, leaving the men on foot. Had it not been for two mounted men who were on guard duty, the Indians would have killed this witness and the ten companions who were with him watching the pass.

The next morning Francisco Vázquez arrived with the rest of the men and learned of what had happened during the night. From there they set out all together in order and marched toward Cíbola. About a league before coming to Cíbola they saw four or five Indians. Upon seeing them, this witness again stopped his men, and he went ahead of the others, alone, to talk to the said Indians, making signs and demonstrations of peace to them. They did not wait for him. In view of this, the Spaniards marched in the same order as before until they came close to Cíbola. Here they found all the Indians of Cíbola and the people of other places who had gathered to meet them with force.[8] On seeing this, this witness, together with a certain Fray Luis of the order of Saint Francis, and a notary,[9] who served as secretary to Francisco Vázquez, advanced ahead of the other people and approached the place where the said Indians were. They coaxed them and made signs of peace to them, putting aside their weapons in order that they should come to them and so that the Indians should also lay down their weapons. The said Indians refused to do it. On the contrary, they rushed toward this witness and the said friar and secretary, shooting many arrows at them. They pierced the habit of the friar with an arrow and lodged another in the clothing and armor of the said notary.

When Francisco Vázquez saw this, he came with all the rest

8. This statement that a large number of Indians from other pueblos as well as those from the first pueblo itself had gathered to oppose the Spaniards is contained in Coronado's testimony as well.

9. This was Hernando Bermejo, according to Coronado's testimony on the management of the expedition.

of the people he had with him to help this witness. Upon his arrival and before they began hostilities with the Indians, Francisco Vázquez again summoned them to peace, but they would not submit. Then Francisco Vázquez ordered that they be attacked because the said Indians rejected their offers of peace. In that attack they killed some Indians and the others fled to the pueblo of Cíbola; it seemed to this witness that not more than ten or twelve of the Indians were killed. After the Indians took refuge in the pueblo, Francisco Vázquez again summoned them to peace.

While this was taking place, Fray Marcos de Niza, a Franciscan friar, who was guiding the Spanish army, arrived. Francisco Vázquez told him of all that had happened, and when the said friar heard it and saw that the Indians were fortified, he said: "Take your shields and go after them." So Francisco Vázquez and some of the others who were with him did so and attacked the Indians. At the entrance to the pueblo of Cíbola, the Indians struck Francisco Vázquez two or three heavy stone blows that knocked him to the ground. If this witness and others who were with him had not come to his rescue they would have killed him. With Francisco Vázquez badly injured, they withdrew.[10]

After this the Indians asked this witness through signs not to harm them any more, as they wanted to leave the pueblo. This witness told the said Indians that they could remain if they wished, and that all would be at peace. But they wanted to leave, and so they went away without being harmed by the Spaniards. They abandoned the said pueblo of Cíbola and left it to the Spaniards, who entered it and quartered themselves there, and all of them remained there for two or three months, more or less.

Asked if, in the taking of Cíbola, this witness, the captain general, or the others who accompanied him had perpetrated any cruelties or abuses, or whether they had beaten the natives of the said province, wherefore the Indians would not submit to the service and obedience of his Majesty, he reaffirmed, he

10. Accounts of this incident are given by Castañeda, p. 208; by Coronado in his letter of August 3, 1540, p. 169; and by Coronado at his trial, p. 323.

stated, what he has said in the question preceding this one, and that nothing else happened in the taking of Cíbola.

Don García Ramírez was asked if it is true that while the army of the Spaniards was quartered in Cíbola, many of the Indians who had left it, and others from other places in the vicinity, came to bring them presents and food, and that they came in peace and always remained so.

He said that what happened was that after the Spaniards entered Cíbola and the Indians had left, Francisco Vázquez Coronado sent some of their own captains to the Indians to bring them to peace and to obedience to his Majesty. Some of them came, and the Spaniards received them well and treated them as friends. The Indians brought some blankets and other little things which he does not remember.

This witness was asked where he and the others went from this province of Cíbola, what entradas they made, and whether they had any encounters with any Indians.

He stated that what happened was that, as the said general and his people saw that the land was sterile and that they had been deceived, they decided to explore in order to see if they could find a better land where God, our Lord, and his Majesty would be served and they themselves benefitted. They set out, agreed that this witness, with twenty-five horsemen, should go to explore the region to the west, and that another captain, with other men, should go to the east, while General Francisco Vázquez remained in Cíbola with the rest of the people. In this entrada this witness went almost one hundred leagues inland, without finding in all this distance any Indian settlements other than those that had already been discovered around Cíbola. They endured much thirst and hunger, as he has stated, and he and his men returned to Cíbola, where they found Francisco Vázquez.[11]

Asked what interpreters this witness took on these journeys, he said that as far as Cíbola they conversed through three or four interpreters, and that they made little use of them because the Spaniards understood the Indians' signs, and that, on his

11. This was the expedition which discovered the Grand Canyon of the Colorado. The story is told more fully by Castañeda, pp. 213-217.

exploration to the west, he did not take any interpreter, nor did he need one.

Asked whether he made other trips, and what trips he carried out after he returned from his exploration to the west, he said that soon after his return to Cíbola from the west, General Francisco Vázquez sent him to Tiguex to prepare quarters for the whole army, as he had already sent for Don Tristán, who had remained at San Miguel with some people, and, as he has stated, this witness went to Tiguex to prepare the said lodgings. He took along thirteen or fourteen horsemen.[12]

This witness found the Indians of the said province of Tiguex friendly and began to prepare the lodgings outside of the pueblos in order not to cause any hardship to the Indians of the said pueblos. And as he saw that the winter was setting in severely, with snow, he begged the Indians to clear a pueblo in order that the soldiers might establish their lodgings in it. The Indians could find homes in the other pueblos, as there were in that province of Tiguex as many as twelve or thirteen pueblos. The Indians did so, and left a pueblo to this witness, which, from what he remembers, was called Alcanfor.[13] This witness and his companions lodged themselves there and prepared quarters for the entire army, as the said Francisco Vázquez had ordered. The general came there, and also the people who had remained at San Miguel with Don Tristán, and Alvarado with the men he had taken with him. As far as he remembers, they remained in peace three months altogether, more or less.

Asked where they went from the said pueblo of Alcanfor and why they left it, he replied that, at the end of the time he has stated in the question before this one, one morning some of the Mexican Indians with the army came to tell that they had found one of their companions killed. With the approval of the general, this witness went with about seven or eight mounted men to investigate and report what had happened.

12. Hernando de Alvarado had already discovered and reported the advantages of the Rio Grande valley, wherefore López de Cárdenas was sent to arrange winter quarters there.

13. Called Coofor by Coronado, p. 326.

When he reached another pueblo which was about a fourth
of a league from the place where the army was quartered, he
found it abandoned. A little farther on he found two or three
horses killed by arrows.[14] Following the tracks of the said
horses, he continued until he crossed the river of Tiguex where
the Indians had crossed with all the horses they could round up
of those in the fields. He found up to twenty-five or twenty-six
of the said horses killed in the field and in the pueblos, on this
side and on the other side of the river.[15]

This witness rounded up the horses he found alive, and,
while returning to where the general was, as he passed near the
pueblos, the Indians shouted a great deal and shot arrows at
this witness and at those who were with him. This witness
stopped to talk to the said Indians through signs, for by now
they understood each other quite well. He told them that he
did not care at all that they had killed the horses, since they
had many, and he asked them to be friends, saying that the
Spaniards would not harm them, but the natives would not
consent to it. When he came to the place where Francisco Vázquez was, he informed him of what had happened. Then Francisco Vázquez again sent this witness with a few horsemen to
talk peace with the Indians once more. He summoned them to
peace, but without any success, and this witness returned to
where Francisco Vázquez was.[16]

Don García Ramírez was asked the reason why the Indians
of the said pueblos rose and rebelled, since he says that the
whole army was lodged at Alcanfor for three months, at peace
with the Indians of the neighboring pueblos, and that they
associated and traded with them; and he was asked what abuses
this witness perpetrated against them or consented to be done.

This witness replied, in accordance with the oath he has
taken, that neither he nor any one he knew ever caused them
any outrage or annoyance, unless it had been to ask them for the
pueblo in which the Spaniards were quartered and the food

14. In the second [new] set of questions framed by Licentiate Tejada in
the investigation of Coronado, it is clear that the incident of the horses took
place at the pueblo of Arenal.

15. Castañeda also tells of this attack on the horses, p. 225.

16. This subject is resumed a little later. See p. 352.

the Indians gave them. It is true that before Francisco Vázquez arrived there, two or three Indians came to complain to
this witness. By means of signs, they complained that an unruly
Spaniard had gone to a nearby pueblo and had seized an Indian woman. And by the signs they made, they indicated that
the said soldier had tried to have relations with the said Indian
woman. At other times, it seemed that they wanted to say by
their signs that he had tried to take a blanket from her. This
witness assembled all his soldiers and made them enter a room.
The Indian went to identify the one against whom he complained, but he was not able to recognize him, nor was the
accused found out by this method, nor by any other means that
this witness resorted to.[17]

Moreover, this witness is certain that no cause had been
given by the Spaniards nor any harm done them by the Spaniards wherefore they should rebel, but that they did it of their
own accord. For soon after the Spaniards entered the province
of Tiguex, while the army was camped in the country, the Indians used to come to the quarters of the Spaniards to wrestle
with them and try their strength. And although the Indians
had very fine estufas in which to sleep, they used to come among
the Spaniards in order to see whether they were on their guard.
By these and other signs which he observed, this witness knew
from the moment he arrived there that they wanted to revolt,
and all the Spaniards who were with this witness had the same
suspicion and were on their guard.

Asked whether this witness took part in the entradas made
by Hernando de Alvarado, and whether he went with him, he
said that he did not.

Asked whether the said Hernando de Alvarado was quartered in the said pueblo of Alcanfor with the general during the
time he says they remained there, he answered that he was,
because Alvarado had returned from the entrada he had undertaken to the east, and the captain general had come from Cíbola.

Don García Ramírez was asked what entradas Alvarado had
told about making in the land he said he had traversed and what

17. The soldier referred to was apparently Juan de Villegas. See Castañeda,
pp. 224-225, and Coronado's testimony, p. 330.

Indians he brought with him, and what had happened to him.

He replied that he heard him say that nineteen or twenty leagues from where they were lodged he had found an Indian pueblo named Ciquique,[18] where he found two Indians who told him of the country ahead. Taking them as guides, he had traveled over some plains until his allotted time had expired. Then the said Alvarado returned to the place where the general, Francisco Vázquez, was. He brought with him certain Indians as prisoners. One of them was called Bigotes, another the Turk, and a third Ysopete. Alvarado gave a detailed account of his expedition to the general, Francisco Vázquez. This witness did not hear it, nor was he present at the conversation.

Asked whether this witness knew these three Indians, the Turk, Ysopete, and Bigotes, he said that he did know them because he had them in his quarters for a long time, as the general had ordered them delivered to him so that he might guard them.

Asked from what provinces the three Indians came, he replied that Bigotes said he was from Ciquique, and that the other two said they were from Quivira, very far in the interior of the land.

Don García Ramírez was asked to state the nature of the abuses, the wounds inflicted on the three Indians by harassing them with dogs, who had done it and by whose command, and whether this witness ordered it and why.

He responded that soon after the arrival of the general and Hernando de Alvarado at Tiguex, where this witness had lodged the three Indians, this witness became sick. And as to what he is asked about in this question, he does not know anything except that when they delivered the three Indians at his quarters, the Indian, Bigotes, showed certain bites which it was said had been caused by dogs. These bites were on both legs and one arm. He heard it said that the Indian, Bigotes, was questioned about it, but he does not remember whether it was the general, or Alvarado by his command, who had ordered the dogs set on him. The Turk told about a certain land, and of a little bracelet of gold, and these Indians claimed there was gold

18. Pecos. See Alvarado's own report, pp. 182-184.

in their land, and because he did not want to show it they threatened him with a dog, and from this misfortune must have originated the story of the said dog. What this witness heard at the time was that he had been bitten, and this witness took care of him at his lodging. He did not hear it told nor did he see that the three Indians had suffered any harm or bad treatment after they came to Tiguex. On the contrary, they were well treated because the Spaniards believed them and thought that they would guide them and show them a fine country, such as the Indian called the Turk had described.

Don García Ramírez was asked whether the province of Tiguex, which was at peace, rose and rebelled on account of the cruelties and abuses committed by the general, this witness, and the other captains against the Indians of the said province; whether it was caused also by a certain Villegas, who, in one of the said pueblos, took an Indian woman by force and raped her; whether the Spaniards seized the blankets, valuables, and clothing they found in the pueblos.

He replied that he repeats what he has stated in regard to this matter. As for the clothing, he remembers that the general, seeing that winter was setting in very severely and that some of the Indians and negroes who were with him had frozen and died of cold, ordered this witness and others to go in different directions through the pueblos to ask the Indians for some clothes in order to be able to withstand the winter. Some of the Indians gave some clothing of their own will, and others against their will, although they were not at all ill treated on this account, nor did this witness permit it where he went.

Asked if the general was in the pueblo when what has been stated in the previous question took place, he answered that he repeats what he has said: that in the affair of the Indian woman, he always tried to apprehend the soldier who had done it in order to punish him; that it was never established that Villegas was the one who attacked the Indian woman, nor was any one else found guilty, because this witness would have punished him if he had learned about it, as he had punished other less serious offenses that had taken place.

Don García Ramírez was asked whether the ill treatment

and unleashing of dogs on Indian Bigotes, in the province of Tiguex, and the taking of the Indians as prisoners and keeping them in chains was sufficient and evident cause for the natives of the said province to revolt as they did.

He replied that it seemed to him and to all that this was not the cause, because the Indians of the said province could not have seen or learned of the unleashing of the dogs on the three Indians. Rather, the causes were as he has explained in another question before this one.

Asked if he knew whether the said general punished Captain Hernando de Alvarado for having unleashed the said dog on Bigotes, he answered that the general did not punish him because this witness believes and knows that Alvarado did not set the dog on Bigotes by his own authority, but that the general was aware of it. For this reason this witness, as maestre de campo, did not punish Alvarado, inasmuch as the general was lenient with him.

Don García Ramírez was asked what the general, this witness, and the people who were with them did when they saw that the Indians of the province of Tiguex were in open rebellion, since this witness states that he had twice summoned them to peace.

He said that the last time this witness returned to tell the general that the Indians refused to submit to or accept peace,[19] the general assembled the captains, this witness, and the friars who were with the army, and when they were all gathered, it was decided, by the agreement of all, to wage war on the Indians. They sent this witness to summon them once more to accept peace, and, if they refused to submit, having first issued his summons, to do them what harm he could. In fulfillment of this commission, he set out from the said place where they were quartered,[20] with sixty horsemen, a number of footmen, and some of the Indians from Mexico who were along. The first pueblo at which he arrived—he did not remember its name—

19. See above, p. 348.
20. At the pueblo of Alcanfor.

must have been half a league from the place where he left.[21] He found that the Indians were haughty and jeered at him. Then this witness, with a few of the captains who were with him, separated from the other people and for a period of two hours summoned them to peace. As the said Indians would not accept peace, this witness waged war and ordered his men to attack them. They did so, and the Indians entrenched themselves. This fight lasted a long time, until the Spaniards gained the terraces of the said pueblo and entered them. In that attack some Mexican Indians were killed and thirteen or fourteen Spaniards were badly wounded. After taking the terraces, the Spaniards remained in them, because night fell. Early the next morning this witness again summoned the said Indians to peace. He himself offered peace to them, but they never accepted. Then the Spaniards fought them again until they defeated them. They entered the houses of these natives one by one. As to whether he knew if any native Indians had been slain in this attack, he does not remember how many.

When the pueblo had been taken by the Spaniards, this witness informed Francisco Vázquez Coronado of what had happened, and Francisco Vázquez sent this witness at the said pueblo the three Indians, Bigotes, the Turk, and Ysopete, whom he had given him to guard. This witness left them in the care of a servant of his at the camp of the said Francisco Vázquez when this witness went to take part in the conquest which he has just narrated. The general sent the three Indians to the scene of battle so that they might see the power with which the pueblo was taken, and the punishment that he inflicted on the said Indians who were apprehended, in order that they should be warned and counsel others not to rebel, but to come and make friends.

Asked whether, after this witness had taken the terraces of the pueblo he was attacking, the Indians there made signs of peace to this witness, and whether they sued for it, he replied

21. This was the pueblo of Arenal. The name is supplied by Coronado in his testimony in regard to the same affair, above, p. 333, and is also mentioned by many of the witnesses at the Coronado and Cárdenas trials.

that they never asked for peace either by signs or in any other manner.

Don García Ramírez was asked whether he made signs of peace to the Indians, whether he promised them peace on a cross he made, and whether he assured them that their lives would be safe if they capitulated.[22]

This witness stated that he always summoned them to peace. He does not remember whether or not it was by the sign of the cross, but that this summons to peace was made before the attack began. Once hostilities started, he never summoned them again until the fight was over, nor did he observe that the Indians asked for peace.

Don García Ramírez was asked whether it was true that, under the word of peace he gave the said Indians, they immediately submitted to obedience and set out from their pueblo in the direction of the Spaniards, unarmed, believing that this witness would keep his word.

He said he repeats what he has already said, that never had any Indian surrendered to this witness on his word, nor did he see any one leave except when they were driven out by force.

Asked whether it was true that the Indians left the said pueblo, trusting in the word he had given them, and that he then sent them to his tent as prisoners, he affirmed what he has already said; the rest he denies.

Don García Ramírez was asked whether the other Indians, who remained in the pueblo, withdrew to their houses when they saw that the Indians who had come to offer obedience were carried away as prisoners; whether this witness ordered the Spaniards to go in and bring them out, and that the said Spaniards brought out up to eighty Indians and placed them in the tent of this witness with other Indians who were under arrest.

He said that, as he has stated, no Indian came to offer obedience, that there was no command other than when this witness ordered the attack on the pueblo, and that in the said attack some Indians were killed, both in the pueblo and beyond it. They were seized as they emerged from the pueblo. Others

22. For Castañeda's story of this episode, see pp. 225-227.

were apprehended and taken to the tent of this witness, and some fled. The pueblo remained in the hands of the Spaniards.

Asked whether he knows a certain Melchior Pérez, resident of Guadalajara, who was with this witness on the said expedition, he said that he knew every one who went on the said expedition, but could not remember him through his name.[23]

Don García Ramírez was asked whether it was true that the said Melchior Pérez told this witness that if he was not going to keep his word to the Indians he should not make promises to them on the sign of the cross, and that this witness replied to him that he was not making the crosses genuinely.

He said that he never told him such a thing, nor had this witness ever answered anything as stated in the question, nor does he remember such a man.

Don García Ramírez was asked whether he had commanded that thirty of the Indians which he had ordered apprehended or held as prisoners in his tent, be burned in the field, each one tied to a stake.

He said that, at the time the pueblo was being attacked, as the Indians would not surrender, the Spaniards lighted some firebrands outside of the pueblo to throw inside in order to set the houses on fire. When the pueblo had already been taken, this witness went with all speed here and there to provide what was necessary and to see what was being done. While engaged in this he heard a great commotion outside the pueblo and went to see what it was; and this witness found that the soldiers had some of these Indians in a tent, which did not belong to this witness. He saw that the soldiers were lancing and killing them. He saw that others had been cast into the fires, tied, and that some were burned, stabbed, and others dead. The said soldiers told this witness that they had done this because the Indians whom they had put in the tent had tried to offer resistance inside of it. And this deponent did not order done what was done in the heat of battle. On the contrary, he wanted all to be spared and no one to be killed. The rest he denied.

23. Melchior Pérez was one of the soldiers listed in the muster roll. He brought four horses and equipment.

Asked whether, when the other Indians in the tent saw that the Spaniards had taken out their friends to burn them, it was not through fear that they would be burned, too, that they rebelled and resisted in the said tent, where this witness and the others lanced and killed them, he reaffirmed what he has already stated, and the rest he denies.

Don García Ramírez was asked whether the burning and killing of the Indians had been by orders of this witness, and whether, if he had not ordered the said burnings and killings, the said soldiers would not have perpetrated them.

He replied that, as he has stated, this witness had been ordered to wage war by blood and fire if the Indians refused to submit. After summoning them to peace, as he has stated, the said Indians still refused, and he ordered that war be waged on them by fire and sword. Through this order the soldiers killed and burned the said Indians without other orders. As to what the question says about the tent, he does not know more about it than what he has stated.

Don García Ramírez was asked why it was that on the second day he ordered the Indians attacked by fire when he says that he gained the terraces of the said pueblo on the first day.

He said that he had ordered the houses in which the Indians had barricaded themselves to be set on fire in order that the war could be waged with less risk for the Spaniards, as the houses were solid and there would have been great risk for them if they had tried to go in, especially since every one of the said houses was narrow and the entrance small. So, as the Indians were harassed by the smoke, they came out, and the soldiers killed them and cast them into the fire as they emerged, as he has said.

Asked what punishment he imposed on the soldiers, who, after taking the pueblo, lanced and stabbed the Indians who were in the tent and burned the others whom they held as prisoners, he said that he did not see it. This witness said that he did not inflict any punishment on the soldiers, because the incident occurred during the excitement and heat of the battle, and it was done by all the soldiers. If they exceeded themselves in severity in this case, it was to warn other pueblos in the neighborhood, in order that some would see it and others hear about it, and none should offer resistance to the Spaniards. It was done thus to spare other pueblos greater harm, as was the case. The said burnings and killings were not done on account of any particular booty they expected from the Indians, because they possessed neither silver nor gold, nor did they have any knowledge of them. It was done in order that the expedition might be carried out more peacefully.

Asked why, after the pueblo was conquered and taken by the Spaniards, he ordered it set on fire and allowed it to be burned, he testified that he had not especially ordered the pueblo to be set on fire, but only that it be taken, and that some fires started from this, a few houses were burned, and others remained standing.

Asked to state what captains and persons were with this witness at the taking of this pueblo, he said that the captains and principal persons with him were Juan de Zaldívar, Don Rodrigo Maldonado, Diego López, alderman from Seville, and others.

Asked whether the pueblo was conquered and calm at the time he ordered the said Indians who were in the tent to be taken out and burned and the others who remained inside to be killed, he said that he repeats what he has already stated, and that when he came out on account of their shouting and saw some Indians burned, and the others who were in the tent wounded and killed, the pueblo had not been completely pacified and conquered, as there were still Indians inside many houses of the pueblo.

Don García Ramírez was asked whether he notified the general that there were many Indians imprisoned in the tents [*sic*], and what he ordered done with them, or whether this witness ordered them burned and killed without notifying him.

He said he reaffirms his previous statements, that he did not order the burning or killing of the Indians in the tent, that it happened during the excitement of the battle, as he has stated. It is true that when he was engaged in the attack on the said pueblo, after he had taken the terraces, he sent word to the general, telling him of the progress of the war, as he was close by; he does not remember what the general answered him.

Asked to tell where he went and what he did after he took the said pueblo, Don García said that it seemed to him that the punishment he had inflicted on the said pueblo was sufficient to warn the Indians of the other pueblos of the province of Tiguex and the surrounding provinces. Even though he had been ordered to wage war on them, after discussing this decision with the general, this witness returned to Alcanfor, where the general was. The latter came out to meet this witness, accompanied by some of the people he had with him. He received him very well and accepted and approved what this witness had done and praised him for it.

Don García Ramírez was asked what the general, this witness, and the other people who were with them did after the taking and burning of the said pueblo and where they went.

He said that within five or six days after this witness had returned to Alcanfor, as he has stated, the general ordered him to go out again with more people to summon the other people of the province of Tiguex to peace, and if they refused to submit peacefully, to wage war on them. Complying with this order, this witness set out from this place of Alcanfor with some forty horsemen, more or less, and some footmen. This witness, together with the said people, crossed to the other side of the river. He did not find people in any pueblo on that side of the river, because, as the Indians of the said pueblos saw him cross, they fled. At the last pueblo on the opposite side of the river, the smallest of them, they found seven or eight dead horses in the plaza. And in order to teach the Indians not to kill any more Spaniards or their horses, this witness ordered the said pueblo set on fire. Some houses were burned and others remained standing.

This done, this witness did not want to linger any longer in the other pueblos, or to do them any harm. So he returned to Alcanfor, where General Francisco Vázquez was. After he had remained there a few days, information reached the general to the effect that in a pueblo in the province of Tiguex, located three or four leagues from Alcanfor—where the said general and Spaniards were quartered—the Indians of that pueblo, and those from the other pueblos that had been abandoned, were entrenched in the said pueblo, the name of which he does not remember. On receipt of this news, the general sent this witness to the said pueblo. This witness went to the said place with some horsemen and found the said Indians prepared for war and fortified in the said pueblo. This witness separated from the rest of the people and advanced all alone near the pueblo. He told them by signs and a few words which they already understood that they should be friends and associate with the Spaniards in peace, that the latter would be glad to do it, and that they would accord them good treatment and friendship.

An Indian named Xauian, who knew this witness, said that he was pleased and asked this witness to approach and embrace and seal their peace. This witness put aside a lance he was carrying and went closer to the Indian. The latter drew back and indicated by signs that he was not afraid of the lance, but of the horse and sword, and that if this witness wished to come nearer in order to establish peace, he should leave his horse and sword and come close to him. This witness, being eager for peace and that there should be no more destruction and deaths, put aside everything and approached. He left three horsemen as his guard and a youth to hold his horse, lance, and sword. Then this witness approached the Indian and offered him peace. The said Indian embraced this witness, and some other Indians sallied out and struck this witness four or five mace blows on his helmet, which stunned him. The Indians were about to carry him inside their pueblo, and had it not been for the three mounted men who came to his rescue, the Indians would have carried him inside the said pueblo. The other people who were with this witness also came to his aid. The Indians of the pueblo came out to fight them and wounded some of the said Spaniards; they wounded this witness on one leg with an arrow. The Indians withdrew to the pueblo.[24]

This witness left them and went to another pueblo which

24. Castañeda calls the pueblo, where this incident took place, Tiguex. See p. 227 of his history. It is called Moho by Coronado. Above, p. 333. The killing of Francisco de Ovando in this siege is related in each of these accounts.

was near by, to summon the natives there to peace. Approaching them, this witness again summoned them to peace, but they refused to accept it. So this witness and his people returned to Alcanfor, where the general was, and gave him an account of what had happened.

Asked where the general, this witness, and the rest of the soldiers went and what they did after this expedition, he replied that a few days after he had returned from the said expedition, the general, together with the entire army and this witness, left Alcanfor and went to the said pueblo where this witness had just come from. Arriving at the said pueblo, they summoned it to peace, and as the said Indians refused to submit peacefully the entire army surrounded the said pueblo. The day following the arrival of the said general, when the siege had been established, he again summoned the said Indians to submit peacefully and said that he would not do them any harm. They continued to refuse, and he ordered that they be attacked, and they were. Some fifty Spaniards climbed up on the terraces on one side of the said pueblo. Five or six of the men were killed and many others wounded. The Indians, in their resistance, dislodged the Spaniards from the terraces, and the fight ceased for the day.

The siege of the said pueblo continued for many more days, without doing the Indians any harm, and they were summoned to peace every day. Seeing that they would not grant it, that the winter was severe and the Spaniards could not stand it, the general ordered that they be attacked again, and they were. In the attack the said Indians captured alive a caballero named Francisco de Ovando. They killed him, committing great barbarities with him, and cutting him into pieces.[25] The fight ceased for that day.

Some days later, after they had been besieged for what must have been eighty days, the said Indians rushed out one night on one side of the pueblo, and as they came out they ran into the Spanish sentries and killed one. Some Indians were killed there, and all the others fled, abandoning the said pueblo.

25. Castañeda says that the Indians did not mutilate his body but preserved it for a long time! P. 256.

Seeing that the Indians had abandoned the pueblo, the Spaniards entered it, and by order of the general they set fire to some houses in it and left others untouched. From there the entire army returned to Alcanfor, from where it had set out.

Asked what clothes, jewels, and other things they found in the said pueblo when they entered it after the Indians had fled, he responded that they found some maize there, as the Indians of that land do not possess anything other than their food, and some blankets with which they clothe themselves.

Asked why the general ordered and permitted the burning of the said pueblo, since the Indians had abandoned it, he said he believed that the general ordered it in order to warn the Indians, and also because some undisciplined soldiers were doing it.

Asked where the three Indians, Bigotes, the Turk, and Ysopete, were while this witness was on the expeditions he said he made and the one he made with the general and all the soldiers to this pueblo, he said that they remained at Alcanfor until they were brought to see how the said pueblo was conquered. Then the army and the Indians returned to Alcanfor, as he has stated.

Asked what other pueblos, in addition to the ones he has stated, this witness knows were burned and destroyed when he was present, he said that when the entire force was at this last pueblo which the Indians had left, information reached the army that the Indians of the region who had abandoned the pueblos were returning to them and were fortifying them. To remedy this situation, the general sent a captain, whose name he does not remember, with some men to go to destroy and level the fortifications that the said Indians were building.[26] He heard it said that these men who had gone to raze the fortifications had set fire to some of the said pueblos.

Don García Ramírez was asked to state and declare what they did after conquering and taking the said province of Tiguex and burning the Indians and pueblos while taking the said places.

26. Evidently Don Rodrigo Maldonado. See Coronado's testimony, above, p. 332.

He said that a few days after they took the last place he has told about, the general, with all his people and army, left Alcanfor, taking along the Indian Turk as guide. The Turk led them toward the province of Quivira.[27] They passed through Cicuique and on their way they left the Indian Bigotes there, as he said he was a native of that place. They proceeded on their journey toward Quivira, as far as the plains of the cattle, where this witness remained, suffering from a broken arm. Some people were left with him, and they had no clashes at all with the Indians, nor did they see any except at two or three places where they saw them wandering like nomads in the field. They had no trouble with them whatever.

The general and the rest of the people continued on their journey toward Quivira, taking as guides the said Indians, Ysopete and the Turk. And as they continued on the march, this witness and the people who had remained with him on the plains returned to Tiguex, where they settled down at Alcanfor until the general returned there with the army he had taken along, without having found anything on the trip to Quivira which they sought.

Asked whether this witness killed or was present at the killing of the Indian called the Turk, this witness said that after the army left the plains where he remained when it set out for Quivira, he never again saw the said Turk, nor did he see them kill Ysopete.

Asked what he knows or heard said about what became of these two Indians, or where they were killed, and by whom and through whose orders, he said that what he knows about this matter is that at the time Francisco Vázquez returned from Quivira to the place where this witness was at Alcanfor, he heard many of those who came with the general say that he had ordered the killing of the Indian Turk because, when they were on this journey, the said Indian through deceit had led them into some uninhabited areas where they thought they

27. Since the departure for Quivira was on April 23, 1541, the siege of Moho must have ended shortly before. Coronado, in his letter, October 20, 1541, gives the date. Castañeda says that the battle ended the last of March. P. 231.

would perish from hunger and thirst. They questioned the said Turk as to why he had taken them there, and he replied that it was in order to kill them all so that they would not go to his country. For this reason the general had ordered him killed. They had left the other Indian, Ysopete, at Quivira, as he said he was a native of that place.

Don García Ramírez was asked what the general, he, and the rest of the people did after they assembled at Alcanfor on their return from Quivira.

He said that he was indisposed because of his arm, that others were sick, and that since winter was setting in and it was very cold in Alcanfor, this witness started back to Mexico to recover. When, on their way back, this witness and the other sick people arrived at Corazones, where Melchior Díaz, with fifty mounted men, more or less, had remained as captain of some people, he found the country up in arms, and the town, where the said Melchior Díaz had remained with the other Spaniards, burned and some of his horses and people burned to death. When they saw this, this witness and those who were with him returned to Alcanfor, where the general had remained. They went back because the Indians of the province of Corazones had taken the passes and they could not continue to San Miguel, where this witness and the other sick people were going.

Within two days after this witness got back and reported to the general what is stated above, the general and the whole army set out on their way to Mexico. They passed through Corazones on their way to San Miguel. At various passes some Indians attacked them and wounded several Spaniards. Thus they reached San Miguel, where the army began to fall apart and each one went where he pleased until it reached Mexico.

Don García Ramírez was asked whether he knew or had heard the reason why the Indians in the provinces of Corazones and of Señora revolted and burned and killed Alcaraz and some Spaniards and horses who had been left there in peace when the general with his army and this witness went inland.

He said that when the whole army reached San Miguel he heard from some of those Spaniards who had escaped when the

Indians burned the town and killed Alcaraz and other people and horses, that they had revolted and taken up arms because of the abuses which the said Alcaraz inflicted on the Indians and their women. Captain Melchior Díaz had left this Alcaraz as his lieutenant in the said province of Corazones, because Captain Melchior Díaz had gone on some exploration.[28]

Don García Ramírez was asked whether, if this witness, the general, and the other captains had not committed the violences, plunderings, outrages, burnings, unleashings of dogs against Indians, and the burning of places in the provinces they traversed, which they did, the said Indians would not have revolted nor taken up arms, but would have remained in the service of and subject to his Majesty and in his royal service and they would have become Christians and been converted to our Catholic faith.

He said that he reaffirms what he has stated, that he did not see any stealing or anything to steal, nor any killings, burnings, or unleashings of dogs against Indians, nor the burning of places in any other way than he has already stated. He knows that Francisco Vázquez and this witness never had such a thought nor any intention of doing as they did, except that the war justified their actions. This witness feels sure that he did not go to excess in anything, nor was there any other principal cause why the said Indians revolted, other than their base intentions, and he says that this fact has always been known about them.

He believes that in the land which this witness has traversed, neither God nor his Majesty would have been served by the people of its provinces, as they are disorganized and have no head, and the land is sterile and has no products, nor has it gold or silver whereby his Majesty could be served, nor would it redound to the benefit of his royal patrimony. And what this witness learned from experience after taking part in the said expedition and journeys is that on account of the base intentions he discovered in the Indians, and because they have

28. Díaz went to the coast to get in touch with Alarcón's sea expedition. It was at this time that he was accidentally killed, and thus Alcaraz was left in command of the post in the Sonora valley.

no leader to follow, it would profit little to pacify them and convert them to our holy Catholic faith. And what some do, others undo, like disorderly people.

Don García Ramírez was asked whether the royal patrimonies of his Majesty had suffered the misfortune and loss of more than five hundred thousand ducats by the rebellion and uprising of the said pueblos and their Indians and the fact that they were not under the service and authority of his Majesty.

He said that according to what this witness saw and understood regarding the land and provinces he had traversed and seen, his Majesty could not have profited by a single ducat; on the contrary, if he should want to maintain this land it would be at great cost to his Majesty. He knows that the one who lost by undertaking the said conquest and exploration was the viceroy of Mexico, Don Antonio de Mendoza, and those who went on the expedition, for they spent more than one hundred thousand ducats in the enterprise. He believes that they spent it all from their own estates, without compensation, in this case, from the treasury of his Majesty or from any other individual.

He says that what he has stated is the truth and is what he knows and saw and heard told, on the oath he has taken. And, everything that he has said in this deposition having been given back to him to read, he said he does not know anything else, and that he affirms and ratifies it. And so he affirmed and ratified what is set forth in it, and signed it with his name, the said Don García Ramírez, and it was also signed by the said Licentiate Cianca, to whom was given the said testimony, which was held before me, Jorge Vázquez, his Majesty's clerk.

All the corrections were registered at the end of each page before the aforesaid signed.

There were present, ALGUACIL TORRES, LICENTIATE CIANCA, DON GARCÍA RAMÍREZ.

Before me, JORGE VÁZQUEZ, clerk. [Rubrics]

SENTENCE OF LOPEZ DE CARDENAS

IN THE LAWSUIT BETWEEN LICENTIATE VILLALOBOS, HIS MAJESTY'S FISCAL, ON THE ONE SIDE, AND DON GARCÍA RAMÍREZ DE CÁRDENAS, RESIDENT OF THE CITY OF MADRID, AND SEBASTIÁN RODRÍGUEZ, HIS ATTORNEY, ON THE OTHER.[1]

We find that the said fiscal proved his accusation and complaint in all that is contained herein and we accept them as fully proved; and that the said Don García Ramírez did not prove his exception or defense of these charges, so we consider them as not proved. Wherefore, for the guilt which results from these proceedings against the said Don García Ramírez, we must and do sentence him to serve his Majesty with his person, arms, and horse at Orán at his own cost for the time and period of thirty months; and he must not default under penalty of the said time being doubled. We sentence him likewise to pay eight hundred gold ducats, one-half of this to be used to defray the passage and sustenance of the friars who may go to the Indies by command of his Majesty, and the other half to be spent in some charitable work in New Spain to be designated by us.

And in order that the above decree may be carried out, we order the said Don García Ramírez to deliver and pay the said eight hundred ducats to Hernando Ochoa Cambío in this city within twenty days after he is served with the executive letter of this our sentence. By this our final sentence, we thus pronounce it and order it, with costs.

LICENTIATE GUTIERRE VELÁZQUEZ
LICENTIATE GREGORIO LÓPEZ
DOCTOR RIBADENEIRA
LICENTIATE BRIBIESCA
[Rubrics]

1. Translated from a photostatic copy of the original in the Archives of the Indies, *Justicia*, legajo 1021.

Sentence passed and pronounced by the members of the Council of the Indies of his Majesty who attached their names thereto. In the city of Valladolid, December 20, 1549.

Notification of this sentence was given in person to Licentiate Villalobos, his Majesty's fiscal, on December 20, 1549.

AMENDED SENTENCE OF CARDENAS

IN THE LAWSUIT BETWEEN DOCTOR BERASTEGUI, HIS MAJESTY'S FISCAL, ON THE ONE SIDE, AND DON GARCÍA RAMÍREZ DE CÁRDENAS, RESIDENT OF MADRID, AND SEBASTIÁN RODRÍGUEZ, HIS ATTORNEY, ON THE OTHER.[1]

We find that the final sentence imposed and pronounced in the said litigation by us, the members of the royal Council of the Indies of his Majesty, which was appealed on the part of Don García Ramírez, was and is good, just, and properly imposed and pronounced. And regardless of the reasons assembled and presented as allegations against it, we must and do confirm it as amended, with the following clarifications and additions: That the thirty months' service in Orán contained and stated in the said sentence shall be interpreted to be one year's service on the frontiers of the kingdom of Navarre, at the part and place which the viceroy shall select for him. This sentence he must set out to serve within the first thirty days after the notification of this our sentence, and within another fifteen days he must send authentic testimony to this said royal council of how he is serving the said sentence. The fine of eight hundred ducats contained in the said sentence shall be interpreted to be two hundred ducats, and not more, distributed in the manner as stated in our said sentence. Further, we sentence the said Don García Ramírez to ten years' banishment from all the Indies, islands, and continent of the ocean sea, and he must not disobey under penalty of having this banish-

---

1. Translated from a photostatic copy of the original in the Archives of the Indies, *Justicia,* legajo 1021.

ment doubled. By this our amended sentence, we thus pronounce and order it, with costs.

LICENTIATE GUTIERRE VELÁZQUEZ
LICENTIATE GREGORIO LÓPEZ
DOCTOR RIBADENEIRA
LICENTIATE BRIBIESCA
[Rubrics]

This sentence was passed and pronounced by the members of the Council of the Indies of his Majesty, and they added their names thereto at Valladolid, July 17, 1551.

Doctor Berastegui, his Majesty's fiscal, was notified in person on July 18, 1551, at Valladolid.

Sebastián Rodríguez, attorney for Don García Ramírez, was notified in person on July 18, 1551, at Valladolid.

RESIDENCIA OF CORONADO

Charges Brought Against Francisco Vázquez de Coronado Resulting from the Investigation of His Administration as Governor of New Galicia Conducted by Licentiate Lorenzo de Tejada, a Member of the Audiencia of New Spain, and Visitador and Juez de Residencia in That Province, Together With Coronado's Testimony Refuting These Charges.[1] Guadalajara, September 1, 1544.

1. Francisco Vázquez de Coronado is charged with receiving a horse valued at one hundred pesos in gold bullion from a certain Ximénez, priest of Culiacán, in order that he should not remove him from his post.

To this Francisco Vázquez stated that the facts as to the horse were that when this witness was on his way back from the new land of Cíbola, upon arriving at the town of San Miguel in the province of Culiacán, a priest named Ximénez, located in the said town, came to see him and told him that he had a good horse for him, a horse he had raised, planning to send it to him in the new land, and, since he was back and he had bought and raised it for him, he should do him the favor of accepting it. However much Francisco Vázquez refused, the said clergyman importuned him so much that he had to accept it. He did so only after giving him a voucher for forty pesos gold bullion which the priest said it had cost him. He was to pay him when he passed through his province, or any one who should come to collect in his name, or he would return the said horse. And, while led by the bridle by a servant of this

<hr />

1. In the original documents, the charges against Coronado and his testimony in answer to them are given in separate documents, and the charges in the legal proceedings are referred to by number. We have combined them here to facilitate reading and to avoid needless repetition. Translated from photostatic copies of the originals in the Archives of the Indies, *Justicia*, legajo 339.

witness, the horse drowned in a river on the way, and he never paid the forty pesos because the said priest has not come nor asked for them.

Francisco Vázquez was asked how many gold pesos this horse was worth at the time he received it, whether it was worth more than the said forty.

Francisco Vázquez said the horse was good, and it seemed to him that it was worth more than forty pesos, but he did not know how much more. He said that this is all he knows about this matter.[2]

2. Francisco Vázquez is charged with receiving, gratis, from Cristóbal de Oñate another horse of a reddish-black color, valued at one hundred pesos in gold bullion.

Francisco Vázquez replied that the truth was that while he was at the city of Compostela, preparing to leave for Mexico, Cristóbal de Oñate told him that he knew he was short of horses and that he would need them in Mexico, where he himself had two of them in care of the alcaide, Lope de Samaniego, and that he could have and use them. Francisco Vázquez replied that he did not need them, otherwise he would be glad to accept them as from a friend. On his reaching Mexico, one day when he was riding with the viceroy, the alcaide, Lope de Samaniego, told this witness that Cristóbal de Oñate had written to him, telling him to give Coronado the horse he was riding, which was of a reddish-black color. Thus he sent it to his quarters. And coming to this province with the army to go on the expedition to the discovery of the new land, Francisco Vázquez said to Cristóbal de Oñate: "I have your horse with me; send for it, as I brought it back to you, for I have plenty of horses for the expedition." The said Cristóbal de Oñate, although this witness importuned him considerably, refused to take it back, saying he regretted that he did not have a dozen other horses to give him since he was going on an expedition in which he would have such great need of them. See-

2. Coronado's attorney presented an affidavit signed by the priest, Diego de Ximénez, showing that payment for the horse had been arranged. Coronado was acquitted on this charge. Archives of the Indies, *Justicia*, legajo 339.

ing that this witness insisted on not accepting it, Oñate said that Coronado should take it along and that both he and the alcaide Samaniego might use it and then return it to him. As this witness always considered the horse as belonging to the said Cristóbal de Oñate, he ordered, in a codicil which he made, that it be paid for or returned to him, as may be seen in a clause in the said codicil.[3] Then when he was bringing it back on his return from the said land to this province, it died.

He was asked how much the said horse might be worth at the time he received it.

He said that in his estimate and judging by other horses he had bought, he thought that it might be worth fifty pesos in gold bullion.

   3. Francisco Vázquez is charged with receiving from Juan Hernández de Ijar a chestnut-colored horse worth thirty pesos in gold bullion.

He declared that it is true that when he was going on the expedition to the discovery of the new land, the said Juan Fernández de Ijar gave him a swift horse that might be worth about fifteen or twenty pesos in gold bullion. He did not pay for it because it was presented to him as a gift for the said expedition.[4]

   4. Francisco Vázquez is charged with receiving another mottled horse lent by Francisco de Godoy which he requested in order to go from Compostela to Mexico city, and which he used for almost two years, and which he did not return to him until about a month or a month and a half ago when he learned that I was coming to hold his residencia.

Francisco Vázquez stated that as he was coming back in a litter from the discovery of the new land, since he was ill,

---

3. This codicil was introduced by the defense, but the judge sentenced Coronado to pay a fine of 150 pesos on this count. *Ibid.*

4. Coronado was fined sixty pesos on this charge. Juan Fernández de Hijar, a former alcalde mayor of Purificación, was himself convicted in his residencia, Judge Tejada sentencing him to pay seven pesos gold dust, six pesos gold bullion, ten fanegas (1.6 bushel) of maize, and fifty pesos in common gold. He paid without appealing the sentence. *Ibid.*

Francisco de Godoy told him that he had a tame horse that walked at an even pace, and that he could take it in case he wanted to leave his litter some time. Francisco Vázquez thanked him and told him that he would borrow it and return it to him. And a year ago, more or less, while at Compostela, he told the said Francisco de Godoy that he was back from Mexico, that he had brought along his horse, and that he could send for it and take it. The said Godoy replied that he had not given it to him with the intention of taking it back, but if he so wished he could pay him what the said horse had cost him or return it. Francisco Vázquez asked him to state how much it had cost him and whether he preferred to be paid or to have the horse returned to him. The said Godoy replied that he would let him know. Then a servant of Francisco Vázquez took the horse to Querétaro and some months passed before his return.[5] About three months past, more or less, this witness ordered that it be delivered to a Montesinos, a friend of Godoy who is in charge of his estate, so that he might return it to him.

> 5. Francisco Vázquez is charged with accepting a small jewel and a little gold chain presented by Juan de Villareal to Doña Isabel, daughter of the said Francisco Vázquez. It was presented to her in his presence and he never paid for it. It was valued at twenty pesos in gold bullion.

Replying to this charge, Francisco Vázquez said that some two years past, more or less, when he was coming from Mexico to this province, Juan de Villareal came out to meet him. He noticed that the said Villareal, approaching his daughter, Doña Isabel, presented her with a small gold chain with a small jewel. When Francisco Vázquez saw this, he told him that she could not accept it and that he should not offer it to her, and that he knows she did not accept it then. Later he saw the little chain and small jewel in the possession of his daughter, and he told the said Villareal that she had to return it to him because his Majesty, while he permits officials to give to others, does not

---

5. Francisco de Godoy was major-domo of Nuño de Guzmán. His administration of the town of Tepic was investigated by Judge Tejada. *Ibid.*

allow them to accept anything from any one. The said Villareal asked that he be not offended, since he had not given it to him but to his daughter as a child. Francisco Vázquez insisted that he was to take it back, or he would pay for it. As to the pay, Villareal said that it should be as Francisco Vázquez pleased, but that he would not take the chain back since he had presented it to the little girl. Later, in a report and account that the said Villareal sent of the bills owed him by Francisco Vázquez, the latter found stated therein the value of the said little chain. He paid him what was included in these invoices, leaving unpaid only the sum of twelve pesos; and a month past, more or less, this witness sent the wife of the said Juan de Villareal, through Francisco Pico, a bar of silver weighing three pounds, more or less, in payment of the said little chain.[6]

Asked how much the little chain and small jewel given by the said Villareal to Doña Isabel could be worth, he replied that he believed it might be worth twenty pesos in gold bullion.

> 6. Francisco Vázquez is charged with receiving from Juan del Camino the houses in which he lives in this city, in order that he transfer to Andrés de Villanueva the pueblo of Coiná which he sold to him. The houses with the adjoining lots are worth one hundred and fifty pesos gold bullion.

In reply, Francisco Vázquez denies what is contained in the charge, as it is not true, because he bought from the said Juan del Camino the said houses and lots that belonged to him for the sum of one hundred and fifty pesos in bullion, which he actually paid for them, and of which there exists a notarial contract of sale. He believes that he sent him the payment through Francisco Godoy.[7]

> 7. Francisco Vázquez is charged with frequently accepting gifts of fowl, fish, maize, and fruit from the Indian chieftains and governors of this province who came to visit him.

6. Coronado was fined sixty pesos on this charge. Villareal, alcalde of Guadalajara, was sentenced to pay a fine of thirty pesos gold. *Ibid.*

7. Coronado's attorney produced contracts of sale to refute this charge. *Ibid.*

He declared that it is true that sometimes the Indian chieftains of this province came to call on him. At times he received from them as many as twenty birds at the price set by himself. On other occasions they brought fresh fish and fruit. But neither did this witness ask it of them, nor did they give it, as far as he remembers, on account of any business that they had pending with him.

> 8. Francisco Vázquez is charged with giving in encomienda to Cristóbal de Oñate the Indians formerly held by Bracamonte. And while they remained assigned to Cristóbal de Oñate, the said Francisco Vázquez collected and enjoyed the tributes of the said pueblos, which amounted to one thousand pesos in gold bullion.

In regard to this, Francisco Vázquez admitted the charge, but said that he did not know how much the said tributes might be worth, and that although they were assigned to the said Cristóbal de Oñate, Francisco Vázquez told him they were for him.

> 9. Francisco Vázquez is charged with having taken married Indians to Mexico city from the towns of Aguatlán and Xala, which he held in encomienda in company with Alvaro de Bracamonte. They returned to this city of Compostela bearing burdens and some of them died on the way or in the hospital at Pazcuaro.

Francisco Vázquez replied that when he went from Compostela to Mexico he took some Indians from the said pueblos to carry his belongings. He believes that this must have happened two or three times, and that each time he took some twenty or thirty Indians, that they came with their loads to this city, and that he sent them back from here and ordered them paid for their work. He never took along more than ten or twelve Indians to look after his belongings, because he took carriers in each pueblo reached. Some he paid, others would not accept payment. This refers to carriers going outside of this province. And he said that the Indians who cared for his belongings as well as others whom he sent with letters or after something, he paid for their work. Sometimes they returned from Mexico city to this province laden with certain articles that were needed and could not be obtained in this province. He paid everyone for his work as he has stated. He does not know that any of them have died on the way.[8]

10. Francisco Vázquez is charged with having brought Indian carriers many times from Aguacatlán and Xala to this city of Guadalajara without paying them.

He denies this, and he reaffirms what he has said in answer to the charge preceding this one.

11. Francisco Vázquez is charged with having taken from Aguacatlán and Xala six free, single Indian women of marriageable age and with taking them against their will to the town of Arçomala which he holds in encomienda in the province of Mechuacán, a hot and unhealthful land. He took them so that they might be taught to make reed mats for beds. They have never been returned to their homes.

Francisco Vázquez denies what is contained in this charge, as he never ordered such a thing.

12. Francisco Vázquez is charged with having sent three free Indian women from Culiacán to his home in Mexico, saying that he was sending them to his wife, Doña Beatriz.

In reply, Francisco Vázquez stated it is true that he sent two from Culiacán, in this province of New Galicia, to his home in Mexico so that they might serve Doña Beatriz, his wife, in order that she might have them instructed in the matters of our holy faith, and so that they could be taught embroidery, sewing, and other occupations appropriate to women. One married and died, and the other is with Doña Beatriz, his wife. He said that Melchior Díaz sent them to the said Doña Beatriz, his wife, and that he remonstrated against sending them because it was too far and the trip long. Upon confessing

8. In his letter to the king, December 15, 1538, Coronado reported that he had put a stop to abuses of this nature.

with Fray Antonio de Castilblanco of the order of Saint Francis and explaining the matter to him, the friar charged him upon his conscience to have them sent, because at his home and in such company they would become Christians and would increase in the knowledge of God, and by allowing them to remain where they were they would continue in their heathenism.

13. Francisco Vázquez is charged that although his Majesty had ordered him through his royal audiencia to go in company with the protector to visit the pueblos of this province and jurisdiction and deal directly with them, he never did so, even when the cabildo and regidores of the city of Compostela urged him.

Francisco Vázquez stated that it was true that his Majesty, in his royal order and cédula which he received after his return from the new land, ordered that this witness and the protector of the Indians, after attending a mass to the Holy Spirit, were to take solemn oath to appraise the pueblos of the province, each one according to its means, after first inspecting them or sending some one to inspect them if for any reason they could not comply with the said order. Francisco Vázquez and the protector attended the said mass and took the said oath in the church of the city of Compostela. And since this witness was busy with matters pertaining to the service of his Majesty, and since, also, part of the province was in rebellion, he could not go out to make the inspection but entrusted it to the protector. The latter, having set out to make the inspection, died before it was completed.[9]

14. Francisco Vázquez is charged with knowing that Diego de Colio, while alcalde of this city, and a certain Juan González, a relative of his, stabbed and beat Andrés de Villanueva, whom Diego de Colio was holding in jail in shackles, and that Francisco Vázquez not only dissimulated and failed to punish the offense, but even when one Pedro Sánchez appeared before him to com-

9. For Coronado's report on this problem of appraising the Indian tribute, see his letter to the king, December 15, 1538.

plain in the name of and with authority from the said Villanueva, who remained in jail, he refused to hear him or to allow him to appear before him and demand justice, saying that if he lodged a complaint with him he would punish severely the said Villanueva, and other words. Whereby the said Villanueva was left without redress, for he did not dare to demand justice.[10]

To this charge Francisco Vázquez stated that it was true that the said Pedro Sánchez, in the name of Andrés de Villa, complained before him at the city of Compostela or presented a document of complaint about the case mentioned in the charge. Francisco Vázquez heard him and ordered a report drawn of his complaint and demand, and was ready to render judgment, but as the said Pedro Sánchez did not furnish him a report nor speak to him again about the matter that he remembers, and, in going over the case, as some told it in one way and some in another, he did not proceed in the matter against any person. This is what he knows has happened; the rest he denies.

15. Francisco Vázquez is charged with being remiss and negligent in administering justice to litigants and in the cases and complaints brought before him, as he did not wish to decide or settle them so as not to displease or annoy any of the contending parties.

He said he denied this charge, because if there had been any delay in the dispatch of some matters it had been, not with the intent of not rendering justice or to shelter any one, but in order to consult with jurists and thus reach a better decision.

16. Francisco Vázquez is charged with being remiss and negligent in the pacification of the pueblos of this province that rebelled, both after he returned from

---

10. This was one of the offenses severely punished by Judge Tejada. The residencia of Diego de Colio, former alcalde ordinario of Guadalajara, covers many folios. Tejada sentenced Colio to pay fifty pesos common gold and fifty pesos fine gold as well as to suspension from office for two years. Fiscal Villalobos, of the Council of the Indies, appealed the sentence in the name of the crown as being too light. Colio also filed an appeal, after depositing the amount of the fines. A. G. I., *Justicia*, legajo 339.

the new land and while he was on his way, during which he found the pueblo of Acatlán and other adjacent towns in revolt, when he could easily have pacified them with the army under his command.

Asked about this charge, Francisco Vázquez said that at the time he came to hold the residencia of Licentiate de la Torre he learned that in the province of Culiacán a chieftain named Ayapín was in open rebellion, keeping a portion of the province disturbed. He had killed a large number of natives because they served the Spaniards. Learning of the matter, he went to the province of Culiacán with some forces that he had brought to his province. Being informed that the said chieftain was up in arms, and of the damage he had caused, he sent Melchior Díaz, alcalde mayor of the town of San Miguel, to arrest him. This he did; once arrested and proved guilty, he meted out justice to him.[11] He pacified the province and returned to Mexico to give the viceroy an account of what had been done. He came back with the army through this province on his way to the conquest and discovery of the new land. It is true that when he passed through this province he heard that at Zacatula the Indians had killed two Spaniards. He does not remember whether or not they were in rebellion and at war. He refrained from going there so as not to lay waste the country with the large army he was leading. Later, after his return from the new land, when he found some pueblos in revolt in the province, he tried to induce them to accept peace without waging war on them. In this manner he brought some of the said pueblos to obedience. He waged war on others which refused to submit on being summoned, as in the case of the Tecosquinos, of Casuchiles and Çacatlán. Likewise, being informed that a chieftain named Ximón was in rebellion in the province and had set fire to a pueblo, killing some Indians and perpetrating other offenses, he went out to apprehend him and restore order. Once apprehended and his guilt proved, Coronado meted out justice to him and pacified the region that Ximón had led to revolt.

11. This subject is also dealt with in Coronado's letter to the king, July 15, 1539.

17. Francisco Vázquez is charged with failure to order and bring about the settling of the Indians who dwelled in cliffs, barrancas, and strong positions in level and suitable places where they could live in orderly manner and where they could be more easily instructed in the matters pertaining to our holy Catholic faith.

Asked about this, Francisco Vázquez stated that he tried to get some towns which were located in barrancas and on rivers to assemble and unite, and he asked the friars to urge this on the Indians, and some have congregated. He did not press this more on the others because he did not have orders or authority from his Majesty to round them up and remove them from their locations. He realizes, however, that to bring them together and remove them from their cliffs and canyons would be very pious and very beneficial to the natives. In this manner they would be spared the occasion to revolt and to commit other crimes and excesses.

18. Francisco Vázquez is charged with being remiss and negligent in not having ordered that the natives of this province be taught and instructed in the matters of our holy Catholic faith and in not ordering appropriate churches built in the Indian pueblos.

In reply, Francisco Vázquez said that he had ordered, in the name of his Majesty, that all Spaniards who have Indians assigned to them in this province shall build and maintain churches under penalty. He charged them to exercise care in teaching the natives the matters pertaining to our holy Catholic faith and to treat them well. And to the Indians of these pueblos he gave instructions that they should be assembled. He ordered and commanded that the Spaniards assemble the natives on certain days of the week at the churches where they might be taught the Christian doctrine.

Francisco Vázquez was asked whether he had enforced the penalty of the said edict on the encomenderos who failed to provide churches in their pueblos, or who did not try to teach Christianity to the natives. He replied that he had not heard of any one who had not done it, and for that reason he did not execute the said edict.

19. Francisco Vázquez is charged with failure to carry out or urge that the Spaniards residing in this province, particularly those who have Indians in encomienda, move to and establish their residences in the Spanish cities and towns of this province, and that those who had the means should build stone or adobe houses.

Replying, Francisco Vázquez said that, complying with an order from his Majesty, he published an edict in all the Spanish towns of this jurisdiction prescribing that all Spaniards residing there who have repartimientos should build houses in the Spanish cities and towns, each one in the town or city in whose jurisdiction his repartimientos may be located.

He was asked whether the said order and penalties were enforced against those who refused to settle in those towns and build stone or adobe houses. He said that, up to the present, they have not been enforced against any person because some lacked the means to comply, and in other cases because, shortly afterward, this witness proclaimed that they could be built of earth. He believes that he issued this proclamation about fifty days ago.

20. Francisco Vázquez is charged that, having failed to order the building of a bridge or to provide barges, boats, or rafts at the Rio Grande,[12] both at the ford at this city of Guadalajara and at Cintiquepaque, many natives and some Spaniards and horses have drowned in both places and have been devoured by the caymans.

To this charge Francisco Vázquez said that the disasters mentioned in the charge had not come to his attention. After he learned about it and on receiving a cédula from his Majesty granting his city five hundred pesos in gold bullion for building a bridge over the Barranca river,[13] this witness, complying with instructions from his Majesty, went to inspect the place where

12. Rio Grande or Santiago.
13. Barranca river, near Guadalajara.

the said bridge was to be built. He found that an Indian had just been drowned. In view of this he disbursed at once the five hundred pesos, made assignments in the surrounding towns of what each one should do, and ordered that the royal arms be placed on the said bridge. He thought it was the Cintiquipaque crossing because at the ford there is a barranca. He ordered that wages be paid to the person who should be in charge of it. He said that he had planned to send a report to his Majesty so that he might so provide what was proper, for he has now learned that the caymans have done and are doing much harm.

21. Francisco Vázquez is charged with having taken, from the time he was appointed governor to the present, numerous free persons, men, women, and children, from the pueblos he held in encomienda in partnership with Alvaro de Bracamonte,[14] to the mines of Tepuzuacán, to mine gold, to dig, wash, and crush dirt and stone by hand, and to grind maize and make Indian shovels for the workers. It is charged that he took more than one hundred and twenty persons there.

Francisco Vázquez denied having brought any Indian men or women from the said pueblos to the said mines to dig, mine, or wash gold, grind stone, or make bread. He said that he had notified Alvaro de Bracamonte by letter to let them out if there are any from Jala.

Francisco Vázquez was asked whether he knew that gold was extracted from these mines and that it was divided between himself and Alvaro de Bracamonte, and who was mining it, according to what they told him. He said that Alvaro Bracamonte had come to him with a certain amount of gold which he said was part of what he held for him. As far as this witness remembers, he never told him who mined it, nor where.

Francisco Vázquez was asked if he had spent some days at the said mines of Tepuzhuacán, and whether he had seen if

14. Judge Tejada sentenced Bracamonte to surrender one-half of his pueblos, Indians, and lands to the crown or to share equally with the crown in all tributes and benefits. A. G. I., *Justicia*, legajo 339.

the three hundred persons, men, women, and children, were employed there extracting gold; whether he was told or learned, on the day he came to the said mines and spent the night there that the said Indian men and women who mined the gold belonged to the towns which he and Alvaro de Bracamonte held in encomienda in partnership. He said he remembers having visited the said mines three times, once when he came to this province and spent a night there; the second time was when he was going to Purificación, some fourteen months ago, and arrived at the mines in the afternoon and spent the night there. The other time he arrived in time for dinner; he ate and then continued on his way. He saw people in the mines but he did not know who they were, nor whether they were the ones mining gold for himself and Bracamonte.

He was asked whether, upon his asking Carmona, the calpisque [cacique?] of the said pueblo, for Indians to serve in his house, the said Carmona replied that there were no Naguales who knew how to serve except the ones who were in the said mines, and this witness told him that he did not want any one who was extracting gold taken from the mines, that he should find them elsewhere; he was asked what happened in this connection. He said he did not remember that such a thing took place between him and the said Carmona, nor has it come to his knowledge that any Indian women from the said pueblos are mining gold.

He was asked whether he knew that for the past one, two, three, four and more years the Indians who were mining gold in the mines were from the towns which the said Alvaro de Bracamonte held in encomienda, and that they were kept there continuously without being relieved. He said that he knew and had known from that time to the present that Alvaro de Bracamonte had Indians from the towns he exploited and held in encomienda in the said mines extracting gold, but whether or not they were relieved he did not know.

22. Francisco Vázquez is charged that the Indian men and women who worked in the said mines, at least those who did the washing and grinding, were not relieved during

all this time, but were kept continuously at the mines like slaves.

To this charge he said he repeats what he has stated in the charge preceding this one.

23. Francisco Vázquez is charged with enjoying, without authority, the salary of governor during the three years he was absent from this province, which salary amounted to fifteen hundred ducats per year in good money.

To this he replied that he had authority from his Majesty and from the viceroy in his name to undertake the expedition that he led to the new land and to enjoy the salary as governor during the entire time he should be absent on the said expedition and engaged in it. So this witness, and Alvaro de Bracamonte in his name, received and collected the said whole salary.

24. Francisco Vázquez is charged that, holding in encomienda in partnership with Alvaro de Bracamonte all of the pueblos which the said Bracamonte had and the ones which became vacant by the death of Francisco de Villegas,[15] and being aware of the chapters and new ordinances, and after these were formulated and promulgated, he divided the said pueblos with Alvaro de Bracamonte, giving him three times as many Indians and three times more profit than was left to his Majesty and his royal treasury. It was clearly fraudulent, because the Indians remaining to the said Francisco Vázquez are at war and render no service, and the others are of very little benefit.

He said he denied the charge absolutely and in its entirety.

He was asked how long it had been since the said division was made between this witness and Alvaro de Bracamonte. In reply he refers to the cédula of encomienda he gave Bracamonte, executed at Compostela on January 7, 1544, by Antonio

15. Indians that were held in encomienda reverted to the crown on the death of the holders, according to the "New Laws." Francisco de Villegas had been an agent of Nuño de Guzmán. See Pacheco y Cárdenas, XVI, pp. 539-547.

Ruiz de Haro, notary, of the Indians he granted Alvaro de Bracamonte, for the said division was made then, as had been agreed on before. He was asked if, when the said division was made, wishing to place it in the hands of notaries, Alvaro de Bracamonte told this witness not to do it because the notaries did not know the towns nor their value, but that they should choose and divide them, and let Alvaro de Bracamonte make the selection. Thus they reached an agreement that Alvaro de Bracamonte should divide them, and that this witness should choose.

Francisco Vázquez replied that he did not remember whether or not what was stated in the question had taken place; what he knows is that the pueblos and farms mentioned in the cédula in the question preceding this one were assigned to the said Alvaro de Bracamonte.

> 25. Francisco Vázquez is charged that, the head town of Aguacatlán having fallen to him in the said partition and the said Alvaro de Bracamonte having relinquished it and other pueblos contained in the relinquishment— because, during his absence, he could not comply if he held them—the said Francisco Vázquez, to defraud his Majesty further, assigned them again in encomienda to Alvaro de Bracamonte.

Francisco Vázquez said he denies that the said head town of Aguacatlán fell to him, because, when he asked for it, Bracamonte was offended, saying that if he took this town from him he would leave him everything. He knows that in the end it fell to Bracamonte with the other towns. It was agreed that in the meantime, while Francisco Vázquez was at Compostela, the said head town of Agutlán [sic] should serve him, which is the one that used to be governed by Guzmán and is now governed by Francisco. This witness never attempted to defraud his Majesty, but to serve him as he has always done.

> 26. Francisco Vázquez is charged with gambling often and for large sums at forbidden games, which resulted in a bad example for the Indians and hindered dispatch

of the matters and cases pending and brought before him.

To this charge he admitted that he has sometimes played *primera* and *triunfo* to while away the time, but not to such an extent that it had set a bad example or interfered with the dispatch of business.[16]

27. Francisco Vázquez is charged that, in all the time that he held the governorship, never did he take pains to order and compel the judges and notaries of the cities and towns of this jurisdiction to fix a schedule of the fees they were to charge, nor did the said Francisco Vázquez have one at the quarters where he dispatched the matters pending before him.

To this charge he stated that as he never charged any fees for the business that came before him, he did not deem it necessary to have a schedule in his home. He did not know for sure whether the judges in the other towns had one, but he believes that they did as no one complained to him of being charged excessive fees.

28. Francisco Vázquez is charged that, when he went to inspect the town of Purificación and held the residencia of Juan Hernández de Ijar, he told those who came to lodge complaints against him that it was not possible that the said Juan Fernández could have done such a thing, as he was a gentleman. He demonstrated that he was a constant friend and favorable to Juan Fernández. For this reason those who had grievances against Juan Fernández refrained from seeking redress, seeing that the governor favored him so openly.

He said he denies this charge, as he favored the said Juan Fernández only in that he treated him as a gentleman and as a man who had held office.

29. Francisco Vázquez is charged that, in a litigation and controversy brought before him at the town of Purifi-

16. These card games are still played in Spain. See *Enciclopedia Ilustrada Espasa-Calpe*.

cación, a lawsuit between Juan Hernández de Ijar and Martín de Rifarache more than forty or fifty Indians who in time of war had moved from a pueblo of the said Rifarache, of which they were natives, to another pueblo belonging to Juan Fernández, and later they had returned to a pueblo belonging to Rifarache where they formerly lived, the said Francisco Vázquez removed the Indians against their will and ordered them to move to the pueblos of Juan Fernández. He caused the said Rifarache to wander for many days, looking for them in the woods to which they had fled because they wanted to move them from their natural home where they dwelled of their own wish. In this he showed himself by deed and word partial and favorable to Juan Fernández de Ijar.

This charge he said he denied absolutely and in its entirety.

30. Francisco Vázquez is charged with having handed over to Juan Fernández de Ijar the cacique of the pueblo and plantation named Carrión, which is assigned in encomienda to Antonio de Aguayo, thus depriving the cacique of his authority without knowing or inquiring as to his will, whether he wanted to reside in the said province whose governor he was, or move to the pueblo of the said Juan Fernández, or inquire about returning to the said Antonio de Aguayo.

Francisco Vázquez denied this charge. The facts of the matter are that an Indian woman came from a pueblo by order of this witness. When she arrived he asked her, at the request of Juan Fernández or Antonio de Aguayo, where she wanted to live, that she should know that she was free and could do whatever she wished. She replied that she wanted to live at a pueblo belonging to Juan Fernández de Ijar, of which she was a native. Coronado was told by the said Aguayo that she had been bribed and was not expressing her own will. Francisco Vázquez ordered her placed in the plaza and that there she should be made to understand that she was free and could go wherever she wished. There she said that she wanted to go to the town of Juan Fernández. After this, she went to the house of Francisco Vázquez and asked that he order a son of hers to be returned to her. He ordered the son returned to her without being told that he was a governor or where he was. Later, as the said Aguayo complained to him, Francisco Vázquez entrusted the matter to Fernán Ruiz de la Peña, so that, upon hearing all sides, he should assign him to whomever he belonged.

31. Francisco Vázquez is charged that, after coming to the the town of Purificación and after proclaiming the residencia of Juan Fernández de Ijar, he would never consent to accept or carry out his secret investigation even though this was urged upon him. For this reason many refrained from seeking redress and telling what they knew.

To this charge Francisco Vázquez said it was true that he had ordered the announcing of the residencia, but that officially he did not conduct any secret hearing, nor did any one appear to ask anything of him.

32. Francisco Vázquez is charged that Juan de Almesto, as mayor and administrator of the estates of the deceased, having urged the said governor to do his duty and press the said Juan Fernández de Ijar to find out who had received payment from the estates of certain Spaniards who had drowned and others who were killed by the Indians on the coast some twelve years before when the brigantines of the Marqués del Valle foundered and the said Juan Fernández was entrusted with their estates, he would not do justice in this matter; on the contrary, he tried to hush it up or induce the said governor to leave the said city, and to the present the payments remain uncollected.

Francisco Vázquez said that he submits to what transpired before Acebedo, notary of the said town, where there will be found what this witness provided in connection with the said summons. This is the truth and what he knows about the matter under the oath he has taken. He signed it with his name. This statement and testimony were read to him soon after he finished giving it and he corrected it. It was signed by the said judge, LICENTIATE TEJADA, and FRANCISCO VÁZQUEZ DE CORONADO.

After the aforesaid, in the city of Guadalajara, on September 3 of the said year, Francisco Vázquez, former governor of this province, again took oath in due legal form. He was asked about the thirty-third charge, which was formulated but had not been brought before him.

> 33. Francisco Vázquez is charged that, in the forty days he remained at Purificación in the preceding year of 1543, he received from the residents of the said town all the food and provisions needed during the entire time by himself, his servants, and horses. It was worth one peso common gold per day. He received it gratis, without paying anything for it. Likewise he received from Alvaro Núñez and Juan Gallego an arroba of wine, which was worth four pesos and two tomines in gold bullion. Likewise he received from Juan de Almesto two steers, forty sheep, and some fowl, which were consumed during this time by him and his men.

To this charge Francisco Vázquez stated that the facts are that, when he was at Compostela, he received a letter from the viceroy to the effect that a portion of the Indians at Purificación were aroused and in rebellion, and that he should go forthwith to restore peace and punish the leaders of the disturbance. As he had information of the matter before the letter arrived, he hastened his departure, and, as the time was so short, he was not as well provisioned as was necessary for the maintenance and upkeep of his person and house. It is true that he received from the residents of the said town of Purificación the food and wine mentioned in the charge, but he had ordered his servant, Francisco Italiano, when they left Compostela, that wherever they should stay, he was to pay for the provisions and food furnished them. But he did not know whether or not the servant paid, other than that he had provided him with funds for the purpose. However, he believed that he did not pay. The wine he accepted, expecting to return it in kind, as there was none for sale at the place.

34. Francisco Vázquez is charged that, in the preceding year of 1543, after the cabildo and council of this city had elected Diego de Colio and Juan Sánchez as alcaldes, the said Francisco Vázquez de Coronado appointed Juan de Villareal as alcalde when the council had not concurred in any vote, without in fact having any votes, and that against the practice and custom prevailing in this city he ordered the staff of office given to the said Juan de Villareal. Although he was asked and urged, he would not give it to the men whom, since they were conquistadores and competent persons, the cabildo had chosen and elected.

To this Francisco Vázquez replied that it was true that the cabildo and regimiento of the city chose and elected as alcaldes the men mentioned in the charge, but the said Juan de Villareal and Juan Miguel received one or more votes. This witness confirmed the said Juan de Villareal and ordered the staff given to him, as he considered him a person competent for the post; it seems to him that he had fewer votes than stated in the charge, but, in accordance with a cédula from his Majesty, when the governor is present the cabildo has no power of election and the governor makes the appointment. He refers to this cédula.

Francisco Vázquez was asked if it was not true that the said Diego de Colio and Juan Sánchez, elected by the cabildo, were conquistadores and prudent persons, honorable, married, and residents of this city, while the said Juan de Villareal was not a conquistador nor married at the time the said election and appointment was made, and whether there was any blemish on the person of the said Juan Sánchez, wherefore he did not confirm the said election. He said he knew that, at the time the said election and appointment were made, Juan Sánchez and Diego de Colio were married and residents of this city, and that he had heard that Juan Sánchez had been a conquistador in this province and that Juan de Villareal was neither married nor a conquistador. He did not know that there was any blemish on the character of Juan Sánchez or on Colio which should prevent their confirmation in the appointment. This is what he knows. It is true that Miguel de Ibarra requested him, in the name of the cabildo of this city, not to appoint Juan de Villareal, as he was not a conquistador, and it was more appropriate that the conquistadores should be preferred in the appointments to those who were not. This witness told him that if he had not already appointed him, and if the election and appointment of Juan de Villareal had not taken place at the cabildo, he might consider what they were asking.

This is the truth and what he knows of the matter in conformity with the oath he has taken. He signed the statement with his name. This testimony was read to him again and he ratified it. It was signed by the said judge, LICENTIATE TEJADA, and by FRANCISCO VÁZQUEZ DE CORONADO.

A copy of this testimony, the charges, and his replies was given to Francisco Vázquez de Coronado by order of Licentiate Tejada, oidor and juez, on September 2, 1544. Witnesses: Francisco Italiano, Alvaro de Toro, and Pedro Ruiz de Faro [Haro].

After the above, on September 6, 1544, at Guadalajara, New Galicia, Pedro Ruiz de Faro presented to Licentiate Tejada, judge of the royal audiencia of New Spain and visitador of New Galicia, a notorized power of attorney and a letter from Francisco Vázquez de Coronado.[17]

17. This letter signed by Coronado is in reality a petition by his attorney, Pedro Ruiz de Haro, asking that the charges against Coronado be dropped and that he be set free. This petition, covering twenty-two pages, retells Coronado's testimony without adding anything new.

SENTENCE OF VAZQUEZ DE CORONADO ON RESIDENCIA CHARGES[1]

In view of the secret residencia of Francisco Vázquez de Coronado, held by order of his Majesty, for the time he was governor of this province of New Galicia, and the charges against him which resulted from this residencia, and his rebuttal of them:

I find, considering the proceedings and merits of the case, that, with respect to the second charge, I must and do sentence him to pay 150 pesos in gold bullion into the treasury of his Majesty.

Further: With respect to the third charge, I must and do sentence him to pay sixty pesos in gold bullion into the treasury of his Majesty.

Further: On the fifth charge, I must and do sentence him to pay sixty pesos gold bullion into the treasury of his Majesty.

Further: For his guilt on charges 13, 14, 15, and 16, I must and do sentence him to pay 200 pesos gold bullion, one-half for the royal treasury and the other half for public works in the cities of Compostela and Guadalajara, and to help pay for the barge or large canoe that is to be built at the Barranca river at the Cintiquipaque crossing.

Further: With respect to charges 27, 28, 29, 30, 31, and 32, I must and do sentence him to pay 150 pesos common gold, one-half for the royal treasury and the other half for public works in the cities of Compostela and Guadalajara and the town of Purificación, and to build the said barge.

Further: With respect to charge 33, I sentence him to pay eighty pesos common gold into the treasury of his Majesty.

With respect to charges 17, 18, 20, 21, 22, 24, 25, and 26, I must and do refer them to his Majesty and the members of his royal Council of the Indies. On all other charges I must and do

1. Translated from a photostatic copy of the original in the Archives of the Indies, *Justicia,* legajo 339, pieza 1.

absolve the said Francisco Vázquez de Coronado. In all the aforesaid sentences, I must and do submit them to his Majesty and members of his royal Council of the Indies to increase or reduce the said sentences as they see fitting and suitable to his royal service.

He must pay to the treasurer of his Majesty in this New Galicia and to the major-domos of the said cities and towns, within the next nine days, what has been assigned to each one of them. And being so judged by this my final sentence, I so decree and order it by these documents, with costs. Licentiate Tejada.

In the city of Guadalajara of New Galicia, on September 16, 1544, Licentiate Tejada, judge of New Spain and judge of residencia for New Galicia, being present in his quarters where the residencia was held, passed and pronounced the above-stated sentence in the presence of Pedro Ramírez de Haro, attorney for the said Francisco Vázquez, who was notified. Witnesses, CRISTÓBAL DE OÑATE, MIGUEL DE YBARRA, and JUAN FERNÁNDEZ DIJAR. PEDRO DE REQUENA, clerk.[2]

2. After this sentence had been imposed, Coronado presented a petition to the Council of the Indies appealing the sentence. His petition was accepted and appeal granted upon his depositing the amount of the sentence. He posted the deposit in silver bars, which were weighed in the presence of Judge Tejada. The silver was entrusted to Cristóbal de Oñate, who guaranteed it with his estates. The appeal was signed by Viceroy Mendoza, and Judges Ceynos, Tejada, and Santillán, and dated at Mexico, November 22, 1544.

The amount reckoned by Coronado was 607 pesos, one tomin, and three grains in gold bullion. This must have been the result of figuring the amount from the sums of common gold and bullion imposed by Judge Tejada.

We have found no documents to show this appeal was acted upon by the Council of the Indies in Spain. In 1533, Coronado's attorney, in the suit before the audiencia of Guadalajara to recover the pueblos taken from his client, introduced as evidence Coronado's appointment as captain general of the expedition to Cíbola, the charges filed against him in connection with its management, and the final sentence by the audiencia clearing him of all charges. It seems that if a similar sentence absolving him of all charges of maladministration as governor of New Galicia were available his attorney would not have failed to produce it. Perhaps the appeal was still pending at the time of Coronado's death in the following year, 1554, and no more was done about it.

CHARGES AGAINST CORONADO

CHARGES AGAINST CORONADO RESULTING FROM THE INVESTIGATION INTO THE MANAGEMENT OF THE EXPEDITION, SEPTEMBER 3, 1544.[1]

It seems that Licentiate Tejada, our judge, held an inquiry in the presence of Pedro de Requena, our notary, and before witnesses, both at Mexico city, and Guadalajara, New Galicia. Upon his examination of the report and the testimony he obtained from Francisco Vázquez de Coronado, he ordered the latter, within fifty days from date, to appear personally before the president and judges of our audiencia at Mexico. Having presented himself before them, he would be placed under whatever restrictions they should choose for him, and he must not break them in any way under penalty of a fine of one thousand pesos in gold bullion for our treasury. This notice, it seems, was delivered to the said Francisco Vázquez de Coronado, and in compliance with it he appeared personally at the audiencia before our said president and judges. After this, our judge, Licentiate Tejada, ordered the said Francisco Vázquez de Coronado that he remain in custody at his home by reason of what is stated above and that he could not leave or break away without his permission or order, under the said penalty. Tejada ordered the said legal report delivered to Licentiate Cristóbal de Benavente, our fiscal, in order that he might lodge any charges against Francisco Vázquez that might result from the report and whatever else should be desirable for our service for the execution of justice. When he has formulated them, he is to hear and accept the testimony of Francisco Vázquez and remit the entire matter to our audiencia, as he has been ordered by

1. Translated from a photostatic copy of the original in the Archives of the Indies, *Justicia*, legajo 336. In 1553, Pedro Ramírez de Haro, Coronado's attorney, brought suit at Guadalajara in an attempt to recover for his client the pueblos that had been taken from him in 1544 by Judge Tejada. To prove Coronado's innocence and his right to the towns in question, his attorney presented a copy of these charges and the absolutory sentence of Coronado.

us in our letter of appointment. This notification, it appears, was given to the said Francisco Vázquez de Coronado.

Thereupon, on March 21 of last year, 1545, in compliance with the aforesaid, our said fiscal appeared before our said judge, Licentiate Tejada, and, in a written document which he laid before him, filed criminal charges against the said Francisco Vázquez de Coronado.

And, explaining the case of the said accusation, presupposing the legal formalities, he stated that as Francisco Vázquez had been appointed by both our viceroy and our audiencia of New Spain as captain general of the newly discovered land and the province of Cíbola, and as he had received our royal orders and instructions to discover, pacify, and settle whatever should be discovered in these provinces to the west, and the order he was to observe and practice in waging this war, in subduing and attracting the natives to the knowledge of our holy Catholic faith and our royal authority and obedience: having taken for this purpose an army of more than two hundred cavalrymen and many footmen, well armed and equipped with everything necessary to carry out the said expedition, the said Francisco Vázquez de Coronado, acting contrary to what had been charged and ordered in our royal letters, orders, and instructions on the said journey, he, and his captains and lieutenants by his command, committed the following offenses:

First: In the province of Chiametla, without any legitimate cause or reason, when its natives were at peace, he took eight Indian men and women, more or less, and some he had hanged and others quartered.

Further: Having established a Spanish town in the valley of Corazones, he should have placed some able and reliable person in charge of it to administer justice and pacify the said province.[2] Because the said captain general was remiss in not choosing a competent person to govern the town and its people and because of the evil deeds and ill treatment shown to the natives by the person or persons he left there, the natives of the prov-

---

2. The man chosen was Melchior Díaz, a competent officer, but he was killed on the expedition to the Gulf of California, leaving Diego de Alcaraz in charge at San Gerónimo in the Sonora valley.

ince rebelled and killed many Spaniards, and the town was abandoned, and the neighboring people revolted.

Further: When the army and its people arrived at the province of Cíbola, the natives of the head pueblo came out to meet them peaceably, furnishing them the needed food and provisions. And the said Francisco Vázquez and his captains, without any legitimate cause whatsoever, waged war, burned the pueblo, and killed many people.[3] For this reason a large portion of the said province and many of its people rebelled and took up arms.

Further: After traveling sixty or seventy leagues farther, the general came to the province of Tiguex, abounding in people, provisions, and many buildings constructed like those of Spain. The natives received the Spaniards peaceably and rendered obedience to us and furnished the army and its people with plenty of maize, fowl, and other provisions. While they were at peace, without any legitimate cause, the general, and his captains by his command, set dogs on the chiefs of the said pueblo and those adjoining. He set the dogs on them so that they should bite them, and they did bite them. As a result of this, the said chiefs and natives of these pueblos and provinces rebelled and took up arms. By waging war against them anew, the Spaniards destroyed and burned many of these pueblos, and in others the natives offered resistance. So the province turned from peace to war and remained at war. As a result the natives killed many Spaniards, and the whole army was endangered. And because of it all, many of the natives were burned alive and put to the sword.

Further: In the same manner, the said general, proceeding with his journey and going farther on, came to the province of Quivira. He had taken as interpreter and guide an Indian named the Turk. After discovering the said province, which was very rich, populated, and had abundant provisions, and the natives meeting them peacefully and furnishing food for all the people of the whole army, he ordered the said guide killed, without any cause or reason at all. Even if there had been any

3. This paragraph seems to indicate that Coronado was charged with burning one of the Zuñi pueblos, which is clearly a mistake, since the only pueblos destroyed were in the valley of the Rio Grande.

reason, the punishment should have been public and not secret as it was.

Further: The said provinces being densely populated and abounding in provisions and numerous cattle, consisting of wild cattle,[4] when the said provinces could have been easily settled, not only did he fail to do so, but he even hindered and prevented some Spaniards who wanted to colonize from doing so. He caused them to abandon the provinces and leave them unsettled, and in revolt and at war.[5] He used up and wasted all of the equipment, articles of trade, munitions, and weapons that had been furnished him for the said war. In all of this the said Francisco Vázquez de Coronado and his captains committed great offenses. Wherefore, he, the fiscal, said that he would and did ask our said commissioned judge that, upon obtaining a report of the aforesaid, he should order proceedings against them or any one of them who might seem guilty and impose on them the heaviest and most severe civil and criminal penalties legally provided for such cases. He should order the penalties against their persons and estates in order that such crimes should not remain unpunished, and, in addition, that they should be sentenced with costs. And he presented the said brief.

Our said judge, upon taking and accepting the report containing all the aforesaid, ordered a copy furnished to Francisco Vázquez de Coronado. He ordered that at the first meeting of the audiencia he might reply and adduce whatever information he thought pertinent to the case. He appeared before our said judge and laid before him a document of exceptions setting forth that the accusation did not apply to him as he had not committed any crime—etc., etc. [There follow some ten pages of allegations repeating his previous testimony.]

Thus the said prosecution was brought to a close. At this stage our said judge issued an act stating in effect that in accord-

4. These were the buffalo, roaming over the plains of what are now eastern New Mexico and the areas to the east.

5. Castañeda wrote that some of the people in the expedition begged Coronado to give them sixty picked men in order to continue the search for a rich country. Several witnesses likewise testified that sixty people wanted to remain in the new land with Fray Juan de Padilla, but that Coronado threatened them and forced them to return. A. G. I., *Justicia*, legajo 1021, pieza 4.

ance with what he had been ordered by us in our said letter and decree of appointment incorporated above, he would and did refer the disposition of the said case to the president and judges of our said audiencia. The proceedings of the case were brought before them, and, upon examining all of the proceedings and the merits of the case, they gave and pronounced a final sentence in the case, the tenor of which is given here.

ABSOLUTORY SENTENCE OF CORONADO[1]

In the criminal suit between Licentiate Cristóbal de Benavente, his Majesty's fiscal in this royal audiencia, on the one hand, and on the other Francisco Vázquez de Coronado, former governor for his Majesty in the province of New Galicia, who was selected and appointed captain general and the king's attorney in his name for the province of Cíbola and the newly discovered land: We find, in view of the proceedings and merits of the case, that Licentiate Benavente, the fiscal, did not prove the accusations and charges he presented against the said Francisco Vázquez de Coronado for the offenses which he says he had committed in the newly discovered land; we find them and pronounce them not proved; and that the said Francisco Vázquez de Coronado proved his exceptions and defenses, and we find and pronounce them well proved. Therefore, we must and do absolve the said Francisco Vázquez of all that he has been and is being charged with in this case by the said fiscal, whom we enjoin to perpetual silence so that neither now nor at any time in the future may he accuse or bring charges against him for anything contained and judged in this our sentence. We so pronounce and order: DON ANTONIO DE MENDOZA, LICENTIATE TELLO DE SANDOVAL, LICENTIATE CEYNOS, LICENTIATE TEJADA, LICENTIATE SANTILLÁN.

This sentence the aforesaid, our president and judges, imposed and pronounced at the said city of Mexico, in a public meeting of the audiencia, February 19, 1546; there were present our said fiscal, to whom and to the attorney for the said Francisco Vázquez notice was given in person.

1. Translated from a photostatic copy of the original in the Archives of the Indies, *Justicia*, legajo 1021.

GLOSSARY

abra—a valley; dale; an opening in the mountains; an inlet or bay.

adelantado—military governor of a frontier province.

alcaide—commander of a fortress or arsenal; a warden or jailer.

alcalde mayor—head of a smaller division of a province, exercising judicial and civil power.

alcalde ordinario—justice of the peace.

alguacil mayor—chief constable.

arroba—weight equivalent to twenty-five pounds.

arroyo—a stream or small river.

audiencia—a judicial body which also possessed wide administrative power.

bachiller—one who holds a first degree from a college or university.

barranca—a gorge; cliff; canyon.

caballero—a member of the nobility; a titled person; a gentleman.

cabildo—municipal council; chapter of a cathedral church.

cacique—an Indian chief or ruler.

cántaro—wine measure of variable content.

Casa de Contratación—the "House of Trade," located in Seville, Spain, in control of trade between Spain and its colonies.

cedros—juniper trees.

cédula—decree or order.

comendador—knight commander of a military order.

conquistador—conqueror; explorer.

contador—comptroller; cashier; accountant; paymaster.

corregidor—magistrate and chief official of a town.

despoblado—uninhabited place; wilderness.

encinal—a grove of *encinos* (oaks).

encomienda—an estate consisting of land and its Indian inhabitants, assigned or granted to an individual for a period of time for its protection and exploitation.

entrada—military exploring or reconnoitering expedition.

escudero—page; squire; shield bearer.

estado—measure of length equivalent to the height of a man.

estufa—kiva or ceremonial chamber of the Pueblo Indians.

factor—commissioner; victualer.

fanega—grain measure equivalent to about 1.60 bushels.

fiscal—attorney general; prosecutor.

gallina de la tierra—the turkey.

henequén—sisal, the fiber of the agave plant.

jornada—journey; expedition; one-day march.

labrado—tattooed; painted; decorated.

legajo—file or bundle of documents.

licenciado—a licentiate, one who holds a high college degree.

maestre (or *maese*) *de campo*—chief army officer; commanding officer.

manta—a blanket.

maravedi—the smallest Spanish coin; a fraction of a cent.

mayorazgo—right of primogeniture; family estate.

monte—jungle; wooded section; brush; hills.

pintado—painted or tattooed.

piñol (piñón)—piñon nuts.

pitahaya—a large cactus bearing an edible fruit.
probanza—attested evidence; proof; testimonial.
procurador—solicitor; procurator.
ranchería—a cluster of *ranchos* or huts; a settlement.
rayado—tattooed; painted; striped.
real—old Spanish coin of variable value, at present one-fourth of a *peseta*.
regidor—councilman or alderman of a city.
repartimiento—allotment of land made to an individual.
requerimiento—legal summons to peace or submission.
residencia—inquiry into the administration of a public official at the close of his
    tenure of office.
sargento mayor—sergeant major, second in command in the army.
tomín—weight equivalent to one-sixth part of a dram.
torta, tortilla—a pancake made of Indian corn and baked.
vaca de la tierra—the buffalo.
visita—inspection; hearing.
visitador—inspector; investigator.

ERRATA

Page 35, note 2, line 8, *for* Martías *read* Matías
Page 52, line 9, *for* Vásquez *read* Vázquez
Page 114, line 34, and page 115, line 27, *read* Bejarano
Page 117, note 1, line 2, *for* vairos *read* varios
Page 126, line 6, *for* breath *read* breathe
Page 131, line 11, *for* then *read* than
Page 147, line 25, *for* distant *read* distance
Page 150, line 10, *for* Quicana *read* Quicama
Page 155, line 28, *for* sent *read* send
Page 197, note 3, *for* Hollenbeck *read* Hallenbeck

INDEX

A

Acaxes: language group, 249

Acebedo: notary, 387

Acha: described by Castañeda, 254

Acoma: visited by Alvarado, 18, 182n, 218; passed by army, 28, 223; cross found near, 280

Acus, kingdom of: Fray Marcos learns of, 68, 72-73; discussion of, by Coronado, 173; mentioned, 84

Adobe: 254n

Adultery: punishment of, 139

Advance guard of expedition: leaves Culiacán, 15, 162, 206, 284; route of, 15-17, 295-298

Aguas Calientes: pueblos of, 259

Aguatlán (Aguacatlán), town of: 374, 375, 384

Aguayaval: location of, 125

Aguayo, Antonio de: 386

Agundez, Diego: 86

Ahacus: Fray Marcos learns of, 72; discussion of, by Coronado, 173

Alameda, pueblo of: location of, 22n, 335

Alarcón, Hernando de: instructions to, 117-123; sea expedition of, 124-155, 7, 9, 15, 16, 20, 21, 202-203; equipment of, 121-123; poses as child of sun, 132-135, 143; his messages found, 211

Alba, Hernando de: 99

Albuquerque: mentioned, 219n

Alcanfor, pueblo of: army quartered in, 22, 219-220, 326, 347

Alcántara, Francisco de: 98

Alcántara, Pedro de: 102

Alcaraz, Diego de: left in command at San Gerónimo, 21, 210, 231n, 268n, 269; reports disturbance in San Gerónimo, 231-232; death of, 28, 104, 363-364

Alemán, Juan: talks with Coronado about clothing, 224; attacks Cárdenas, 227

Alligators: Alarcón hears of, 144; Castañeda tells of, 275

Almaguer, Antonio de: 82, 86, 116

Almesto, Juan de: 387, 388

Alonso, Domingo: 98

Alonso de Astorga, Martín: 102

Alvarado, Hernando de: identified, 88; exploration by, 19-20, 22n, 217-221, 244, 288, 325-326, 328-329, 349-350; report of, 182-184; in battle at Cíbola, 169, 208; mentioned, 202

Alvarado, Pedro de: mentioned, 155n, 198, 277

Alvarez, Alonso: 103

Alvarez, Antonio: 95

Alvarez, Gaspar: 13, 100

Alvarez, Lorenzo: 98

Alvarez, Pedro: 97

Alvarez, Roque: 101

Alvarez de Zafra, Rodrigo: 101

Animals: taken on expedition, 7, 16, 206, 235, 236, 278; in the new land, 172-173, 252, 258; on plains, 262; described to Alarcón, 146; described by Díaz, 158

Aorta: 13, 100

Arache, Arehe: see *Harahey*

Aranda, Alonso de: 92

Arce, Juan de: 105

Arellano, Tristán de: identified, 93; as commander of the main army, 15, 206, 320; establishes town at Corazones, 209; mentioned, 201, 210, 240

Arenal: battle of, 24, 226, 230n, 333-335, 352-358

Arias de Saabedra, Hernando: 105

Arizpe: 16

Arjona, Gonzalo de: 100

Arkansas river: 291n, 303

Armor: listed in muster roll, 87-108

Army, main body of: departure of, from Culiacán, 209; departure of,